The Elections in Israel

2006

Published in cooperation with the Israel Democracy Institute.

The Israel Democracy Institute is an independent, non-partisan body on the seam of academia and politics. The Institute plans policy and devises reforms for government and public administration agencies, and for the institutions of democracy.

In its plans and endeavors, the Institute strives to support the institutions of Israel's developing democracy and consolidate its values. The Institute's serious research work is followed up by practical recommendations, seeking to improve governance in Israel and foster a long-term vision for a stable democratic regime adapted to the structure, the values, and the norms of Israeli society. The Institute aspires to further public discourse in Israel on the issues placed on the national agenda, to promote structural, political, and economic reforms, to serve as a consulting body to decision-makers and the broad public, to provide information and present comparative research.

Researchers at the Israel Democracy Institute are leading academics directing projects in various areas of society and governance in Israel. The Institute's publications department produces, markets, and distributes the results of their work in several series of books ("The Democracy Library"), policy studies, the Caesarea Forum, periodicals, and conferences proceedings.

Translator   Dorothea Shefer-Vanson

Language Editor (English)   Rachel Wind Wiesen

Language Editor (Hebrew)   Iris Avner

The Elections in Israel

2006

Edited by Asher Arian and Michal Shamir

THE ISRAEL DEMOCRACY INSTITUTE

Transaction Publishers

New Brunswick (U.S.A.) and London (U.K.)

Library of Congress Catalog Number: 2007039347
ISBN: 978-0-7658-0388-7
Printed in the United States of America

Library of Congress Cataloging-in-Publication Data

The elections in Israel, 2006 / Asher Arian and Michal Shamir, editors.
    p. cm.
"Published in cooperation with the Israel Democracy Institute."
Includes bibliographical references and index.
ISBN 978-0-7658-0388-7 (alk. paper)
    1. Elections—Israel—History. 2. Israel. Knesset—Elections, 2006.
3. Israel—Politics and government—21st century. I. Arian, Asher. II. Shamir, Michal, 1951- III. The Israel Democracy Institute.

JQ1830.A95E435 2008
324.95694'054—dc22

2007039347

Contents

45 ~66

Acknowledgements

Our sincere thanks to Edna Granit, Anat Bernstein, and Nadav Shtechman for their generous help in the production process, to Dorothea Shefer-Vanson for her translation, to Rachel Wind Wiesen for her editorial work, to Amnon Lahad, who provided the drawing of the Knesset building at the age of 11 in 1971, to Daphne Kanellopoulos for her work in producing the English version, to Adi Livny for constructing the index, to the scholars who agreed to review anonymously the articles submitted to this volume, and to Tel Aviv University's Alvin Z. Rubinstein Chair of Political Science for its financial support.

A. A.

M. S.

Introduction

Asher Arian and Michal Shamir

Several dramatic events preceded the elections to the Seventeenth Knesset on March 28, 2006, beginning with the unilateral withdrawal from Gaza in August 2005 and its attendant and unprecedented removal of Jewish settlements and settlers, followed by major shifts among and within the various political parties. Most dramatic was the split in Likud when Prime Minister Ariel Sharon decided to form a new party, Kadima, leading to the breakup of the Likud party that Sharon had formed in 1973. Both Labor and Likud found themselves with new leaders—Amir Peretz and Binyamin Netanyahu—and with depleted ranks. Shinui, a party that had soared in 2003 under the leadership of Tommy Lapid, but whose second-tier activists soured on the leadership and ruptured it three years later, imploded before the elections. And Sharon, prime minister since 2001, succumbed to a stroke soon after he had formed Kadima and arranged for elections to be held at the end of March 2006. He was succeeded by his deputy prime minister, Ehud Olmert.

However, despite the preponderance of dramatic events, the Israeli electorate was not enthusiastic, and voted at the lowest rate ever in Knesset elections. There were indications that this would occur from polls taken prior to the elections, yet its actual occurrence firmly established that Israel joined the trend of declining electoral participation evidenced in other industrialized democracies.

The elections resulted in a clear winner, Kadima (see table 1). It obtained less votes than expected based on pre-election polls, but still outdistanced the other parties with its 29 seats in the Knesset, followed by Labor, its closest competitor with only 19 members of Knesset (MKs). Olmert formed a coalition government supported by 67 members of the 120-person Knesset with Labor (19), Shas (12), and the new Pensioners party (7), and presented it to the Knesset on May 4, 2006. With no party achieving a decisive majority, the overall fragmentation of the Knesset increased; it reached levels of party volatility not witnessed since the 1977 realignment. The legal threshold for representation in the Knesset elections was raised from 1.5 to 2 percent of the valid votes before these elections, and the smallest party to win representation was Balad with 2.3 percent of the vote. In all, 12 parties are represented in the Seventeenth Knesset.

Table 1
Results of the 2006 Knesset Elections[a]

	Valid Votes	% of Valid Votes	No. of Knesset Seats
Kadima	690,901	22.0	29
Labor-Meimad	472,366	15.1	19
Shas	299,054	9.5	12
Likud	281,996	9.0	12
Israel Beiteinu	281,880	9.0	11
National Unity-Mafdal	224,083	7.1	9
Pensioners Party	185,759	5.9	7
Torah and Shabbat Judaism	147,091	4.7	6
Meretz	118,302	3.8	5
United Arab List - Arab Renewal	94,786	3.0	4
Democratic Front for Peace & Equality (Hadash)	86,092	2.7	3
National Democratic Assembly (Balad)	72,066	2.3	3
Greens	47,595	1.5	0
Green Leaf (Aleh Yarok)	40,353	1.3	0
National Jewish Front	24,824	0.8	0
Tafnit (Uzi Dayan)	18,753	0.6	0
One Future	14,005	0.4	0
Hetz	10,113	0.3	0
Shinui	4,675	0.1	0
Tzedek Lakol	3,819	0.1	0
Democratic Action Organization (Daam)	3,692	0.1	0
Herut	2,387	0.1	0
Party for the Struggle with the Banks	2,163	0.1	0
Brit Olam	2,011	0.1	0
Lev	1,765	0.1	0
Lechem	1,381	[b]	0
Tzomet	1,342	[b]	0
New Zionism	1,278	[b]	0
Strength to the Poor	1,214	[b]	0
National Arab Party	738	[b]	0
Leeder	580	[b]	0
TOTAL	3,137,064	99.7%	120

Source: http://www.knesset.gov.il/elections17/heb/results/Main_Results.asp
[a] There were 5,014,622 eligible voters; 3,186,739 participated in the elections. Of those who voted, the ballots of 49,675 (1.6%) were disqualified. Qualifying threshold for representation (2%) - 62,742 votes. Quota per Knesset seat - 24,619 votes. 180,525 voters (5.7 %) cast ballots for parties that received less than the 2% minimum required.
[b] Less than 0.1% of the vote.

I. Disengagement

The unilateral separation plan that Sharon announced in December 2003, and executed between August 15 and September 12, 2005, held a particular irony in light of the fact that the defeated Labor party's candidate, Amram Mitzna, had championed the very same plan in the January 2003 elections and lost as badly as any major party leader ever lost in the history of Israeli elections. After that defeat Mitzna resigned as head of the Labor party and Shimon Peres was named acting chairman. In January 2005, with Sharon facing extreme difficulties in having his own Likud Knesset delegation accept his plan for Gaza, Peres led Labor into the Sharon cabinet, thus bolstering Prime Minister Sharon and ensuring the votes needed for approving the withdrawal.

Sharon paid a heavy price for the disengagement within his Likud party. Many Likud cabinet members as well as other Likud members opposed the move; in fact, in a referendum held among Likud members in May 2004, the proposition was defeated by a vote of 60:40, with about half of the 193,000 Likud members participating. In June 2004, Sharon removed two ministers, Avigdor Lieberman and Benny Elon of the far-right National Union party, from his coalition. Both had opposed his plan to withdraw unilaterally from Gaza. Their dismissal gave Sharon a majority within his cabinet for the crucial vote on the plan, and in October the Knesset voted 67-45 in favor of the plan.

Opposition to the disengagement was substantial and vocal, and in the months leading to the disengagement, the settlers' protest was expressed by means of massive acts of illegal civil disobedience, including confrontations with the police and the security forces. The unilateral withdrawal from Gaza, however, which involved relocating about 9,000 Jewish settlers, was completed in a relatively peaceful and efficient manner. Rockets were still being fired at Israel from Gaza but the public seemed to be relieved that the burden of defending isolated settlements and manning army outposts in the Gaza Strip was no longer on the long list of challenges the army had to face. Moreover, the unilateral withdrawal was carried out with almost no casualties among the settlers, the police, or the army units involved. The withdrawal dealt a harsh blow to the settlers and to many in the religious community, especially the National Zionist camp, but Israeli and international public opinion applauded Sharon for his daring and for the relative efficiency of the operation.

II. From the Disengagement to Early Elections

A. The "Big Bang"

The difficulties Sharon faced in the Likud led to rumors that the prime minister was planning a "big bang," breaking up the existing party structures and forming a new party comprised of Sharon and his followers from Likud, as well as members of parties more to the left and center than Likud, perhaps from Shinui and Labor. Shinui was a centrist party that had done well in the 2003 elections, only to implode by late 2005. Most observers felt that the emergence of a new party at the center of Israel's political map would attract many voters and perhaps succeed in winning a majority of the votes, a feat never accomplished by any political party in Israel's electoral history. The Shamir et al. and Mendilow chapters in this volume discuss many of these developments in depth.

By the fall of 2005, Peres's Labor party was providing the votes necessary for the Likud-led government to maintain its majority support in the Knesset. They were willing to provide this support as Sharon's newly adopted dovish policies were more in line with their beliefs. But it was clear that Labor would leave the coalition before the 2006 elections. An internal leadership contest was held among Labor members between Peres and Amir Peretz, a labor union leader of North African heritage who had previously split from Labor to form the Am Ehad (One Nation) list and had recently rejoined the party to run for party leader. Running in the November 10, 2005 primary on a platform that included withdrawing Labor from the Sharon-led coalition, Peretz received 42.4 percent of the vote to 40 percent for Peres. Peretz called for government emphasis on social and economic justice and a more conciliatory stance toward the Palestinians. Peretz's selection represented the first time a major political party had nominated a Sephardi candidate for prime minister. An extensive analysis of the selection of leaders and lists is presented in Rahat's article in this volume. Two days after the primary the Labor ministers resigned from the Cabinet, leaving Sharon and his government without a majority in the Knesset.

Sharon's intra-party difficulties were evident throughout this period, most clearly when he failed to win Knesset approval for several ministerial appointments he proposed. Likud MKs joined the opposition in voting against his proposal. It was also clear that former Prime Minister Binyamin Netanyahu would challenge Sharon's leadership of Likud.

Charges of corruption and favoritism were also in the air and probably played a role in the decisions made. Allegations were leveled against Sharon and his sons, Omri and Gilad, regarding shady affairs that included nepotism, accepting bribes, misconduct in the office, and breach of faith. Sharon's sons were accused of being involved in illegal fundraising to finance their father's election campaign in the 1999 Likud primary, culminating in the Cyril Kern affair. The state comptroller pointed out Sharon's disregard for the conflict of interest between his official role and his son's ownership of agricultural land affected by a proposed transaction. Another embarrassing revelation was the agreement signed between contractor David Appel and Gilad Sharon whereby the prime minister's son would receive three million dollars in return for helping to promote Appel's plan to set up an island resort in Greece. This inquiry into bribery charges was closed by Attorney General Mazuz, but Omri was indicted in the scandal relating to fundraising for his father's 1999 bid to lead the Likud party, and on November 15, 2005, he pleaded guilty in a deal with prosecutors.

He was sentenced to nine months in prison, a nine-month suspended sentence, and a fine of almost $80,000, although the start of his prison term was delayed by six months because of his father's health. Many of these issues of corruption are discussed in Navot's article.

With all of these incidents as background, Sharon decided to set up Kadima, an act that would inevitably lead to a split in Likud. This move was loaded with symbolism beyond its obvious political significance, because it was Sharon's efforts in 1973 that had initially brought about the formation of Likud. On November 21, 2005, Sharon announced that he was leaving Likud to form a new, more centrist party, which was eventually named Kadima. Thirteen other Likud ministers and Knesset members joined him. Labor's Shimon Peres—who had just lost the Labor leadership election to Peretz—Haim Ramon, and Dalia Itzik soon after announced their support for the new party. Tzachi Hanegbi and Shaul Mofaz also deserted Likud to join Kadima, as did other Knesset members and individuals not then active in party politics. On December 18, the members of Likud selected Netanyahu to head its list with less than half of the members voting; Netanyahu received 44 percent of the votes, compared to Foreign Minister Silvan Shalom's 33 percent.

The formation of Kadima turned the election into a three-way race among Kadima (the new party), Labor, and Likud. Polls taken through the end of 2005 showed Sharon's Kadima party enjoying a commanding lead over both Labor and Likud. Led by Sharon, the stage seemed set for a Kadima landslide by appealing to the center of Israel's political map with Labor's Peres at his side, rejecting the stridency of the right, and presenting himself as the only leader who could achieve both security and peace. Moreover, Labor could be portrayed as out-of-touch since it continued to campaign on a social-economic platform, and Likud seemed to retain its recalcitrant role. In addition, Peretz gained a reputation as a representative of sectoral interests after heading the Histadrut Labor Federation for many years, and Netanyahu's recent tenure as finance minister branded him as a heartless capitalist willing to take benefits away from children and the disabled.

A dramatic change in Sharon's health altered the calculations. Sharon suffered two strokes before the elections; the first was on December 18, 2005, the very day that Likud held elections to select its leader. Sharon was released from the hospital two days later and continued to function as prime minister. The second stroke, on January 4, 2006, left him in a coma and ended his political career.

Sharon, as founder of Kadima and the incumbent prime minister, was universally expected to lead the new party into the March 2006 election. When Kadima submitted its list of candidates, Sharon was absent from the list due to his inability to sign the necessary documents to be a candidate. Ehud Olmert, who had become acting prime minister and acting chairman of Kadima when Sharon became incapacitated, was now officially the new party's candidate for prime minister. Peres was in second place on Kadima's list of candidates. Foreign

Minister Tzipi Livni was third on the Kadima list, with the understanding that she would be the senior vice premier if Kadima formed the next government.

In the Shinui primaries, Tel Aviv council member Ron Leventhal defeated Avraham Poraz for the number two spot. Poraz, a close ally of party leader Yosef ("Tommy") Lapid, subsequently resigned from Shinui, as did most Shinui Knesset members, forming a breakaway party called Hetz (Arrow). Neither Shinui nor Hetz received sufficient votes to win any seats in the Seventeenth Knesset. Shinui had won fifteen seats in the 2003 election and was the third largest party in the Sixteenth Knesset.

On January 30, 2006 the right-wing National Union (HaIchud HaIeumi), a coalition of three small parties (Moledet, Tkuma, Tzionut Datit Leumit Mitchadeshet), submitted a joint list with the National Religious Party (Mafdal). The merged list was headed by Binyamin Elon. The largely Russian immigrant Israel Beiteinu (Israel Is Our Home) party separated from National Union and ran a separate list. It did well in the election, and this is discussed in the articles by Konstantinov and by Philippov in this volume. This separation occurred following polls that predicted that, when running separately, these two major rightist blocs would receive between twenty to twenty-five seats (in the previous elections, they had received only seven), and it turned out to be true: the National Union bloc received nine seats and Israel Beiteinu received eleven.

B. Setting the Election Date

The date of the election was set for March 28, 2006. Determining the date of Knesset elections is both a constitutional and a political act. By law, elections are to be held every four years unless earlier elections are called. Earlier elections can be decided on by the Knesset, or by the prime minister with the concurrence of the country's president; they can disband the Knesset and thus bring about early elections.

Setting the date for the 2006 elections became embroiled in controversy before the politicians began discussing the matter. The issue over whether the Knesset's full term would expire in November 2006 or in October 2007 erupted in 2005 when a reporter discovered that a mistake had been made while passing a relatively minor amendment to the Basic Law: Government. The oversight occurred when the Knesset voted to abandon the direct election of the prime minister and to reinstate the parliamentary system that Israel had historically used.

According to the Basic Law: Knesset, if parliament votes to disperse before the end of its legal term in office, the next parliament will hold office until the month of Heshvan after it has completed four full years in office. If the Knesset serves its full term in office, the next parliament will hold office until the month of Heshvan, which comes before the end of its fourth year. Furthermore, according to the original Basic Law: Government, if the prime minister disbands parliament, it will be regarded as if the Knesset dispersed itself. Therefore, the next Knesset can serve more than four full years.

Prior to the 2003 elections, the Knesset passed an amendment to the Basic Law: Government, which extended the time between the dispersal of parliament until the next election from sixty days to ninety days. In writing the amendment, and evidently due to an oversight, the words that had appeared in the Basic Law: Government to the effect that if the prime minister disbands parliament it is to be regarded as though the Knesset dispersed itself were not included.

In 2002, Prime Minister Sharon and President Katsav disbanded parliament and brought about the elections of 2003 rather than have the Knesset disperse itself. According to the original law, this act would have been regarded as if parliament had disbanded itself. But the amendment to the law extending the election period from sixty to ninety days forgot to specify that fact. Everyone agreed that the words were deleted in error, but the Supreme Court ruled that it could not assume the Knesset's intentions when the provision was not specifically mentioned. Accordingly, the court ruled that elections would have to be held no later than the end of 2006, and not in 2007 as many politicians preferred.

In the end these matters were not that important because conditions were ripe for early elections well before the final possible date. Sharon was frustrated in his fighting with coalition partners and members of his own Likud party and approached the President of Israel, Moshe Katsav, to ask for his consent in disbanding the Knesset and holding new elections shortly after announcing his resignation from Likud and the formation of Kadima. The president offered to consider the request. In the meantime, some Knesset members proposed legislation which would bring about elections on a date of their choosing, a date later than the one that the prime minister preferred. A parallel move was made by other Knesset members to try to form an alternative government to the one led by Sharon that would avert the early elections. After two days of intense negotiations, an agreed upon date was reached. President Katsav and Prime Minister Sharon announced that elections would be held on March 28, 2006.

III. The Campaign

Polls conducted from January through March showed Kadima enjoying a substantial lead over all the other parties. It reached its highest levels of support in January, well after Sharon's incapacitation, with a projection of over forty seats in the Knesset. Later on its support declined, and the polls closest to election day gave it thirty-four to thirty-six seats.

Sharon remained part of Kadima's message throughout the campaign, and its Internet site continued to be titled http://kadimasharon.co.il. In their electoral campaign, Kadima and the parties of the right vowed to continue the relentless fight against the Palestinian militants, which Sharon had lead since 2001. During the al-Aqsa Intifada, more than a thousand Israelis were killed in Palestinian terrorist attacks. Sharon's security policy during that time focused on arresting or killing members of the militant organizations, by means of frequent military excursions into the Palestinian territories and somewhat controversial targeted assassinations, as well as curbing the movement of suspected militants—especially would-be suicide bombers—through the use of checkpoints. This policy won the support of the Jewish mainstream, but elements in the Jewish left, as well as the vast majority of the Arab population, vehemently opposed what they viewed as an excessive response to the security threat. Some claimed that Israel's policy was actually encouraging more violence from the Palestinian side. Despite the decrease in violence during 2005 and 2006, or perhaps because of it, popular support for the security policy remained high among the Israeli public, which continued to fear suicide bombings and Qassam rocket attacks. The continuation of Palestinian violence in spite of the unilateral disengagement, and the results of the January 2006 parliamentary elections in the Palestinian Authority, which brought Hamas to power, ensured that security and foreign affairs issues would not lose their dominant place in the election campaign. Even Labor, traditionally thought of as a more dovish party, put "combating terrorism" at the top of its agenda on the conflict, alongside the social economic plank in its platform.

Notwithstanding the prominent place of the Israeli-Palestinian conflict, the election of Amir Peretz as the head of Labor firmly positioned the social agenda in the forefront of the campaign. As outlined in Weimann et al., the media and much of the parties' advertisements focused on poverty, education, health, and welfare, with the campaign adapting itself to the climate of opinion rather than leading it. On the public's agenda, internal social, economic and political issues took the lead over conflict-related concerns.

The article by Weimann et al. also portrays a "spiral of cynicism" that characterized the media and the public regarding the campaign, and by extension, the parties, the elections, and politics overall. Indeed, the weakening attachment to political parties and the increasing rates of rejection and derision regarding the political parties are major characteristics of the changing Israeli party system, as discussed in Shamir et al. The Internet is one mechanism used by the parties to increase contact with the public, and the article by Atmor indicates the uses and the limitations of that medium. In any case, the 2006 campaign exhibited low efficacy and high levels of alienation and disdain from politics. In the Israel National Election Study (INES) post-election survey, we asked our respondents about the reasons for the low turnout. The most frequent explanation was that politics and politicians were viewed derisively by the public.

The pre-election polls overestimated the vote for the establishment parties, in particular for Kadima, and underestimated the vote for new parties and for niche parties whose voters are not distributed widely throughout the population. The contraction of the Kadima vote from the optimistic projections of the pollsters is attributed to a large extent to the withdrawal of Sharon from the campaign as a result of his illness, and the appeal of Lieberman to the Russian voters as discussed in the article by Philippov in this volume, and to the Pensioners party campaign appeals. The interest generated by the Pensioners party increased dramatically in the last days of the campaign and its appeal spread by word of mouth. Many voters evidently sensed the shift and switched their own votes as well. Voters flocked to it once it was projected in the last polls of the campaign as passing the 2 percent threshold needed for representation.[1] The success of the Pensioners party can thus be seen as an example of strategic vote considerations, in addition to its being a protest vote. Other strategic voting considerations concern coalition preferences and prospects, and those were also evident, even if rarer in 2006 than in other recent Israeli elections; these are analyzed in Abramson et al. Tepe and Baum discuss Shas, another niche party, and compare its position and ideology with similar parties in Turkey. Rekhess's article on the vote of the Israeli Arabs sheds light on a series of electoral issues that are different from those facing most Jewish voters.

IV. Voting Turnout

Voter turnout in the 2006 elections for the Seventeenth Knesset stood at 63.5% of all the citizens in the electoral register (3,186,739 out of 5,014,622 people, 294,547 more than in the 2003 elections).[2] Figure 1 presents turnout rates for each of the national elections held in Israel since it became a state in 1948. The lowest rate was recorded in the special elections for prime minister in 2001. The 2006 Knesset elections turnout was, however, the lowest in Knesset election history. Average turnout for Knesset elections in 1949-2006 was 78.6 percent. The turnout rate for 2006 represents a trend of increasing indifference to, and alienation from, elections and politics.

When the turnout rate is calculated based on the voting age population of those who are eighteen and over and residing permanently in Israel, the rate is higher. The Israeli electoral register also includes citizens who have emigrated to other countries. Citizens outside the country's borders do not have the right to vote (except for Israeli emissaries), therefore turnout rates seem lower than they actually are if the base of the calculation were to include those who could potentially vote. Dividing the number of ballots cast by the number of citizens aged eighteen and over, in the population of those residing in the country, results in a turnout in 2006 of 70.8 percent.[3]

The decline in the turnout of Israeli Arabs was even larger and more noteworthy than the decline in the electorate in general. The 19 percent turnout rate in the 2001 special elections for the prime minister was an exception with an unusually low turnout rate, since neither of the candidates for prime minister, Ehud Barak and Ariel Sharon, appealed to Arab leaders or to Arab voters, and the political parties were not up for election. Even if the 2001 turnout is unusually low, the overall picture is one of decline in Arab voter turnout. The phenomenon of abstention from voting which characterizes Arab citizens is evidence of weakened support

Figure 1
Voter Turnout in Israeli Elections, 1949-2006

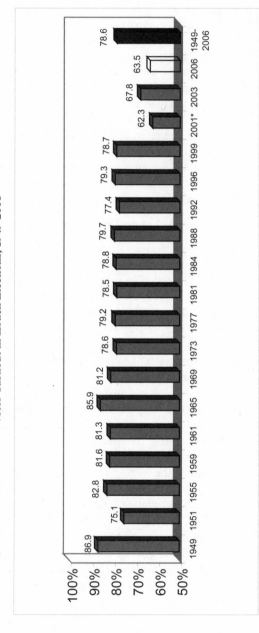

*Special elections for prime minister only

for the political parties, the Knesset, and Israeli democracy overall. Rekhess discusses the issue of turnout among Arab voters, which reached its lowest point in Knesset elections in 2006, with only 56.3 percent voting.

A drop in voter turnout is a phenomenon typical of most Western democracies,[4] reflecting a weakening of social ties and of political parties, a lack of public trust in the traditional party and parliamentary political system, and a growing inclination to resort to alternative, extra-parliamentary channels. In Israel it came about quite abruptly in 2001, and has continued ever since. The low and declining turnout among Israeli voters is arguably the most significant aspect of the 2006 elections. It solidifies a trend begun earlier, and adds yet another topic of dissension to the long list already in play in the Israeli political system. As the system remains unsettled, there are those who call for further reform of the electoral system while others point to the persistent cleavages among Jews and Arabs, religious and secular, doves and hawks, rich and poor, immigrants and veterans, as causes of the unrest and disengagement from politics. Whatever its determinants, there can be no debate about the debilitating effect a lowered rate of participation has on a democratic system. As its most public aspect, elections are a bellwether of democratic life. The turnout rate of 2006 and the downward trend of that rate over the last decade indicate the distress the system is undergoing and signal the need for remedial action by politicians as well as by reformers of the political system.

Notes

1. See Mina Zemach, "Analysis of the Pensioners Party Vote," http://ofakim.org.il/zope/home/he/1138194787/1147681685
2. See http://www.knesset.gov.il/elections17/heb/index.asp and http://www.knesset.gov.il/elections17/heb/results/Main_Results.asp
3. The estimate of the number of people 18 and over permanently living in Israel was taken from a press announcement published by the Central Bureau of Statistics on 22 March 2006. See http://www1.cbs.gov.il/reader/newhodaot/hodaa_template.html?hodaa=200624061
4. R. Dalton, "The Decline of Party Identification," in R. Dalton and M. Wattenberg, eds. *Parties without Partisans: Political Change in Advanced Industrial Democracies* (Oxford: Oxford University Press, 2000) 22.

Part 1

Voting Behavior

Kadima—Forward in a Dealigned Party System

Michal Shamir, Raphael Ventura, Asher Arian, and Orit Kedar

I. Introduction

At a press conference held on November 21, 2005, Prime Minister Ariel Sharon announced the formation of a new party, initially called "National Responsibility," but later renamed "Kadima" ("Forward" or "Onward" in Hebrew). On that same day he resigned from Likud and asked President Moshe Katsav to dissolve the Knesset. Sharon thus set in motion the process leading to early elections in March, and launched the long-rumored "Big Bang."

The background to this dramatic move was multifaceted. The short-term triggers were the loss of Labor as a coalition partner following the surprise victory of Amir Peretz over Shimon Peres in the Labor primaries for the head of the party just eleven days before, and Sharon's difficulties with rebels in his own Likud party. Just two weeks before his move Sharon was unable to get approval by the Knesset for several ministerial appointments he wished to make. Likud MKs joined the opposition in voting against his proposal, a vote which was a source of frustration and personal humiliation for Sharon. Sharon's difficulties within his party were evident from the moment he decided on the disengagement agenda for the Gaza Strip.

The "Big Bang" however, is more properly linked to the stagnation of the Israeli party system and its left and right camps. A pervasive argument was that the major political parties had lost their visions, and that, in terms used by political scientists, a realignment was long overdue. In an article published in *Yediot Aharonot* in March 2005, Haim Ramon suggested that there are three major ideological conceptions in today's Israel: the right, which is hawkish, conservative neo-liberal, and supportive of the hegemony of the religious establishment; the left, which is dovish, socialist, and for separation of the secular and religious; and the center, which is pragmatic in the area of security and foreign affairs, supports unilateral separation from the Palestinians, and is middle-of-the-road in terms of economics and state-religion issues (*Yediot*

Aharonot, March 4, 2005). True to this logic, Ramon anticipated the establishment of a new central movement that would include most of Labor, the new pragmatic Likud, and much of Shinui. It is not surprising to learn that Ramon was one of the leaders of the founding of this type of party.

After Kadima's establishment, many political pundits and politicians attributed its appeal to Sharon's popularity and deemed it opportunistic, non-ideological, inconsistent, and vague on policy—the creation of public relations spins and the brainchild of political consultants (e.g., Eldar, *Haaretz*, Nov. 28, 2005; Lam, *Yediot Aharonot*, March 31, 2006; Sternhall, *Haaretz*, Feb. 10, 2006, Feb. 23, 2006). Despite these criticisms, leading figures from Likud and Labor, as well as non-political figures, were anxious to join Kadima; some out of a sense of identification with Sharon's middle-of-the-road policy path, and others in response to the promising prospects of the party demonstrated by the public opinion surveys.

In December 2005 Sharon suffered a mild stroke, followed in January 2006 by a major cerebral hemorrhage, which left him incapacitated, and Deputy Prime Minister Ehud Olmert replaced him as the leader of Kadima. Sharon continued to be an integral part of Kadima's campaign,[1] and Kadima maintained its popularity. In the polls, its support increased even further, then declined in March, and on election day it obtained 690,901 votes, giving it 29 seats, significantly less than anticipated, but still outdistancing Labor, its closest competitor, by 10 seats.

This chapter focuses on the Kadima party in the electorate. The dense and dramatic events preceding the March 2006 election, from the Gaza disengagement in August 2005, through the establishment of Kadima in November, and the incapacitation of Sharon in January 2006, provide a unique setting for the study of the role of party attachment, leadership, ideology, and policy positions in voters' considerations. We anchor our analysis in the concepts of realignment and dealignment, to which we now turn.

II. Party System Change

There can be no doubt that the Israeli party system has undergone a dealignment process since the 1990s. Dealignment describes a general loosening of the ties between the society and the political parties in response to processes of social and political modernization (Dalton and Wattenberg, 2000). The weakening of the connections with political parties is a feature of all industrialized Western democracies and is a result of the declining role of parties as political institutions as well as changes in the electorate in recent decades, particularly in light of the increase in the number of highly educated voters, the rise in living standards, and the expansion of political knowledge. In an age of abundant information and a better-educated public, coping with political problems is no longer limited to the party system, and alternatives to politicians and traditional parties become available. More and more citizens find political answers by turning to the media, and the parties' traditional function of serving as a com-munication channel is filled by other means.

One manifestation of the slackening party system was the instability of the election results, evident in the growing difficulty of accurately forecasting elec-tion results. As ties weakened, voter turnout declined, identification with the parties decreased, and volatility grew. In addition, the tendency among voters to vote for a party other than the one with which they had identified in the past increased, the number of independents became larger, and the decision about which party to vote for was postponed to a later stage of the election campaign. Doubts about parties as political institutions grew and confidence in them sank. As party identification weakened, there was a rise in issue and one-issue voting, and in voting according to the performance of the party candidates, resulting in a fragmentation of the political party system, the disappearance of veteran parties, and the swift rise and fall of new parties in the political system (Crotty, 2006; Dalton, Flanagan and Beck, 1984; Dalton and Wattenberg, 2000; Webb, Farrell and Holliday, 2002).

A second concept used to analyze party system change is realignment. It refers to change in the cleavages underlying a party system on their three dimensions: their social structural bases, their value or collective identity characteristics, and their organizational expressions. A realignment involves a shift in the traditional balance of power among parties, a reorganization of ideological and social coalitional bases of major parties, and shifting group alignments, which persist for several succeeding elections. A critical election or realigning set of elections are characterized by great and highly involved voter participation, increased ideological polarization and issue-distances among parties, and the emergence of a new cleavage or substitution of one cleavage for another. After these critical elections, a new balance is in place and persists for several subsequent election campaigns (Burnham, 1970; Crotty, 2006; Key, 1955, 1959). The "Big Bang" discussed in Israeli politics in connection with Kadima is part of what a partisan realignment entails: it focuses on change in the party balance of power based on value and policy dimensions, and it also points to a long-term rather than temporary impact.

The weakening of the party system is a general phenomenon that is char-acteristic of Israel (Arian and Shamir, 2005). In Israel, the 1992 change in the Law of Direct Election for the Prime Minister may have been a catalyst in the acceleration of this trend (Arian and Shamir, 2002), but not its major source. The emergence of Kadima in the 2006 elections can be read either as another manifestation of dealignment or as an indication that the system has embarked on a process of realignment. In the next section we establish the dealignment features of the Israeli party system, further strengthened in the 2006 elections. After that, we analyze the support for Kadima from several perspectives, using various types of empirical data. In the concluding section we return to Kadima to determine whether its emergence and attendant activity were but temporary blips in the pattern of dealignment in Israel or if they indicated a break with the past and were a sign of movement toward the realignment of the party system.

III. A Dealigned System

A. Electoral Volatility

Kadima tapped into a growing predisposition on the part of Israeli voters to change their votes from one election to the next. This phenomenon is typical of voting behavior in many democracies (Dalton, McAllister, and Wattenberg, 2000). A measure that assesses the extent of change in voters' behavior and in party fortunes is the index of electoral volatility, measuring the shift of votes between parties between one election and the next (Pedersen, 1979). The electoral volatility index ranges between a score of 0, indicating lack of volatility between parties, and a score of 100, indicating full volatility.[2] Figure 1 presents electoral volatility in Israel since the end of the 1960s using three measures: volatility of political parties, volatility of political blocs, and individual-level volatility, measured on the basis of voters' report of their past and intended vote in the INES pre-election surveys.[3] All three measures point to the same pattern. The highest level of volatility is of individuals; the two aggregate measures computed for the Knesset parties and for political blocs are lower but follow a similar pattern. We see a trend of increasing volatility in the 1990s, which peaked in the 2006 elections. It is also apparent that instability between parties within blocs has increased at a higher rate than between blocs, as the two lines grow farther apart. This pattern may be taken as further evidence of the erosion of party ties, but less of left-right bloc demarcations. Aggregate party instability reached the same level in the mid-1990s as in the 1977 realignment and by 2006 it exceeded it by 17.4 points. Bloc instability almost reached its 1977 high point in 2006 with individual-level switching reaching a higher level in 2006 than in the 1977 realignment (63 to 50 percent).

When direct elections for the prime minister were instituted in the 1996 elections, a rise in electoral volatility was recorded, but the combination of the three measures, as well as the longer time perspective afforded after the reform was annulled, do not support the conclusion that this institutional reform was a major factor associated with this instability. In the 2006 elections, individual-level instability reached 63 percent and party instability rose to 42.7 percent—the highest ever. The rise of Kadima at the center of the political map, the decline in Likud's power, the disappearance of Shinui and the success of the Pensioners' Party, are all signs of high electoral volatility. It is interesting to note that a comparative perspective demonstrates these levels of volatility as high but not exceptionally so. In terms of party volatility Israel ranks in the upper third of 29 countries, compared in Mainwaring and Torcal (2006; see in Arian et al., 2006, Figure 44, p. 75).

Figure 1
Electoral Volatility in Knesset Parties, Knesset Blocs and in Vote,
1969–2006 (percentages)

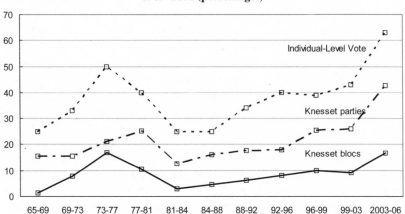

Electoral Volatility is computed according to Pedersen (1979), once for Knesset Parties, once for Knesset Blocs (Left, Center, and Right-Religious), and once for individual-level vote. See endnote 3.

B. Weakening Party Attachment

The diminishing attachment on the part of voters to political parties is a major aspect of dealignment. This weakened attachment is most beneficial to a new party such as Kadima. This quality is characteristic of the Israeli party system as it is of other countries in which the party system is waning (Wattenberg, 1998; Dalton, 2000).

A prominent measure of the parties' strength and functions is the number of their supporters, members, and activists. Party membership was once considered to be significant for many reasons, the primary one being the need for fundraising. Members' dues were vital to ensure the party's existence and its organizational renewal. In the course of time, income from membership dues dropped drastically and in 1973 the parties promoted the Political Parties (Financing) Law which became an alternative source of funds. Political parties had in the past provided many important services for their members: housing, health, education, cultural services, and mediation between their members and state institutions. Parties had activists, members, and many supporters, but the numbers eventually dwindled, and the attraction of political parties progressively dimmed. Over time, we find a long-standing and moderate trend of detachment from the parties. More and more people profess no support for any specific party and are not active in, nor are they members of, any party. Based on INES data for Jewish respondents[4] in 1969, 58 percent indicated that they supported a specific party or were active in or members of a party, whereas in the 2000s, their number dropped to about 40 percent. The rate of respondents who indicated they were party members but were not active also dropped sharply: from a height of 18 percent in 1969 to 16 percent in 1973, to 8–10 percent in 1981 through 1996, and to 5–7 percent in 1999, 2003, and 2006 (Arian et al., 2006, p. 82).

Data from the Comparative Study of Electoral Systems (CSES)[5] allow us to compare the electorate's closeness to parties over the last decade, and they indicate a similar trend. These surveys posed two relevant questions: "In general, do you see yourself close to a particular party?" and "How close do you feel to the party you indicated?" The answers to these questions were obtained in three post-election surveys in 1996, 2003, and 2006, and the data point to a drop in citizens' identification with political parties, suggesting a weakening of the party structure in general. In 1996, 64 percent saw themselves close to a party; in 2003, 62 percent; and in 2006, only 54 percent. Out of those, 37 percent felt very close to a party in 1996, dropping to 28 percent in 2003 and to 24 percent in 2006.

C. Disaffection

The skeptical attitude that many Israelis have developed toward the parties and toward the Knesset was another factor that made Sharon's break with his Likud party attractive to many. The low and declining trust in the parties and the legislature, and a propensity to indifference toward them, are once again, not unique to Israel (see Arian et al., 2006, p. 78; Norris, 1999; Pharr and Putnam, 2000; Sapanov, 2002). The trust of the Israeli public in the parties and in the Knesset is not high, and it is ranked lowest in a series of surveyed political institutions (Arian et al. 2006, figure 18, p. 41). According to surveys of the Israel Democracy Institute, only 22 percent of respondents in 2006 stated that they trust political parties to a large extent or to some degree, similar to a 2005 rate, but lower than the rates of 27 percent and 32 percent respectively observed in 2003 and 2004. In 2006, 42 percent indicated they do not trust political parties at all, and 36 percent had little trust in them.

Political corruption is a prominent factor in the public's attitude toward the parties. Revelations of corruption during the previous Knesset term, together with the ensuing legal discussions and decisions, created a growing sense of unease toward the political system among many voters. In the 2006 Israel Democracy Institute survey, 62 percent felt that the system was corrupt to a large extent, and only 9 percent thought that the extent of corruption was small or non-existent. Furthermore, the public thought that a political career meant renouncing integrity: 49 percent of respondents noted that getting to the top in politics requires one to be corrupt. Respondents also thought that politicians do not keep their promises: only 17 percent agreed with the statement: "The politicians we elect try to keep the promises they made in the election campaign."

In sum, skeptical attitudes toward the parties are endemic to Israeli politics and have increased over time. The evidence points to increasing distrust of political parties and politicians' promises. This atmosphere worked to the advantage of Kadima, although in the final days of the campaign it seemed to benefit the Pensioners' Party.

IV. The Support for Kadima in 2006

A. Voters Attracted to Kadima: The Role of Sharon, Policy, and Party Identification

Kadima attracted most of its votes from those who had previously voted for three parties: Likud, Labor, and Shinui. Our INES post-election survey in April 2006[6] revealed that 42 percent of the Kadima vote came from voters who had selected Likud in 2003, 23 percent from past Labor voters and 17 percent from Shinui. New voters made up only 4 percent of Kadima's total. Most of the analysis in this section is based on a three-wave panel study conducted at three critical junctures: in July 2005, shortly before the Gaza disengagement; in December 2005, right after the establishment of Kadima and the announcement of early elections;[7] and in April 2006, following the elections.[8] This unique data set enables us to track voters, their attitudes, and their vote intentions from the period prior to the disengagement, through the establishment of Kadima and until after the elections. According to the December phase of this survey, 53 percent of respondents who revealed their 2006 vote intention, and who reported that they voted for Likud in 2003, 37 percent of 2003 Labor voters, and 74 percent of Shinui voters said they would vote for Kadima. In the end, according to the April post-election survey, these figures were 31 percent of 2003 Likud voters, 27 percent of former Labor voters and 42 percent of Shinui voters. The bulk of the votes that Kadima lost in that period from former Likud voters went to the Pensioners' party. Most of the votes lost to Kadima from former Labor voters reverted to Labor, and many of the votes Kadima lost from former Shinui voters went to Israel Beiteinu (Avigdor Lieberman's party). Many of those in the last group were immigrants from the former Soviet Union. Moreover, in comparing the characteristics of the respondents who stayed loyal to Kadima until election day with those who said in December that they intended to vote for Kadima but eventually voted for another party, we see that the former were those who better fit the profile of the typical Kadima voter, as we shall demonstrate.[9]

In the analysis below we focus on those Kadima voters whose previous choice was Likud, Labor, and Shinui—the bulk of Kadima voters. When asked why they chose Kadima instead of their 2003 party in an open-ended question in the December survey, a wide variety of responses were collected and grouped according to the major reason offered (see table 1). More than half of former Likud voters cited personal support for Ariel Sharon. Former Labor voters talked most often about Sharon's and Kadima's policy, and former Shinui voters pointed out their dissatisfaction with their former party and its leaders. It appears, therefore, that the factors influencing former Likud and Labor voters to switch to Kadima were mainly "pull" factors, while former Shinui voters were more influenced by "push" factors (since their former party was no longer a viable electoral option).

These data suggest the pivotal role of Sharon in propelling the defection to Kadima. Likud adherents pointed out their personal support for him (56 percent) and former Labor voters emphasized his policy and performance (51 percent). Whether these differences reflected actual differences or a form of expression, the first panel in table 2 shows the high levels of evaluative and affective support for Sharon among all groups that supported him, as measured in July 2005, before Kadima was founded. We offer a comparison between five groups:[10] Loyal Likud voters; switchers from Likud to Kadima; loyal Labor voters; switchers from Labor to Kadima; and switchers from Shinui to Kadima. There is no group of loyal Shinui voters because there were almost no Shinui voters left by the end of 2005. Among those who had voted Likud in 2003 but later said they planned to vote Kadima, 18 percent said Sharon was the best prime minister Israel ever had. Among those who remained with Likud, only 4 percent chose Sharon. Among those who had voted Labor but said they would vote Kadima, 14 percent chose Sharon compared with 3 percent who chose Sharon among those who continued to vote Labor. Sharon's love-hate feeling thermometer means tell the same story: Support for Sharon seems to be the common denominator for those who selected Kadima.

Table 1
Major Reason Given for Voting Kadima[1] by 2003 Vote (percentages)

| | 2003 Vote | | |
	Likud (N=88)	Labor (N=37)	Shinui (N=45)
Personal support for Ariel Sharon	56	5	9
Positive performance evaluation of Sharon	3	19	9
Disappointment with former party or its leadership	16	22	55
Support for Kadima's candidates	3	11	4
Support for Kadima/Sharon's policies	7	32	7
Kadima is a better choice	8	8	2
Change in the public agenda	2	3	9
Other	5	-	5

[1] December 2005 survey

Table 2
Voter Characteristics by Transition/Loyalty Groups, 2003 and 2006

2003 vote choice	Likud	Labor	Shinui		
2006 vote choice	Kadima	Likud	Kadima	Labor	Kadima
Reaction to Ariel Sharon					
Mean Sharon thermometer score[1, 3, 4]	7.05	5.25	6.41	4.90	7.13
% seeing Sharon as the best PM in Israel's history[1, 4]	18%	4%	14%	3%	11%
N	(101)	(48)	(37)	(60)	(46)
Major Factor Determining Vote Choice[2, 4]					
Party identification	6%	23%	11%	26%	22%
Party's candidate for prime minister	52	45	51	16	33
Party's stand on certain issues	33	28	30	55	40
Status of party in coalition or opposition	9	4	8	3	5
N	(98)	(47)	(37)	(62)	(46)
Party Identification, Membership and Activity[1, 5]					
Neither identifier nor active in any party	82%	83%	90%	71%	85%
Identifier with a party but not a member	14	13	5	21	15
Party member (active/non-active)	4	4	5	8	-
N	(101)	(48)	(37)	(60)	(46)

[1] Questions asked in July 2005.

[2] Question asked in December 2005.

[3] Scale 1–10 (1 – hate; 10 – love).

[4] Differences between Likud loyalists and switchers and between Labor loyalists and switchers statistically significant (p<.05).

[5] Differences between Likud loyalists and switchers not statistically significant (p=.97); differences between Labor loyalists and switchers statistically significant at p=.08.

The critical role played by Sharon in the establishment and success of Kadima may also be understood by examining what supporters of Kadima coming from both Likud and Labor said was the most important factor that determined their vote compared to Likud and Labor loyalists. Over 50 percent in each group of these switchers said in December that they chose their party because of the candidate for the prime ministry (see second panel in table 2). Loyal Likud voters were not much different (45 percent offered the same rationale), but those loyal to Labor were more likely to say that their voting choice was based on ideology (55 percent), and only 16 percent said that it was determined by the candidate for prime minister. A third of 2003 Shinui voters chose the candidate for prime minister as the determining factor of their vote.

Likud and Labor loyalists also mentioned party identification as the factor determining their vote more often than Likud and Labor deserters, although they amounted only to about a quarter of each group (23 and 26 percent respectively). A better basis for assessing the role of party identification in electoral behavior in 2006 is provided by examining the distinction between respondents defining themselves as party members, activists, or identifiers (see last panel in table 2). Among 2003 Likud voters, party identification did not matter at all in determining their support for Kadima in December, but among 2003 Labor voters, 21 percent of those who remained loyal to Labor defined themselves as identifiers compared to only five percent of the switchers to Kadima (p=.08).

Further support for this difference between Labor and Likud with regard to support for Kadima is obtained from an open-ended question we asked in the December 2005 survey about the political atmosphere in the home in which the respondent grew up. In table 3 we can see that many of those who chose Kadima after having voted Likud in 2003 identified their home environment as committed to one of the parties that made up the Likud (41 percent), more than among those who remained loyal to the Likud (13 percent). By contrast, those who remained loyal to Labor were more likely to label their home as committed to constituent parties of Labor than those who switched to Kadima (38 and 18 percent respectively). Although based on small Ns and not statistically significant, these results reinforce those in table 2 to suggest that party identification was still of significance in determining vote intention for Laborites but not for Likudniks.

The self-reports of switchers to Kadima (table 1) seemed to indicate that for 2003 Likud voters Sharon himself was the major factor rather than policy, whereas for 2003 Labor voters Sharon's policy and performance were what mattered. However when we examine the ideological and policy underpinnings of

Table 3
The Political Environment at Home[1] by Transition/Loyalty Groups
(by percentages)

Former vote choice	Likud		Labor		Shinui
Present vote choice	Kadima	Likud	Kadima	Labor	Kadima
Socialist, Communist	13	6	11	9	7
Left, radical left, moderate left	4	19	39	35	14
Labor, Alignment, Mapai	8	12	18	38	25
Center, center-left, center-right	10	-	11	6	7
Liberal, Bourgeois	-	-	-	-	11
Likud, Herut, Beitar	41	13	11	6	7
Right, radical right, moderate right	16	31	-	-	18
Religious, National Religious	-	6	5	3	4
Other	8	13	5	3	7
N	(51)	(16)	(18)	(32)	(28)

[1] December 2005 survey.

 Chi square test for full table statistically significant p<.01; former vote choice Likud only: p=.12; former vote choice Labor only: p=.40.

the move to Kadima in greater depth, by means of further comparisons of Likud and Labor loyalists and switchers to Kadima, a different picture emerges.

Based on cross-sectional survey data usually used in election studies, it is difficult to ascertain the role voters' attitudes play in electoral shifts, given the likelihood of voters adopting the positions of the new party to which they have shifted for other reasons. Our panel design offers information on a respondent's attitudes espoused in July 2005, before the establishment of Kadima, and even before the implementation of the Gaza disengagement. We can therefore confidently establish the role of policy positions in voters' transition to Kadima. Even though only few of the Likud switchers to Kadima attributed their move to policy considerations, table 4 shows that they were significantly different from Likud loyalists in their attitudes on security and foreign policy issues, with differences reaching thirty to forty percentage points on some items. Compared with Likud voters who remained with Likud, Likud switchers to Kadima were more inclined to remove settlements, to support the unilateral disengagement, and to believe that it was possible to reach an agreement with the Arabs. They were also more moderate in their assessment of the aspirations of the Arabs and more willing to compromise on the Golan Heights (although these two differences are statistically significant only at $p=.09$ and .08 respectively).

Labor voters who shifted their support to Kadima did not differ significantly in their security and foreign affairs positions from those who continued to support Labor. The two Labor groups were similar in their support of the disengagement plan, in their belief in a settlement with the Palestinians, and in the degree of outright opposition to compromise (although more Labor loyalists compared to Labor deserters supported wide-scale territorial compromise in the West Bank and the Golan Heights, but these differences were not statistically significant). Kadima voters from Shinui were more similar to Kadima voters who came from Labor than to those who came from Likud.

There were no significant differences between Likud switchers and loyalists and between Labor switchers and loyalists in terms of a socio-economic viewpoint, although Labor-Labor voters were more likely to identify themselves as strong supporters of socialism (47 percent) compared to the Labor voters who shifted to Kadima (35 percent; not shown in table). In terms of state-religion relations, Kadima switchers from both Likud and Labor espoused somewhat more secular points of view than loyalists, although these differences were not statistically significant.

As to socio-demographic characteristics, there were no significant differences between those loyal to the party and those who defected by age, ethnic origin, gender, and education. Two differences are worth noting, however. Among loyal Likud voters 14 percent reported being religiously observant, compared to 3 percent among those who switched to Kadima (statistically significant at $p=.09$). Among loyal Labor voters, 29 percent reported a living density higher

Table 4
Voter Issue Positions[1] by Transition/Loyalty Groups (percentages)

2003 vote	Likud		Labor		Shinui
2006 vote	Kadima	Likud	Kadima	Labor	Kadima
1. No settlement evacuation whatsoever	18	52	14	13	9
Evacuate only small and isolated settlements	60	33	51	43	50
All settlements should be evacuated	22	15	35	44	41
2. Should not return any part of the Golan Heights	59	75	30	29	35
Return only a small part	26	21	35	20	43
Return a significant part	15	4	35	51	22
3. Support the disengagement plan	76	31	92	92	95
4. Arabs aspire to conquer all of Israel	60	71	22	28	46
5. Not possible to achieve peace agreement with the Palestinians	59	77	33	34	47
6. Government should see to it that public life is conducted according to Jewish tradition	54	60	30	41	36
7. Capitalist (rather than socialist) economic structure	51	57	38	36	58
N	(100)	(48)	(37)	(61)	(46)

[1] July 2005 survey
All chi square tests for Labor loyalists and switchers non-significant. For Likud loyalists and switchers, questions 1, 3, and 5: $p<.05$; question 2: $p=.08$; question 4: $p=.09$; questions 6 and 7 beyond standard levels of significance.

than one person per room, compared with only 14 percent among Labor switchers to Kadima (statistically significant at $p=0.08$).

Given these results, the most interesting questions relate to the impact of party identification, issue positions, and affect toward Sharon on voters' decision to remain loyal or desert their party in favor of Kadima. Table 5 presents multivariate analyses allowing for more incisive scrutiny of electoral choice and changes during the campaign. We performed binary logistic regression analysis separately for past Labor and past Likud voters to assess the combined effect of (1) Sharon's evaluation, (2) attitudes in the areas of security and foreign affairs, social-economic policy, and state-religion relations, and (3) party identification on their vote intention in December 2005 and in their actual vote as they reported it in the post-election (April 2006) survey.[11]

The upper panel of table 5 displays the results for 2003 Likud voters. The major factors that distinguish Likud loyalists from Likud switchers to Kadima are their evaluation of Sharon and their policy position in the area of security and foreign affairs (indicated in the model by their position on the evacuation of settlements). Both effects are greater in April than in December, and this increase is most striking with regard to the voters' policy position. In other words, in the end, when it came to the actual vote, policy mattered more than at an earlier stage, and it mattered more than affect toward Sharon.[12] None of the other variables reached standard levels of statistical significance, however it is worth noting that two more variables grew in importance in April and reached a level of statistical significance of .11: party identification and the voter's position on state-religion relations. While not statistically significant under commonly used criteria, there is an indication that among past Likud voters, those less strongly identified with the party were more likely to actually desert it (even though in December there was no sign that party identification made any difference—b was .20 and non-significant). The same was true of those holding a more secular position on the state-religion dilemma. But above all, more dovish voters, and voters with greater sympathy toward Sharon, were the ones to switch to Kadima.

The lower panel of table 5 presents the same logistic regressions for 2003 Labor voters. The number of observations we have here is smaller, and all goodness of fit measures indicate that we are much less successful in predicting their vote than the vote of those who voted Likud in 2003, both with respect to vote intention revealed in December and the vote reported in April after the elections. Socialist vs. capitalist orientation is the only factor with an appreciable effect on voters' loyalty to Labor or switching to Kadima (in the April equation), meaning that (other things being equal) 2003 Labor supporters who switched to Kadima were more capitalistic in their socio-economic orientation, whereas those loyal to Labor (and Amir Peretz) were more socialist in their orientation. The party identification coefficient is not statistically significant, although it is in the predicted direction in both equations.

In summary, the Kadima electorate that voted for Likud in 2003 did so because of their affinity for Prime Minister Sharon, and even more so, because of Kadima's more moderate position on foreign and security matters, with which they concurred. We are less successful in explaining the shift to Kadima by former Labor voters; however, what is most pronounced in the multivariate analysis is that those who agreed with the party's economic policies formulated by the new leader, Amir Peretz, were more likely to remain loyal to Labor than those who tended toward a more capitalistic orientation. These results concur with the voters' agenda as they stated it in our post-election survey. Past Likud voters, and in particular those who moved to Kadima, stated more often that negotiations with the Arabs and the security situation were the topics that most affected their vote rather than the socio-economic situation. Among 2003 Labor

Table 5
Logistic Regression for Labor and Likud loyalists and Kadima switchers

	December 2005		April 2006	
2003 Likud voters	b	(SE)	b	(SE)
Party attachment	0.20	(0.57)	-1.57	(0.97)
Sharon affect	0.19*	(0.08)	0.26*	(0.13)
Evacuate settlements	0.78*	(0.35)	1.94**	(0.69)
Oppose Halakha in public life	0.08	(0.21)	0.60	(0.37)
Support socialist over capitalist approach	0.20	(0.18)	0.28	(0.30)
Constant	-2.70*	(1.23)	-5.00*	(2.24)
N	(130)		(68)	
LL	-70.5		-29.7	
Nagelkerke R2	.18		.48	
Chi Square (significance)	17.8 (.003)		28.9 (<.001)	
2003 Labor voters	b	(SE)	b	(SE)
Party attachment	-0.57	(0.70)	-0.88	(0.96)
Sharon affect	0.16	(0.10)	0.17	(0.16)
Evacuate settlements	-0.19	(0.40)	-0.47	(0.54)
Oppose Halakha in public life	-0.02	(0.25)	0.58	(0.37)
Support socialist over capitalist approach	-0.39	(0.23)	-0.91**	(0.34)
Constant	0.95	(1.67)	1.28	(2.36)
N	(75)		(57)	
LL	-47.4		-29.7	
Nagelkerke R2	.12		.29	
Chi Square (significance)	7.0 (.218)		13.2 (.002)	

Dependent variable: 0 – party loyalist; 1 – Kadima switcher
* p<.05 ; ** p<.01

voters, the picture was more complex, and it was therefore harder to predict their vote. Loyal Labor voters overwhelmingly mentioned the socio-economic situation as the factor that most affected their vote. The priority of Labor switchers to Kadima lay in the realm of security and foreign affairs.[13] As to Shinui voters who voted Kadima, here the explanation is much simpler—they were utterly disaffected with Shinui and were looking for another center option which Kadima naturally offered.

B. Accounting for the Kadima Vote versus Other Parties

We will now examine the Kadima electorate in comparison to the other parties, beginning with their views on major policy issues. Table 6 presents policy positions of voters for the major parties, and we find Kadima voters in-between the left and right parties. They are similar to Labor voters in terms of unilateral moves, territorial compromise, and the Arab neighborhoods of Jerusalem. Regarding the concessions to which they are ready to agree (such as the evacuation of settlements in Judea and Samaria or withdrawal from the Golan Heights), the Kadima voters are somewhere in between the Likud and Labor groups. They reject solutions that call for "not one inch" and for complete withdrawal. They are also between the two other groups regarding the aspirations of the Arabs.

On socio-economic matters, Kadima voters are more similar to Likud voters than to Labor voters. Regarding religious matters, Kadima voters are more similar to voters of Labor and hold more secular views than Likud voters.

But are these ideological and policy differences between Kadima voters and the voters of the other parties maintained once other factors are taken into consideration? To conduct a more in-depth exploration of the vote for Kadima, we analyzed the differences between Kadima and the other party voters by means of a multinomial logistic regression. In this analysis, Kadima served as a reference in comparison to other parties: Meretz, Labor, Likud, Israel Beiteinu, Yahadut Hatorah, Shas, and Ihud Leumi-Mafdal. The vote predictors included socio-demographic background characteristics of voters (education, density of living, age, gender, immigrant vs. veteran, and religiosity); the issues of territories, state-religion relations, and socio-economic policy; prospective performance evaluations in the security, economic, and social realms, and affect toward Sharon.[14] The detailed results are presented in Appendix 1.

The results bolster the analysis of loyal Likud and Labor voters versus switchers to Kadima (tables 4 and 5), and the differences we observed between the vote groups in table 6. Policy issues and prospective performance evaluations significantly discriminate between Kadima and the other party voters, and security and foreign affairs are pivotal, both in terms of issue position and in terms of prospective performance evaluation when comparing Kadima to other party voters. Voters' position relative to territorial compromise in the West Bank is significant in all comparisons with Kadima (except for Yahadut Hatorah for which only the issue of religion and state is significant). Kadima voters are more hawkish than Labor and Meretz voters, and more dovish than all the parties to the right of it. With respect to the parties to the left of Kadima, voters' positions on social-economic policy also matter. Only for these parties does prospective performance on welfare-oriented policies reach standard levels of statistical significance. Compared to Kadima, left-wing party voters tend to have a socialist position on the structure of the economy (although this difference is only significant for Labor). Right-wing party voters tend to be more capitalistic, but the differences are not statistically significant (except for Israel Beiteinu). For all parties to the right of Kadima (except for Israel Beiteinu), the issue of state-religion is significant.

Table 6
Voter issue positions by vote choice[1]

	Meretz	Labor	Kadima	Israel Beiteinu	Likud	Shas + Yahadut Hatorah	Ihud Leumi-Mafdal
No settlement evacuation whatsoever	-	13%	18%	46%	54%	62%	82%
Evacuate only small and isolated settlements	38%	42%	65%	50%	38%	38%	18%
All settlements should be evacuated	62%	45%	17%	4%	8%	-	-
N	(21)	(93)	(127)	(50)	(60)	(37)	(38)
Should not return any part of the Golan Heights	5%	28%	48%	81%	80%	86%	95%
Return only a small part	33%	29%	32%	15%	12%	9%	5%
Return a significant part	62%	43%	20%	4%	8%	5%	-
N	(21)	(93)	(126)	(52)	(61)	(35)	(38)
Support further unilateral withdrawal	86%	72%	62%	17%	18%	14%	8%
N	(72)	(247)	(407)	(153)	(181)	(132)	(104)
Arabs aspire to conquer all of Israel	22%	31%	49%	83%	72%	86%	88%
N	(74)	(239)	(412)	(156)	(181)	(132)	(104)
Should give up Arab neighborhoods of Jerusalem	81%	70%	62%	66%	30%	25%	21%
N	(21)	(92)	(126)	(50)	(60)	(36)	(38)
Government should see to it that public life be conducted according to Jewish tradition	20%	32%	37%	35%	69%	95%	88%
N	(71)	(191)	(379)	(156)	(169)	(129)	(104)
Capitalist (rather than socialist) economic structure	27%	21%	49%	80%	49%	30%	40%
N	(74)	(247)	(402)	(154)	(179)	(129)	(100)

[1] March 2006 survey.
All chi square tests statistically significant p< 0.001.

Another interesting result of this analysis is that controlling for all the other variables in the model, affect toward Sharon was a factor in people's support for Kadima versus all the other parties, even though Sharon was incapacitated and not an active candidate or potential office-holder.

In terms of the social underpinnings of the vote, religiosity stands out as the most persistent variable determining vote choice, statistically significant in the Meretz equation, just about significant in the Likud equation (p=.06), and significant for all religious parties. Kadima voters are less secular than Meretz voters, similar to Labor and Israel Beiteinu voters, and less religious than all other parties to the right of it. Our class indicator (household density) has an effect for Likud, Yahadut Hatorah, and Shas, indicating that voters of a higher economic class are more likely to endorse Kadima than these three parties. Compared to Israel Beiteinu, Kadima was much less likely to attract FSU immigrants, but more likely to do so than Labor.

Figure 2 presents probabilities of voting for Kadima, Likud, and Labor, based on our multivariate model.[15] Here we vary respondents' positions on territorial compromise, government involvement in the economy, and state-religion relations, while setting all other variables at their means. Nominal variables are set such that the hypothetical respondent is a female, and not an immigrant from the former Soviet Union. The probabilities on the vertical axis then are the predicted probabilities of endorsing each of the three parties for a hypothetical "average" individual given the relevant range of positions on the three issues.

The first panel of the figure presents a voter's inclination to endorse each of the three parties as she moves from supporting a territorial compromise as part of a permanent agreement with the Palestinians to opposing it. As the figure shows, the less a voter is willing to compromise , the less likely she is to endorse both Kadima and Labor, with a decline of about 16 percentage points in the likelihood of endorsing Kadima and about 30 percentage points in the likelihood of endorsing Labor. The likelihood of endorsing Likud, on the other hand, increases from about 6 to 30 as the voter becomes more apprehensive about territorial compromise. While the pattern for Labor and Likud is linear, the pattern for Kadima is curvilinear, reflecting its center position on this dimension. The highest probability for voting Kadima is among moderate doves. Among the most dovish voters, the highest probability is for voting Labor (and very close to it—voting for Kadima). Among the two middle categories, Kadima is the most likely choice. Among the three parties, Likud is the most likely choice for the most hawkish respondents.

While voters seem to be reacting similarly to Labor and Kadima on the peace-security dimension, a different pattern emerges from the economic dimension, as seen in the second panel of the figure. Kadima voters are indifferent to government involvement in markets, while Labor voters clearly prefer such involvement. As we move from those expressing support for a capitalist way of life to those endorsing socialism, the likelihood of supporting Labor increases

Figure 2
Probabilities of voting Kadima, Labor, and Likud, by issue positions.

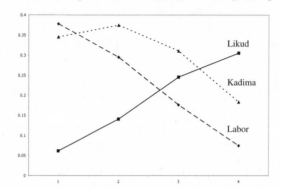

Territorial compromise (agree to disagree)

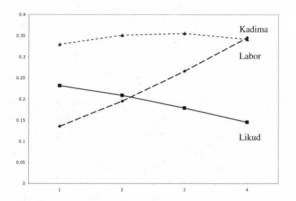

Economic position (capitalist to socialist)

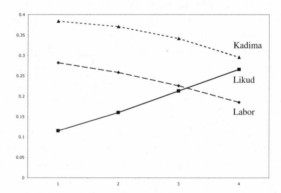

Separation of state and religion (yes to no)

by 20 percentage points. The opposite holds true for Likud support: the likelihood of supporting Likud moderately decreases with greater preference for government involvement in the economy.

An examination of the third issue regarding the relations between religion and state reveals an interesting pattern. It is similar in its general outline to the peace-security dimension and consistent with the interpretation of these two dimensions as internal and external dimensions of collective identity in Israeli politics (Shamir and Arian, 1999). Here, too, Labor supporters resemble Kadima supporters, and both groups show a mild decline in their vote intention as we move toward involvement of the state in maintaining Jewish life. Likud voters are also set apart; supporting involvement of the state defining Jewish life increases one's likelihood of endorsing Likud by 15 percentage points. However, the potency of this internal identity dimension in the 2006 elections (with respect to the three parties examined here) is significantly weaker than that of the external dimension—as in the past. The primacy of the security-peace dimension over the other issue dimensions in electoral behavior is clearly established.

C. Kadima as a Center Party

As demonstrated so far, and in accordance with the Big Bang thesis, the story of Kadima is more than just Sharon's whim. The unilateral withdrawal from Gaza and Sharon's leaving Likud were the catalysts for the formation of Kadima but only offer a partial explanation. It is likely that Kadima would not have been established without Sharon, but it is also true that Kadima was more than a one-man show, and it would not have endured were it not for its resonance with the public's preferences. Perhaps the best evidence was its continued existence after Sharon's strokes removed him from the political scene. The party tapped into fertile soil in offering the Israeli electorate a party alternative that epitomized the median voter's stance—a specific combination of the left and the right: a growing willingness for compromise from the left together with deep mistrust of the Palestinians (and Arabs in general) from the right. These were the distinctive features of Sharon's policy and heritage, embodied in the unilateral disengagement and the separation fence. This is the thrust of the meaning of the center—falling between Labor and Likud and between left and right: a pragmatic middle ground with a specific platform detailing well-defined foreign and security policies. Unlike most new and center parties, Kadima came to the elections with a platform which was already being put into effect by Sharon. In 2005 post-disengagement Israel, Sharon was inescapably associated with the disengagement and with unilateralism, as was Kadima. In this sense Kadima was different from other center parties Israel has known. Examples include the Democratic Movement for Change (DMC) which conquered the center of the political map in 1977 after gaining 15 Knesset seats, and Shinui which repeated this success in 2003.

Table 7
Left-right self-placement, by vote[1]

Vote Choice	Left-Right Placement Mean	N
Hazit Leumit Yehudit	1.00	5
Ihud Leumi-Mafdal	3.03	37
Yahadut Hatorah	3.38	13
Likud	3.39	41
Shas	3.45	22
Israel Beiteinu	3.67	48
The Pensioners	3.88	17
Kadima	3.93	86
Labor	5.13	61
Meretz	5.62	13
Hadash	6.11	9

[1] INES data: Vote report from April post-election survey; left-right self-placement from March pre-election survey. Differences statistically significant at p<.001.

In 2006, Kadima captured 29 seats in the 2006 elections to the Seventeenth Knesset. Another new party—the Pensioners party—gained 7 seats As the Pensioners party did not have a clearly defined position on political and defense issues, and its mandate was to protect the civil rights of the elderly in Israel, it cannot be defined as either a leftist or rightist party. Thus 36 of the 120 Knesset seats (30 percent) went to center parties, at the same time that 29 percent of the 2006 respondents placed themselves in the center of the left-right political continuum.

The size of the center vote and bloc in the 2006 Knesset is unprecedented; not so with the percentage of citizens identifying themselves as center rather than left or right. This was the average size of the center-identifiers since the beginning of the Israeli election studies in 1969 through the mid-1980s (Arian and Shamir, 2005, Table 1.2, p. 17).

There is clearly a less than full correspondence between center self-iden-tification and the vote. Indeed, as in previous election years, there is the least amount of correspondence between self-placement and a vote for the center, compared to the left and the right. Fifty-seven percent of center identifiers voted for one of the two center parties, but 73 percent of right-wingers voted for a right-wing/religious party, and 71 percent of the left-wingers for a left party. Looked at from the other direction, 51 percent of the vote for Kadima and the Pensioners party came from voters identifying themselves as center. This compares with 72 percent of the left-wing party vote which came from left-wingers, and 78 percent of the vote for the right coming from voters identifying with the right. This is the general pattern also observed in previous elections, although the differences are somewhat attenuated because in 2006 more voters of all groups voted for a center party.[16]

The interpretation of Kadima as center is well supported by an examination of voters' self-placement on the left-right scale, defined in Israel primarily by the security and foreign affairs dimension. Table 7 presents the mean self-identification scores of the INES respondents on a 1–7 right-left scale as measured shortly before the elections in March, grouped by their vote report. Kadima voters are located pretty much in the middle of the scale (3.93), next to the Pensioners party (3.88), and the order of parties we obtain spreads across almost the full spectrum and corresponds to common placement of the political parties in Israeli politics. It is worth noting that the order of parties according to a left-right self-placement mean, as presented in table 7, is identical to the order of parties relative to security and foreign affairs positions, as reflected in table 6. Our July–December panel data allow us to assess voters' stability on this scale. During the six turbulent months between July and December 2005, there were no significant differences between the placement of the voters planning to vote for Kadima (paired samples t-test p=.867), nor for that matter for any of the other party groupings.[17]

It has been argued that over time the left-right division in the Israeli multi-party system has become more meaningful, useful, and prevalent (Arian and Shamir, 2002), and in intergenerational socialization the left and right labels have become more important and relevant than a specific party identification, especially since the structural change from a dominant party system to a competitive system (Ventura, 2001). Within this context it is interesting to return to table 3, which provides a glimpse at political socialization sources. It shows that Kadima attracted voters from both right-wing and left-wing political homes. Offspring tend to choose a party acceptable to their parents; in multi-party systems of the Israeli type, this is a party from the same political bloc, defined primarily in left and right terms (Ventura, 2001). The fact that Kadima's leadership included prominent figures from both Likud and Labor made it easier for voters from different political backgrounds to opt for Kadima, without alienating themselves from their political homes. Whether center has become or will become another identification category on this continuum is questionable, but it is clear that new center parties like Kadima enjoy advantages in attracting voters over parties on the left and on the right.

V. Conclusion

The unprecedented success of Kadima in winning an election a few months after its establishment is far beyond that achieved by any other center party in Israel's electoral history. In the past, the Israeli party system has been inhospitable to center parties, and their historical course deserves attention. The Democratic Movement for Change (DMC) aroused great enthusiasm in the 1977 elections, gaining fifteen seats, but disbanded after about a year. Its heir, Shinui, gained only two seats in the 1981 elections. The Center Party headed by Yitzhak Mordechai participated in the 1999 elections and captured only six seats. Its members soon abandoned it and the party sank into oblivion. Shinui, under the leadership of Tommy Lapid, was the surprise of the 2003 elections, gaining fifteen seats. In the Seventeenth Knesset it too obtained no representation, following its dissolution after internal elections in the party council on the eve of the 2006 elections. Other center parties, like Moshe Dayan's party, Ezer Weizman's party, and the Third Way fared even worse, and were also short-lived.

How can we explain Kadima's extraordinary achievement? Will Kadima's future be different from other center parties?

Like other center parties, Kadima also drew together figures from both sides of the political spectrum. It talked about new politics and about change, and placed itself in the center of the policy space. However, unlike any of its predecessors, Kadima ran as the ruling party, with a perceived strong chance at forming the next government. In the past, Israeli voters who opted for a center party waived the opportunity to determine who would be the next ruling party in government. In 2006, for the first time in Israel's electoral history, people could vote for a center party that was also a potential ruling party. As a newly established party it was also the outgoing ruling party, headed by an experienced leader who had just pulled off the unprecedented unilateral disengagement from the Gaza Strip. Furthermore, it did not locate itself simply in the middle of the policy space, but rather raised a clearly defined policy banner—unilateralism—which combined growing willingness for compromise together with deep mistrust of the Palestinians. The policy of disengagement had become the reference point in the political discourse, and Kadima entered the campaign with a platform and a suggested policy path. While it was not a policy outgrowth of a grand vision such as Greater Israel or a New Middle East, but rather the product of pragmatic adjustment to pressing and changing realities, at the time of the elections of 2006 it seemed that this path would in some sense be duplicated in the West Bank as well. Other major factors in favor of Kadima were Ariel Sharon—present and absent—and the gallery of senior and eminent leaders from both the left and the right. The Likud brought Ehud Olmert, Tzipi Livni, Shaul Mofaz, and Tzachi Hanegbi. Labor offered Shimon Peres, Haim Ramon, and Dalia Itzik. Other popular non-political figures included ex-chief of the Shin Bet Avi Dichter and Professor Uriel Reichman. But above all, as we amply demonstrated, Kadima fit the median voter's stand on the major issue dimension of Israeli politics relating to the Israeli-Palestinian conflict.

Sharon is no longer part of Israeli politics, and the policy of unilateralism has become obsolete since Hamas' rise to power in the Palestinian Authority in January 2006, the Kassam rockets fired from the Gaza strip into Southern Israel, and the second Lebanon war in the summer of 2006. Sharon's Gaza disengagement did not produce the hoped-for results, Olmert's convergence or realignment plan was shelved, and the unique policy blend Kadima offered dissipated. Above and beyond the difficulties encountered by the unilateralism policy, the question of agency is of course crucial for the future of Kadima: Leadership and organization are vital. However, as our focus is on Kadima in the electorate, the major question in this context is whether the Israeli party system has been undergoing a realignment or a dealignment.

Our conclusion, in accordance with previous research, is that the Israeli party system has undergone dealignment, and the striking success of Kadima was made possible by the depth of this dealignment, at the same time that it contributed to it. However, in a dealigned system a new party may thrive for a variety of reasons. In the political discourse about Kadima, two theses were presented. One was the "Big Bang" thesis, and the other the spin and ideology vacuum interpretation. Our analysis firmly established the "Big Bang" interpretation over the ideological vacuum interpretation. Our panel data on voter issue positions, as well as our multinomial choice analysis, demonstrated the solid policy basis of Kadima in the electorate, in particular on the major issue of contention in Israeli politics—the Israeli-Palestinian and Israeli-Arab conflict. Kadima was thus not a spin, nor merely the making or remaking of Sharon, but a timely response of the party system to voter preferences, grounded in policy. Indeed many voters of moderate and middle-of-the road views on the Israeli-Arab conflict found their place in Kadima.

The 2006 elections were characterized by a dramatic change in party balance. This restructuring was unmistakably based on policy, and was also buttressed by the prevailing social divides of religiosity, class, and ethnicity. Their role seems to have been heightened, as the more religious and less affluent past Likud voters, as well as FSU immigrants, were less likely to vote for Kadima, leaving Likud more religious and less well off than ever before. Thus, with the Likud split, the right has become more homogenous on these social characteristics. But the shifting vote patterns were not grounded in changing social coalitions or issue dimensions. They restated the existing ones. No significant new dimension emerged, nor did we find any indication for a shake-up of the traditional social bases of the vote. The social economic agenda promoted by Amir Peretz, which seemed to eclipse security concerns in November and December 2005, lost its lead as the campaign dragged on. Most significantly, the social-economic cleavage did not emerge as a significant dimension in voters' considerations (except for voters of the left parties) nor did it materialize in a significant redrawing of the social basis of the vote. Amir Peretz as minister of defense, and the insignificance of Labor in the formulation of social and economic policy in Olmert's government, banished the thought that this cleavage would emerge as a dominant force in Israeli politics in the foreseeable future.

In terms of policy dimensions, security and foreign affairs remained the major issue of contention on which Kadima occupied a central position (see figure 2). There was no emergence of a new cleavage or substitution of one cleavage for another. Moreover, the 2006 elections did not exhibit any of the typical symptoms of realignment—particularly high electoral involvement, concern and turnout, and increased ideological polarization. If anything, there was no electoral enthusiasm, turnout dropped to a record low, and perceptions of party differences were smaller than in the past (Arian et al., 2006, Figure 54, p 92).

Above and beyond all these findings which negate a realignment interpretation, our conclusion that a lasting partisan realignment is not on the horizon is based on the depth of the dealignment of the Israeli party system, which in the most fundamental sense works against such a possibility. The establishment and success of Kadima befits the dealignment model much more than it does a realignment model.

Our results agree with the dealignment model, which posits, as we found, volatile, unattached voters with weak party identification which, in turn, has limited effect on vote choice, as well as great weight of issues and candidates in voters' considerations. In the vote choice model, apart from social affiliations, issues and performance evaluations mattered, as well as affect for Sharon. Kadima was the beneficiary of this dealigned party system in 2006, but in future elections it may well be on the losing side. Despite the appearances of a realignment, and despite the apparent correspondence of Kadima to the median voter on security and foreign affairs, the emergence of Kadima is primarily one more milestone on the long road of the dealignment of the Israeli party system.

Notes

1. Months after the election, Kadima's Internet site was still labeled http://kadimasha-ron.co.il.
2. The formula for calculating the index is to subtract the votes that each party (bloc) received in the previous election from the votes it received in the current election, total the absolute values of the differences, and divide it in two.
3. The Israel National Election Study (INES) surveys have been conducted since 1969. The surveys between 1969 through 1977 were carried out by the Israel Institute of Applied Social Research and were based on a representative sample of the adult urban Jewish population. Later surveys were representative of the adult Jewish population, excluding kibbutzim and settlements in the territories. Since 1996 all election surveys included both Jews and Arabs. Interviews through 1999 were face-to-face interviews. Since 2001 the surveys have been conducted by telephone and are representative of the adult population, including kibbutzim and settlements. All surveys were pre-election surveys, although in some of them (including the 2006 elections) they were complemented by post-election surveys. The following institutes have carried out the surveys since 1981: Dahaf between 1981 and 1992; Modi'in Ezrachi in 1996; and Mahshov since 1999 (http://isdc.huji.ac.il/ehold1.shtml).

   Individual-level vote volatility is computed from cross-tabulations of voters' vote intention by their report of past vote in INES pre-election surveys. The categories comprise: Left, Labor, Center, Likud, Religious, Right, and no answer. The number reported is the percent that generated a change in category over the two periods. The figures are based on Jewish respondents only, since until 1992 the samples were of the Jewish population only. Respondents with no previous election vote report (no vote or no right to vote) were excluded. Respondents who gave "no answer" once were considered volatile. Those who gave "no answer" to both questions were not included in the calculations.

The two aggregate volatility measures were computed according to the following rules (see Mainwaring and Torcal, 2006, p. 222): When a party splits into two or more parties from election T1 to T2, we compared its T1 total with the largest split off. We then treated the smaller new splinter party as if it had no votes in election T1. When two or more parties merged and created a new organization, we calculated volatility using the original party with the highest percentage. Thus if two or more parties merged for election T2, but competed in election T1 as separate parties, we assumed that the one(s) with fewer votes disappeared in election T2. We gave a zero value to this party in T2 and counted its share of the vote in T1 as its percentage of change. When a party changed its name but had an obvious continuity with a previous party, we counted them as being the same organization. Kadima in 2006 was counted as a new party, as was Tehiya in 1981. We included only parties that passed the threshold and were represented in the Knesset. If a party had seat(s) in one election but in the previous or next election received votes but no seats, we counted their vote in that election as 0 percent (even if they received some non-zero share of the vote).

The Left bloc includes Israel One, Labor, Maarach, Mapai, Ahdut Haavoda, Rafi, Mapam, Civil Rights Movement, Ratz, Meretz, Maki, Haolam Haze, Sheli, Am Echad, and Arab parties. The Right-Religious Bloc includes Likud, Herut, Liberals, Merkaz Hofshi, ShlomZion, Tehiya, Moledet, Kach, Israel Beiteinu, HaIchud Haleumi, Mafdal, Agudat Israel, Poalei Agudat Israel, Degel Hatora, Yahadut Hatorah, Tami, Shas, Zomet, and Israel B'Aliya. The Center Bloc includes the Independent Liberals, DMC, Shinu, Hareshima Hamamlachtit, Telem, Yachad, Flatto-Sharon, Ometz, Merkaz party, Haderech Hashlishit, Kadima, and Gil (Pensioners).

We wish to acknowledge the research assistance of Nir Atmor in the volatility measurement.

4. For appropriate comparison over time, the figures are based on Jewish respondents only, since until 1992 the INES samples were of the Jewish population only.

5. The Comparative Study of Electoral Systems (http://www.umich.edu/~cses).

6. The 2006 INES was carried out in a panel design. Our pre-election sample of the Israeli electorate included 1,919 respondents interviewed by phone in the month before the March 28 elections, in Hebrew, Arabic, and Russian. Our post-election survey returned in April to 1,411 of the respondents. The field work was carried out by Mahshov Survey Research Institute. Of the 1,411 interviewees, 272 indicated that they had voted for Kadima. The two waves are well representative of the population on gender, age, education, and ethnicity, although somewhat biased toward the more highly educated and older as well as second-generation Israeli-born Jews and Israeli-born Jews of European origin. In the April wave, there is also a slight bias toward European-born respondents, and a further slight bias in favor of university graduates and older respondents.

7. The December poll entered the field on December 28, and the last interviews were conducted on January 22, 2006. Most interviews (over 70 percent) were conducted before Sharon's second cerebral event on January 4, 2006.

8. The July 2005 survey was conducted among a representative sample of the Israeli adult population, N=2004. The second wave was collected in December and 898

respondents were re-interviewed. The third wave was carried out in April 2006, following the March 28 elections, and returned to 744 of the 898 respondents interviewed in the December survey. The interviews were conducted by phone in Hebrew, Arabic, and Russian by Mahshov Institute. All three waves are well representative of the population on gender, age, education, and ethnicity, although somewhat biased toward the more highly educated and Israeli-born Jews of Ashkenazic origin; and the successive waves become slightly more biased in the direction of women, middle-age, and older respondents.

9.   Voters who remained loyal to Kadima until election day were significantly more moderate in their views on peace and security; they had a stronger tendency to support capitalistic economic policies, they were more secular, and they had a much more positive view regarding Ariel Sharon and the Kadima party. They were also older on average and of higher socio-economic status than those who intended to vote Kadima (in our December survey) but eventually switched to another party (in our April 2006 survey).

10.   The transition/loyalty groups in tables 2 to 4 are defined on the basis of vote intention and past (2003) vote reported in the December 2005 survey.

11.   We used one indicator for each policy dimension. In none of the analyses was there any multicollinearity problem which might have blurred the results.

12.   We computed the probabilities of voting Kadima for voters being one standard deviation above and one standard deviation below the mean, once for Sharon's affect, and once for the evacuation of settlements variable, while setting all other variables at their means. The difference in these probabilities of voting Kadima between Sharon moderately weak and strong supporters in December 2005 was .21, and in April 2006, .30. The difference in the probabilities of voting Kadima between moderate hawkish and moderate dovish voters (so defined in terms of their position on settlements in the West Bank) was .25 in December, and in April, .49.

13.   These results stipulate an interaction specification between issue position and priority, but our N is too small for such analysis.

14.   We performed this analysis on the general sample but the dummy variable for Arabs caused serious multicollinearity problems which forced us to leave Arab voters out. The results thus pertain only to Jewish voters.

We performed the analysis with several specifications and measures. We did it twice, once with the pre-election vote intention and once with the post-election vote report as dependent variable (in the latter specification we also included the Pensioners' party as a category; we could not include it in the first specification because there were too few respondents who indicated a vote intention for this party before the elections). For both dependent variable specifications, we performed the analysis once with ethnicity coded as one dummy variable with veteran Israeli Jews as reference and FSU immigrants as 1; and also with ethnicity represented by 3 dummy variables for former Soviet Union (FSU) immigrants from the 1990s, for Ashkenazim (first and second generation), and for Mizrahiyyim (first and second generation), with second generation Israeli-born as the reference category. The results for the different models were robust and in most cases similar, and none of the Ashkenazi or Mizrahi dummies were statistically significant. We present the model with the pre-election vote intention—with the larger N—and the one ethnicity distinction (the full model is reported in Appendix 1). The model includes as predictors: socio-economic status indicated by density of living (high score, high density); education (in years); ethnicity (with veteran Israeli Jews as reference and FSU immigrants as 1); age (in years), gender (1 – female); and self-defined religiosity (in terms of religious practice; high score, religious); three issue dimensions: territories (measured by agreement to territorial compromise and evacuation of settlements in the West Bank); state-religion relations (measured by agreement that the government should see to it that public life be conducted according to Jewish religious tradition), and socio-economic policy indicated by Rs preference for capitalist (rather than socialist) economic structure; comparative prospective performance evaluations of the Kadima team in the areas of security and foreign affairs, economic policy, and social policy; and affect toward Sharon.

15. Other probabilities can be calculated from the table as well.
16. In 2003, 32 percent of center identifiers voted for a center party compared to 82 percent of left-wingers who voted for a left-wing party and 88 percent of right-wingers who voted for a right-wing party. In 1999, the corresponding figures were 51 percent for the center, 88 percent for the left and 90 percent for the right. In 2006 thus the overall correspondence between identification and vote was somewhat weaker than in the previous elections, although the percentage of consistent center identifiers and voters was slightly higher than in 1999 and significantly higher than in 2003.
17. The overall stability of the two placements is high: between July and December 2005, 37 percent of the panel respondents placed themselves exactly on the same point on the 1–7 right-left scale, 33 percent changed their self-placement by only one place, 15 percent moved two places, 10 percent—three places, and 5 percent—four or more places (N=864). Only 9 percent moved from one side to the other. As a benchmark, we may point out that the probability of an Israeli voter marking exactly the same point on the scale twice if the two events are independent is 0.17 (based on data from 2005–06).

References

Arian, Asher, Nir Atmor, and Yael Hadar. 2006. *Auditing Israeli Democracy—Changes in Israel's Party System: Dealignment or Realignment?* Jerusalem: Israel Democracy Institute.

------, and Michal Shamir. 2002. "Candidates, Parties, and Blocs." In idem, eds. *The Elections in Israel—1999*. Jerusalem: The Israel Democracy Institute, 11-33.

------, and Michal Shamir. 2005. "On Mistaking a Dominant Party in a Dealigning System." In *idem*, eds. *The Elections in Israel—2003*. Jerusalem: The Israel Democracy Institute, 13-31.

Burnham, Walter D. 1970. *Critical Elections and the Mainsprings of American Politics.* New York: Norton and Company.

Crotty, William J. 2006. "Party Transformation: The United States and Western Europe." In Richard S. Katz and William J. Crotty, eds. *Handbook of Party Politics*. London: Sage, 499-514.

Dalton, Russell J. 2000. "The Decline of Party Identification." In Russell J. Dalton and Martin P. Wattenberg, eds. *Parties without Partisans: Political Change in Advanced Industrial Democracies.* Oxford: Oxford University Press, 19-36.

------, Scott C. Flanagan, and Paul A. Beck, eds. 1984. *Electoral Change in Advanced Industrial Democracies: Realignment or Dealignment?* Princeton, NJ: Princeton University Press.

------, Ian McAllister, and Martin P. Wattenberg. 2000. "The Consequences of Partisan Dealignment." In Russell J. Dalton and Martin P. Wattenberg, eds. *Parties without Partisans: Political Change in Advanced Industrial Democracies.* Oxford: Oxford University Press, 37-63.

------, and Martin P. Wattenberg, eds. 2000. *Parties without Partisans: Political Change in Advanced Industrial Democracies.* Oxford: Oxford University Press.

Key, V. O., Jr. 1959. "Secular Realignment and the Party System." *Journal of Politics* 21: 198-210.

Key, V. O., Jr. 1955. "A Theory of Critical Elections." *Journal of Politics* 17: 2-18.

Mainwaring, Scott, and Mariano Torcal. 2006. "Party System Institutionalization and Party System Theory after the Third Wave of Democratization." In Richard S. Katz and William J. Crotty, eds. *Handbook of Party Politics*. London: Sage, 204-227.

Norris, Pippa, ed. 1999. *Critical Citizens—Global Support for Democratic Governance*. Oxford: Oxford University Press.

Pedersen, Mogens N. 1979. "The Dynamics of European Party Systems: Changing Patterns of Electoral Volatility." *European Journal of Political Research* 7: 1-26.

Pharr, Susan J. and Robert D. Putnam, eds. 2000. *Disaffected Democracies—What's Troubling the Trilateral Countries?* Princeton: Princeton University Press.

Sapanov, Shiri. 2002. *Political Efficacy in Israel in Comparative and Historical Perspective*. M.A. Thesis, Tel-Aviv University.

Ventura, Raphael. 2001. "Family Political Socialization in Multi-Party Systems." *Comparative Political Studies* 34: 666-691.

Shamir, Michal, and Asher Arian. 1999. "Collective Identity and Electoral Competition in Israel." *American Political Science Review* 93: 265-277.

Wattenberg, Martin. 1998. *The Decline of American Political Parties 1952-1996*. Cambridge, MA: Harvard University Press.

------. 2000. "The Decline of Party Mobilization." In Russell J. Dalton and Martin P. Wattenberg, eds. *Parties without Partisans: Political Change in Advanced Industrial Democracies*. Oxford: Oxford University Press, 64-76.

Webb, Paul, David Farrell, and Ian Holliday, eds. 2002. *Political Parties in Advanced Industrial Democracies*. Oxford: Oxford University Press.

Appendix 1
Multinomial logit analysis

	Meretz	Labor	Likud	Israel Beiteinu	Yahadut Hatorah	Shas	Ihud Leumi-Mafdal
Household density	-0.03 (0.56)	0.10 (0.40)	0.80* (0.39)	0.32 (0.43)	1.10* (0.50)	1.51** (0.44)	0.21 (0.45)
Former Soviet Union	-0.29 (0.72)	-1.91* (0.79)	0.61 (0.42)	2.30** (0.39)	--***	-0.37 (1.13)	-0.48 (0.68)
Religiosity	(-1.13)** (0.32)	-0.11 (0.22)	0.41 (0.22)	0.25 (0.24)	3.94** (0.67)	1.56** (0.28)	0.99** (0.26)
Age	-0.01 (0.01)	-0.01 (0.01)	0.01 (0.01)	-.003 (0.01)	-0.04* (0.02)	-0.03 (0.01)	-0.01 (0.01)
Female	0.93** (0.36)	0.01 (0.27)	-0.39 (0.29)	-0.23 (0.30)	-0.51 (0.53)	-1.08** (0.41)	-0.38 (0.37)
Education	-0.01 (0.06)	0.01 (0.05)	-0.03 (0.05)	0.08 (0.06)	0.17 (0.10)	0.02 (0.07)	0.13* (0.06)
Religion and state	-0.27 (0.20)	-0.05 (0.14)	0.37* (0.15)	-0.07 (0.16)	1.13* (0.51)	0.73** (0.25)	0.67** (0.21)
Economy	0.32 (0.18)	0.30* (0.14)	-0.17 (0.14)	-0.40* (0.16)	-0.35 (0.24)	-0.06 (0.19)	-0.28 (0.18)
Territorial compromise	-0.95** (0.27)	-0.33* (0.16)	0.74** (0.16)	0.59** (0.16)	0.40 (0.29)	0.89** (0.23)	1.55** (0.22)
Kadima prospective Performance: economy	-0.37 (0.22)	-1.15** (0.20)	-1.08** (0.22)	-0.74** (0.20)	-0.73 (0.45)	-0.55 (0.30)	-0.80** (0.30)
Kadima prospective Performance: social	-0.71** (0.23)	-1.14** (0.21)	-0.29 (0.21)	-0.31 (0.20)	-0.24 (0.45)	-0.10 (0.29)	-0.48 (0.29)
Kadima prospective Performance: security	-0.90** (0.21)	-0.92** (0.16)	-1.59** (0.19)	-0.91** (0.19)	-0.79 (0.42)	-0.96** (0.27)	-1.10** (0.26)
Sharon affect	-0.37** (0.07)	-0.27** (0.06)	-0.29** (0.06)	-0.32** (0.06)	-0.49** (0.09)	-0.38** (0.07)	-0.47** (0.07)
Constant	8.73** 1.75	7.50** (1.31)	3.34* (1.39)	2.72 (1.48)	-12.91** (3.62)	-4.06* (2.00)	-2.53 (1.77)

March 2006 survey: Reference category is Kadima. N=997, LL = -1026.89; Chi Square (significance) 1692.34 (p<.001).

Standard errors in parentheses.*=p-value<0.05. **=p-value<0.001. *** None of the 185 immigrants from the FSU included in this model endorsed Yahadut Hatorah.

Coalition Considerations and the Vote

Paul R. Abramson, John H. Aldrich, André Blais,
Daniel Lee, and Renan Levine

1. Introduction

New parties form in Israel before almost every election and often gain
representation, but they rarely win enough votes to become contenders to lead
the ensuing government. Yet from the outset of the 2006 Knesset election campaign, it was clear that the newly formed Kadima Party would emerge with a
significant share of the vote and provide the leadership for the next government.
Kadima's popularity, however, never approached the levels that would enable it
to win a majority of votes in 2006. It was apparent that the government formed
after the March 28 election would be, like all previous Israeli governments, a
multi-party coalition.

Almost all studies of voting behavior in proportional representation systems
presuppose that voters vote for representatives who are most similar to them
either ideologically or programmatically. We argue that this assumption misses
an important aspect of voting behavior: voters anticipate post-election coalition
bargaining and some votes are cast to at least partially influence that bargaining.
In the days preceding election day in 2006, much of the talk in Israel by both
media commentators and party leaders focused on the composition of the governing coalition. Parties like Meretz-Yahad and Shas, which had been outside the
governing coalition, promised potential voters that they would seek to enter the
next government, and they openly discussed the terms under which they might
join a coalition. Meanwhile, Likud suggested various coalition possibilities that
would exclude Kadima from the coalition. Might this have influenced voters to
the extent that they voted for a party other than their favorite?

In all multi-candidate or multi-party elections there are some voters that
vote for candidates and parties that are not their first choice. Because there is
no way to vote for a particular government, instrumental, utility-maximizing
voters who wish to shape policy outcomes can only communicate their coalition preferences indirectly, through their vote for a party. We examine survey
data in 2006 to test the hypothesis that some Israelis in 2006 did not vote for

their preferred party, but instead opted to vote for another party in an attempt to influence the composition of the governing coalition after the election. Indeed, we find that there was a significant amount of strategic voting, but with fewer voters planning to cast a coalition-oriented strategic vote in 2006 than in 2003 (see Aldrich et al., 2005).

2. Strategic Voting in Israeli Elections

The likelihood of voting strategically for a party or candidate other than one's favorite may vary depending upon the election rules. For example, Gary W. Cox (1997) concludes that strategic voting is most likely to occur in plural-ity-vote-win systems, such as in the U.S. and Britain, and least likely to occur under proportional representation. Moreover, the level of strategic voting under proportional representation will tend to vary: systems with relatively small dis-trict magnitudes, or with relatively high thresholds, tend to encourage strategic voting; those that have high district magnitudes and low thresholds, such as in Israel, will encourage voters to vote for their first choice. The high district magnitude and low threshold make it highly unlikely that one's vote would be wasted, unlike a vote for the third-place or lower ranking candidate in a first-past-the-post system. Even so, in such systems, some voters may abandon their first choice because they want one of the larger parties to lead the next coalition (see Felsenthal 1990; Nixon et al., 1996) or otherwise affect the composition of the governing coalition (e.g., Kedar, 2005).

Most studies of strategic voting focus on what Maurice Duverger called the "psychological factor" (Duverger, 1963, 226) or "facteur psychologique" (Duverger, 1958, 256). It postulates that voters do not want to waste their votes on parties likely to lose, thereby causing defections in plurality-vote systems. In contrast to plurality-vote systems, under proportional representation (PR) there are rewards for coming in second or third, especially in a country like Israel where multi-party governments are the norm. Rather than "wasting" a vote on the third-place party, every vote directly contributes to the size of that party's Knesset representation. These additional seats traditionally give the party increased clout in coalition negotiations with the other parties. As a result, many scholars expect that there is less incentive for voters to defect from their preferred party in PR systems.

Duverger's wasted-vote logic does not apply in situations where some par-ties risk failing to cross the threshold for minimum representation. In 2006, the threshold for representation for the Knesset was raised from 1.5 percent to 2.0 percent.[1] While the change was small, it did have a substantive effect since the Green Party gained just over 1.5 percent of the valid vote, falling short of the newly raised threshold and therefore did not win any seats. Ultimately, this concern influenced only a small number of voters, as less than six percent of the valid vote was cast for parties which did not make the cutoff.[2] Rather than considering threshold effects, our analysis focuses on a variety of aspects relative to the outcome Israeli voters anticipate will occur: (i) expectations about the likely winner; (ii) preferences among prime ministerial candidates; and (iii) expectations about and preferences over potential governing coalitions.

We concentrated our analyses on these aspects in two recent volumes of this series. For the 1999 election we demonstrated the importance of viability estimates in affecting voting choices among the three leading prime ministerial candidates (see Abramson and Aldrich, 2002; Abramson et al., 2004) in an election in which Israeli voters cast a separate vote for prime minister. Our analyses revealed two basic findings. First, whereas respondents who ranked Binyamin Netanyahu (Likud) and Ehud Barak (One Israel, a coalition of Labor and allies) first on a "love/hate" scale were very likely to vote for them (81 percent and 92 percent, respectively), only three out of five respondents (59 percent) who ranked Yitzhak Mordecai (Center Party) first intended to vote for him. Much of Mordecai's failure to hold on to his supporters resulted from the perception that he would not win. While over eight in ten supporters of Netanyahu or Barak thought their candidate would win, only half of Mordecai's supporters (51 percent) thought he would win.

We also (Abramson et al., 2005) found that the second vote these voters cast for the Knesset under the nation's traditional PR rules was also likely to be strategic. In particular, we found that such votes appear to have been based in part on voters' preferences for prime ministerial candidates, even though they voted separately for this office. These analyses demonstrated that strategic voting in the 1999 Knesset election occurred at nearly the same rate as strategic voting in elections with plurality voting.

By 2003, the direct election of the prime minister had been abandoned, but we found that strategic voting was still relatively common. Expectations relative to how the election results would affect coalition negotiations appeared to have influenced voters' decision making. Given published pre-election polls forecasting that Likud would win the most Knesset seats on election day, some voters cast their votes in an apparent effort to influence negotiations with Likud (see Aldrich et al., 2005). Hawkish voters, who desired a broad, national-unity government over a narrow, right-religious coalition, were more likely to vote for a party other than their favorite. Secular voters who supported a secular government and thought a secular coalition likely, tended to vote for Shinui more frequently than those who thought a broad, secular coalition unlikely. Our findings suggested that whenever there is a reasonable possibility of multi-party considerations playing a major role in parliamentary systems, models of voting behavior must take into account the voters' preferences about shaping the governing coalition (see also Blais et al, 2006).

In a more recent study we compared these Israeli results with those of the multi-candidate U.S. presidential contests since 1968, the 1988 U.S. presidential primaries, and results from two recent elections in the Netherlands (Abramson et al., 2006).[3] Comparing models from U.S. data with those based upon the recent Dutch and Israeli elections, we found more similarities than differences. We concluded that strategic voting is not only found in plurality-vote systems where theorists expect it, but is also likely to occur in a system where many would not expect strategic voting: in a system of proportional representation with high district magnitude and a low threshold.

Based on these results, we anticipated finding evidence of strategic voting in Israel in 2006, but of an uncertain magnitude. On the one hand, the consequences of raising the threshold and the dynamics of the election campaign created circumstances that provided another reasonably rich environment for strategic voting. On the other hand, the high likelihood of Kadima winning the election might moderate the influence of party viability measures on strategic voting, and the near certainty that Kadima's leader, Ehud Olmert, would become prime minister would greatly attenuate the effect of preferences over prime ministerial candidates on strategic voting. Thus, much as in 2003, attention should be expected to focus primarily on the influence of preferences and expectations over governing coalitions as the locus for strategic voting.

3. The Electoral Context for Strategic Choice in 2006

Kadima was formed as a centrist alternative to Likud and Labor. Kadima led by a wide margin in the polls leading up to election day, similar to the lead enjoyed by Likud in 2003. Even though its support declined from its peak in late January and early February, Kadima still held a wide lead over the other parties when the Israel Election Study began interviews on February 28. While the survey was being conducted, pollsters for Yediot Aharonot, Haaretz and the Jerusalem Post estimated that support for Kadima ranged from a peak estimate of between thirty-six and thirty-nine mandates to thirty-four.[4] No other party polled within ten seats of Kadima during this period. With such a sizeable lead throughout the campaign, it was apparent to even the most marginally attentive voters that Kadima would be the leading party in the next coalition. If voters could assume that Kadima would be the largest party, we would not expect a great deal of strategic voting for parties, per se, or over candidates for prime minister, but we might expect some to vote strategically in an effort to influence the coalition Kadima would lead.

The likelihood of Kadima leading the coalition was enhanced by Kadima's location in the center of Israel's party system. By occupying the center, Kadima retained the greatest flexibility in choosing coalition partners, while making it extremely difficult for parties on the left or the right to form a coalition excluding Kadima. While Likud leader Binyamin Netanyahu argued that a coalition of right-wing and religious parties could be formed without Kadima, commentators thought such a scenario unlikely, barring a much better showing for Likud than predicted by the polls.[5]

Survey respondents echoed the pundits' expectations that Kadima, not Likud nor Labor, would form the government after the election. Of the 1,207 respondents who speculated as to the chances of Kadima being in the next coalition, 41 percent thought it had a 100 percent chance, 79 percent gave it a better than 50 percent chance,[6] and 77.7 percent of all respondents expected Kadima to be the largest party. The average expectation for Kadima was 33 seats, compared to 21 for Labor and 20 for Likud.[7]

4. The Logic of Coalition Voting

Voters who felt certain that Kadima would be in the coalition might choose to vote for a smaller party, in hopes that by gaining additional mandates the smaller party would be able to claim wider support from the electorate. Moreover, additional mandates would enable the party to become a more likely coalition partner, and/or be given more influence in a coalition. Consequently, Kadima's strength, much like Likud's success in 2003, might prove to be an incentive to vote for a smaller party.

However, Kadima's strength could also be a disincentive to vote strategically. Felsenthal and Brichta (1985) suggested that many strategic voters were motivated by an interest in influencing which party would be the largest one in the Knesset. The largest party in the Knesset is traditionally given the first opportunity to be the coalition *formateur* (and if successful, traditionally supplies the prime minister). Although the Labor campaign emphasized the prospect of Amir Peretz becoming prime minister, there was little doubt that the leader of Kadima, acting Prime Minister Ehud Olmert, would lead the new coalition, eliminating the impetus of strategic behavior identified by Felsenthal and Brichta.

Unlike 2003, the polls at various points in the campaign suggested that two parties alone, Kadima and Labor, might win enough seats to be able to form a majority government. Almost 19 percent of the Israeli Election Study sample expected Kadima and Labor together to win 61 or more seats. The prospect of two parties being able to form a coalition without any of the small parties, whose support is normally crucial to the governing coalition, might also have motivated respondents to cast votes for either Kadima or Labor in hopes that such a coalition would indeed be feasible. At the same time, others who do not like the narrow Kadima-Labor coalition might choose to vote for a party other than Kadima and Labor in hopes of a broader coalition taking shape, even though one of those two parties is the voter's favorite.

Respondents who were optimistic yet uncertain that the large party they preferred would join the coalition, would seem to be among the voters most likely to cast a vote for that party, even if they preferred a smaller party (Abramson et al., 2005). This may be motivated by a desire to influence the composition of the coalition, or the relative influence of each party in the coalition, since cabinet ministries are typically distributed relative to party size. In contrast, parties viewed as unlikely to join the coalition would not attract the support of voters seeking to influence the composition of the coalition and might lose supporters to parties more likely to join the government.

5. Preferences over the Parties

A centrist strategy like Kadima's is not only valuable in coalition negotiations, but may also be appealing to voters. These voters might prefer moderation or compromise, or find parties in the center to be an acceptable alternative to their most preferred option. To measure preferences over parties, respondents were asked to express their level of "love" or "hate" on a 1 to 10 scale for the following seven parties in the 2006 election: Kadima, Labor, Likud, Meretz, Ihud Leumi-Mafdal, Israel Beiteinu, and Shas.[8] As table 1 indicates, Kadima's average rating on the thermometer scale was the highest. About one in three respondents rated Kadima highest, nearly double the next most highly evaluated party, Labor. Note as well that the average evaluations of the six parties other than Kadima are quite low, and the proportions ranking each of them highest are similarly quite low.

Another way to gauge the popularity of individual parties is to compare the results of a head-to-head competition using the respondent's thermometer evaluations. In table 2 we compare the relative thermometer evaluations among all seven parties. It seems very likely that Kadima was the Condorcet winner, and that it would have defeated each party in pair-wise voting.[9] Kadima has a majority over five of its six rivals. It leads Labor among 42 percent of the electorate and ties with Labor among another 28 percent. It therefore trails Labor among only 30 percent. Labor, on the other hand, maintains a majority only over Shas, although it enjoys plurality support over the other four remaining parties. Even Israel Beiteinu was preferred over Likud by more respondents. A plurality of respondents strongly preferred the Likud to only two parties, Meretz and Shas.

That Kadima appears very likely to have been the Condorcet winner suggests that Kadima was successful in positioning itself as the centrist party to Israelis. Duncan Black (1956) demonstrated that the Condorcet winner was the median

Table 1
Evaluation of Parties
Mean "Love/Hate" Scores for each Party and Percentage of
Respondents who Ranked each Party Highest

Party	Mean	% ranked highest
Kadima	5.0	31.9
Labor	4.6	16.5
Likud	3.9	9.9
Meretz	3.7	12.1
Ihud Leumi- Mafdal	3.9	8.4
Israel Beiteinu	4.0	10.8
Shas	3.4	10.5

A total of 1,473 observations in the full sample reported thermometer scores for all 7 parties, of which 1,440 had a strict highest preference.

party, in his "median voter theorem." Thus, even if Kadima had not won the most votes and been given the opportunity to form the governing coalition, it would have been an essential member of any viable majority government, a subject to which we now turn.

As the 1999 election demonstrated, merely being in the center in Israel is not sufficient to guarantee great popular support, but in 2006, Kadima was the party that respondents indicated they were most likely to vote for. Respondents

Table 2
Party Preferences
Percent of voters who prefer party (on left) in pair-wise comparison competition with party listed by column and correlation between the two feeling thermometers.

		Shas	Meretz	I. Leumi-Mafdal	Likud	Israel Beiteinu	Labor
Kadima	Preferred	**58.3**	**51.4**	**53.6**	**51.5**	**50.3**	41.8
	Tied	16.4	24.8	18.0	20.5	17.9	27.9
	Pearson's $r =$	-.14	.22	-.13	.04	-.08	.34
Labor	Preferred	54.3	49.7	48.4	44.0	45.3	
	Tied	19.6	29.7	18.5	21.1	17.5	
	$r =$	-.05	.52	-.12	-.06	-.18	
Israel Beiteinu	Preferred	41.6	43.5	28.2	34.7		
	Tied	35.1	20.4	45.4	32.9		
	$r =$	.34	-.21	.63	.46		
Likud	Preferred	45.4	44.0	35.8			
	Tied	28.3	21.2	32.4			
	$r =$	.28	-.14	.48			
Ihud Leumi-Mafdal	Preferred	41.5	39.2				
	Tied	34.5	23.7				
	$r =$	.47	-.18				
Meretz	Preferred	44.8					
	Tied	22.4					
	$r =$	-.18					

Based upon all respondents using 11-point "love/hate" scale.

The first comparison shows that 58.3 percent of the respondents preferred Kadima to Shas on the "love/hate" scale with 16.4 reporting the same level of affect for the two parties. The remainder (25.3 percent) rank Kadima higher than Shas. The correlation between the two sets of feeling thermometers is -0.14.

The cells in bold indicate that the majority of respondents rank this party first in this head-to-head comparison.

The number of respondents upon which these results are based range from a low of 1,790 to a high of 1,853. The correlations were based on an N of 1,743.

were asked, "If the elections for the Knesset were held today, which party would you vote for?" Among the 1,512 respondents who expressed a vote intention, 28 percent planned to vote for Kadima, 17 percent for Labor, 12 percent for the Likud, and 10 percent for Israel Beiteinu.[10]

6. Preferences over Potential Coalitions

Although Israeli voters cast a single ballot for a party-list, voters recognize that their preferred party will not win a majority of the seats in the Knesset. Israel had held sixteen elections since its inception, and no party or list had ever won a majority of the 120 Knesset seats. All Israeli governments have been based upon coalitions, although there have been occasional minority governments (Strøm, 1990). Therefore, informed Israelis must think in terms of the coalition likely to be formed after the election. The Arian and Shamir survey asked respondents to evaluate seven coalition possibilities: a coalition formed between Kadima and Labor; between Kadima and Likud; among Kadima, Likud, and the Haredi parties;[11] among Kadima, Labor, and the Haredi parties; among Kadima, Likud, and the right; among Kadima, Labor, and Meretz; and among Kadima, Labor, Likud, right, and the Haredi parties, that is, "a national-unity government."[12] The results of these ratings are reported in table 3.

We studied four coalition types in our analysis of the 2003 election (Aldrich, 2005). A national-unity government was strongly preferred to both a left-leaning and a right-leaning narrow coalition, and was weakly preferred to a secular coalition. But in 2006, a national-unity coalition was the second *least*-preferred coalition. A "narrow" left coalition of Kadima and Labor received the highest average thermometer rating by far, and was the highest rated coalition for nearly

Table 3
Evaluation of Potential Coalitions

Coalition	Mean	% ranked highest
Kadima-Labor	5.7	36.2
Kadima-Likud	4.4	11.5
Kadima-Likud-Haredi	3.7	6.8
Kadima-Labor-Haredi	4.1	3.6
Kadima-Likud-Right	4.2	13.7
Kadima-Labor-Meretz	4.5	14.6
National Unity*	4.1	13.6

1,147 respondents reported thermometer scores for all 7 potential coalitions. After settling ties for first preference using the responses to the question following the feeling thermometers identifying the respondent's favorite party, we calculated the percentage that ranked each coalition the highest from a total of 990 respondents.

* National Unity was defined in the survey as a coalition including Kadima, Labor, the Likud, right, and Haredi parties.

two out of five Israelis. The next highest average score went to the "wider" left coalition of Kadima, Labor, and Meretz. The average thermometer rating for the six other coalition options closely followed the level of approval for the wider left coalition. A coalition composed of Kadima, Labor and Meretz was favored by 14.6 percent of the respondents. A similar percentage preferred a National Unity coalition (despite its lack of general support), or a right-coalition led by Kadima. Coalitions including Kadima, Labor or Likud, and the Haredi parties were the least popular both in terms of average feeling thermometer and the percentage of respondents who preferred these coalitions over all others.

The popularity of a Kadima-Labor coalition can also be seen in the pair-wise comparisons as reported in table 4. Kadima-Labor is even closer to a Condorcet winner among coalitions than Kadima is among parties. A pure majority preferred it to all but two coalitions, and in these two it came quite close, making the large percentage of ties on this limited-range scale all but certain to yield a majority favoring it over every other coalition. The second-favorite coalition by this standard was Kadima-Likud (followed closely by the three-party coalition of the left), which might seem surprising as Likud was not among the three most popular parties in this survey. The least popular coalitions included the Ultra-Orthodox "Haredi" parties.

The government formed after the election was a close approximation of the Kadima-Labor-Haredi option, although it also included Gil, the small Pensioners' Party.[13] This coalition was not as popular as Kadima-Labor-Meretz, especially for supporters of Kadima and Labor. Including Shas changes the coalition median on security issues as Shas's commitment to a pullback from the territories is not as clear as Kadima's or Labor's. Including Shas also affects policies on budgetary and religious matters. Adding Meretz would theoretically have moved the coalition's policies towards the left, closer to Labor. These data suggest that supporters of a Kadima-Labor coalition would have been quite comfortable with a coalition that included Meretz, since the correlation between evaluations of a Kadima-Labor coalition and Kadima-Labor-Meretz coalition was .61. In contrast, the correlation between evaluations of a Kadima-Labor coalition and a Kadima-Labor-Shas coalition was still positive, but it was a weaker .36. Meretz did not win enough seats in the election to enable Kadima-Labor-Meretz, or even Kadima-Labor-Gil-Meretz, to form a majority coalition, thus thwarting the hopes of these voters.

7. Thermometer Evaluations of the Parties and Vote Intentions

If all actors voted sincerely, we would expect them to vote for their first choice from among the available alternatives. In table 5 we show the first choice of potential voters among seven parties and their voting intentions. As with our analyses of the 2003 Arian and Shamir survey, we display voting intentions only for those parties toward whom affect has been measured on the "love/hate" scales.

Table 4
Coalition Preferences
Percent of voters who prefer coalition in pair-wise comparison with coalition listed by column and correlation between the two coalitions' feeling thermometer scores.

		Kadima-Likud	Nat'l	Kadima-Labor-	Kadima-Likud-	Kadima-Labor-	Kadima-
		Haredi	Unity*	Haredi	Right	Meretz	Likud
Kadima-	Preferred	54.9	52.9	53.4	51.4	48.2	44.6
Labor	Tied	18.1	19.3	27.4	16.9	34.8	23.9
	Pearson's $r =$	-.14	-.08	.36	-.22	.62	-.01
Kadima-	Preferred	41.7	39.1	43.2	38.2	42.6	
Likud	Tied	40.5	31.6	26.3	35.3	22.7	
	$r =$	.55	.39	.15	.59	-.03	
Kadima-	Preferred	42.0	39.6	37.8	37.5		
Labor-	Tied	24.9	26.4	31.6	26.6		
Meretz	$r =$	-.13	-.04	.25	-.13		
Kadima-	Preferred	34.8	32.3	37.2			
Likud-	Tied	41.1	38.3	27.7			
Right	$r =$	.54	.47	.15			
Kadima-	Preferred	30.7	36.3				
Labor-	Tied	43.1	31.1				
Haredi	$r =$	.43	.29				
National	Preferred	34.5					
Unity	Tied	37.4					
	$r =$	.48					

The first comparison shows that 54.9 percent of the respondents prefer a Kadima-Labor coalition to a Kadima-Likud-Haredi coalition on a "support/reject" scale and that 18.1 percent tie the two coalitions. The remainder (27 percent) rank a Kadima-Likud-Haredi coalition higher than a Kadima-Labor coalition.

The cells in bold indicate that the majority of respondents rank this coalition first in this head-to-head comparison.

The number of respondents upon which these results are based range from a low of 1,158 to a high of 1,176.

Compared to 2003, a greater percentage of voters intended to vote for their favorite party, with supporters of the largest parties more likely to cast a sincere vote than supporters of smaller parties.[14] According to the 2003 Israeli survey, 78.6 percent intended to vote for the party they ranked first. In 2006, 86.3 percent planned to vote for the party they ranked first on the feeling thermometers. In each of the last two elections this broke down into two distinct groups. Among respondents who ranked Labor and Likud first in 2003 (N = 277), 87.4 percent planned to vote for their favored party; among supporters of six smaller parties (N = 334), 71.3 percent did.

As table 5 demonstrates, the three parties expected to be the largest in 2006 did a remarkably good job holding on to the respondents who ranked them first on the feeling thermometers. Among the respondents who ranked Kadima, Labor, and Likud highest on the feeling thermometer (N = 655), 91.9 percent intended to vote for their favorite parties; among those who ranked one of the

Table 5
Party Preference and Vote Intention

Highest Ranked Party	Intended Vote for							
	Kadima	Labor	Likud	Meretz	Mafdal	Israel Beiteinu	Shas	Total
Tie	25.2	24.4	19.5	3.3	12.2	11.4	4.1	100
	31	30	24	4	15	14	5	123
Kadima	91.0	4.6	1.9	0.5	0.3	1.4	0.3	100
	335	17	7	2	1	5	1	368
Labor	2.4	93.5	1.8	2.4	0.0	0.0	0.0	100
	4	157	3	4	0	0	0	168
Likud	3.4	0.0	92.4	0.0	0.8	3.4	0.0	100
	4	0	110	0	1	4	0	119
Meretz	6.2	23.7	2.1	67.0	0.0	0.0	1.0	100
	6	23	2	65	0	0	1	97
Ihud Leumi-Mafdal	1.0	3.1	7.1	0.0	82.7	4.1	2.0	100
	1	3	7	0	81	4	2	98
Israel Beiteinu	7.8	2.6	9.5	0.0	2.6	76.7	0.9	100
	9	3	11	0	3	89	1	116
Shas	1.3	6.6	7.9	1.3	1.3	0.0	81.6	100
	1	5	6	1	1	0	62	76
Total	33.6	20.4	14.6	6.5	8.8	10.0	6.2	100
	391	238	170	76	102	116	72	1165

four remaining parties first (N = 387), 76.7 percent planned to vote for the party they ranked highest. In 2003, each of the three parties on the right, Mafdal, Ihud Leumi, and Israel B'Aliya, retained less than 50 percent of their supporters. In 2006, each party retained more than 65 percent of its supporters.[15]

While the number of respondents who intended to vote sincerely appears higher than in previous elections, a substantial number of voters chose not to vote for their favorite party. In the following section we will show how strategic considerations most likely motivated many of these insincere voters. At the same time, we will explain why strategic defections were less prevalent in the context of the 2006 election and how the context of the election in particular affected the larger parties. This will enable us to answer the following two questions: First, why were Kadima, Labor, and Likud so much more successful in retaining their supporters than the other four parties? Second, why did the smaller parties have a greater, if incomplete, success in holding onto their supporters than in previous elections?

8. Loyalty and Defection

One possible explanation for the loyalty of the large party supporters could be their interest in ensuring that their party provides the next prime minister by becoming the largest party. Since Kadima voters expected both Labor and Likud, on average, to win between eighteen and twenty-one seats compared to thirty-seven for Kadima, this may not have been a very strong consideration for Kadima voters. However, this might have been a consideration for both Likud and Labor voters. Likud and Labor supporters had inflated expectations of their favorite party's success on election day. Even though pre-election polls and respondents to the Israel Election Study as a whole gave Labor a slight edge over Likud, respondents to the survey who favored Likud expected their party to receive the second highest number of mandates; twenty-eight for Likud but only twenty-one for Labor. The mean number of expected mandates Likud supporters gave Kadima was only thirty-one, affording Kadima only a small advantage over Likud. Similarly, Labor supporters had a slightly biased expectation of their own electoral success, anticipating twenty-five mandates for Labor compared to only seventeen for Likud. If these partisans thought their favorite party still had a chance to be the largest party, there would be little incentive to defect. In contrast, in 2003, even most Labor supporters expected Likud to become the largest party.

Other voters on the right did not share the Likud partisans' optimism about the strength of Likud relative to Kadima, although they did expect Likud to be larger than Labor. Similarly, Meretz supporters expected Kadima to win eleven more mandates than Labor, the second-largest party. There was little incentive for many of these voters to help create the largest party since these voters already expected Kadima's Ehud Olmert to form the coalition. However, the uncertainty as to which party would be the second largest party provided an incentive to vote strategically in an effort to increase the likelihood of their favorite coalition forming (with their favorite party).

9. Coalition Preferences, Expectations and Party Choices

As we pointed out above, coalition preferences were substantially different in 2006 than in 2003. In 2003, a national-unity government was the most popular preference. Table 6 shows thermometer evaluations for the coalitions grouped by the respondents' favorite party (as measured by the "love/hate" scale for parties). The last column of the table indicates that a national-unity government was disliked by supporters of every party other than Ihud Leumi-Mafdal and Shas.[16]

In examining these scores for coalition preferences among the supporters of the seven parties, we find that most coalition preferences are consistent with party preferences. For instance, Labor supporters strongly favored a Kadima-Labor coalition, followed (at a considerable remove) by a Kadima-Labor-Meretz coalition. Meretz supporters preferred these same two coalitions. Likud supporters

Table 6
Mean Coalition "Love/Hate" Scores, by
Party Ranked First on "Love/Hate" Scales

Mean Coalition Score	Kadima-Labor	Kadima-Likud	Kadima-Likud-Haredi	Kadima-Labor-Haredi	Kadima-Likud-Right	Kadima-Labor-Meretz	National Unity	Number
Party Ranked First								
Kadima	**7.4**	4.6	3.4	4.5	3.9	5.3	4.0	330
Labor	**7.4**	3.5	2.8	5.0	2.8	6.2	3.4	157
Likud	4.2	**6.4**	4.8	3.9	5.5	3.3	4.6	96
Meretz	**6.8**	3.0	2.1	3.2	2.4	6.4	2.7	121
Ihud Leumi-Mafdal	2.5	4.2	4.6	3.5	**6.1**	2.3	5.4	77
Israel Beiteinu	3.4	4.6	3.7	3.2	5.3	2.8	4.2	92
Shas	3.7	4.9	**6.8**	**6.0**	5.3	2.7	**5.5**	92
Total	5.9	4.4	3.7	4.3	4.1	4.7	4.1	965

Only includes respondents who rated all seven parties.

The entries are mean scores for each coalition based on a scale ranging from 1 "strong rejection" to 10 "strong support." The first entry shows that respondents who ranked Kadima first on the "love/hate" scale gave an average score of 7.4 for a Kadima-Labor coalition.

Only respondents with a strict highest party preference are included here, so total mean coalition scores differ from values in table 3.

The cells in bold denote the highest coalition score for each row.

preferred Kadima-Likud, followed by the Kadima-Likud-right coalition. On average, supporters of the right-wing parties, Israel Beiteinu and Ihud Leumi-Mafdal, preferred a Kadima-Likud-right coalition over a Kadima-Likud or a national-unity coalition.

In light of these findings, in table 7 we more closely examine the relationship between partisan evaluations and coalition preferences. First, we ask if the respondent's favored party is also in his or her favored coalition. The evidence in table 6 suggests that the favored party is likely to be in the favored coalition, but the evidence in table 7 provides additional proof. Part A of table 7 displays the percentage of respondents whose most highly rated party is in their favorite coalition; part B shows the percentage of respondents who intended to vote for the party that was in their favorite coalition, and part C indicates the percentage who plan to vote for a party in what they view as the most likely coalition.

Further evidence of the impact of party preference is illustrated in figure 1, which denotes the mean score on the "love/hate" scale when controlling for vote intention. The average affect for the respondent's favorite party is 8.4.[17] There is a sizable gap in the emerging pattern between the respondent's favorite and second-favorite parties. The mean thermometer score for the second party exceeded the mid-point (5.5) only for Meretz and Ihud Leumi. The survey data suggests that voters in this election had a clear favorite party as well as a general dislike for all the significant alternatives. These are hardly conditions where voters would be eager to cast strategic votes for a party other than their favorite, regardless of their assessment of the coalition probabilities.

Because Kadima was a member of every hypothetical coalition for which we have information on voter preferences, Kadima supporters by definition had to choose a coalition with their favorite party.[18] But this is not true for supporters of the six other parties. Part A of table 7 demonstrates that a clear majority of each party's supporters chose a coalition, which included their party. Almost 95 percent of Labor supporters most preferred a coalition that included Labor. For those ranking Likud or Shas first, more than four out of five preferred a coalition, which included their favorite party. Of the remaining parties, Israel Beiteinu had the lowest proportion of supporters for a coalition that included their favorite party, and even then the proportion was nearly three in five.[19]

Many voters who did not intend to vote for their favorite party intended to vote for one of their favorite party's coalition partners, or chose to vote for a party in their favorite coalition, rather than casting a vote for their favorite party. Almost 90 percent of all respondents planned to vote for a party in their favorite coalition (see table 7 – B). The respondents least likely to intend to vote for a party in their favorite coalition were those respondents who most preferred a coalition with the Haredi voters. Respondents who liked the most ideologically extreme coalitions, Kadima-Labor-Meretz and Kadima-Likud-parties on the right, were the most likely to vote for a party in their favorite coalition. Labor

Table 7
Coalition Preferences and Party Preferences

Part A: Is the respondent's most highly ranked party in his or her favorite coalition, by political party?

Highest Party on Love/Hate Scales	Is party in favorite coalition?		
	Yes	No	Total
Labor	126	9	135
	93.3%	6.7%	100%
Likud	75	13	88
	85.2%	14.8%	100%
Meretz	66	42	108
	61.1%	38.9%	100%
Mafdal	50	20	70
	71.4%	28.6%	100%
Israel Beiteinu	44	32	76
	57.9%	42.1%	100%
Shas	72	15	87
	82.8%	17.2%	100%
Total	433	131	564
	76.8%	23.2%	100%

Excludes voters who intended to vote for Kadima.

Part B. Does the respondent intend to vote for a party in his or her favorite coalition?

Highest Coalition on Love/Hate Scales	Does the respondent intend to vote for a party in this coalition?		
	Yes	No	Total
Kadima-Labor	230	30	260
	88.5%	11.5%	100%
Kadima-Likud	72	12	84
	85.7%	14.3%	100%
Kadima-Likud-Haredi	30	15	45
	66.7%	33.3%	100%
Kadima-Labor-Haredi	23	6	29
	79.3%	20.7%	100%
Kadima-Likud-Right	114	2	116
	98.3%	1.7%	100%
Kadima-Labor-Meretz	105	5	110
	95.5%	4.5%	100%
Total	574	70	644
	89.1%	10.9%	100%

Table 7 (cont.)

Part C. Does the respondent intend to vote for a party in the most likely coalition?

Most Likely Coalition	Does the respondent intend to vote for party in the most likely coalition?		
	Yes	No	Total
Kadima-Labor	152	75	227
	67.0%	33.0%	100%
Kadima-Likud	25	19	44
	56.8%	43.2%	100%
Kadima-Likud-Haredi	14	17	31
	45.2%	54.8%	100%
Kadima-Labor-Haredi	17	6	23
	73.9%	26.1%	100%
Kadima-Likud-Right	38	6	44
	86.4%	13.6%	100%
Kadima-Labor-Meretz	27	20	47
	57.4%	42.6%	100%
Total	273	143	416
	65.6%	34.4%	100%

Includes only respondents who rated all seven parties.

For Part A, we have excluded respondents who rated Kadima first on the "love/hate" scales. Since Kadima was included in all seven possible coalitions, any respondent who ranked Kadima first had to vote for a party in his or her favorite coalition.

For Parts B and C we exclude respondents who favored a national-unity coalition. By definition they had to rank as highest one of the parties in such a coalition.

and Likud were the most likely recipients of insincere votes cast by supporters of smaller, more extreme parties on their respective flanks.

Part C illustrates that the tendency to vote for a party in their favorite coalition was reinforced by people's expectations. For every coalition except one, a majority of respondents intended to vote for a party in the coalition they thought was most likely be formed.[20] Two thirds of the respondents who thought the coalition of Kadima-Labor was most likely to form voted for either Kadima or Labor. Even though the polls during the campaign suggested that it was improbable that Kadima and Likud would have enough seats to form a coalition together without any other parties, 44 respondents thought the coalition would form, with 25 of those respondents planning to vote for Likud or Kadima. Another 44 respondents thought that a Kadima-Likud-right coalition would form, 86.4 percent of whom intended to vote for a party that would be included in this coalition.

In table 8 we provide evidence of biased expectations by presenting the average odds of a coalition forming by the party ranked first on the "love/hate"

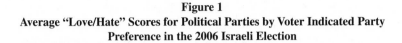

Figure 1
Average "Love/Hate" Scores for Political Parties by Voter Indicated Party
Preference in the 2006 Israeli Election

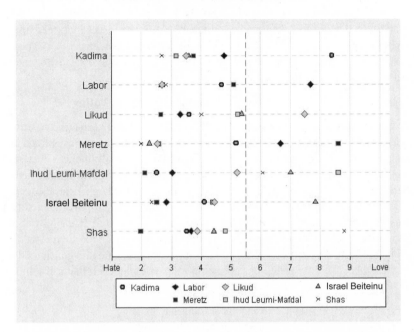

scales. If a coalition included the respondents' favorite party, it was viewed on average as more likely to be formed. For example, respondents who like Labor best, on average, estimated the odds of a Kadima-Labor coalition forming at 66.6 percent. Respondents who on average preferred Likud best, gave the same coalition only a 55.0 percent chance of forming; the same odds they gave Kadima-Likud. Supporters of both the left, Labor and Meretz, and the far right, Ihud Leumi-Mafdal and Israel Beiteinu, agreed that the odds of Kadima-Likud forming were about ten percentage points less than what Likud supporters estimated the odds to be.

To calculate the bias of these expectations, we first took into account the differences between the prediction of each party's supporters and the overall average odds. This allowed us to control for coalitions seen as more likely to occur. We then calculated the average difference for the coalitions that included the party, and the average difference for the coalitions that did not include the party. In the last row of table 8 we present what we call the net bias, the difference between these two averages.[21] The higher the net bias, the more the respondents overestimate the chances of coalitions including their favorite party, and underestimate the chances of coalitions which do not include their favorite party, when compared to the chances perceived by all respondents. For

Labor supporters, the average odds of a coalition forming that includes Labor was, on average, 4.6 points higher than the odds estimated by the total sample. Since Labor supporters slightly underestimated the odds of coalitions that did not include Labor, the net bias is 6.1 points. For Likud, the net bias was more than twice that number. Compared to the entire sample, Shas supporters similarly thought that the odds of a coalition including Shas were higher. Those who preferred the remaining, smaller parties had lower expectations for their parties' inclusion in any coalition.

10. Coalition Considerations and Strategic Voting

How did coalition considerations affect strategic voting? First, the positive bias in coalition expectations helps to reinforce the respondents' likelihood of supporting their most preferred party because they generally believe there is a good chance that their most preferred party will be in the next government. Second, this tendency is strongest among supporters of the largest parties, helping to account for the success of these parties in retaining their potential voters. Respondents ranking Labor the highest felt, even more strongly than non-Labor supporters, that Kadima-Labor was the most likely coalition. They therefore had no incentive to defect to any other party. Similarly, those who ranked Likud the highest were the only group of party supporters who believed that a Kadima-

Table 8
Subjective Odds of Coalition Forming,
by Party Ranked First on "Love/Hate" Scales

	Party with Highest Love/Hate Score							
Odds of Coalition Forming	Kadima	Labor	Likud	Meretz	Mafdal	Israel Beiteinu	Shas	All
Kadima-Labor	69.9	66.6	55.0	69.7	65.0	54.8	62.1	65.3
Kadima-Likud	46.6	43.6	55.0	46.4	43.0	44.7	50.0	46.7
Kadima-Likud-Haredi	37.1	41.8	49.3	43.7	45.1	39.4	56.0	42.6
Kadima-Labor-Haredi	47.5	56.6	44.8	46.0	42.4	41.2	53.1	48.1
Kadima-Likud-Right	38.1	41.5	50.1	42.9	39.0	38.4	52.8	41.9
Kadima-Labor-Meretz	48.2	51.9	43.8	50.2	52.2	36.6	47.7	47.8
National Unity	30.2	30.0	35.5	30.3	30.8	27.4	42.8	31.7
Number	315	151	88	117	79	88	90	928
Net Bias (excluding Nat'l Unity)	--	6.1	13.6	1.5	-2.4	3.3	9.8	--

Only includes respondents who rated all seven parties. Respondents who rate Kadima first are excluded since all the coalition possibilities included Kadima.

In assessing the chances for each coalition, scores could range from a low of 0 (no chance) to 100 (the respondent is certain this coalition will exist). The first entry shows that respondents who ranked Kadima first on the "love/hate" scale on average said there was a 69.9 percent chance of a Kadima-Labor coalition.

Likud coalition was most likely to form. This expectation of coalition odds is consistent with the lack of strategic defections from Likud.

Third, party preferences and coalition preferences tended to reinforce one another, thus providing yet another means of modulating the extent of incentives for strategic voting. Although supporters of the smaller right parties attributed a high probability to the formation of a Kadima-Labor coalition, their dislike for that coalition reduced the incentives for strategic defection. The Kadima-Labor coalition was the second-lowest ranked coalition for Mafdal, the third-lowest for Israel Beiteinu, and the second-lowest for Shas supporters (see table 6). Furthermore, unlike Likud supporters, the supporters of the smaller right parties did not believe the Kadima-Likud coalition had an equal or better chance of forming than Kadima-Labor, and (observing the means in table 6) these respondents overall preferred the Kadima-Likud-right coalition to Kadima-Likud. These factors attenuated the incentives of those with a preference for a small right party to strategically vote for Likud, or for another party in their preferred coalition. Supporters of the Kadima-Likud-Haredi coalition were most likely to vote for a favorite party, which was not in their preferred coalition.

Finally, supporters of the smaller parties—the ones for whom "defections" were more likely—would tend to favor coalitions which did not include their preferred party. Such "defectors" tended to vote for the ideologically compatible party that was in the coalition they preferred (e.g., Labor for voters who preferred Meretz, Likud for supporters of Ihud Leumi-Mafdal and Israel Beiteinu). Since Labor and Likud are ideologically located closer to Kadima, and are larger parties, it would be highly unlikely that Kadima would form a coalition with the parties closer to the extremes, without the extremist's larger ally being closer to the center. Among respondents favoring Meretz, six of seven defectors voted for Labor, bolstering the prospects for their favored coalitions of Kadima-Labor and Kadima-Labor-Meretz. Defectors from the small right-wing parties also tended to vote for a party in their favored coalition. The small number of Shas defectors split six to three for Likud over Labor. Once again, this is logical for a party whose leaders are primarily concerned with religious issues and who are not clearly "hawkish" or "dovish" on peace and security issues.

11. Conclusions

The central finding of this chapter is that a significant number of voters in the 2006 Israeli election took into account more than their preferences among the parties in determining for whom they intended to vote. We have found a similar conclusion to be true in other recent elections as well. Indeed, such strategic voting is more common in proportional than in plurality electoral systems (see Abramson, et al., 2005). What made the 2006 election different from other proportional elections we have studied in these terms was that the electoral context was only one aspect contributing to the relevancy of the anticipated outcome. In earlier elections voters conditioned their vote, in part, on the basis of expected seat shares of the parties, on who was likely to serve as formateur and therefore prime minister, or which governing coalition was likely to form and how their vote might assist the chances of a favored coalition forming. In 2006, only the last option was relevant. Kadima held a solid lead and, as figure 1 illustrates, respondents reported a large gap between their first and second most preferred party. Combining those two points with the common bias of expecting one's favored party to win more mandates than the polls predict, made party probability considerations largely irrelevant. Similarly, most expected Ehud Olmert to form the next government and to serve as its prime minister.

The only major outcome with an attendant measure of uncertainty was what type of governing coalition Olmert could be expected to form. The vast majority of voters preferred a centrist two-party coalition and/or a coalition that included their favorite party. Many disliked their favorite party's potential coalition partners. The result was that strategic voting was less prevalent in 2006 than in other recent Israeli contests. The Condorcet-preferred coalition did not win enough votes to form a majority government, as both large and small parties held on to more of their supporters than in the other elections. Yet a significant amount of strategic voting remained. Most of those who intended to vote strategically were concentrated among those favoring the smaller parties, and they acted strategically in an attempt to influence Kadima in forming a favorable coalition.

Notes

1. The higher threshold provided a greater incentive for voters to cast votes for small parties they fear may not cross the threshold without their vote.
2. And, of course, we are unlikely to detect such considerations in the data, because most surveys, including the Israel Election Study we utilize, only ask about the larger parties, which means they only ask about parties likely to be well above the threshold.
3. For the U.S. results see Abramson et al. 1992, 1995, and Abramson, Aldrich, and Rohde, 2003.
4. All of these polls were monitored via the websites for these newspapers.
5. In the event, Kadima clearly held the pivotal position after the election (see Diskin and Hazan, forthcoming).
6. Respondents were asked: "And now we would like to ask you about the chance of each one of the following parties to be a member of the coalition after the elections. Here you have a scale between 0 to 100, where 0 means you think there is no chance the party will be a member of the coalition, 50 means that the party's chances are half and half, and 100 means that it will certainly be a member of the coalition."
7. Respondents thought that Labor had the best chance of joining Kadima in government. Ten percent gave Labor a 100 percent chance of being in the next coalition, and almost half the sample gave Labor a better than fifty-fifty chance. Relatively fewer respondents agreed with Netanyahu: only 7 percent gave Likud a 100 percent chance and 36 percent gave them a better than even chance of being in the government.
8. Respondents were asked, "Here is a scale from 1 to 10 to express support or rejection of a group or a person. '1' describes strong rejection/hate, and '10' describes strong love/support."

9. Even though we only have data for seven parties we are reasonably confident that a plurality of voters would prefer Kadima to any other party in a head-to-head comparison because the other parties are smaller than the seven we have data for, and only a few (Gil, Hetz and Shinui) made centrist appeals that might draw support away from Kadima.

10. These percentages are all somewhat lower than the percentage that plans to vote for these parties shown in the final column of table 5. This is because we are reporting here about the vote intention among all respondents who planned to vote for any party, whereas in table 5 we report the vote intentions only among respondents who i) had a first choice among the seven ranked parties, ii) who planned to vote for one of these parties, and iii) reported a preference for each of the seven parties.

11. Haredi is a colloquial term for Ultra-Orthodox Jews. The Israel Election Study questionnaire described the coalition as Kadima, Likud and the Haredi Parties ("Miflagot Harediot") explicitly defined in the questionnaire as Shas and/or United Torah Judaism.

12. Respondents were asked, "And how supportive would you be of the following coalitions after the elections . . . on a '10' point scale where '1' means strong rejection and '10' means strong support, and the rest are levels in between."

13. As part of the bargaining process after the election, the Pensioners' Party merged into Kadima. This coalition lasted until October 30, 2006, when Israel Beiteinu joined the coalition.

14. Our discussion ignores the results for "ties" presented in the ninth column of Aldrich et al., 2005, Table 7.3, as well as the results for "ties" presented in the first row of table 3.

15. As in 2003, the difference between the retention rate of the large parties and of the small parties is statistically significant. But this difference is smaller than in 2003, and smaller still than the differences observed in either prime ministerial or Knesset voting in 1999. The 2006 data may overestimate sincere support for the largest parties since the data does not include Gil and predicts more mandates than Kadima ultimately won.

16. For a head-to-head comparison of coalition preferences among the entire electorate, see table 4.

17. The median is 8.3. Thus here, as throughout, the difference between the mean and median is small, and so we will report the mean scores.

18. When asked to name their preferred coalition in a follow-up question, no Kadima supporter mentioned a coalition that did not include that party.

19. The relatively low percentage of Israel Beiteinu voters who preferred a coalition with Israel Beiteinu may be a function of the survey not including their preferred coalition. None of the coalition options included the coalition with both Israel Beiteinu and Labor that formed on October 30, 2006.

20. Respondents were asked, "And now we want to ask you about the chances of different coalitions after the election. On a scale of 0 to 100, 0 means you give no chance for a certain coalition, 50 means the coalition's chances are half and half, and 100 means that you are sure this coalition will exist. Naturally you can give any number between 0 and 100. On such a scale, what are the chances that after the elections there will be a coalition between . . ."

21. We exclude respondents who prefer Kadima and the national unity government.

References

Abramson, Paul R. and John H. Aldrich. 2002. "Were Voters Strategic?" In Asher Arian and Michal Shamir, eds. *The Elections in Israel—1999.* Albany: State University of New York Press, 33-44.

Abramson, Paul R., John H. Aldrich, André Blais, Matthew Diamond, Abraham Diskin, Indridi H. Indridason, Daniel Lee, and Renan Levine. 2005. "Preferences and Choices in First-Past-the-Post and Proportional Elections." Paper presented at the annual meeting of the American Political Science Association, Washington, DC.

------. 2006. "Preferences and Choices In Voting Choices in the United States, Israel, and the Netherlands." Unpublished Paper, Duke University.

Abramson, Paul R., John H. Aldrich, Matthew Diamond, Abraham Diskin, RenanLevine, and Thomas J. Scotto. 2001. "Prime Minister and Parliament: Strategic Split-Ticket Voting." Paper presented at the annual meeting of the American Political Science Association, San Francisco.

------. 2004. "Strategic Abandonment or Sincerely Second Best? The 1999 Israeli Prime Ministerial Election." *Journal of Politics* 66 (3): 706-728.

Abramson, Paul R., John H. Aldrich, Phil Paolino, and David W. Rohde. 1992. "'Sophisticated' Voting in the 1988 Presidential Primaries." *American Political Science Review* 88 (1): 55-69.

------. 1995. "Third-Party and Independent Candidates in American Politics: Wallace, Anderson, and Perot." *Political Science Quarterly* 110 (3): 349-367.

Abramson, Paul R., John H. Aldrich, and David W. Rohde. 2003. *Change and Continuity in the 2000 and 2002 Elections*. Washington, DC: CQ Press.

Aldrich, John H., André Blais, Indridi H. Indridason, and Renan Levine. 2005. "Coalition Considerations and the Vote." In Asher Arian and Michal Shamir, eds. *The Elections in Israel—2003*. New Brunswick, NJ: Transaction Publishers, 143-166.

Blais, André, John H. Aldrich, Indridi H. Indridason, and Renan Levine. 2006. "Do Voters Vote for Government Coalitions? Testing Downs' Pessimistic Conclusion." *Party Politics* 12 (6): 691-705.

Cox, Gary W. 1997. *Making Votes Count: Strategic Considerations in the World's Electoral Systems*. Cambridge: Cambridge University Press.

Diskin, Abraham, and Reuven Y. Hazan. Forthcoming. "The Knesset Election in Israel, March 2006." *Electoral Studies*.

Duverger, Maurice. 1958. *Les partis politiques*, 3e ed. Paris: Armand Colin.

------. 1963. *Political Parties: Their Organization and Activity in the Modern State*. Barbara North and Robert North, trans. New York: Wiley.

Felsenthal, Dan S. 1990. *Topics in Social Choice: Sophisticated Voting, Efficacy, and Proportional Representation*. New York: Praeger.

Felsenthal, Dan S., and Avraham Brichta. 1985. "Sincere and Strategic Voting: An Israeli Study." *Political Behavior* 7 (4): 587-601.

Kedar, Orit. 2005. "When Moderate Voters Prefer Extreme Parties: Policy Balancing in Parliamentary Elections." *American Political Science Review*, 99(2): 185-199.

Nixon, David, Dganit Olomoki, Norman Schofield, and Itai Sened. 1996. "Multiparty Probability Voting: An Application to the Knesset." *Political Economy Working Paper* 186, Washington University, St. Louis, Missouri.

Strøm, Kaare. 1990. *Minority Government and Majority Rule*. Cambridge: Cambridge University Press.

Part 2

Parties and Groups

Shas' Transformation to "Likud with Kippa?" A Comparative Assessment of the Moderation of Religious Parties

Sultan Tepe and Roni Baum

Since its establishment Shas has been regarded as a party whose support would inevitably decline. Following the tradition of the previous elections, the pollsters prior to the 2006 elections underestimated the party's electoral appeal and predicted a final cut of nine to eleven mandates (seats). Many contended that after having spent three years in the opposition Shas would be cut off from its financial sources, thereby losing the supporters who came to the party mostly for its schools and other welfare services. It was only reasonable to expect that Shas would lose much of its electoral power. However, Shas not only maintained its power, but increased its total number of votes, gaining an additional mandate. In the current parliament the party holds twelve seats and constitutes the third largest bloc, holding the same number of seats as Likud. This situation has led some observers to describe Shas as "Likud with Kippa."[1] While Israeli politics is witnessing yet another major reshuffling of party lines with the emergence of Kadima, Shas has silently confirmed that it has established itself as a major force in Israeli politics (see figure 1).

A review of the recent elections confirms both the resiliency of Shas and also raises questions regarding the structural and ideological conditions contributing to this resiliency: What are the factors that led Shas to survive and to also consolidate its power against all odds? Has the party become a more moderate or radical party after participating in seven elections with astonishing success? While Shas has established itself as a pivotal actor in Israeli politics, has it also transformed itself from an ultra-orthodox to a less orthodox social party? To what extent is Shas merely the "social struggle party" it claims to be? What is the real political ideology of Shas, and to what extent does it affect the success of the party? Is Shas' resiliency and moderation a unique development in Israel, or can it be assessed within the broader context of the rise of religious parties in other parliamentary democracies in the Middle East? Is there any resemblance between Shas' trajectory of change and electoral successes and those of the pro-Islamic parties in Turkey?

Figure 1
1984–2006 Shas' Share of the Total Votes and Knesset Seats

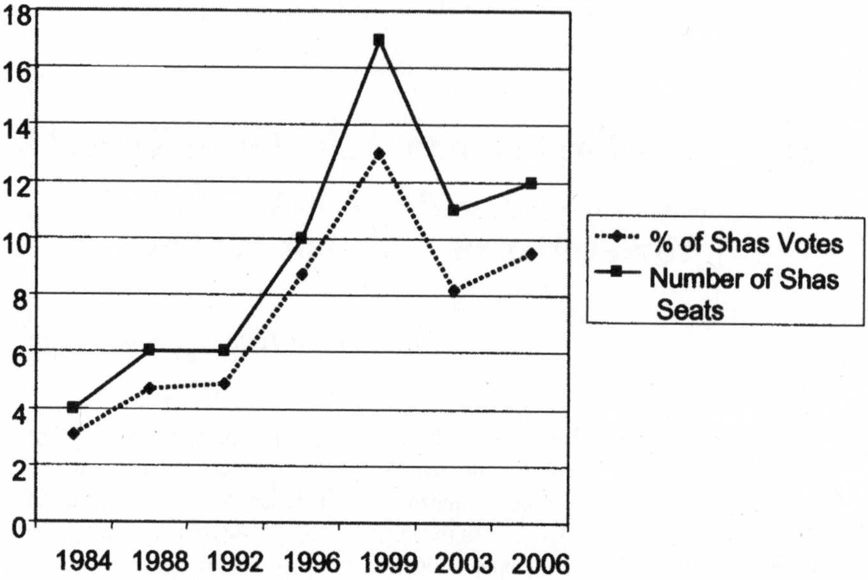

Legend:
···◆··· % of Shas Votes
—■— Number of Shas Seats

X-axis: 1984 1988 1992 1996 1999 2003 2006

Determinants of Shas' Success and Resiliency

The Shas party was founded in 1984 after Israeli politics witnessed the decline of the hegemony of the Labor Party. The political restructuring reflected the increasing importance of ethnic votes, in part due to the changing role of Sephardim. As their experience in Israel increasingly unified the Sephardim as a voting bloc and strained their relationship with Mafdal and Labor, they realigned themselves with Likud (Ben-Rafael and Sharot, 1991). Despite the initial dominance of one party (Labor), and later on that of two parties (Labor and Likud in the late 1970s), the sudden emergence and disappearance of small parties has been part and parcel of Israeli politics since its inception. The intense political competition and volatility of the electorate often led to a short life span (three or four elections) for the small parties.

Against this rather simplified electoral background, Shas' success emerges as a striking development by any account. Notwithstanding the overall fluctuations in its electoral support over the last 20 years, Shas has not only preserved, but tripled its power. As the party sailed through several elections, it never fell back to its core vote level of 3.1 percent in 1984. Taking into account both the electoral failure of former ethnic movements as well as the inability of ultra-orthodox parties to expand their support base, the long lasting electoral achievements of Shas are critical to understanding the overall map of Israeli politics. When placed within the historical and political context of Israeli politics, the path-breaking survival of Shas offers a solution to the conundrum of why, despite revealing characteristics of both an ethnic and orthodox party, it not only survived the challenges of Israel's tumultuous politics but also expanded its political power.

In the following section we posit that any questions regarding Shas' political power cannot be thoroughly answered without taking into account the internal (leadership, ideology, grassroots activities) and external (neo-liberal policies and the context of the elections) determinants of Shas' electoral performance. This analysis seeks to deepen the understanding of Shas by placing it in a broader comparative context. Such contextualization allows us to see that Shas, like other religious parties, was born into its unique political system, grew up in it, and developed as a result of its political environment, and not necessarily in opposition to it. To this end, we explore the commonalities and differences between Shas and the pro-Islamic parties in Turkey. This comparative inquiry demonstrates that Shas' organizational foundations and ideology, and their adjustment throughout the elections, is by no means unique to Israeli politics. As in the case of other religious parties, Shas' moderation is not a question of either/or. The party's ideological positioning and the direction of its change cannot be determined by identifying which of its components, namely ethnic (Sephardi), ultra-orthodox, or social issues dominate its policies. Shas' moderation relates more to how the various components of its ideology and party institutions interact and generate somewhat contradictory consequences. A comparative look at Shas' experience vis-à-vis the Turkish parties reveals that electoral competitions do in fact transform religious parties. However, this change alone cannot be taken as a sign of their substantial moderation. Religious parties constantly adapt to the surrounding environment of electoral competition and shift their ideological focus from the state to the community. But their transformation brings about mixed results. As they defy definite categorizations, these parties can be described as moderate radicals at best or fundamentalist pragmatists.

Internal Determinants

1. Leadership:

Shas was once blessed with two charismatic, spiritual, and political leaders, Rabbi Ovadia Yosef and Aryeh Deri. Rabbi Ovadia Yosef provided the spiritual guidance, while Aryeh Deri's pragmatic policies brought the party increased political clout. A division of labor ensued: the spiritual leader's authority as a diligent Torah scholar legitimized the party's policies and the political leadership balanced the internal division and presented a unified face: a critical role in Israeli politics where internal party rivalries often end up splitting parties. As a result, Shas benefited from the fusion of Aryeh Deri's political maneuvering and authority and Rabbi Ovadia Yosef's spiritual patronage. It was not surprising therefore, that after Deri's conviction, many observers of Israeli politics believed that the party's future was uncertain. In fact, after the removal of its first charismatic political leader, Aryeh Deri's Shas was on the brink of splitting into two camps: Eli Yishai's followers and those of Aryeh Deri. Initially it appeared that Rabbi Ovadia Yosef and Eli Yishai could not control the majority of Shas voters. Shas' pirate radio stations (the holy channels) did not hesitate to accuse Shas' Knesset members of not doing enough for Aryeh Deri. They regarded Deri as the undisputed leader to such an extent that some even argued he could continue to lead Shas from prison. Shas' major achievement was its ability to survive the end of Deri's leadership and his replacement with the once obscure Eli Yishai.

Eli Yishai resembles and differs from Aryeh Deri in many ways, and consequently shifts the party's image in opposing directions. Many observers of Shas have focused on the negative and expanded on Yishai's lack of Deri's charismatic appeal and pragmatism. But it is this lack of charisma and pragmatism that has unexpectedly contributed to Shas' resiliency. A closer look at the two leaders indicates that like Deri, Yishai comes from a modest background. It is this shared background that made Deri credible and continues to empower Yishai, especially when the party appeals to the masses on social issues. Unlike Deri, Yishai was born in Israel and worked for the party in different capacities before becoming the leader. In fact, Yishai began his political career representing Shas as a member of the Jerusalem city hall council. In 1988 he was appointed assistant to the internal affairs minister—Aryeh Deri. He served as secretary-general of Shas from 1990 to 1996 and as the chairman of the "El-Hamaayan" association. Climbing the internal ladder of power, Yishai also served as Shas' head of the municipality department, establishing its youth movement—"Bnei Chayil" and the women's organization "Margalit Em BeIsrael." In 1996 he was elected to the Knesset for the first time. Yishai is therefore well connected and informed about the party's grassroots, and this constitutes the foundation of his political power. Aside from his standing within the party as a young politician, Yishai was given many responsibilities at the national level. He served as welfare minister under Netanyahu and Barak and was appointed minister of internal affairs and deputy prime minister between 2001 and 2003.

Despite what Deri and Yishai have in common, the party's first major leadership change, from Deri to Yishai, was a major challenge to Shas' political survival. The successful transition in itself marked the central role of religious leadership and the resiliency of the party's network. Facing the challenge of a possible split after the forced resignation of Deri, Yishai's Rabbi Ovadia Yosef praised Eli Yishai in his weekly oration on the Saturday night after the last convention. He once introduced Yishai and proclaimed "we have never had someone like him," thereby offering an implied criticism of Aryeh Deri, effectively declaring Yishai to be the sole leader of the movement. As a result of this endorsement, in spite of the strong opposition against his leadership,

Eli Yishai gradually succeeded in attaining his own personal stature as a political leader of Shas. In contrast to Deri who legitimized his power mostly through his own political wit and strategy, Yishai derived his strength from Rabbi Ovadia Yosef's unqualified support and experience in the party circles. Rabbi Ovadia Yosef firmly supported him and his service to the party network. Deri's and Yishai's different sources of legitimacy and style of leadership impacted significantly on the party and also revealed its vulnerabilities and strengths; the ability of Yishai to establish himself by means of a gradual and less controversial process attested to two important traits of the party: (i) its ability to secure its continuity as a political party, moving beyond the shadow of its first charismatic political leadership; and (ii) the critical role its spiritual leader, Rabbi Ovadia Yosef, plays in minimizing the impact of the potentially destabilizing changes on the party.

The short yet tumultuous history of Shas leadership presents an unclear picture regarding the extent to which Shas has institutionalized its party apparatus and is able to handle the changes in its post-Yosef era. After all, Rabbi Ovadia Yosef is by no means a conventional spiritual leader. His statements play a critical role in resolving political crises, and in some cases ignite crises. He reveals the qualities of an astute practical politician as well as those of a highly regarded Torah scholar. His decisions often blend "Real Politics" and spiritual considerations with remarkable pragmatism, thereby creating carefully crafted decisions with religious legitimacy. Traditionally, religious leaders do not need to attend to everyday practical concerns and accommodate them into their religious opinions. In fact, spiritual leadership can often manage to maintain a firm and uncompromising position on a wide range of issues, relating them only to the "religious world" (Kopelowitz and Diamond, 1998, pp. 671–708). In contrast, Rabbi Ovadia Yosef's statements embody flexibility and adaptation to current conditions in light of existing political conditions and he therefore personifies both ultra-orthodoxy as well as the change in the movement with his highly controversial rulings. It is this combination of spiritual leadership and pragmatism that enabled Shas to join Rabin's government in 1992 as the only religious party. Likewise, the spiritual leadership did not hesitate to relinquish Deri's services as a political leader in 1999 and accepted Shas' inclusion into Olmert's government without waiting for the Ashkenazic-Orthodox party "Yahadut Hatorah." Shas' political decisions often invite severe criticism from Ashkenazi *haredi* parties on the grounds that Shas is not *Haredi* enough, or capable of leading a religious community.

The expectation that Shas was about to sign a coalition agreement with Kadima brought about a wave of intense denigration from Yahadut Hatorah elders, to the extent that they confirmed Rabbi Shach's very divisive assessment which had initially paved the way for the formation of Shas as a Sephardi orthodox movement:

"...they (sephardi religious block) are not worthy of carrying a leadership...how right he [Shach] was" (*Yom Leyom*, April 12, 2006, p. 2). Yahadut Hatorah Knesset members claimed that accepting a coalition agreement with Kadima without receiving the consent of a majority of the rabbis over certain matters like education, religious courts, and religiously improper marriages would be detrimental to their struggle over religious issues. Notwithstanding the opposition from the ultra-orthodox bloc, Rabbi Ovadia Yosef ordered Eli Yishai to sign the agreement with Kadima, without discussing the possibility of joining forces with Yahadut Hatorah to form an ultra-orthodox bloc. In comparable decisions a pattern emerges: Rabbi Ovadiah Yosef offers religious justification for the party's policies as well as changes in the party's structure, despite the opposition of the religious bloc. While the spiritual leadership serves as a powerful force in legitimizing unconventional positions, the political leadership emerges as the effective executor of decisions. Eli Yishai's recent campaign picture, without showing his kippa, was an unprecedented campaign image for a religious party, presenting him as an able manager who attends solely to the needs of the poor. It is this combination of spiritual capital offered by Rabbi Ovadia Yosef and the tactful political leadership of Eli Yishai that distinguishes Shas from other parties. The same division of labor within the party suggests that unless Shas develops a strong party structure, it is likely to face difficulties when there is a change in its religious leadership.

2. Ideology: Transformation of Shas From A Party of "Haredim" to a Party of "Social Warriors"

Since its entrance into the Israeli political system with an ideology that displayed the characteristics of Sephardi, ultra-orthodox, and social empowerment movements, Shas' political identity has been at the center of an intense political debate. Given the intricate nature of Shas' identity, several analyses of the party's appeal surfaced. The first views Shas as a social class movement—the Sephardim comprise the semi-periphery of Israeli society, thus its ideology is often a class discourse under the guise of religion (Peled, 1998, pp. 703–727). For others, Shas simply represents another branch of ultra-orthodoxy which emerged in reaction to the Lithuanian (Ashkenazi) domination of the religious bloc (Kamil, 2000). The dominant accounts and their derivatives leave us with contradictory images, and the absence of a common ground between them attests to the complexity of the party and indicates that treating Shas as a party of the periphery, or as a new brand of ultra-orthodoxy alone, does not enable us to understand the full spectrum of its ideology.[2]

A closer examination of the different strata of factors contributing to Shas' overall political discourse clearly demonstrates that its rhetoric is anything but monolithic and blends both social and religious-spiritual messages. With its roots in the ultra-orthodox *Haredi* movement, Shas' message underscores the importance of the Torah world, and Torah as a source of lifestyle. To understand its position in the *Haredi* world, it is important to note that aside from the conventional *Haredi* beliefs and practices, Shas also extensively employs other traditional spiritual messages and symbols, especially *kame'ot* (blessed objects, amulets), blessings and curses.[3] The party's use of *kame'ot*, and its call for support in the 1996 elections, was so extensive as to result in a correction to election law 122 (Knesset Election Law, 1969). According to the revised version, a person who encourages voters to either vote, or abstain from voting, by distributing *kame'ot*, can be imprisoned for up to 5 years. This new law notwithstanding, Shas continued to draw on many spiritual icons and symbols in its electoral campaign which struck a chord with its traditional Sephardi audience. The frequent use of "a Jewish home," "family life," rabbis, talismans, and letter purchasing for blessings not only brings together a wide range of people who share similar symbols, but also creates a substantial information bank and increased interaction via shared addresses for letters, and an exchange of spiritual messages imbued with political meanings. Overall, the party's messages are filled with both the promises of social justice and spiritual benefits, thereby posing the question of whether Shas is a *miflaga hevratit lohemet* (a party of social warriors) or a religious party resorting to social issues and traditional symbols to disguise its ultra-orthodox agenda.

What makes answering this question complicated is that a cursory review of Shas' public appeal offers evidence leading to different conclusions. A historical review of the party discourse reveals that the party's ideology has not only been significantly transformed, but is also multilayered. Despite the critical and central role of religious and spiritual symbols, it is the social issues which increasingly play a central role in the party's electoral campaign. The 2006 election campaign constituted a turning point in the party's rhetoric: the leadership introduced the party's campaign to the public as a social road map (in contrast to Sharon's political road map). However, a quick review fails to recognize the increasing centrality of social issues which is a rather new phenomenon. The historical review of the party's rhetoric indicates, despite their continuous importance, that social issues moved to the core of the party's appeal only in 1999, the party's hitherto most successful campaign. It is in this campaign that the captivating *J'accuse* (I accuse) surfaced as the party's main slogan. The tape distributed under the same title portrayed Aryeh Deri's trial as an unfair ethnic prosecution resembling that of Dreyfus. Its 2006 campaign evidenced the consolidation of social issues in the party's agenda. Under the leadership of Eli Yishai, the party this time sought to mobilize the non-religious and traditional voters by bringing to the fore "the social plan of Shas." The Shas mission, in the words of Eli Yishai, was first and foremost the fight against the social apartheid (Guerowitch, March 7, 2006).

It is important to note that the rising salience of social issues has been accompanied by the *de-Haredization* of the party's rhetoric. *Haredization* is used here to refer to views that promote cultural isolation, as well as a single-minded commitment to promoting the needs of the religious community. Although the party's religious messages remained intact, its exclusively religious demands have been put on the backburner. The *de-Haredization*, and concern for the religious needs of the non-religious public, reached such a level that the party declared its support for non-religious burials, should it attain control of the internal affairs ministry: "I am sorry there are people who would rather be buried this way" said Yishai, "but once I get back to the internal affair office, I will secure approval for allocating a non-religious burial ground" (*Maariv*, February 24, 2006, p. 5). Comparable statements again evoked severe criticism from the Ashkenazi-religious world, thereby assigning Shas an odd place in the *Haredi* world. It is not rare to see statements such as the one made by Rabbi Elyashiv, the leading rabbi of the Yahadut Hatorah Lithuanian stream: "The chairman of Shas, Eli Yishai does not represent 'Bnei Torah'… he is not a representative of the Yeshivot, he walks in front of discotheques, watching who comes and goes, this is not an orthodox party" (*Maariv*, February 21, 2006, p. 2). Inundated with such criticisms, Shas finds itself in a position that forces it to constantly negotiate its *Harediness* vis-à-vis other groups.

It is this all-inclusive electoral campaign that, according to Michael Avigded, the key strategic advisor for Shas, explains Shas' electoral miracles:

> The campaign which carried a promise of restoring the stipends for children along with the critique of Likud's chairman, Binyamin Netanyahu, allowed us to reach an audience that never voted for Shas before. The highlight of the social issues defined the campaign's main tone. Shas aimed at meeting the people which in return opened a door to increase its power in the future…. As of today Shas has three kinds of audiences: Sephardi Orthodox, Sephardi Traditional, and a new public. Some of them are not religious: we spoke right to their guts…what I wanted to emphasize was; the rabbi cares about them more than any other party. We have shown his tears over a hungry boy. I wanted to show to the Israeli people that he is like our grandfather who thinks about all of us…. (Etinger, *Haaretz*, March 31, 2006, p. 7-B)

In fact, Shas' shift towards social issues best manifests itself in the 2006 Shas central campaign advertisement entitled "Burning heart—the country's tears." In a 36-minute videotaped advertisement, the party leadership presents the deterioration of the middle class, the detachment of young people from religion, and the pervasive effect of poverty, and it describes the party's unique efforts to fight against these developments (Shas, 2006). The image of a hungry boy epitomized "the general collapse felt by Israeli citizens." Party chairman Yishai's voice explains that poverty does not discriminate among ethnicity and religiosity: "a hungry boy is a hungry boy regardless of his religious beliefs and ethnicity." The depiction also hammers home the message that poverty is not just a social problem: a hungry person cannot fulfill his or her religious obligations and study Torah. Thus fighting against poverty also becomes a mission to create a vibrant Torah community. According to the party, 600,000 free copies of this message were distributed to a wide range of groups while the party received the votes of 300,000 Israelis.

Representing the three layers of its ideology in its recent campaign, the party presented three images: (i) an a-religious party with a strong social agenda, (ii) a *haredi* party that best addresses the needs of the Torah community – a community that is expanding along with the party's efforts, and (iii) a Sephardi traditional party that still cherishes *kame'ot*. Although the party tactfully separates its three facets, the messages remain intertwined: Poverty hurts religious communities, the expansion of the religious community requires a minimum level of welfare, and many of the disadvantaged share traditional Sephardi beliefs.

3. Party Centered Network: Permanent Campaign and Continuous Social Engagement

> "Shas is the only party in Israeli politics that starts its election campaign right after winning the election, and against all the experts' evaluations, hard and devoted work for the voters is the winning motive...." (*Yom Leyom*, March 30, 2006, p. 2)

Unlike other self-assessments that are not always reliable, Shas' assertion that it is a party that constantly campaigns has proven to be accurate. In fact, Shas' permanent campaign serves as a venue for a large group of people from the periphery to improve their conditions (especially in the local municipalities). The party activists are often rewarded with jobs and in return they become party advocates and participants in the party's network. But rather than creating a circle of machine politics based on a loosely connected patron-client relationship, the party's permanent campaign and constant recruitment from local groups strengthens its social ties to the local communities. Each local representative knows the local community well, uses the existing relationships for party-related activities, and keeps in close contact with everyone in the community. In the municipalities, Shas' activists hold key positions, enabling them to attend to those in need and to reach out to multiple segments in each community. Preferring positions at welfare-related agencies, the party activists consolidate the role of Shas as a social service deliverer, handling the concerns of those in need on a daily basis, and use the opportunity to recruit more supporters for the next election.

When Shas' network is viewed as a whole, it becomes clear that the party has quietly formed one of the most effective social network systems in the country (Leon, 2005). In their entirety, the party services form a surrogate state, providing social services for its target population. This is what led to the prediction of the party's demise when Shas was left out of the governing coalition. Not holding any government position deprives the party of the state funds on which it has increasingly depended. Indeed, the party faced a severe crisis in its social institutions, especially in its education system. The party's ability to survive this crisis and its years in opposition highlights another dimension often neglected by observers: Rabbi Ovadia Yosef established a special fund to deal with the financial crisis: "a rescue fund for the religiously observant."

The party collected donations, particularly from abroad, in order to prevent "Maayan hahinuch hatorani" from closing down, and it successfully raised NIS 26 million (Hahazala, 2003). The Shas movement proved that it has the capacity to maintain its system when it is not part of the governing coalition. This survival, however, cannot be taken as a sign of full autonomy. Although the party network remains dependent on state funding sources, it also successfully mobilizes funds, mostly from Sephardi communities abroad.

In assessing the general profile of Shas voters and the party's political discourse, a complex picture emerges. Shas support cannot be reduced to unilinear ethnic religious identities and a shared uniform social economic status. It is the socio-economic services of the party that reinforce the supporters' ethnic identities. The party's religious discourse brings to the fore traditional Sephardic religious beliefs and plays an important role in redefining Sephardi identity. In fact, according to census data collected by the Central Bureau of Statistics, so called "traditionals," those who stand between the ultra-orthodox and secular worlds, have a limited place in the Ashkenazic population (Liebman, 1982). In contrast, among Jews originating from Africa and Asia, which are mostly Islamic countries, there is a broad range of traditional Jews (see figure 2).

Unlike its Ashkenazic counterparts, Shas targets not only ultra-orthodox or religious Jews, but also traditional Jews who are observant enough to receive

Figure 2*
Ethnicity and Religious Identity

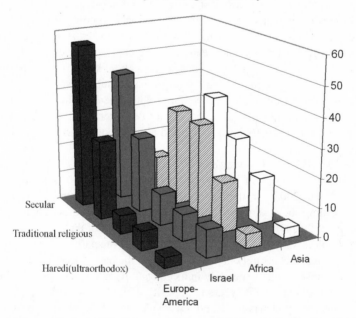

* Israel Central Bureau of Statistics, www.cbs.gov.il/hodaot2006n/19_06_02005

religious messages without being uncompromisingly religious.[4] It is not merely a discursive appeal but a strategic electoral choice taken by Eli Yishai, similar to Arye Deri, directing his messages at the non-orthodox community. Consequently, it is not the expansion of the *Haredim*, but the increasing support among "traditionals" that explains the continued growth of Shas' voter strength, while the political growth of their Ashkenazic-orthodox counterparts remains limited. The range of services provided by Shas attests to a popular support base that does not draw solely on religious and ethnic identity, or economic standing, but on an interplay of them all. Ultra-orthodox practices and spirituality serve as an important venue to convey the message and legitimize policies rather than being just the source of policies. The party services use both social economic services and "return to religion" campaigns to recruit new members.

Understanding the complexity of the party services requires us to note the importance of Torah tradition to the Sephardi community, as well as the huge gap between disadvantaged mizrahim and other mizrahim who are inseparable from Israel's multi-ethnic middle class. With its move towards social issues Shas obtained a unique place in the Israeli political system and the *Haredi* world. The predominant *haredi* party, Agudat Israel, Shas' ultra-orthodox competitor, launched a campaign based on a moderate religious appeal, but remained within the framework of religion without resorting to any social class appeal. Labor, on the other hand, failed to draw on the nuances of Sephardi ethnic identity, leaving a vast political area for Shas to cover. Shas, on the other hand, fused social and religious issues and introduced spiritual strength as an answer to social problems. After all, Shas argued, a good Torah-based education and a strong social life strengthens those who are disadvantaged and have fallen behind for various reasons, not only spiritually but also socially and politically.

External Conditions:

Fallout of Neo-Liberalism: Shas as a Critique of an Aggressive Free Market Economy

The prevalent idea that Shas is a unique case often results in analyses that treat the party in a political vacuum. Nevertheless, just like that of any party, Shas' success cannot be understood without taking into account the immediate context of the election and the broader socio-economic conditions of the party's policies. As Michal Shamir and Asher Arian have described, Israeli politics suffered from the dual process of political dealignment and realignment, where changes in the position of the parties coincided with shifts in voter allegiance (Arian and Shamir, 2001; and Arian and Shamir, 2004, pp. 13–33). Shas has found a niche in this fluid political arena that has enabled it to benefit from the countervailing forces which have eroded the foundations of other parties. It is also important to note that attacks by other parties portraying Shas "as political outsiders" have not weakened but in some cases expanded Shas' political appeal. Given this background, what distinguished the 2006 election was that Shas did not face an attractive secularist enemy like Shinui, but rather the formation of a new party, Kadima. This new political scene provides the backdrop for Avishai Benhaim's argument that Shas focused its campaign on the implications of the policies represented by Netanyahu and Likud by excluding Shas. "...Before the previous government he [Dimona's voter] was not poor. Today, when Shas is in the opposition, he is poor. If, with the help of God, Shas will be back in the coalition, he will be extracted from poverty..." (*Cohen*, March 1, 2006).

In fact, in the 2006 election, Shas' agenda shifted from religious to exclusively social issues. The policies adopted by Binyamin Netanyahu symbolized aggressive privatization and the repercussions of the decline of the welfare policies. For many Sephardim, these policies not only failed to ameliorate the conditions of the socially disadvantaged, but further deteriorated them. Disregarding the existing income gap, the Likud government cut the child stipend and sponsored five other reductions in the education budget. Low-income and large families, in particular, viewed the reduction of the child stipend as epitomizing the mainstream parties' indifference to the problems of those who struggle to make ends meet. Shas asserts that their indispensable role results from their efforts to correct discriminatory policies. Claiming for itself the role once played by Mafdal as the moderator between religious and secular parties, Shas presented itself as the much needed coalition partner promoting the rights of the religious and the disadvantaged. Most of Shas' voters were not protected from aggressive market-driven policies while Shas was in the opposition. Accordingly, support for Shas meant ensuring that the party in power provides for those in need. After all, if Shas had been part of the governing coalition for the past three years, those decrees and unfortunate situations affecting the poor would not have occurred, and its voters would not have been so badly hurt.

This new political approach that centered on social issues appears to match the expectations of its supporters in *Haredi* neighborhoods. According to the party, when asked which messages the parties should focus on, more than 64 percent of *Haredi* neighborhood residents reported education and welfare as the most important issues (see figure 3).

Only 19 percent identified issues related to the Torah world alone as the most salient ones (*Yom Leyom*, March 26, 2006). At the same time the party's message seems in tune with its non-*Haredi* supporters' expectations. Shas' focus on compensatory policies also appeals to the attentive ears of those who were adversely affected by neo-liberal policies—especially the disadvantaged, most of them non-religious Sephardim who are disappointed with Likud. For them, Shas' political presence is viewed as an antidote to aggressive neo-liberal policies that left social issues at the mercy of private initiative.

Figure 3
Salient Issues for the Shas Supporters 2006

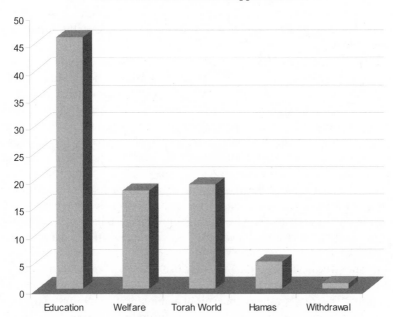

Normalization of Religious Parties in the Public Perception and the Media

Since its inception Shas has often been described as a threat to Israeli democracy. The party leadership has been brought to public attention as a result of their inflammatory remarks, especially about the courts and judges. The meteoric rise of the party and its subsequent successes have often, therefore, been perceived in the public eye as an embodiment of a dramatic rebellion against, and a challenge to, the secular democratic values of the Israeli state. Despite this image, perpetuated by the media, Shas managed to be a part of almost all governments, and took part in the formation of economic decisions that did not always protect its voters' interests. While Shas accepted various parties as coalition partners, this did not prevent its leaders from coming out strongly against the establishment in every election campaign. In the 2006 election, Binyamin Netanyahu embodied the policies against religious and disadvantaged communities and was therefore singled out as a target for the party's attacks.

In addition to the fear of having a new anti-systemic party, the allegation of corruption involving Shas' leaders further portrayed the party as a drain on government resources. More often than not, Shas and its leaders have been characterized as *mushchatim* (corrupt and deceitful actors) in the non-religious press. The often stated conclusion was that "The Shas movement and its leaders are a strategic threat to the state of Israel" (*Free People*, March 18, 1999). Nevertheless, since Eli Yishai took over the party, Shas' image has substantially shifted. A process that can be called "the normalization of Shas" altered it from a party slandered by the media to a party perceived as politically serious and responsible.

Yaacov Eichler of *Kol Ha-Ir* metaphorically described the transformation of the party in the media as follows: "Eli Yishai turned the public's attitude toward Shas from being treated as an *arava* [willow branch] to be beaten to that of an *Etrog* [citron] that needs to be preserved." The change in the media's perception of Shas was not an independent process but in part reflected the newly adopted strategy of Shas' political leadership. Instead of ignoring the media image, the new leadership actively challenged the controversial statements and actions of the party leadership. There have been discernable concerted efforts over the past three years to recreate the party's popular image by minimizing the impact of the party leadership's statements; statements that not only brought about the secularists' uproar but also reinforced the party's image as habitual violators of the law. Since Eli Yishai was never involved in criminal affairs, the changing party leadership made the party's public perception as deceitful and corrupt less tenable. The new leadership promoted itself in pursuit of the party's social mission as the lawful, honest manager of a wide range of services, immune to corruption. The party's various channels of communication reinforced the idea that the party had no interest in attacking state institutions, especially the Israeli courts. It is no coincidence, therefore, that Eli Yishai pledged that any Knesset member convicted of corruption will be forced to resign from the Knesset. This promise was put to the test shortly afterward during Shlomo Benizri's trial. Even though there was no resignation, four days after Shlomo Benizri was to be indicted, his standing was lowered from second place to sixth by the Torah council, symbolically punishing him while still securing his Knesset seat.

Aside from Shas' own campaign to battle its image as corrupt and anti-systemic, the events surrounding the 2006 election further contributed to the normalization of the party's image. Among others, the elections were marked by the establishment of Kadima (November 21), Ariel Sharon's stroke (January 4), Shinui's split (January 25), the evacuation of Amona (February 1), and the success of Hamas. All this contributed to deflecting attention away from Shas as an anti-systemic party. The culmination of the developments and their ensuing monopolization of public attention granted the party additional space to mold its image. Just prior to the elections, Eli Yishai challenged the establishment, and only then was the original image of the party as anti-systemic and ultra-orthodox restored to a certain extent. Even then Shas centered its appeal on fighting corruption and refrained from provoking any antagonism. The shift in the party's discursive practice suggests that Shas both assumed and consolidated a new role for itself in Israeli politics. It is this very new role that does not answer but increases the salience of many questions regarding the direction of the party's ongoing transformation. Is Shas' new campaign against corruption and poverty another sign of its metamorphosis from an ultra-orthodox to a moderate religious party? Is Shas attempting to reconcile its religious social class agenda and become more of a social class party? Underlying these questions is the overarching issue of whether Shas has truly moderated its agenda, or adopted a new rhetorical strategy for the sake of its political survival.

Reinvention or Increasing Elusiveness of Shas' Ideology?

As opposed to Ashkenazi orthodox parties, Shas came into existence after the establishment of Israel. It therefore did not carry the historical baggage of Agudat Israel, which was established as an exile party in the Diaspora. Perhaps this is why Shas could face the current political reality and the important issues of daily life without being limited to conventional *Haredi* predispositions. But the absence of this predisposition did not amount to a clear and consistent ideology. Shas' conduct in the political system since its establishment, and the declarations of its various leaders, present a rather vague ideological picture as well as a political standpoint which is unclear. In some cases Shas' rhetoric contained ideological components of the radical right, while its actions and Knesset voting record supported left-wing positions. In some other cases its rhetoric was surprisingly moderate while its actions were more radical. Given the wide range of positions and discrepancies between its practice and ideology, an extremely cautious approach is necessary before reducing Shas' ideology to one consistent position. The party's mixed rhetoric places it in a strategic position to serve as a perfect coalition candidate for both the left and the right. As long as the government continued support for Shas' social network, providing financial support for the party's long-term goals, Rabbi Ovadia Yosef did not hesitate to instruct Shas to join the right-wing coalition. Likewise, irrespective of his religious anti-liberal stands, he also endorsed the party's participation in coalitions consisting of secularist left and non-religious parties (Baum-Banai, 2004, p. 160).

The ability of Shas to place itself between commonly used ideological poles stems from its ideology that defies the accepted alliances. Instrumental to this end is the party's embracing unclear and foggy ideological positions which revealed themselves in numerous statements:

> ...Sitting in the opposition for three years being loyal to our path, we have struggled. Today no other party is willing to commit to what Shas stands for—the social road map. They say it will take years, 750,000 children are going to sleep hungry. This is the cost that needs to be charged to the coalition and the Israeli government.... We are neither "right," nor "left." Neither are we at "center".... (Yishai, 2006)

In other statements we find additional examples of Shas as a political party moving beyond the conventional parameters of party politics. For instance, "Shas is not another party and its activists are not center people" is repeatedly stated by the party affiliated daily. "We don't have primaries and don't need encouragement. Shas has what no other party has. Our merchandise is unique: values, tradition, father's house, Judaism" (*Yom Leyom*, February 2, 2006, p. 17).

Another striking element of the Shas ideology has been the lack of attention to, or absence of, national issues. While the supporters of the other parties were preoccupied with territorial issues, in the Shas campaign there was no mention of peace or the country's safety. The party's main issues were poverty and social problems on the one hand, and Jewish values on the other, with the emotional value of Judaism overshadowing all other issues. This election strategy demonstrates the victory of traditional-religious populism over the national populism of the Likud which engaged in launching a fear-based campaign about Hamas in the 2006 election and maintaining a compromised policy.

The party's principle of *piku'ah nefesh*, and territorial compromise for permanent peace, offers a perfect example of how their pragmatism displays an internally consistent as well as a politically expedient position. Any debate on the territories is guided by the two rules laid down by Rabbi Ovadia Yosef. Land can be exchanged only for true peace. Therefore, employing the same principle, Rabbi Ovadia Yosef extended support for the Oslo accords and challenged Sharon's disengagement plan: "Thirty years ago I talked about giving land for peace, I still support that but only for a true peace, not a peace of words." Repeating the conventional argument of the right, Rabbi Ovadia Yosef argued that "there is no partner, no one to talk to.... We should wait patiently and not give the terrorists a thing without receiving. They will say: 'We have the upper hand, we have run the Jews off from there, we can do it also in Hebron and Beer Sheva.'" As a result, in this recent election Shas aligned itself with the anti-disengagement block, arguing that "we mustn't leave this place for terrorists to sit there and kill people...every Jew should know that. We are all the sons of Isaac and Jacob." But in reading between the lines one can discern Shas' original thesis, *pikuah nefesh*, and if the agreement had secured Jewish lives, it would have been deemed acceptable. Rabbi Ovadia Yosef concluded by saying: "I call upon all 'Likud' people and the rest of the parties—you have a conscience, you give your reports to God. If they will shoot from there and kill some people, what will you say? How can you risk Israel's welfare doing such a thing?" (Rabbi Ovadia Yosef, 2004).

Similar political positions must be placed within the broader framework of Shas' supporters, the majority of whom are not orthodox but traditional. When viewed from a broader perspective, voting for Shas can be understood as stemming from various motives; social justice, traditional loyalty, Da'at Torah [Torah inspired directions], and the religious instruction of the religious leadership may not be what is most compelling to Shas voters. The traditional Eastern public respects their rabbis; however, it does not mean the rabbis are the ones who decide which political positions to adopt on divisive issues such as disengagement and the peace process. Shas' impressive electoral success was an outcome of its ability to attract voters from the non-orthodox traditional Sephardi community without any connection to political messages. For some, the bundle of Shas' specific political positions was secondary to the voter's decision. Shas' role needs to be seen within the broader ideological space of Israeli politics.

A Unique Movement or a Reflection of Global Patterns? Shas in Comparative Perspective

Although Shas appears as a culmination of factors unique to Israeli politics, one can find remarkable parallels in Shas' trajectory of transformation in Islamist parties in Turkey.[5] Before presenting the Turkish case it is important to note that several parties representing Turkey's Islamist movement were formed and disbanded as a result of repeated closures by the constitutional court (see table 1).

The first ideological representative of Turkey's Islamist movement was National View, *Milli Görüş* (*milli* in Turkish means national but also referred to the Ottoman system of religious communities). The National View movement attributed the woes of the Turkish economic and political systems to Turkey's state system which marginalized the role of Islam. Even though the party names changed, all parties had their roots in the National View movement. Attesting to

Table 1
Genealogy of Turkey's Pro-Islamic Parties

The National Order Party (1970–1971)
(Closed Down by the Constitutional Court, May 20, 1971)

The National Salvation Party (1972–1980)
(Closed Down by the 1980 Military Coup d'etat)

The Welfare Party (1983–1998)
(Closed Down by the Constitutional Court, January 16, 1998)

Virtue Party (1998–2001)
(Closed Down by the Constitutional Court, June 22, 2001)

| **The Prosperity Party** | **The Justice and Development Party** |
| (2001–present) | (2001–present) |

the importance of structural and global forces shortly after Shas entered Israeli politics, Turkish politics witnessed the unprecedented electoral victory of its pro-Islamic Welfare party. In the 1987 election the Welfare party managed to establish itself in Turkish politics as a significant political force for the first time, only to further increase its power over the next five elections (see figure 4).

After the decline of the political leadership of Necmeddin Erbakan and the Virtue Party, Tayyip Erdogan and his party, the Justice and Development Party, became the new face of Turkey's Islamist politics.[6] What distinguishes the JDP and its predecessors from other parties in Turkish politics and aligns them with Shas are their massive grassroots movements, permanent campaigns, elusive ideology and the parties' ability to fill the ideological vacuum left by the declining secular left and right political parties as well as the adoption of neo-liberal reforms with broad social costs.

A historical look at Turkish Islamists demonstrates that the first wave of the Islamists' discourse focused overtly on the state. The National View parties opposed Turkey's secularism as a threat to the Islamic community. They carried on a developmental discourse by assigning a major role to the presence of a moral economy. The party called for the establishment of a *milli* economy whereby local sources would be used more effectively in conjunction with the moral guidance of Islam. Only this type of system could serve as a panacea for the problems of the disadvantaged (Bugra, 2002). "The only solution is in Islam" emerged as one of the powerful popular mottos of the movement in its early years. Given the prevalence of its state-centered and anti-secularist rhetoric, the emergence of the JDP marked a turning point in Turkey's Islamist movements. Unlike its predecessors, the JDP introduced itself more as a party attentive to the problems of economic redistribution and the restoration of secularism. Most strikingly, although the JDP leadership served under Erbakan and once shared his rhetoric against Turkey's secular establishment since the late 1990s, Islam was relegated to the background of the movement.

A closer look at the transformation of Turkey's Islamist movement highlights that although religious symbols and explanations were frequently and overtly employed, a *de-Islamization* of the party's messages has marked the Islamist parties' public appeal over the last several years. Similar to Shas, the JDP's ideology differed from those of its predecessors as the party developed a hybrid political language and practice that has become more attentive to the community and to non-state institutions. One can argue that this transformation was a forced one as the Islamist parties' anti-systemic rhetoric risks their closure. Nevertheless, this *de-Islamization* seemed to occur as the parties' constant confrontation with the state alienated their moderate supporters, thereby causing a loss of support for the Welfare party after the 1995 elections. It is the Islamist movement's search to expand its appeal that can be viewed as the main driving force for its change. *De-Islamization* thus meant more than simply redefining religion's role in relation to social issues. In the party's current rhetoric, Islamic society

Figure 4
Support for Pro-Islamic Parties 1987-2006

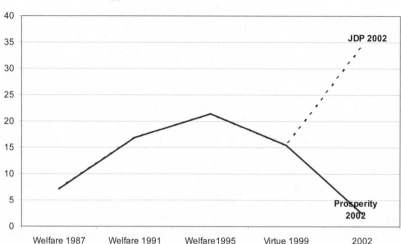

is presented not as an end in itself but as a means to restore social justice. As a result of this transformation the party introduced its ideology as Conservative Democracy, a term that had never been used in Turkish politics.[7]

When the party leadership is asked to define this new ideology, the clarifications resonate with the Shas rhetoric in that the party explains what its ideology is not, rather than what it is and what it entails. Mirroring this approach, the party program focuses on how the party is not Islamist, and thus the search for more religious rights is subsumed under expanding the rights of individuals against the state. According to the party program, it is the enforcement of secularism which amounts to a ban on religious practices and attire in state institutions and which in turn generates the Islamist political agenda. As a result, the party program is aimed, among others, at increasing individual welfare and moral capital. The party's specific objective to re-strengthen religious education and practices is designed to emphasize secularism not as the state's control of religious practices, but as the state's disengagement from religious affairs altogether. This is why, according to the JDP's program, it is not in opposition to but as a requirement of the principle of secularism, that all facilities should be provided to enable citizens to learn their religion (Justice and Development Party Program, 2002). By strengthening this message of saving Turkey's secularism from its antireligious outlook and not destroying it, the party also changes its public image. It is not a coincidence that many of the JDP's municipal candidates' campaign and hold public positions without a beard—having a beard is considered as a *sunnah* and is a common practice among religious males. Likewise perhaps the most controversial symbolic issue, the turban headscarf issue (i.e, the ban on the use of turbans in the state institutions as it represents a religious symbol) has been put on the backburner of the party's agenda.

According to this neo-Islamist ideology, only by tapping into the "shared values" defined by Islam can Turkey secure the foundations of a moral community and secure social justice. The role of Islamist parties, therefore, is to ensure that Islamic values and "sensitivities" will be reflected in government decisions and that funds and political power will be allocated to institutions and organizations that champion the rights of the oppressed. Only when these values are restored and civil society institutions are strengthened can people then be protected, and the social problems addressed more effectively. Although this overall position informs the party's ideology, the party centers its policies on the income gap. Contradicting its overarching rhetoric, the word "Islam" has almost disappeared from the party's public appeal when it speaks to its "traditional" constituency. This presentation of the politics of Islam without any overt reference to Islam has generated two contradictory results: given the party's anti-establishment and controversial history, some skeptics view the JDP like any pro-Islamic party as *takiyyeci*, a party concealing the true aims in what it perceives to be an adversarial political environment. This elusiveness, however, makes it more appealing to Turkish traditionals (e.g., those who define themselves between religious and secularists) presenting the party as a viable alternative to other parties.

Due to its multilayered and ambiguous ideology, similar to that of Shas, the voters for JDP turn to the party not to reestablish a Muslim community but for a wide range of reasons. The effectiveness of the pro-Islamists' approach becomes particularly visible in the case of Kurdish groups (Yavuz, 2005). The Islamist parties in general and the JDP in particular have been successful in mobilizing the Kurdish electorate as the parties do not employ nationalist rhetoric. They define the common denominator of Turkishness as its Muslimness. According to Erdogan "it is Islam that serves as the cement of Turkish society" (*Yeni Safak*, December 12, 2005). The question of Kurdishness is thus an artificial problem that can be solved when collective identities are defined without the tight grip of a nationalist secularist discourse. Such rhetoric enhances its appeal to ethnic groups that feel estranged from the once hegemonic secular Turkish nationalism.

It is important to note, however, that the root of the party's appeal lies not only in its multifaceted ideology that simultaneously broadcasts different messages to different communities, but also in its national network that creates a well-connected welfare system. A wide range of services, from training courses to food stipends, is offered by highly organized party members and activists. The backbone of the system, however, draws on volunteers. The party has a representative in each neighborhood, *mahalle*, the main unit of society. These representatives collect data and communicate the party's messages to the electorate directly, using a political language that eludes the scrutiny to which the party's national discourse is subjected. The party's community leadership and political leadership often overlap, blurring the boundaries between the organization's activities in civil society and the political domain. The party representative visits to identify problems and extend help in a manner that often blends political and religious messages. The party, therefore, becomes a place where people seek help from committed believers when they must deal with a social or bureaucratic problem. The party's local centers often serve as training houses and community centers where a good society becomes a good Islamic community, where injustices are addressed promptly by a team of dedicated believers and party supporters. As in the case of Shas, women play the most substantial role in recruitment and campaigning, while being excluded from the party's upper echelons. Interestingly enough, when asked why women are not represented in the parliament, both Yishai and Erdogan offered identical answers: it is the lack of interest by women activists that explains the under-representation of women in parliament (Erdogan, 2004; Guerowitch, 2006).

The scope and strength of the Islamist parties' grassroots movements has led many observers to attribute the Islamists' popularity to the parties' social service network. Despite this appealing argument, the extent to which the Islamist party constituency hails from among the fundamentalists, or becomes fundamentalist after supporting the party, still constitutes one of the most vexing questions in Turkish politics (Ozdalga, 1997). When viewed from the bottom up, by using the self-assessments of the electorate that voted for the JDP, those who consider themselves very religious constitute only 16 percent (see Figure 5). [8]

Figure 5*
Religious Identities in Turkey—2005

* The 2005 Turkish Religious Party Support Survey (for more details see footnote 8).

The majority of JDP voters refrain from identifying themselves as on the extremes. Similar to the profiles of those who support Shas, we need to discuss different concentric circles of supporters for Turkey's Islamist parties, from traditionalist to ultra-orthodox, and the core supporters who hail more from the religious and traditional circles (Tessler, 2004).

The direct question of why supporters voted for the JDP offers us more insight into the thoughts of JDP voters. When asked why they chose the JDP, more than 33 percent reported that they turned to the party in reaction to the economic crises that preceded the elections (see figure 6). This reaction is in part in response to one of the country's most severe crises, affecting people from different socio-economic segments of society (Onis, 2001 and 2006). The following political reactions manifested themselves in the narrowing of the political sphere in Turkish politics. The main parties' socio-economic policies converged around similar positions, creating a consensus on market-oriented policies. As a result, notwithstanding the increasing rivalry among the main parties, they all advocated the disengagement of the state from welfare-related areas (Cizre and Yeldan, 2005). It is this convergence that created an important political gap in the representation, especially of the disadvantaged, as the main parties increasingly shied away from discussing redistributive policies. Given the hegemony of neo-liberalism, Turkish Islamists distinguished themselves from others as adamant critics of socially irresponsible market-oriented policies. A

Figure 6
Reasons to Support the JDP

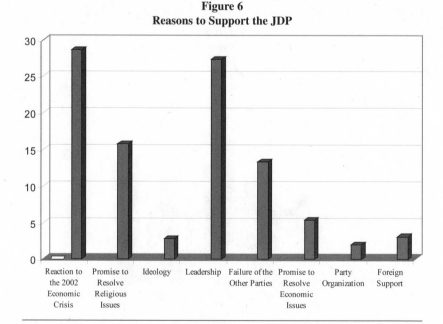

* The 2005 Turkish Religious Party Support Survey

closer look at the JDP indicates that instead of criticizing the rationality and mechanism of neo-liberal policies, the JDP views the weakening of the nation's moral cement, Islam, as the main reason for its current social ills. This is why the once popular slogan of the pro-Islamic groups—"Islam is the answer"—has been gradually replaced by "the JDP is the main tool for an 'enlightened Turkey'" (Justice and Development Party Program, 2002).

Similar to Shas' rejection of accepted fault lines in Israeli politics not only in its recent appeals, but since the mid-1990s, the Islamist parties viewed their political positions as beyond the conventional parameters of Turkish politics. According to the Prosperity Party's current leader, one of the earlier mentors of the leader of JDP's Erdogan, Recai Kutan, it is futile to attempt to understand the Islamist stance on a left-right spectrum:

> We are asked often if we are on the Left or Right or if we are trying to become a center party. First, we do not accept the conventional definition of Left and Right. But if you ask who represents the center, the reasonable answer should be based upon whoever represents the beliefs, world views, visions and desires of the nation defines the center. The most essential criterion [to decide which party is at the center] is the nation's views. Whichever party distances itself from the desires of the nation becomes a fringe party. We believe that we represent our people's views and beliefs best. Therefore, the Virtue must be the center party. (Kutan, 1998)

Although such statements first appear to be rhetorical maneuvering, they reflect the Islamist parties' rejection of the dominant categories and social and economic policies. This discursive and practical refutation makes them both unique and attractive to those who view existing parties as ineffective. Politically alienated supporters in search of novel political identities turn to Islamists not merely out of religious conviction, but due to the Islamist parties' ability to offer an unconventional ideology and place the supporters within a national network of support (Tessler, 2004). Consequently, the JDP's success needs to be seen in the context of other parties' weakening grassroots support, ideological foundations, and consensual commitments to neo-liberal reforms. The end of center, right and left parties unleashed a process similar to Israel's concurrent processes of dealignment and realignment (Yesilada, 2002). It is in this context that the JDP holds a unique place, not only as a result of its own strategic choices, but also as a result of other parties' failure. Accordingly, the Islamist parties' success and their expansion results from their ability to fill the political vacuum generated by other parties. It is not a coincidence that both Israel and Turkey witnessed their highest non-participation rates (36.8 percent and 20.9 percent respectively) in their most recent election.

The Direction of Shas' Transformation:
From Fundamentalist Believers to Pious Social Servants?

When Shas' emergence and transformation are placed under a comparative lens it becomes clear that, just like other religious parties, the changes the party underwent put it at a crossroads: the party currently exhibits signs of both moderation as well as a tendency to become more radical. Determining which of these currents will prevail requires an understanding of the party's religious identity and the way in which its adaptation unfolded. The party's ideological journey and the reconfiguration of its religious identity is best revealed in the party's shifting slogans. Shas' once very effective motto, "restoring the past glory" (i.e., restoring the Sephardi ethnic religious tradition to its original dominant place), withered away. The newer slogans, "a hungry boy cannot study," "Eli Yishai is a genuine social leader," "they hurt you, cut you down – we have to have a strong Shas," emerged to capture and create the party's new role. It is this rhetoric that has led some observers to describe the party as a "merchant of poverty." Along with shifting the social issues to center stage, the leadership emphasized the party's acceptance of the state apparatus and was even photographed with three flags of the State of Israel, reinforcing the party's image as not anti-systemic. This attempt to normalize the party also marked the efforts of many other vote maximizing religious parties, such as the JDP. Yet this normalization cannot be simplified as a decisive shift from a religious to a social agenda. Both policies continue, but their relative importance has changed. In the words of the chairman of election headquarters, Mr. Yitzchak Cohen (2006), these are signs of the coexistence of somewhat contradictory tenets in the party's agenda:

> Shas presents its platform clearly: it includes proven activity and strong will to continue its social care.... Being an orthodox party it must obey the "Rabbinical Council." Therefore, the orthodox public has no other party to look for.... (p. 8)

Due to their ideological inconsistencies, the true nature of these religious parties and the real direction of their transformation have often been questioned. Much of the scrutiny devoted to them has been dedicated to weighing the party's role as a warrior for social justice against its *Haredi* activist side which seeks the restoration of religious community. This is why Yitzchak Cohen is often asked for his reactions to *Haredi* criticism of Shas, which among others claimed that "it does not represent the Torah world as it demanded a children's stipend, but no budget for the Torah world." Cohen argued that these perceptions attempt to damage the religious foundations of the party, while *Haredi* leaders like Abraham Friedman, the head of the Yeshiva's organization, confirm that Shas has dealt most effectively with the problems in the Torah world (*Kol Ha'Ir*, March 1, 2006).

Aside from its investment in the *Haredi* sector, the party leaderships' own messages suggest that ultimately it is the party's ultra-orthodox identity which defines its political messages and agenda. The most significant of these messages was offered by Rabbi Ovadia Yosef who described voting for Shas as *mitzvah* and that: "a partner for a good deed has a place in heaven." Such calls resonate with Erbakan's statements dividing Turkish citizens into real Muslims who support the party and those who belong to the religion of potatoes (i.e., those who belong to an invented, unholy, and meaningless religion). Bringing the electoral rules closer to those in the Turkish system, the chairman of the Israeli election committee, Judge Dorit Beinish, ordered the Shas campaign to stop broadcasting a statement that equates voting to a religious practice. The party's reaction to the ban affords a reflection of Shas' religious paradigm that surfaces infrequently, yet quickly overshadows the party's image as a social issue party. In the words of Eli Yishai:

> Whoever silences the Torah words leans on the perception of hatred and destruction of Judaism...the assumed policing of thoughts disqualifies Jewish words with no one to contradict them...I feel sorry that in the Jewish state Torah words are being censored...our voters will not bow down to the judge, that is why Maran Maor Israel Shalita repeatedly says those who vote for Shas will have a place in heaven (March 16, 2006, p. 2).

An inside-out look at Shas' message to its audience offers further examples of how the party assigns religious meaning to political practices.[9] The party's newspaper, *Yom Leyom*, defines voting for Shas as, in essence, a political action in service of religious ends. Voting for Shas, according to Shmuel Asulin, will result in more religious schools, *yeshivot*, *mikva'ot*, more observers of *mitzvot*, and additional prerogatives in the world to come. The rabbi's words are geared toward our mistaken brothers, who are "unaware of the huge privilege they have been given during election time, one which unfortunately they do not get every day." The critical and religious significance of voting often concluded such statements: "Those people should know the critical meaning of the note they put in the ballot boxes, the one that will find, a day after the election, the face of the country more Jewish or God forbid not...." (Asulin, March 16, 2006, p. 2)

In its appeal geared toward its hardcore supporters, the party's rhetoric brings the secular-religious conflict to the fore and presents its view as the protection of the latter. In this dichotomous world Shinui represents the secular "other", and Shas' participation in politics is presented as a result of religious obligation:

> We are facing an important battle now. In the previous election "Shinui" achieved more seats than Shas, therefore we were not in the coalition. We have gone through a hard and desperate time. This election is destined for more *yeshivot*, children's Torah schools, *mikva'ot*—so how can we be indifferent? Our job in the Knesset is to stop the destruction of the Israeli people. *That is why we allow ourselves to join "the golden calf.* Otherwise what do we have to look for in the Knesset? The Israeli Torah is our law. " (Baadny, March 1, 2006)[10]

When we look at Shas' public appeal in its entirety, beyond the dichotomy of secular and religious, ultra-orthodox and others, what distinguishes Shas from other parties is its ability to move beyond these dualities. Shas carefully imbues its spiritual messages with social messages and vice versa, and reaches out to those refusing to accept a clear-cut distinction between the secular and the religious. For instance, fighting against poverty becomes a precondition for fulfilling desired religious ends. After all, a religious community first and foremost needs individuals who are able to meet their basic needs. As a result, "a hungry boy cannot pray" indicates to party supporters the obligation to attend more to the needs of the disadvantaged, so that they can then attend to their religious obligations. Given this dual position, it is not surprising that Shas' leadership views the party not only in competition with Likud but also with Labor:

> ...The Labor party used, and is still using, the social vision of Shas, and even if we lost some thousand votes to Amir Peretz, they are still our votes, they will come back to us for the real house is the Jewish house. Yet beyond everything, beyond welfare, beyond the dignity of the people who were pushed towards poverty, Shas still stands with its huge flag of religious education maintenance and brings the Israeli hearts closer to the holy Torah, to our Father in the sky. (*Yom Leyom*, March 30, 2006, p. 5)

In light of Shas' own ideological positioning, it is not that easy to decisively conclude whether Shas is a moderate or fundamentalist party or, more importantly, to ascertain the direction of its transformation. At the risk of simplification, we argue that a religious party can be defined as fundamentalist, if it does not recognize the legitimacy of the existing order and seeks to alter it. Political engagement becomes a means for initiating a radical and massive transformation of society thereby enabling its rules to be altered.[11] When faced with political resistance, fundamentalist parties have the potential of not subscribing to a gradual change from within, but to large-scale sudden changes, and resorting to coercive methods. A quick review demonstrates that Shas' policies do not display the basic characteristics of an anti-systemic movement. Shas was born into the political system, it grew up there, and developed as a result of it, not against it. Neither does it represent only those who are estranged from the system. Shas' policies focus on an incremental bottom-to-top change. In this regard, attributing Shas to the family of fundamentalist parties requires cautionary notes. Unlike fundamentalist parties, Shas accepts the existing system as a given and participates with its institutions, even if it is for sectarian reasons and interest in the community rather than on national or Zionist grounds.

Although Shas does not display the immediate attributes of a party seeking the radical transformation of society, it does have, like any religious party, a subgroup of supporters who promote the transformation of Israel to an *halakhic* community. Nevertheless, they do not constitute the majority of Shas voters, and their fundamentalism is "quiescent." During Deri's trial some observers felt that Shas would turn into a separatist party, should Aryeh Deri be convicted. While the party seemed to be turning to the "protest tent" and issuing "the lion's roar," the protests gradually faded away and Shas did not become a separatist party. It would be fair to argue that the political and spiritual leadership of Shas declares its primary obligation to *halakhah*. The party attempts to encourage as many people as possible to repent, uses rhetoric derived strictly from religious texts and tradition, and implements social activities that target those who are disadvantaged. Therefore, those who view Shas as an extremist religious party, or a social struggle party, can find justification for their opinions.

At the theological-ideological level of Rabbi Ovadia Yosef's ruling, there is no direct call for resolutions of the conflicts by force. Once again, we need to realize that some elements of radical religious and transformative ideas can be found, especially among Sephardi yeshivah students who were educated in Ashkenazic institutions, and among newly recruited "repentant" supporters. Shas' political appeal is not rooted in the promise of a drastic alteration of the existing social order, nor are the party's activities coercive per se. Shas does also not regard the existing system as its adversary. Poverty and ethnic injustices appear as the enemy, and they are presented in abstract terms without a clear explanation as to why they exist. Therefore, in its current form, Shas does not appear to be a radical transformative party. Nevertheless, Shas was and remains an orthodox religious party, even though most of its voters are not orthodox. Unless we acknowledge the novelty and intricacy of its ideology, and its unconventional politics of religion without religion, just like its Turkish counterpart, an analysis of Shas can be highly misleading.

Conclusions

In attempting to analyze Shas and the Islamist parties in Turkey, we must pay closer attention to the multifaceted nature of religious parties, and warn against the consequences of hastily drawn conclusions that conflate one aspect with the entire movement. Both parties suggest that beyond their specific religious beliefs a new genre of religious parties is in the making: one that defies our conceptual tools and requires nuanced explanations. For example, the debate on Shas' identity must move beyond whether and to what extent it is an ethnic party, to how it draws on ethnicity in its appeal. Similarly, the policies of Turkey's JDP require a perspective that avoids assessing whether the party is an anti-systemic party or not. It is also important to note that the leadership plays a critical role in religious parties, just as it does for other parties. Yet one needs to be extremely cautious before presenting these parties simply as parties of charismatic leaders or movements. The Shas party has already survived three political leaders (Peretz, Deri, and Yishai), and the charismatic leadership of Deri. Similarly, Turkey's Islamist parties easily shifted their support from the charismatic leadership of Necmeddin Erbakan to Tayyip Erdogan, which only expanded the movement's power. Given the strong roots of these parties in their respective communities, single-track assessments, such as Shas is Rabbi Ovadia Yosef's party, or the JDP is Erdogan's party, do not allow us to grasp the depth of these movements. It is also important to note that none of these leaders are merely ideologues or pragmatists. Instead of presenting a clear ideology, or justifying politically expedient decisions, both groups of leaders define the main parameters of the party's policies in religious terms yet also promote policies that are relevant and accessible to different groups. Religious parties in general, and Shas and the JDP in particular, benefit from their charismatic leadership, and from their justification of the policies as religiously informed and acceptable. They not only facilitate critical and unconventional decisions by granting them religious legitimacy, but also provide party discipline and minimize the impact of challenges. However, these parties' appeal and roots extend beyond the popularity of their leadership.

As political alienation reaches its peak in both countries, Shas and JDP differ from other parties with respect to their connection with local communities. Both Shas and the JDP grew out of local movements, and they continue to maintain representatives in each neighborhood. The party representatives act as community leaders and ombudsmen, and bring the issues and concerns of local people to the relevant institutions, or to the local representatives. The continual and active party presence in the communities amounts to a permanent campaign. The uninterrupted efforts of the party advocates, and their ability to use traditional symbols and ideas, give these parties a presence and depth of communication that competing parties do not enjoy. Given that both parties' political leadership hail from modest backgrounds, they reach out to people who experience the similar problems they once did.

Perhaps as a result of their widespread roots in their respective communities, the overall profiles of the Shas and JDP constituencies demonstrate that religious parties do not appeal solely to religious or ultra-orthodox, but mostly to "traditional voters." The mixed nature of support confirms that parties do not attract supporters in order to transform their society into a more religious one. Both parties promise to revive the assumed-to-be shared traditional religious values, but they, in fact, create some new ones. One of the striking qualities shared by Shas and the JDP is their dual rhetoric that reconciles religious and social themes. On the one hand, both parties present their agenda as a social transformation project: a social revolution in the case of Shas, or a social development and enlightenment project in the case of the JDP. In the case of Shas, the social and spiritual campaigns are visible in the public sphere. Due to existing laws, Turkey's religious parties cannot overtly launch religious and spiritual campaigns, while such campaigns do remain powerful at the local level. Thus, in a hybrid language, party activists often mention their "devotion and service" *hizmet*, which literally means serving a higher cause without any expectation, but also means serving God. Erbakan openly linked voting for the party to religious duty. Erdogan's language at first appears to be free of such references, yet the party uses a rather secularized language to express religious demands. It is not coincidental that the JDP's program differs from others in that it defines itself as a project for democracy and asks for God's help in executing it—a rare statement in Turkey's secular political world. The party's community level activities draw heavily on religious references and one can speak of a continuous spiritual campaign.

When viewed together, Shas' and the JDP's rhetoric exhibit striking similarities, thereby suggesting that religious parties' religious and social projects are compartmentalized, but eventually form a rather coherent political vision. Implicit in the social projects is the idea that all social problems have two roots: (i) the misguided policies of the state and (ii) people's detachment from their religious roots and the lack of religious mobilization. Ironically enough, when Shas and the JDP's election campaigns are reviewed, one finds a language that resonates with those of the left wing parties. The assessment of the problems focuses on the negative impacts brought about as a result of the free market economy. These parties present their role as a "detector and articulator of social problems," a role ignored by others. They reach out and act as power brokers, not only for the disadvantaged, but also for those who are trying to cope with the challenges of the changing market economy. Likewise, both parties' rhetoric embodies a language of protest, and describes other parties as paying only lip service to the people's problems. The center parties, both parties argue, not only fail to attend to the problems but also fail to understand that creating moral communities does not aggravate but rather alleviates social ills. The rhetoric of both parties details an imagined religious community that serves as an ideal political community. Religion, in essence, helps to restore the social fabric, uniting and not undermining the stability and overall welfare of the political community. Perhaps because of these parties' emphasis on strengthening community, education emerges as one of the fundamental issues. After all, only education can assist the new generation in acquiring the right values.

Despite their references to "lost communities," the electorally successful and expanding religious parties are very much products of the political currents and conditions that have shaped and continue to mold their respective societies. The resiliency of Shas, the JDP, and its predecessors can be attributed not to their reactionary nature but to their proactive role, one that results in a careful and continuous adjustment of their policies relative to the demands of their broadening constituencies. While it is a narrow Sephardi ultra-orthodox movement, Shas re-invented itself as a Sephardi Social Movement Party. In its current form Shas accentuates its social agenda, popularizes ultra-orthodox appeal, and downplays exclusive ethnic ideas to reach the secular and the religious, Sephardi and non-Sephardi public alike. It is not a coincidence that in its recent election campaign Shas never once used the word "Sephardi" in its main advertisement of thirty-six minutes. According to Yishai, it does not matter if a hungry boy is Russian or Ethiopian. Likewise, Turkish Islamists have broadened their scope and established themselves more as a mass party with a strong social agenda. Their public appeal rarely uses the word Islam alone. "Our common values" and "genuine and real values of the nation" are used as a proxy for Islamic values. What matters is restoring the moral community for the benefit of all.

The shift in the rhetoric of religious parties at first suggests that these parties have moderated their positions and that they increasingly embrace non-religious actors and ideas. However, when the actions of these parties are carefully reviewed, their practices remain loyal to the idea of creating a broad religious community. They refrain from questioning certain issues, like the status of women and the social consequences of a "pious life style." Despite their idealized society which is rooted in religion, and their constant efforts at achieving it, this society is also constantly being redefined. These parties are therefore by no means fundamentalist with a single-minded dedication to restoring a religious community. None of these parties target seizing state power, or aim to drastically and completely transform their respective societies into historical and religious ones. They carry a rather accommodating ideology which seeks to introduce necessary social processes, guiding their society in the right direction. Thus both Shas and the JDP warn against reducing these parties' versatile appeals and programs to conventional labels of fundamentalist or moderate. They are pragmatic fundamentalists or moderate radicals, depending which side of the movement and party apparatus we examine. Their very success and resiliency is rooted in their multifaceted structure, and their new position between fundamentalist and moderate religious parties.

Notes

1. It is important to note that Shas' leadership never overtly declared that they want to be a "Likud with Kippa." However, according to the reporter, Ilan Marciano (*Yediot Aharonot*), "important elements in the party have endorsed the 'Likud with Kippa' comparison within the party circles," *Yediot Aharonot* (March 29, 2006).
2. For an analysis of the complicated foundations of Shas that combine ethnic religious and social messages see Herzog (1987).
3. For an analysis of the use of amulets see Fisher (c. 2004).
4. The distinction between Sephardi and Mizrahi is important, yet it is beyond the scope of this analysis. Both terms are used to indicate groups that immigrated from Muslim countries. But Mizrahi is a geographical and cultural indicator that refers to the Jews of the Maghreb and the Middle East, while Sephardi emphasizes the religious tradition of Sefarad (Spain) and its followers. We use Sephardi, as Shas describes itself as a Sephardi party.
5. As any use of religion for political end is seen as unconstitutional, the welfare party and its antecedents were closed down by the constitutional court. It is important to note that the closures did not eliminate the party; rather, they only resulted in the reestablishment of the closed party under a different name. The pro-Islamic movement was unified, and split only in 2002. Given that one of the splinters, the Prosperity party, received only 2 percent, the pro-Islamist bloc gathered under the Justice and Development party.
6. Among others, one of the reasons for the leadership change was Erbakan's consent to the Secularist National Security Council's advisory decisions to curb the power of Islamists, his own hard-core constituency, when he became Turkey's first Islamist Prime minister.

7. For more details on the Justice and Development Party's ideology see Tepe (July 2005) as well as Hakan Yavuz (2006) and Akdogan, (2004).

8. The sample of The 2005 Turkish Religious Party Support Survey includes 1,016 representatives of the Turkish electorate. The questionnaire was designed by Sultan Tepe and included 120 questions pertaining to the assessment of Turkish politics in general, the European Union membership process, and the policies of the Justice and Development party in particular. A set of open-ended questions were used, such as "what laicism means to you?" and "why do you support or oppose Turkey's EU membership?" The interviews were conducted face-to-face by trained interviewers. Each lasted approximately forty-five minutes. All the figures and findings regarding the public perceptions reported in this analysis are derived from this survey.

9. For another detailed discussion of how religious meanings are attributed to political practices in general, and in Kiryat-Gat in the early 1960s in particular, see _Deshen_ (1970).

10. Rabbi Shimon Baadny is a member of Shas' Council of Sages.

11. According to Samuel C. Heilman, fundamentalism reinvents the past by selectively retrieving from it those elements that challenge the alternative truths offered by contemporary culture. As such, it constitutes a kind of counterculture and society and is often engaged in an intense battle against forces in the contemporary world that, in its view, seek to undermine or to defile the world as it sees it. For more see Heilman (2005) and Heilman and Friedman (1991).

References

Akdogan, Y. 2004. *Muhafazakar Demokrasi* [Conservative Democracy]. Ankara.

Arian, Asher and Michal Shamir, eds. 2004. "On Mistaking a Dominant Party in a Dealigning System." In *The Elections in Israel—2003*. New Brunswick: Transaction Publishers, 13–33.

------. 2001. "Candidates, Parties and Blocs, Israel in the 1990s." *Party Politics* 7 (6): 689–710.

Asulin, S. 2006. *Yom Leyom*, 16 March.

Baadny, R. S. 2006. Yad Eliyahu, *YNET*, 1 March.

Baum-Banai, R. 2004. *The Rise and Solidification of Shas: A Chapter in the Ethnic Social History of the State of Israel*. Doctoral Thesis, University of Tel Aviv.

Ben-Rafael, E and Stephen Sharot. 1991. *Ethnicity, Religion and Class in Israeli society*. Cambridge: Cambridge University Press.

Bugra, A. 2002. "Labour, Capital, and Religion: Harmony and Conflict among the Constituency of Political Islam in Turkey," *Middle Eastern Studies* 38 (2): 187–204.

Cizre, U., and E. Yeldan. 2005. "Turkish Encounter with Neo-Liberalism: Economics and Politics in the 2000-2001 Crises." *Review of International Political Economy* 12 (3): 387–408.

Cohen, I. 2006. Interview by *Kol Ha'Ir*, 1 March.

Deshen, S. A. 1970. *Immigrant Voters in Israel: Parties and Congregations in a Local Election Campaign*. Manchester: Manchester University Press.

------, and Moshe Shokeid. 1974. *The Predicament of Homecoming: Cultural and Social Life of North African Immigrants in Israel*. Ithaca: Cornell University Press, 1974.

Erdogan, T. 2004. "Secim(Election)," *Hurriyet*, 1 March.

Ettinger, Y. 2006. "Welcome the new Shas [*Kablu et Shas ha-Hadasha*]." *Haaretz*, 31 March.

Fisher, S. c. 2004. "Talismans and Political Liberalism: The Conceptual Organization of Reality and the Legitimation of the State According to Shas Movement." In Y. Yonah and Y. Gudman, eds. *Me'arbolet ha-Zekhuyot: Diyyun Biḳorti be-Datiyyut u-ve-Ḥiloniyyut be-Yisrael*, Van Leer Institute. Tel Aviv: Ha-Ḳibbutz ha-Meuḥad [Hebrew].

"Free People." 1999. *Yediot Aharonot*, 18 March.

Guerowitch, Y. 2006. "Elections." 7 March. Retrieved June 12, 2006 from: nana.co.il/ Article.

------. 2006. "Wants a Jewish State?" 7 March. Retrieved June 2, 2006 from: elections. nana.co.il/Article.

Heilman, S. C. 2005. "Jews and Fundamentalism." *Jewish Political Studies Review* 17 (nos. 1–2): 183-191.

------, and M. Friedman. 1991. "Religious Fundamentalism and Religious Jews: the case of the Haredim." In M. E. Marty and R. S. Appleby, eds. *Fundamentalisms Observed.* Chicago: University of Chicago Press, 1991, 229-233.

Herzog, H. 1987. *Contest of Symbols: The Sociology of Election Campaigns through Israeli Ephemera.* Cambridge, MA: Harvard University Library.

------.1988. "Political Ethnicity as a Socially Constructed Reality: The Case of Jews in Israel." In M. J. Esman, I. Rabinovitch, eds. *Ethnicity Pluralism and the State in the Middle East.* Cornell University Press, 140–151.

Inyanim. 2006. 27 February.

The Justice and Development Party Program. 2002. Retrieved July 6, 2006 from: http:// www.akparti.org.tr/

Kamil, O. 2000. "Rabbi Ovadia Yosef and His 'Culture War' in Israel." *Middle East Review of International Affairs* 4 (4): 22-30.

Keren ha-Hatzalah. 2003. Interview with David Gil the CEO of the "salvation fund," *YNET.* 24 August.

Knesset Election Law (Shortened Version). 1969. Ch. 122 (6).

Kol Ha'Ir. 2006. 1 March. Bnei Brak.

Kopelowitz, E., and M. Diamond. 1998. "Religion That Strengthens Democracy: An Analysis of Religious Political Strategies in Israel." *Theory and Society* 27: 671–708.

Kutan, R. 1998. Interview in *Yeni Safak.* 24 May.

Leon, N. 2005. *Sephardic Ultra-Orthodoxy in Israel: Religious and Community Practices.* Tel Aviv University Dissertation

Liebman, C. May 1982. "The Rise of Neo-Traditionalism among Orthodox Jews in Israel." *Megamot* 27:231–50.

Maariv. 2006. 27 January.

Maariv. 2006. 21 February.

Maariv. 2006. 24 February.

Önis, Ziya. 2001. "Political Islam at the Crossroads from Hegemony to Coexistence." *Contemporary Politics* 7 (4): 281–298.

------. 2006. "The Political Economy of Islam and Democracy in Turkey: From the Welfare Party to the AKP." In Dietrich Jung, ed. *Democracy and Development: New Political Strategies for the Middle East.* New York: Palgrave, 103-128.

Özdalga, E. 1997. "Civil Society and Its Enemies: Reflections on a Debate in the Light of Recent Developments within the Islamic Student Movement in Turkey." In Elizabeth Özdalga and Sune Persson eds. *Civil Society Democracy and The Muslim World.* Istanbul: Swedish Research Institute & Curzon Press, 73–84.

Peled, Y. 1998. "Towards a Redefinition of Jewish Nationalism: The Enigma of Shas." *Ethnic and Racial Studies* 21 (4): 703–727.

Shas (Producer). 2006. *Burning heart—the country's tears* [Videotape].

Tepe, S. July 2005. "Turkey's AKP: A Model 'Muslim-Democratic' Party?" *Journal of Democracy* 16 (3): 69–82.

------. 2006 "Promises and Limits of Pro-Islamic Parties." In M. Hakan Yavuz, ed. *The Emergence of a New Turkey: Democracy and the AK Parti*. University of Utah Press, 107-136.

Tessler, M. and E. Altinoglu. 2004. "Political Culture in Turkey: Connections Among Attitudes Toward Democracy, the Military, and Islam," *Democratization* 11 (1): 21-50.

Yavuz, H. M., ed. 2006. *The Emergence of a New Turkey: Democracy and the AK Parti*. University of Utah Press.

------. 2004. "Milli Gorus Hareket; Muhalif Modernist Hareket" [National View Movement: An Oppositional Modernist Movement]. In Yasin Aktay, ed. *Islamcilik*. Istanbul: Iletism, 591-604.

Yesilada, B. 2002. "Realignment and Party Adaptation: The Case of the Refah and Fazilet Parties." In Sabri Sayari and Yilmaz Esmer, eds. *Politics, Parties, and Elections in Turkey*. Boulder, CO: Lynne Rienner Pub., 155-179.

Yeni Safak. 2005. 12 December.

Yishai, E. 2006. Speech given at the opening of the 2006 election campaign. Jerusalem.

------. 2006. *Yom Leyom*, 16 March.

Yom Leyom. 2006. 2 February.

Yom Leyom. 2006. 26 March.

Yom Leyom. 2006. 30 March.

Yom Leyom. 2006. 12 April.

Yosef, O. 2004. 23 October. Address directed mainly to the Knesset members.

The Immigration from the Former Soviet Union and the Elections in Israel, 1992-2006: Is a "Third Israel" Being Created?

Viacheslav Konstantinov

Introduction

From the end of 1989, when the influx of immigrants from the former USSR began, six election campaigns were held in Israel for the Knesset or the office of prime minister—in 1992, 1996, 2001, 2003, and 2006. In this article I examine to what extent the votes of these immigrants impacted on the election results and the political system in Israel.

Beginning in the 1990s, several studies have been conducted on the participation of immigrants from the former USSR in elections in Israel (Weiss, 1997; Horowitz, 1999; Katz, 2000; Gitelman and Goldstein, 2001; Goldstein and Gitelman, 2004; Bick, 1998; Reich et al., 1995; Fein, 1995; Horowitz, 1994; Al-Haj and Leshem, 2000; Khanin, 2001, 2005; Lochery, 2006). These studies deeply analyze both the voting patterns of these immigrants as well as the factors affecting their electoral behavior.

Several theories can be found in the academic literature explaining the electoral behavior of the immigrants. One of them is the protest vote, whereby immigrants generally vote against the current government in protest against their absorption difficulties (Horowitz, 1994, 1999; Fein, 1995). Another theory is that of political assimilation in which the longer immigrants have been in Israel, and as the process of their absorption in other areas (language, accommodation, employment) continues, their electoral behavior more closely approximates that of the general population (Goldstein and Gitelman, 2004; Lochery, 2006). The theory of political multiculturalism maintains that Israeli society is divided into several sectors, each of which—including that of immigrants from the former USSR—has its own voting pattern (Horowitz, 1999; Bick, 1998; Gitelman and Goldstein, 2001).

Within this context there are two interesting questions that present themselves. First, to what extent can these theories explain the voting pattern of the influx of immigrants from the former USSR? Second, in what way does the electoral behavior of the immigrants differ from that of the general Jewish population in the three main areas of Israeli politics—political-security, socio-economic, and the relations between state and religion? An interesting focal point would be to examine whether the trends in these spheres have been consistent over time or have changed from one election to the next. The reference here, of course, is to dominant trends on a group level rather than an individual one. I will attempt to answer these questions by means of statistical analysis.

Most studies of immigrant voting patterns are based on analyzing the results of exit polls or public opinion polls taken prior to an election. The advantage of these types of studies is that they make it possible to analyze voting patterns (including those of immigrants) according to socio-demographic characteristics (gender, age, education, etc.) as well as by social and political attitudes (to the peace process, state and religion, etc.). These polls, however, are limited. They relate to only a minority of immigrants, making it difficult to assess how representative they actually are. Moreover, since exit polls that examine immigrants' voting patterns are generally conducted in areas with large concentrations of immigrants from the former USSR there may be an inherent bias, as immigrants' political attitudes in areas where they constitute a majority differ from those in which they constitute a minority. In addition, most of the studies on this subject deal with one or two election campaigns and do not examine the development of voting patterns over time.

The study presented here, however, examines changes in the electoral behavior of immigrants over time, from 1992 to 2006, and is ecological in character. It is not based on polls but on official statistical data, including a cross-section of immigration by year and ethnic group: Ashkenazi, Caucasian, and Bukharan. It is difficult, on an individual level, to isolate the votes of immigrants from the former USSR from those of the general population in Israel because of the confidentiality of votes cast. I have therefore chosen to examine the electoral behavior of the immigrants indirectly and have analyzed the Pearson correlation coefficients between the proportion of immigrants from the former USSR in the population of a locale and the proportion of votes cast for parties or prime ministerial candidates in that area.

For this purpose I have taken into account all the Jewish locales with a population of over 5,000 in which a majority of immigrants from the former USSR reside. The analysis included 100 areas throughout Israel, including some that are located across the Green Line. The proportion of immigrants from the former USSR was high in some of them and low in others. Correlation coefficients were calculated between the proportion of immigrants from the former USSR (during and after 1989) in the population of the locale—as measured at the end of the year before the elections (1991, 1995, etc.)—and the voting rates in the Knesset elections of 1992, 1996, 1999, 2003, and 2006 for each Jewish party that passed the minimum threshold as well as in the prime ministerial elections of 1996, 1999, and 2001 for all the candidates (Shimon Peres, Binyamin Netanyahu, Ehud Barak, and Ariel Sharon). Since the locales differed in size, all the data were weighted relative to the extent of the area's population.

An ecological study suffers from five restrictions that do not exist for polls:

a. The number of variables in the analysis is limited, because the data is not gathered for research purposes.
b. The second limitation relates to the statistical dependency between two variables—in this case between the proportion of immigrants and the voting rate for a specific party or candidate. The statistical dependency attests to the link between them on a geographical level rather than to its existence at an individual level (Diskin, 1988). In the current study this limitation is even more pronounced, because the unit of measurement constitutes an entire locale. In other words, this study disregards differences between neighborhoods – relative both to the proportion of immigrants and the voting rates for parties or candidates—in the large towns. However, these differences can often be quite large, for example, when comparing neighborhoods of ultra-orthodox Jews to mixed and secular neighborhoods in Jerusalem. It would have been preferable to analyze the data according to polling booths or at the very least statistical areas, but these units are problematic insofar as the availability of data, particularly with regard to the independent variable, i.e., the proportion of immigrants (the figures for the proportion of immigrants from the former USSR by statistical area were published only in the results of the population census held in 1995). Elections in Israel are held more frequently than censuses, and the proportion of immigrants changes from year to year. Therefore up-to-date data were used even though the unit of measurement was larger (locales).
c. The correlation between the proportion of immigrants in an area and the voting rate for parties or candidates are influenced not only by the electoral behavior of the immigrants themselves but also by other factors, the most important being the geographical distribution in Israel of immigrants from the former USSR. The immigrants tend to settle in peripheral areas where the veteran population often votes for certain parties (the reason for this settlement pattern is primarily economic). For example, the positive correlation between the proportion of immigrants from the former USSR and the voting rate for the Shas party does not indicate that these immigrants vote for Shas, but merely that they tend to live in peripheral areas whose veteran population votes for that party. The opposite trend could apply relative to parties like Shinui and Meretz, where many of their veteran supporters reside in prosperous neighborhoods where there are fewer immigrants.

To at least partially overcome this problem all the correlation coefficients were adjusted (by partial correlations) by the proportion of individuals of North African origin in a locale, including the second generation, on the basis of data from the 1995 population census. This index was chosen for two reasons: the first, because of its significance as one of the most important indices affecting election results by areas of residence (Diskin, 1988), and second, because of its availability—this index comprises the data for all the locales included in the study. The adjustment makes it possible to neutralize the effect of the concentration of immigrants in areas of residence where certain voting patterns prevail among the veteran population. Thus, the adjusted correlations more closely reflect voting patterns of the immigrants themselves. In most cases the adjusted correlations between the proportion of immigrants and the voting rate for certain parties or candidates did not differ greatly from the unadjusted ones, except when the votes were for Shas.

As noted above, Arab areas were not included in the analysis. In some Jewish areas, however, such as Haifa, Lod, and Ramle, there is a large Arab population which also participates in the elections. It is difficult to isolate Arab voters from the results of the elections in these areas as many of them vote for Zionist parties. Therefore the proportion of immigrants in these areas was generally calculated on the basis of the total number of inhabitants and not only of the Jewish population. Only in Jerusalem was the proportion of immigrants calculated on the basis of the Jewish population, as only a small proportion of the Arab inhabitants of Jerusalem participated in the elections for the Knesset and the position of prime minister.

d. This limitation is a product of the lack of data. There is a difference between the immigrants and the general population in every locale relative to voting activity rate and the proportion of individuals with the right to vote, but the present study does not deal with this difference. We focus on the proportion of immigrants in the population of the locale and not on voters or legitimate votes.

e. The analysis of the correlations (both weighted and adjusted, as noted earlier) by areas of residence does not allow for a precise calculation of the voting rate of immigrants from the former USSR for one party or another, but offers only an estimate based on a comparison with all voters in Jewish locales. If the coefficient is positive, the voting rate among the immigrants for a given party or candidate will be higher than the average voting rate for that party among the Jewish population, and vice versa if the coefficient is negative.

The analysis is based on data from the Central Bureau of Statistics (CBS) and the Ministry of Immigrant Absorption for the proportion of immigrants from the former USSR (including those from the Caucasus and Bukhara) in the population of a given area (CBS, 1995, 1998, 2000; Ministry of Immigrant Absorption, 2000, 2001, 2003, 2006) as well as the results of the elections by area of residence published by the CBS (CBS, 1993, 1997) and the Israeli press.[1]

1. General trends in immigrant voting in elections, 1992-2006

The 1992 Election

The Knesset election held in 1992 was the first in which immigrants who had arrived as part of the influx of immigrants from the former USSR participated.

This election led to the fall of the right-wing government led by Yitzhak Shamir and the installation of the left-wing government headed by Yitzhak Rabin. It has been stated (Weiss, 1997; Horowitz, 1994) that the immigrants were the deciding factor in that election, as most of them were dissatisfied with the absorption policy adopted by the Shamir government, primarily the policies affecting employment and accommodation. The ecological analysis only partially supports that claim (table 1, below). There was a significant positive correlation (0.47) between the proportion of immigrants in a locale and the voting rate for the Labor party in 1992. Thus, the proportion of immigrants voting for that party was considerably higher than that of the total Jewish population which voted for it, namely, one third. This finding is consistent with the results of the exit polls, according to which the Labor party obtained 47 percent of the immigrants' votes (Reich et al., 1995). A survey conducted by Tamar Horowitz demonstrates that this proportion was even higher—53 percent (Horowitz, 1994). However, the immigrants' support for the Labor party in 1992 was apparently not connected with support for the peace process (which was not the main issue in the Labor party's campaign at that time). Prior to the election more than half the immigrants from the former USSR opposed relinquishing territory for peace (Fein, 1995). The main reasons for the preponderance of immigrant votes for Labor may have been their disappointment with Likud absorption policy (as noted above), but the social-democratic orientation of many of the immigrants in the socio-economic sphere, particularly in the middle and older age-groups, may have also played a role (Horowitz, 1994). Many of the immigrants might have expected the Labor government to construct public housing and create employment in the government sector (as was done in the 1970s), but these hopes were dashed.

In this context it is important to note the following: a series of surveys undertaken by the Tatzpit Institute indicates that most immigrants from the former USSR originally intended to vote for Likud and other right-wing parties, but the situation gradually changed in favor of the parties of the left (and Labor in particular), with the most prominent shift occurring between January and March 1992, when the voting rate for these parties rose from 30 to 43 percent (Fein, 1995). This rise was not coincidental: at the beginning of March 1992 the Shamir government decided to stop payments which the Ministry of Immigrant Absorption had been granting to unemployed immigrant university graduates residing in Israel for more than one year. After one year they could only claim income support from the National Insurance Institution and were required by law to accept any work offered to them, even if it was not what they were professionally trained to do. This decision incensed many immigrants and quite naturally weakened their support of the Shamir government.

The correlation coefficient between the voting rate for Meretz and the proportion of immigrants was negative and almost significant (−0.22), i.e., the immigrants' voting rate for that party was lower than the average vote for it in the Jewish sector, namely 10 percent. This finding reflects a lack of agreement on the part of most of the immigrants with the political views of the left. Both Horowitz's study and the exit polls, however, demonstrate that the voting rate for Meretz among the immigrants was higher—11 percent (Horowitz, 1994; Reich et al., 1995).

The voting rates for Likud yielded a correlation coefficient that was positive and significant (0.35), but lower than that found for the vote for Labor (table 1, below). The voting rate for Likud among the immigrants was higher than that among the general population in Jewish locales (about 25 percent). This finding contradicts those of Horowitz and the exit polls, according to which Likud obtained only 14 and 18 percent respectively of immigrants' votes in 1992 (Horowitz, 1994; Reich et al., 1995).

The correlation coefficient for voting rates for Raphael Eitan's Tzomet party was positive but not significant (table 1, below). That party obtained seven percent of the votes of the entire Jewish population, and could undoubtedly have attracted some of the immigrants with its secular, right-wing platform. This finding also contradicts the exit polls, whereby Tzomet received only 1.4 percent of the immigrants' votes *(ibid.)*. Be that as it may, the results of this study dispel the widely held view that in the 1992 election the majority of immigrants voted for the parties of the left.

We found a negative and significant correlation in the 1992 elections between the proportion of immigrants and voting rates for the religious parties—Mafdal, Yahadut Hatorah, and Shas (table 1, below)—despite the fact that the vast majority of immigrants who came to Israel before 1992 were acknowledged by the Rabbinate to be Jewish. The immigrants' negative attitude toward the religious parties may have increased as a result of the policy of "spiritual absorption" of the minister of absorption at the time, Rabbi Yitzhak Peretz of Shas, who attempted to bring the immigrants into the fold of Orthodox Judaism (Fein, 1995). Moreover, because of their economic difficulties, many immigrants felt that the spiritual absorption policy served as a substitute rather than a supplement, for economic absorption.

An immigrants' party—Da (Democracy and Absorption)—headed by Yuli Kosharovsky, participated for the first time in the 1992 elections. Although it did not pass the election threshold, the current study calculates the correlation coefficient for the voting rate for this party. The correlation appears to be statistically significant (0.42), but too low for a sectoral party. Assuming that all those who voted for Da were immigrants from the former USSR, one may conclude that only 5 percent of the immigrants voted for this party. The immigrants' lack of support for Da may have been a result of Kosharovsky's right-wing tendencies, causing immigrant concern over a possible coalition with Likud, whereas most of the immigrants, who were dissatisfied with their economic situation, wanted to vote the Shamir government out of office. But immigrants who experienced a relatively positive absorption, or who adhered to a right-wing ideology, preferred to support Likud or other right-wing parties.

The 1996 Election

The next election campaign was held in May 1996, following Yitzhak Rabin's assassination. That year the general election introduced a separate vote for the office of prime minister. The race between Binyamin Netanyahu and Shimon Peres was close; 56 percent of the Jewish population voted for Netanyahu and 44 percent for Peres. This could perhaps be explained by a series of acts of terrorism which took place in Israel. An analysis of immigrants' voting pattern for the position of prime minister demonstrates that this was similar to the general Jewish population in Israel (table 2, below). Horowitz's analysis demonstrates that in polling booths, where the vast majority of voters (over 95 percent) were immigrants, Netanyahu's victory (about 70 percent of the vote) was even more decisive (Horowitz, 1999). However, as has been noted above, the electoral behavior of the immigrants in "Russian" areas of residence may have differed from that of immigrants in mixed areas. According to a Gallup poll cited by Horowitz, the immigrants' preferences were divided evenly between the two candidates *(ibid.)*. Shevah Weiss's assessment that 60 percent of the immigrants voted for Netanyahu was closer to the results of the ecological analysis (Weiss, 1997).

As to the Knesset elections (table 1, below), the most outstanding result among immigrants from the former USSR was the success of a new party, Israel Ba'Aliya, founded by Natan Sharansky. According to several studies, this party obtained between 33 and 43 percent of immigrants' votes *(ibid.,* Horowitz, 1999), and seven Knesset seats (a correlation of 0.89). One of the possible reasons for the success of Israel Ba'Aliya in 1996 was the change in the electoral system, affording the possibility of a separate prime ministerial election, thereby demonstrating specific views relative to the peace process and security, as opposed to the Knesset vote which reflected social and community interests *(ibid.;* Bick, 1998; Lochery, 2006). However, I believe that Israel Ba'Aliya would have succeeded in 1996 even without the change in the electoral system, not only because of Sharansky's organizational ability and the immigrants' disillusionment with both major parties, but also because this party combined relatively right-wing political views which aligned with those of most of the immigrants, and with ideas that suited their expectations in the social sphere. The immigrants also lacked appropriate representation in the lists of the major parties (Weiss, 1997; Horowitz, 1999).

As to the veteran Israeli parties, the correlation coefficient in 1996 between the proportion of immigrants and the voting rate for Labor switched from positive to negative, albeit not significantly (-0.15). The voting rate for that party among the immigrants was slightly lower than that among the general Jewish population (28 percent). This finding is consistent with the results presented by other studies (Weiss, 1997; Horowitz, 1999). The negative correlation between the proportion of immigrants and the voting rate for Meretz grew stronger

(–0.36), and the proportion of immigrants who voted for that party appears to have been low (in single digits). There was also a significant negative correlation for Labor defector Avigdor Kahalani's Third Way party (–0.35).

The adjusted correlation coefficient gleaned from the voting figures for Likud was almost significant (0.20), and lower than in 1992 (table 1, below), but support for Likud increased among the general Jewish population and reached 27 percent, and therefore it may be assumed that the immigrants' support for Likud had not changed since 1992. Horowitz assesses that 25 percent of immigrants voted for Likud, while Shevah Weiss estimates that this percentage was 39 percent (Weiss, 1997; Horowitz, 1999).

As with the 1992 election, there was a significant negative correlation in 1996 between the proportion of immigrants and the voting rate for the Mafdal and Yahadut Hatorah parties (–0.38 and –0.27 respectively). But in contrast to the expectations and results of the 1992 elections, there was a weak positive correlation between the proportion of immigrants and the voting rate for Shas (after adjusting for the proportion of the population of North African origin in the locale). There are two possible explanations for this: first, non-Ashkenazi immigrants (from Georgia, the Caucasus, and Bukhara), who arrived in Israel between 1992 and 1995 (see below) and did not want to support the Ashkenazi Israel Ba'Aliya party, may have voted for Shas. Second, some of the immigrants, including Ashkenazi immigrants, may have been attracted by the Shas party's platform on social issues.

In comparison with 1992, the 1996 election showed a decline in support for the parties of the left—Labor and Meretz. There was a concurrent decline in the positive correlation assessed from voting figures for Likud. Many immigrants voted for the new party—Israel Ba'Aliya. Taking into account the similarity of that party's political views to those of Likud, or even to the right of Likud (Horowitz, 1999; Lochery, 2006), there appears to have been a shift to the right in the attitudes of all the immigrants from the former USSR. This shift is explained by three factors. First, disillusionment with the Oslo process, largely as a result of the ensuing series of terror attacks. Second, there was a change in the composition of the immigration, with a larger share of immigrants coming from the Asiatic republics, particularly the "warm" areas of the former USSR (e.g., the Caucasus), where anti-Muslim attitudes were prevalent. And third, the immigrants were disappointed with the Labor government's socio-economic policies. The dissatisfaction with certain ministers may also have had an impact, specifically with the minister of labor and welfare, Ora Namir, who required unemployed individuals (including those with university degrees) to accept whatever work they were offered to be eligible for unemployment benefits (although, as noted above, it was the Shamir government that initiated this policy). However, even the replacement of Ora Namir by the immigrants' representative, Sofa Landver, within the Labor party's list, did not alter this trend.

The 1999 Election

The early elections in May 1999 included elections to the Knesset and the separate election of the prime minister. Ehud Barak defeated Binyamin Netanyahu in the prime ministerial election (56 vis-à-vis 44 percent). Barak's victory was less conclusive in the Jewish population (51.5 vis-à-vis 48.5 percent). The ecological analysis shows that for immigrants from the former USSR, as with the 1996 elections, their voting patterns were similar to those of the general Jewish population. Immigrants' support for Netanyahu declined between the 1996 and 1999 elections, paralleling a similar trend among Jewish voters. Support for the two candidates among the immigrants was almost equal. The findings of the present study contradict those of studies which present Barak as winning an outright victory among immigrants from the former USSR in the 1999 elections (Katz, 2000; Gitelman and Goldstein, 2001; Al-Haj and Leshem, 2000). The different findings may stem from the under-representation of peripheral areas or from the fact that areas beyond the Green Line were not included in those surveys. Barak possessed a clear advantage in the 1999 elections only among one group of the immigrants—those who had immigrated in 1989–1991 (see below).

The immigrants' support for Ehud Barak in 1999 (and for Yitzhak Rabin in 1992) may have stemmed not only from their support for the political process but from other factors as well, such as his plan to create employment and the concept of the "civic revolution" (Gitelman and Goldstein, 2001). Nevertheless, the majority of the immigrants did not concur with the political ideas of the left. This is highlighted by the fact that at the end of July 1999 (two months after the elections) only 38 percent of the immigrants supported Barak's peace plan, while 52 percent opposed it and 75 percent were against returning the Golan Heights to Syria (Khanin, 2005). The decline in terrorist attacks and the development of high-tech industry (in spite of the rise in general unemployment) under Netanyahu must be taken into account for the fact that in 1999 almost half the immigrants still supported him.

The strength of the Israel Ba'Aliya party declined slightly in the 1999 Knesset elections but about one third of the immigrants still voted for this party (Gitelman and Goldstein, 2001; Khanin, 2005). The party's promise to replace Shas in the Ministry of the Interior ("Nash Kontrol") strongly influenced the immigrants. However, about 17 percent of the immigrants voted for a new party, Israel Beiteinu, headed by Avigdor Lieberman (Gitelman and Goldstein, 2001). The correlations between the proportion of immigrants in an area and the voting rate for each of these parties were high (table 1, below).

The negative correlation between the proportion of immigrants and the voting rate for the Labor party and Meretz grew stronger (–0.29 and –0.47 respectively) in the 1999 elections; in other words, among those who voted for those parties the proportion of immigrants was smaller than among the general Jewish population (22 and 8 percent respectively). An interesting correlation was found between the proportion of immigrants and the voting rate for the Am Echad party headed by Amir Peretz. The correlation was positive and significant (0.49), even though the voting rates both among immigrants and the general Jewish population for Am Echad were quite small. This correlation (like others in this analysis) is adjusted for the proportion of individuals of North African origin in the area of residence, and it therefore reflects the voting pattern of the immigrants themselves. The support of some of the immigrants for Amir Peretz's party may be connected with the fact that in contrast with other left-wing parties (Labor and Meretz), Am Echad placed social rather than political issues at the forefront of its campaign. Many immigrants, especially those living in peripheral areas, earned only the minimum wage, and the promise to increase it almost certainly served to garner their support. There was a negative and significant correlation between the proportion of immigrants and the voting rate for Yitzhak Mordechai's Merkaz party (–0.47) in 1999. There was also a negative (but not significant) correlation for the results of the vote for the Shinui party led by Tommy Lapid (table 1, below).

The correlation for the Likud party also changed from positive in the 1996 elections to negative but not significant (–0.15) in the 1999 elections. The voting rate for Likud among immigrants was slightly lower than that among the general Jewish population (15 percent). The correlation coefficient between the proportion of immigrants and the voting rate for Rehavam Ze'evi's party was negative and significant (–0.27) in 1999 when he headed National Front, while in the 1996 elections, when he headed the Moledet party, the coefficient was almost zero (table 1, below). The votes of the immigrants who voted for Likud and Moledet appear to have shifted to Lieberman's party.

The correlation coefficients between the voting rates for the religious parties and the proportion of immigrants in an area in 1999 were similar to those found in 1996. The correlations were negative and significant relative to support for Mafdal and Yahadut Hatorah and the correlation was positive but small relative to Shas (table 1, below). According to Ze'ev Khanin's figures, about 80,000 immigrants voted for Shas in 1999, that is, one immigrant in six (Khanin, 2001). This may have been the protest of the non-Ashkenazi immigrants to the campaign, waged at that time by Israel Ba'Aliya against Shas (table 5, below).

The electoral behavior of immigrants in 1999 was quite ambivalent: on the one hand, their support for the right-wing candidate for prime minister (Binyamin Netanyahu) declined similar to the general Jewish population, while on the other support for the sectoral parties (Israel Ba'Aliya and Israel Beiteinu), which together obtained more seats than Israel Ba'Aliya alone in 1996, increased (10 vis-à-vis 7 respectively).

The 2001 Election

Special prime ministerial elections were held in February 2001, after Ehud Barak resigned due to lack of support in the Knesset. Ariel Sharon defeated

Barak in that election (62.5 vis-à-vis 37.5 percent among the population as a whole, and 65 vis-à-vis 35 percent in the Jewish sector). The correlation coefficient between the proportion of immigrants in an area of residence and the voting rate for Sharon was positive but not significant (table 2, below). Sharon's victory among the immigrants may have been slightly greater than it was among the Jewish population as a whole. The explanation appears to lie in the beginning of the second Intifada and the renewal of the spate of terror attacks after the collapse of the Camp David talks. The fact that the Barak government did not keep its promise to introduce civic reforms and brought Shas into the coalition was a disappointment to many immigrants and may have played a part in these developments.

The 2003 Election

The Knesset election of January 2003 was held after the National Unity Government disbanded and the law for the direct election of the prime minister was revoked. This was the first election since the initial influx of immigration from the former USSR that did not bring about a political turnaround. The Likud party led by Ariel Sharon retained power, although the composition of the Knesset and the coalition changed radically.

One of the noticeable results of the 2003 election among the immigrants from the former USSR was the failure of the Israel Ba'Aliya party, which obtained only two Knesset seats, obtained about 15 percent of immigrants' votes (Goldstein and Gitelman, 2004; Khanin, 2005), and was subsequently incorporated within Likud. The present analysis shows that the correlation coefficient between the proportion of immigrants and the voting rate for that party was lower than in 1999 (table 1, below). There were three reasons for the failure of Israel Ba'Aliya in 2003. First, the grave security situation marginalized social issues and the problem of state and religion. Second, Israel Ba'Aliya concentrated primarily on the problems of senior citizens (only a part of the immigrant sector) and families with non-Jewish members (in which it was in competition with Shinui). And third, the cancellation of the direct election of the prime minister caused many immigrants to vote for Likud in support of Ariel Sharon, who was quite popular among immigrants from the former USSR (Khanin, 2005).

Despite the failure of Israel Ba'Aliya, the results of the 2003 election did not attest to the decline of the sectoral parties among the immigrants from the former USSR, as has been claimed (Lochery, 2006). In effect, Avigdor Lieberman's party, Israel Beiteinu, was the sectoral "Russian" party (even though it joined Moledet and Tekuma in a list known as the National Front). This is indicated by the correlation between the proportion of immigrants and the fact that the voting rate for that party in 2003 was similar to that of Israel Ba'Aliya, 0.81 and 0.80 respectively. Lieberman's party benefited primarily from the votes of immigrants from the former USSR. The immigrants' support for Lieberman's party in 2003 was greater than it had been in 1999, accounting for one quarter of immigrant voters (Goldstein and Gitelman, 2004), even though only three of its seven seats were represented by immigrants from the former USSR. This demonstrates the consistent shift to the right among immigrant voters.

In 2003 there was a positive and significant correlation (0.36) between the proportion of immigrants and the voting rate for Likud, compared with the moderate negative correlation in the 1999 elections (table 1, below). In 2003 the rate of immigrants voting for Likud was higher than that among the Jewish population as a whole. Among Jewish voters in general the rate of Likud voters in 2003 was double that in 1999 (32 vis-à-vis 15 percent respectively), so that among the immigrants the increase was even greater. According to the exit polls only one-quarter of the immigrants voted for Likud (Goldstein and Gitelman, 2004).

For the left-wing parties (except for Am Echad), as in the 1999 election, in 2003 the correlation coefficient of votes for Labor remained negative and significant (-0.26) as did that for Meretz (-0.47) (table 1, below). These correlations changed little since the 1999 election, because the rate of voters for the left declined among the general Jewish population, and also decreased among the immigrant population. The exception, as in 1999, was the Am Echad party, where the correlation coefficient between the voting rate for the party and the proportion of immigrants was positive and significant, although lower than it had been in the previous elections (table 1, below). This result contradicts that of the exit polls, according to which Am Echad did not receive any votes from immigrants (Goldstein and Gitelman, 2004). This discrepancy may be due to the under-representation in the exit polls of peripheral areas of residence.

The voting figures for Shinui indicate that the correlation coefficient for the voting rate and the proportion of immigrants changed from being slightly negative in 1999 to slightly positive (0.16) in 2003. The proportion of immigrants who voted for that party was slightly higher than that of voters in the general Jewish population (15 percent). The 2003 exit polls presented the voting rate of immigrants for Shinui as 22 percent *(ibid.)*.

As in all the previous election campaigns, there was also a negative and significant correlation between the proportion of immigrants and the voting rates for Mafdal and Yahadut Hatorah in the 2003 campaign. In contrast with 1996 and 1999, as in 1992, there was also a negative and significant correlation for voting figures for Shas (after adjusting for the proportion of Jews of North African origin in the locale). According to Khanin's estimate, the rate of voters for Shas among immigrants from the former USSR declined in 2003 to a third of what it had been in 1999, and amounted to 5 percent (Khanin, 2005). Many non-Ashkenazi immigrants may have been disappointed by Shas and switched to Likud.

Immigrants' voting patterns in 2003, in contrast with those of previous election campaigns, indicate support voting for the current government rather than a protest vote. The question then arises as to why, despite the difficult security and economic situation, immigrants' support for the Likud government not only did not decline in 2003 but rose. A partial explanation may have been the personal popularity of Ariel Sharon among the Israeli population in general, and the immigrants in particular. In addition, terrorist attacks always influence public opinion in Israel and shift it rightward. The rate of immigrants injured in such attacks was higher than that among the population as a whole, because immigrants tend to use public transportation and shop at open-air markets with lower prices to a greater extent than the general population, and those were the principal targets of terrorist attacks. About 4 percent of immigrants reported that a relative had been killed by a suicide bomb attack, and 26 percent reported that a friend had been killed (Goldstein and Gitelman, 2004). The attack at the Dolphinarium in Tel Aviv in 2001 impacted strongly on the immigrants.

As to the economics issue, at the beginning of the 1990s, with its nascent economic growth, the economic situation of the immigrants was particularly bad, because most of them belonged to the weaker socio-economic strata. They were unemployed or employed in low-paid, blue-collar jobs. This situation engendered a sharp sense of discrimination among them, so that the harsh economic measures, such as the greater stringency in the terms of eligibility for unemployment benefit or income support, were perceived by the immigrants as being directed against them. This brought about their protest vote against the Likud government (in 1992, and partially in 1999), as well as against the Labor government (in 1996). At the beginning of 2000, however, the situation changed. Many of the immigrants (except for those who had arrived in Israel shortly beforehand) had integrated relatively well into Israeli society. However, the economic crisis and the subsequently introduced measures created a sense of a shared fate, as they impacted equally on veteran residents and immigrants. Many immigrants also blamed the Intifada and the Oslo accords, and therefore the left-wing parties rather than the Sharon government, for their difficult situation.

The 2006 Election

Dramatic changes took place in Israel's political life prior to the 2006 Knesset election. Ariel Sharon's disengagement plan (the evacuation of settlements from the Gaza Strip and northern Samaria), implemented in 2005, brought about a split in the Likud party and the establishment of the Kadima party, headed first by Ariel Sharon, and after his hospitalization by Ehud Olmert. A schism also emerged among the group of immigrants in Likud, mainly former members of the Israel Ba'Aliya party. Some of them (including Natan Sharansky and Yuli Edelstein) remained in Likud, headed by Binyamin Netanyahu, while others (Marina Solodkin and Ze'ev Elkin) switched to Kadima. And the Israel Beiteinu party, led by Avigdor Lieberman, defected from the National Front party, which joined up with Mafdal, so that the party once again became independent. Changes also took place in the parties of the left. Am Echad merged with Labor, and Amir Peretz was chosen to head the party. Shinui (which obtained fifteen seats in the 2003 election) also divided into two parties, neither of which managed to pass the election threshold.

How did all these changes affect the voting patterns of immigrants from the former USSR in the 2006 election? The most marked result was the achievement of Israel Beiteinu, headed by Lieberman, which in effect became Israel's only "Russian" party (although there were several veteran Israelis on its list). According to the Institute for Social and Political Research (ISPR) exit polls, Israel Beiteinu obtained about half (48 percent) of immigrants' votes and 11 seats in the Knesset.[2] The correlation between the proportion of immigrants in a locale and the voting rate for that party reached 0.92 (table 1, below). The predictions that the sectoral immigrants' parties would decline after the failure of Israel Ba'Aliya in 2003 were too hastily made. Israel Beiteinu may have become the party of choice for immigrants who had been disappointed by the Sharon-Olmert government's espousal of the disengagement process, or by the religious right-wing's stand on the issue of state and religion.

The correlation coefficient between the proportion of immigrants and the voting rate for Likud in 2006 was lower than that in 2003 (0.21 vis-à-vis 0.36 respectively), but still remained significant. The proportion of immigrants from the former USSR who voted for Likud was higher than that in the Jewish population as a whole (12 percent). According to the ISPR Institute's exit polls, Likud obtained 15 percent of immigrants' votes.[3] The reasons for Likud's greater popularity among immigrants than among the veteran Israeli population were the disillusionment with the disengagement plan and the fact that Natan Sharansky and Yuli Edelstein had been voted onto Likud's list of Knesset candidates without benefit of any immigrant quotas. Despite the adverse effect on many immigrants of Finance Minister Netanyahu's economic policies, some may have supported these measures, especially the reduction of child allowances in the belief that they served only the Arab and ultra-orthodox segments and came at the expense of other sections of the population.

The correlation between the voting rate for the Kadima party headed by Ehud Olmert and the proportion of immigrants in the population was positive but not significant (0.11). The proportion of immigrants who voted for Kadima was similar to that of the veteran Israeli population, or slightly higher (about 20 percent). According to exit polls, Kadima obtained 18 percent of the immigrants' votes.[4] This is indicated by the general survey of immigrant voting, but when all the newcomers are divided into groups by their year of immigration to Israel it is evident that they differ from one another in support for Kadima (see below).

A weak negative correlation (–0.10) was found between the voting rates for the Labor party and the proportion of immigrants in the population. In the 2003 election the correlation was significant (–0.26). Within this context it is important to note that in the 1999 and 2003 elections there was a positive and significant correlation between the voting rate for the Am Echad party headed by Amir Peretz and the proportion of immigrants in the population. This may be attributed to Amir Peretz's statements on social problems (e.g., his insistence that the minimum wage should be raised) as well as to the fact that he refrained from discussing political issues. As leader of the Labor party he supported the continuation of the Oslo process, and therefore lost the votes of many immigrants. But the negative attitude of many immigrants to the Labor party under his leadership was not as strong as it had been in the previous elections (2003), when Amram Mitzna headed the party. In contrast to Mitzna, Peretz focused primarily on the social issues rather than on the peace process, so that some immigrants—particularly in development towns—voted for Labor.

As in the 2003 elections there was a negative and significant correlation in 2006 between the proportion of immigrants in the population and their voting rate for the religious-nationalist and ultra-orthodox parties, on the one hand, and their proportion in the population and their voting rate for Meretz, on the other (table 1, below).

2. Trend in Immigrants' Voting Patterns, by Year of Immigration

One of the most important factors affecting the behavior of immigrants, in particular their electoral behavior, is the amount of time that has elapsed since their immigration. The current study does not have specific data about immigrants' voting patterns or figures as to how long they have lived in Israel. The data, however, on the proportion of immigrants in certain areas of residence enable us to make an educated guess as to the length of time since their immigration. All the immigrants from the former USSR were divided into four groups by year of immigration: 1989–1991; 1992–1995; 1996–1999; from 2000 on.[5] In all these groups the proportion of immigrants in a given year and area of residence is calculated according to the following equation:

$$\theta_{T1-T0} \, (Te) = (A_1 - A_0) \, {*}100 \, / \, Se$$

Definitions of variables:

θ_{T1-T0} (Te) – proportion of immigrants who came to Israel between years T_0 and T_1 at end of year Te (the one before the election);
A_0 – number of immigrants in locale at end of year T_0;
A_1 – number of immigrants in locale at end of year T_1;
Se – general population in locale at end of year Te (the one before the election).

The proportions of immigrants in the 1992–1995 group at the end of 2005 was calculated as follows: the incremental number of immigrants in the locale

Table 1

Correlation Coefficients[1] Between the Voting Rate for Parties in Knesset
Elections and the Proportion of Immigrants from the Former USSR in the
Population of a Locale, 1992–2006

	1992	1996	1999	2003	2006
No. of immigrants ('000s[2])	312	536	665	860	870
Labor	.47*	-.15	-.29*	-.26**	-.10
Am Echad[3]	-	-	.49*	.37*	-
Meretz	-.22	-.36*	-.47*	-.47*	-.45*
Kadima	-	-	-	-	.11
Gil	-	-	-	-	-.16
Shinui	-	-	-.11	.16	-
Third Way	-	-.35*	-	-	-
Center	-	-	-.47*	-	-
Likud	.35*	.20	-.15	.36*	.21**
Tzomet	.16	-	-	-	-
Da (Democracy and Absorption)	.42*	-	-	-	-
Israel Ba'Aliya[4]	-	.89*	.93*	.80*	-
Israel Beiteinu[5]	-	-	.88*	}.81*	.92*
Moledet/National Front[5]	-.15	-.10	-.27*		}.32*
Mafdal[6]	-.37*	-.38*	-.37*	-.35*	
Yahadut Hatorah	-.45*	-.27**	-.26**	-.34*	-.33*
Shas	-.34*	.08	.05	-.21**	-.20

* P<0.01

**P<0.05

SOURCE: Based on CBS and Ministry of Immigrant Absorption data.

1 The correlation coefficients in all the tables are weighted by population size and
   adjusted for the proportion of the population in the locale which originates from
   North African countries.

2 In this and the other tables, the number of immigrants from the former USSR in a
   locale who arrived in and after 1989 up to end of the year preceding the election is
   included in the analysis.

3 In 2005 the Am Echad party merged with the Labor party.

4 The Israel Ba'Aliya party merged with the Likud party after its defeat in the 2003
   election.

5 In the 2005 election the National Front and Israel Beiteinu parties ran on a joint list
   headed by Avigdor Lieberman. In 2006 the National Front and Mafdal parties ran
   on a joint list headed by Benny Elon.

6 See preceding note.

in 1992–1995 (i.e., the difference between the number of immigrants at the end of 1995 and their number at the end of 1991) divided by the population of the locale at the end of 2005.

$$\theta_{1992-1995} (2005) = (A_{1995}-A_{1991}) * 100 / S_{2005}$$

The figure calculated does not relate to the length of time an immigrant has been in Israel, but rather to the length of time he or she has been in the locale (due to data constraints, this system disregards internal migration), but that is sufficient. The amount of time an immigrant has lived in an area also indirectly reflects the amount of time he or she has been in Israel. In view of the general difference between areas of residence relative to the election results, the length of time immigrants have been in an area itself also has a marked effect on their electoral behavior. Indeed, alongside common trends in the voting patterns of immigrants from the former USSR in the Knesset and prime ministerial elections, there are notable differences between groups of immigrants defined by their year of immigration.

Immigrants in the 1989–1991 Group

This group is the largest one of immigrants from the former USSR. It is characterized by a high level of education, with many of its members originating from the European republics (with a large proportion from Moscow and Leningrad). The vast majority of them are Jews as defined by the Rabbinate and were the first to leave the former USSR. This group arrived in Israel when the Shamir government was in power and has participated in all the elections

Table 2
Correlation Coefficients Between Voting Rate for Prime Ministerial Candidates and Proportion of Immigrants from Former USSR in the Population of a Locale, 1996–2001

	1996	1999	2001
No. of immigrants ('000s)	312	536	816
Shimon Peres	-.01	-	-
Ehud Barak	-	-.03	-.13
Binyamin Netanyahu	.01	.03	-
Ariel Sharon	-	-	.13

Not significant

SOURCE: Based on CBS and Ministry of Immigrant Absorption data.

since 1992. This group, which has been in Israel the longest, has been relatively well absorbed compared with the other groups. According to the CBS Labor Force Survey for 2005, for example, about half of the employed immigrants in this group (46 percent) were employed that year in work requiring an academic qualification, in the liberal and technical professions, or in management and clerical work. Among immigrants in the 1992–1995 group, on the other hand, only 33 percent were employed that year in those professions, and among immigrants who arrived in and after 1996 the rate was only 23 percent.[6] This group was, therefore, also the most politically "Israeli." But the initial absorption difficulties experienced by these immigrants under the Likud government also impacted on their electoral behavior in later years. Their average political stance was more left-wing than that of immigrants in the other groups.

In the 1992 elections, there was a significant correlation between the proportion of immigrants in an area of residence (the vast majority of whom belonged to the 1989–1991 group) and the voting rate for the Labor party (0.47). In subsequent elections (1996–2006) this correlation was weakened, but always remained positive—in contrast to more recent immigrants (table 3, below). The voting rate of immigrants in the 1989–1991 group for the Labor party was therefore similar to that of the entire Jewish population for that party, or even higher. The correlation between the proportion of immigrants in the 1989–1991 group and the voting rate for Meretz was negative and moderate, while among more recent immigrants it was negative and strong (table 3, below).

The correlation between the proportion of immigrants in the 1989–1991 group in an area of residence and the voting rate for Likud was positive and significant in most of the election campaigns (except for those held in 1999 and 2006). Immigrants to the right of this group, which is more veteran than the others, may have preferred to vote for the general Israeli party, Likud, while the more recent arrivals gave their support to the sectoral parties of Sharansky and Lieberman (see below).

The more left-wing inclinations of the immigrants in the 1989–1991 group than those of immigrants from the former USSR in general was also expressed in the direct elections for prime minister (table 4, below). In contrast to immigrants who arrived in Israel later, the immigrants in the 1989–1991 group supported Shimon Peres in the 1996 election and Ehud Barak in the 1999 election to an even greater extent than the general Jewish population. In the 2001 election there was also a positive (although not significant) correlation between the proportion of immigrants in this group and the voting rate for Barak (table 4, below). This does not indicate that most of the immigrants in this group supported Barak in the 2001 election, but that the support of these immigrants for Barak was higher than that of the Jewish population as a whole (35 percent), while their support for Sharon was lower than that of the Jewish population as a whole (65 percent).

Table 3

Correlation Coefficients[1] Between the Voting Rate for Parties in Knesset Elections and the Proportion of Immigrants from the Former USSR in the Population of a Locale, by Year of Immigration, 1992–2006

Year of election	1989-1991					1992-1995				1996-1999			+2000	
	1992	1996	1999	2003	2006	1996	1999	2003	2006	1999	2003	2006	2003	2006
Labor	.47*	.17	.08	.07	.12	-.29*	-.39*	-.40*	-.14	-.27*	-.23**	-.18	-.07	-.04
Am Echad	–	–	.23**	.23**	–	–	.47*	.41*	–	.40*	.25**	–	.11	–
Meretz	-.22	-.19	-.21**	-.20	-.20	-.36*	-.39*	-.39*	-.40*	-.52*	-.51*	-.49*	-.36*	-.22**
Kadima	–	–	–	–	.25**	–	–	–	-.14	–	–	.12	–	.31*
Gil	–	–	–	–	.07	–	–	–	-.44*	–	–	-.08	–	.32*
Shinui	–	–	.17	.21**	–	-.42*	-.27*	-.08	–	-.02	.23**	–	.42*	–
Third Way	–	-.07	-.14	–	–	–	–	–	–	-.36*	–	–	–	–
Center	–	–	–	–	–	–	-.52*	–	–	–	–	–	–	–
Likud	.35*	.29*	.07	.40*	.08	.10	-.22**	.14	.15	-.12	.36*	.21**	.39*	.26**
Tzomet	.16	–	–	–	–	–	–	–	–	–	–	–	–	–
Da (Democracy and Absorption)	.42*	–	–	–	–	–	–	–	–	–	–	–	–	–
Israel Ba'Aliya	–	.58*	.63*	.50*	–	.83*	.77*	.73*	–	.81*	.69*	–	.48*	–
Israel Beiteinu	–	–	.42*	–	.61*	–	.83*	–	.78*	.77*	–	.85*	–	.46*
Moledet/National Front	-.15	.01	-.31*	{.43*	{-.36*	-.13	-.20	{.75*	{-.16	-.16	{.73*	{-.31*	{.53*	{-.19
Mafdal	-.37*	-.39*	-.32*	-.35*	–	-.28*	-.27*	-.22**	–	-.32*	-.34*	–	-.19	–
Yahadut Hatorah	-.45*	-.45*	-.45*	-.46*	-.45*	-.10	-.10	-.12	-.10	-.14	-.29*	-.28*	-.33*	-.30*
Shas	-.34*	-.18	-.20	-.28*	-.27*	.20	.20	.00	.02	.00	-.24**	-.20	-.31*	-.32*

* P<0.01

**P<0.05

SOURCE: Based on CBS and Ministry of Immigrant Absorption data.

[1]Number of immigrants who arrived in 1989–1991 in the locales examined, 312,000; immigrants who arrived in 1992–1995, 224,000; immigrants who arrived in 1996–1999, 234,000; immigrants who arrived in and after 2000: at the end 2002, 91,000, and at the end of 2005, 100,000.

There was a positive and significant correlation between the proportion of immigrants in the 1989–1991 group in a locale and the voting rate for Shinui in 2003 and for Kadima in 2006. Support for the sectoral parties (Israel Ba'Aliya and Israel Beiteinu) among immigrants in the 1989–1991 group was weaker than among immigrants in the 1992–1999 groups. In all the elections a negative and significant correlation was found between the proportion of immigrants in the 1989–1991 group and the voting rate for the religious parties (table 3, below).

Immigrants in the 1992–1995 Group

This group immigrated to Israel after the break-up of the former USSR. Between one quarter and one third of its members were not Ashkenazi. Most of the immigrants in this group arrived in Israel during the period of the Rabin-Peres government and the first elections in which they participated were those of 1996.

The immigrants in the 1992–1995 group (as well as those in the 1996–1999 group) were found to be one of the most right-wing groups of all immigrants from the former USSR. In all the election campaigns other than the last one, the correlation between the proportion of immigrants in the 1992–1995 group in a locale and the voting rate for Labor was extremely negative (–0.29; –0.40). This appears to have been a protest vote in the wake of this group's initial absorption difficulties, which took place under a Labor government, as well as their disappointment with the political process. Voting data for Meretz also displayed a negative and significant correlation in all the election campaigns (–0.36; –0.40), although it was smaller than the correlation for immigrants in the 1996–1999 group (table 3, below). Nevertheless, their support for Amir Peretz's Am Echad party in the 1999 and 2003 elections was very strong (correlation of over 0.40). The explanation for this lies in the difficult economic situation of this group, and especially of those who are not Ashkenazi. Peretz's promises to address social issues apparently caused many of these immigrants to vote for him. However, after Peretz was made chairman of the Labor party and revealed his political views, this group's support for him declined.

As to Likud, there was a weak positive correlation between the proportion of immigrants in the 1992–1995 group in a locale and the voting rate for Likud in the 1996 election, and in the 1999 election it even became negative and significant (–0.22), but in the 2003 and 2006 elections it again became positive, although not significant (table 3, below). The lower level of support for Likud among the members of this group in contrast to the other groups may be linked to their firm support for the parties of Sharansky and Lieberman.

The right-wing inclination of immigrants in the 1992–1995 group was also apparent in the direct prime ministerial elections. Both in 1996 and 1999 there was a positive (but not significant) correlation between the proportion of this group in the population and its voting rate for Netanyahu (0.17), and in 2001 there was a significant correlation between the proportion of this group and the voting rate for Sharon (0.28). Compared with support for Sharon among the other immigrant groups, the highest correlation was found for the voting rates of this group (table 4, below).

Immigrants in the 1992–1995 group displayed another unique trend. In the 1996 and 1999 election campaigns, a positive but not significant correlation (0.20) was found between the proportion of this group and the voting rate for Shas (even after adjusting). While this correlation fell to zero in the 2003 and 2006 elections, it was negative and significant for other groups of immigrants (table 3, below). This finding appears to be linked to the greater proportion of immigrants from the Asiatic republics in this group (34 percent) than in the others—23 percent in the 1989–1991 group, and 18 percent in the 1996–1999 group (CBS, 2001).

As to the other religious parties (Mafdal and Yahadut Hatorah), we found a negative correlation between them and the voting rate among immigrants in the 1992–1995 group, although it was weaker than that of the other groups. This

Table 4

Correlation Coefficients Between the Voting Rate for Prime Ministerial Candidates and the Proportion of Immigrants from the Former USSR in the Population of a Locale, by Year of Immigration, 1996–2001

Year of immigration[1]	1991–1989			1992-1995			1996+[2]	
Year of election	1996	1999	2001	1996	1999	2001	1999	2001
Shimon Peres	.26**	-	-	-.17	-	-	-	-
Ehud Barak	-	.27*	.15	-	-.17	-.28*	-.06	-.07
Binyamin Netanyahu	-.26**	-.27*	-	.17	.17	-	.06	-
Ariel Sharon	-	-	-.15	-	-	.28*	-	.07

* P<0.01
**P<0.05

SOURCE: Based on CBS and Ministry of Immigrant Absorption data.

[1] The number of immigrants in the 1989–1991 group in the areas of residence studied, 312,000; immigrants who arrived in 1992–1995, 224,000; immigrants who arrived in and after 1996: by the end of 1998, 129,000; and by the end of 2000, 280,000.

[2] This group was defined as "immigrants who arrived in and after 1996," because the voting patterns of immigrants who arrived between 1996 and 1998 were taken into account in the 1999 election, while those of immigrants who arrived between 1996 and 2000 were taken into account in the 2001 election (because of the small number of immigrants who arrived in 2000 their voting pattern for the prime minister was incorporated within that of the preceding group).

finding is explained by the higher proportion of traditional Jews in this group. In contrast to immigrants in the 1989–1991 group, there was a negative and significant correlation between those in the 1992–1995 group and their vote for Shinui in the 1999 election (table 3, below).

The correlation coefficients between the proportion of immigrants in the 1992–1995 group in an area of residence and the voting rate for the sectoral parties (Israel Ba'Aliya and Israel Beiteinu) were the highest (table 3, below).

Immigrants in the 1996–1999 Group

Most of the immigrants in this group arrived in Israel when the Likud government, headed by Netanyahu, was in office. They took part in three Knesset elections (1999, 2003, and 2006) as well as in the two prime ministerial elections (1999 and 2001). In contrast with the previous group, the vast majority of immigrants in this group originated from European republics, particularly the Ukraine.

As with the previous group, this group also tended to support the political right. In the 1999 and 2003 elections, there was a negative and significant correlation between their group and their voting rate for Labor, although it was weaker than that of immigrants in the 1992–1995 group. However, the negative correlation between the voting patterns of the 1996–1999 immigrant group and Meretz in all the election campaigns was even stronger (–0.50) compared with the correlation found for the voting patterns of the 1992–1995 immigrant group (table 3, below). As with the previous group, there was a positive and significant correlation between the proportion of immigrants in the 1996–1999 group and their voting rate for the Am Echad party in 1999 and 2003.

In contrast to the previous group, the correlation between the proportion of immigrants in the 1996–1999 group and the voting rate for Likud switched from negative and not significant in 1999 to positive and significant in 2003 and 2006 (0.36 and 0.21 respectively). In the prime ministerial elections of 1999 and 2001 the correlation for the voting data of this group for each candidate was negligible (table 4, below). They voted similarly to the general Jewish population. For purposes of comparison, the voting data of immigrants in the 1989–1991 group revealed a positive correlation in the vote for Barak (significant in 1999), whereas the data for immigrants in the 1992–1995 group revealed a weak positive correlation in the vote for Netanyahu in 1999 and a significant one in the vote for Sharon in 2001.

As with immigrants in the 1992–1995 group, there was a strong correlation between the immigrants in the 1996–1999 group and their vote for the parties of Sharansky and Avigdor Lieberman. However, the negative correlation for the voting data for the national-religious and ultra-orthodox parties (including Shas) among immigrants in the 1996–1999 group was stronger than the negative correlation for the voting data of immigrants in the 1992–1995 group. In contrast with the previous group, the voting data for immigrants in the 1996–1999 group reflect a positive and significant attitude (0.23) in voting for Shinui in the 2003 election, but the support for that party among immigrants who came from 2000 on was even stronger (table 3, below).

Immigrants Who Arrived During and Subsequent to 2000

This group took part in two Knesset elections, in 2003 and 2006. The immigrants who came to Israel in 2000 also participated in the special prime ministerial election of February 2001, but because of their small numbers they were included in the previous group for that election.

The electoral behavior of the immigrants who arrived in Israel from 2000 on differed from the behavior of those who arrived between 1992 and 1999, and to some extent resembled that of those in the 1989–1991 group. There would appear to be two reasons for this. First, like the immigrants who came between 1989 and 1991, these immigrants also experienced initial absorption difficulties, aggravated by the economic crisis and the strict economic measures introduced by the Likud government. Second, in contrast with the immigrants who came earlier, this group included many who were not accepted as Jews by the Rabbinate, and the issue of state and religion was significant to them. According to CBS figures, about 6 percent of the immigrants from the former USSR who arrived in 1990–1991 were not defined as Jews, while 20 percent of those who came in 1992–1995, 43 percent of those who came in 1996–1999, and 56 percent of those who came during and subsequent to 2000 were not defined as Jews (CBS, 2004).

In the elections of 2003 and 2006 the correlation between the proportion of immigrants in a locale who had arrived from 2000 on, and their voting rate for Labor, was almost zero (table 3, below). The correlation found for the voting data of this group for Meretz was negative and significant, but weaker than the correlation found for the voting rate for that party of immigrants who came between 1992 and 1999. However, the correlation between that group and their voting rate for Likud in the 2003 and 2006 elections was positive and significant, and was similar to the average correlation of the voting rate for Likud of all immigrants from the former USSR (table 3, below).

Immigrants who came during and after 2000 displayed stronger support (0.42) for Shinui in 2003. They supported Kadima (0.31) in the 2006 elections, as did immigrants in the 1989–1991 group. The group of immigrants who arrived from 2000 on is the only one whose voting patterns yielded a positive and significant correlation (0.32) for the senior citizens' party in the 2006 election, even though there were no immigrants in that party.

Similar to the immigrants in the 1989–1991 group, those who arrived from 2000 on demonstrated massive support for the Israel Ba'Aliya party (in the 2003 election) and the Israel Beiteinu party (in the 2003 and 2006 elections), but this support was less pronounced than that of the immigrants who arrived between 1992 and 1999. As with all the immigrants, this group also yielded a negative correlation between the proportion of immigrants and their voting rate for the ultra-orthodox parties. The negative correlation found for this group's voting pattern for the national-religious parties (National Front and Mafdal) was not very strong.

3. Immigrants' Voting Patterns by Ethnic Group

The data on the ethnic composition of the immigrants from the former USSR—defined as Ashkenazi, Caucasian (Mountain Jews), or Bukharan—by distribution in areas of residence was only published beginning in 1999 (Ministry of Immigrant Absorption, 2000, 2001, 2003, 2006). The proportion of Ashkenazi immigrants was calculated as the difference between the proportion of all immigrants from the former USSR in the population of a locale and the proportion of those from the Caucasus and Bukhara (there are no data for immigrants from Georgia, but I have disregarded them because their numbers are not large). Hence, only the results of the elections held between 1999 and 2006 could be analyzed by the ethnic origin of immigrants from the former USSR.

In the Knesset elections held in 1999 and 2003, for each ethnic group of immigrants from the former USSR there was a negative correlation between the proportion of groups and their voting rate for the Labor party (with a significant correlation for the Ashkenazim only), while there was a positive and significant correlation with their voting pattern for Amir Peretz's Am Echad party (table 5, below). In the 2006 elections, when Peretz headed Labor, the correlation for the voting pattern of each ethnic group for Labor was almost zero (table 5, below). The voting patterns for Meretz yielded a negative correlation for all the ethnic groups in every election (1999, 2003, and 2006). However, there is a difference between the correlations. The Ashkenazi voting rate for this party yielded a negative and extremely strong correlation, while that of immigrants from Bukhara was negative but not significant (table 5, below). As to Likud, there was a weak negative correlation (–0.15) for the voting pattern of Ashkenazim for that party in 1999, while the correlation for the voting pattern of immigrants from the Caucasus and Bukhara was almost zero. In the 2003 election, the correlation was positive and significant for all three groups, whereas in 2006 it remained significant only for the Ashkenazi group, though it was lower than it had been in 2003. Voting for Kadima in the 2006 election yielded a correlation of almost zero for all three groups (table 5, below).

Voting for the religious parties yielded differences between the ethnic groups of immigrants from the former USSR. Those from the Caucasus, for example, in contrast to those from Bukhara and the Ashkenazi group, did not reject Mafdal in 1999 or 2003, nor did they reject the joint National Front–Mafdal list in 2006. The correlation among immigrants from the Caucasus relative to these parties was almost zero in contrast to negative and significant among the

Table 5
Correlation Coefficients Between the Voting Rate for Parties in the Knesset
Elections and the Proportion of Immigrants from the Former USSR, by Ethnic
Group in the Population of a Locale, 1999–2006

	Ashkenazi			Caucasus			Bukhara		
	1999	2003	2006	1999	2003	2006	1999	2003	2006
No. of immigrants ('000s)	544	729	739	51	54	54	70	77	78
Labor	-.26*	-.22**	-.09	-.19	-.17	.01	-.12	-.06	.04
Am Echad	.39*	.29*	-	.38*	.35*	-	.36*	.26*	-
Meretz	-.42*	-.44*	-.42*	-.28*	-.24**	-.23**	-.06	-.07	-.08
Kadima	-	-	.10	-	-	.01	-	-	.04
Gil	-	-	-.11	-	-	-.17	-	-	.04
Shinui	-.07	.19	-	-.18	-.07	-	-.13	.01	-
Center	-.43*	-	-	-.30*	-	-	-.24**	-	-
Likud	-.16	.33*	.25**	-.03	.26*	.15	-.02	.20**	.10
Israel Ba'Aliya	.95*	.81*	-	.50*	.47*	-	.23**	.21**	-
Israel Beiteinu	.88*		.93*	.42*		.45*	.28*		.39*
Moledet/ National Front	-.14	}.76* }-.22*		-.13	}.33* }-.09		-.11	}.24** }-.26*	
Mafdal	-.31*	-.27*		-.07	-.09		-.29*	-.31*	
Yahadut Hatorah	-.25**	-.33*	-.32*	-.14	-.17	-.17	-.16	-.21**	-.22**
Shas	.02	-.2**	-.21**	.05	-.10	-.08	.14	-.04	-.03

* P<0.01

**P<0.05

SOURCE: Based on CBS and Ministry of Immigrant Absorption data.

other groups. A negative and significant correlation was found only among the Ashkenazi group in the 2003 and 2006 elections relative to Shas. With regard to Yahadut Hatorah, a negative correlation was found for the voting pattern of all the ethnic groups but was strongest among the Ashkenazim. In contrast to this, the correlation for the voting rate for Shinui was almost significant (0.19) among the Ashkenazi group in the 2003 election, while for the groups from the Caucasus and Bukhara it was essentially zero (table 5, below).

The most striking difference between the ethnic groups was expressed in their voting for the sectoral parties, Israel Ba'Aliya and Israel Beiteinu. Among the Ahkenazi group the correlation found for their voting pattern for these parties was high (between 0.80 and 0.90), while among those from the Caucasus it ranged between 0.40 and 0.50, and among those from Bukhara it was even lower, between 0.20 and 0.40.

In the direct elections for prime minister in 1999 the correlation among all the ethnic groups was almost zero in the vote for both candidates (Barak and Netanyahu), and in the 2001 election the correlation was positive and weak (not significant) for Ariel Sharon among the Ashkenazi group and those from the Caucasus (table 6, below).

The main differences between the immigrants from the former USSR based on voting patterns by ethnic group reflect the higher level of traditionalism among the Jews from the Caucasus and Bukhara. The relatively low voting rate for the sectoral parties among these groups may also attest to their stronger integration into general Israeli politics than the Ashkenazi group. In the political sphere, however, the Ashkenazi group and, to a lesser extent, the group from the Caucasus, revealed more right-wing views on average than those of the general Jewish population. But the electoral behavior of the group from Bukhara was closer to that of the Jewish population as a whole.

Table 6
Correlation Coefficients between the Voting Rate for Prime Ministerial Candidates and the Proportion of Immigrants from the Former USSR, by Ethnic Group in the Population of a Locale, 1996–2001

	Ashkenazi		Caucasus		Bukhara	
	1999	2001	1999	2001	1999	2001
No. of immigrants ('000s)	544	687	41	54	70	75
Ehud Barak	-.00	-.09	-.07	-.14	.01	-.01
Binyamin Netanyahu	.00	-	.07	-	-.01	-
Ariel Sharon	-	.09	-	.14	-	.01

Not significant

SOURCE: Based on CBS and Ministry of Immigrant Absorption data.

Conclusion

The analysis gives rise to the following conclusions:

a. The data only partly bear out the protest vote theory, particularly with regard to the elections of 1992, 1996, and 1999 in part. In the other elections, e.g., those of 2003, most of the immigrants from the former USSR supported the government in power, while the protest movements were concentrated mainly among the veteran population. In the 2006 election the votes of the immigrants were distributed among those who supported the government in power and those who opposed it.

b. The data do not support the political assimilation theory. After the defeat of the Israel Ba'Aliya party in 2003, many pundits hastened to announce the demise of the sectoral parties and the successful absorption of the immigrants from the former USSR within the veteran Israeli parties. In the 2006 election, however, the sectoral party Israel Beiteinu gained a fresh impetus. Although there were many differences in the immigrants' voting patterns by year of immigration, fairly consistent voting patterns were discernible within each group by year of immigration, and these changed only slightly over time.

c. The theory of political multiculturalism is borne out by the analysis of the voting patterns of the immigrants from the former USSR. The electoral behavior of these immigrants (despite their differences in age, education, area of origin, etc.) displays certain dominant trends, and these indicate that a new political culture is being formed. This culture differs from that of the established Ashkenazi Israeli population ("First Israel"), which is identified with the Palmach Generation and the Labor Movement, as well as from the traditional Sephardi Israeli population ("Second Israel"), located predominantly in development towns and thought to have engendered the political turnaround of 1977. This phenomenon does not appear to be dependent on transient factors, such as the short period of time since the immigrants' arrival or their continued use of the Russian language. Israelis whose families originated from North African countries—even though many of them are second and even third generation Israelis, speak Hebrew, and have progressed in many spheres—display different electoral behavior as a group than most Ashkenazi Israelis. As the determinants of the new political culture are not transient, the influence of the immigrants from the former USSR on the political system in Israel is not transitory. The question then arises whether we are witnessing the emergence of a "Third Israel."

What are the main characteristics of the political culture now being created among the majority of immigrants from the former USSR?

1. *In the political-security sphere*: most of the immigrants from the former USSR display right-wing tendencies, namely, opposition to making territorial concessions (Weiss, 1997; Horowitz, 1999; Gitelman and Goldstein, 2001;

Goldstein and Gitelman, 2004; Khanin, 2005). In contrast with the "traditional" right, however, which is generally of a religious and even Messianic nature, the immigrants' right-wing views are based primarily on security and the concept of a culture clash, i.e., the struggle between Western civilization, which includes Israel, and a fundamentalist-Muslim culture. These trends arise from the minority status of Jews in the USSR and the discrimination they suffered and the intense competition of Russians as well as of the national entities which belonged to the republics. This discrimination generated a strong sense of national identity among them. Their reaction to the anti-Zionist propaganda prevalent in the USSR for many years should also be taken into account. Many immigrants were also influenced by the terrorist acts perpetrated in various countries, including those from which they originated, as well as in Israel.

The more right-wing stance of most immigrants from the former USSR than that of the general Jewish population on political issues is indicated by various findings. First, this is demonstrated by the negative correlation coefficients found for the voting data for the Labor party (except in the 1992 election) and for Meretz (in all the elections). Second, in most of the elections we found positive and significant correlations for the voting data for the Likud party (the correlations peaked in 2003). Third, even when the immigrants' support for Likud declined (as occurred in the 1999 and 2006 elections), this did not benefit the parties of the left, as it was mainly the sectoral parties of Sharansky and Lieberman which profited (and which also adhered to right-wing political views).

Right-wing views were particularly prominent among immigrants who arrived in Israel between 1992 and 1999. However, those in the 1989–1991 group, as well as those who came from 2000 on, expressed opinions that tended more toward the center (these groups supported the Kadima party in the 2006 election). This may be explained by the fact that both these groups experienced their initial absorption difficulties under a Likud government. There may be another reason for the support for the center displayed by the immigrants who arrived in and after 2000. The fact that a fairly high proportion of them were defined as non-Jews by the Rabbinate may have accounted for their support for Shinui in 2003. This group displayed the greatest support for that party of any group of immigrants.

2. *In the socio-economic sphere*: despite the open rejection of socialist values and the shift to the political right, most of the immigrants from the former USSR oppose "raw capitalism" and in effect support the social-democratic approach which advocates such rights as guaranteed employment in one's profession, public housing, and social security. Their support for this view is connected to a great extent with their difficulties in those spheres (Weiss, 1997; Horowitz, 1994, 1999). This is also demonstrated by the fact that 61 percent of the immigrants supported government intervention in the economy, and the same proportion agreed with the reduction of income differentials (Horowitz, 1999). However,

in contrast with the social movements of "Second Israel," the attitudes of the immigrants from the former USSR in the socio-economic sphere are "elitist" to a great extent, as indicated by their preferences in this area: the development of high-tech industry rather than simply places of work; support for elementary and secondary education, as well as for higher education; assistance for pupils with learning difficulties as well as support for outstanding students. This is not merely the product of their high level of education but also that higher education in their country of origin was free, and the correlation between social status and an individual's economic prosperity was not absolute.

The left-wing views of most of the immigrants from the former USSR in the socio-economic sphere are indicated by their intense support for candidates who placed social issues high on their list of political priorities in their election campaign, e.g., Yitzhak Rabin before the Oslo process and Ehud Barak in his first election campaign. These attitudes also account for the backing given by the immigrants to Amir Peretz's Am Echad party and their partial support for Shas. However, the fact that, in contrast with the established Israeli population, most immigrants did not accept the "package deal" combining political with social issues, cannot be ignored. Even when the immigrants supported left-wing parties and certain candidates on the left (e.g., Yitzhak Rabin in 1992 and Ehud Barak in 1999), this did not stem from their views on the peace process (which, according to public opinion polls, remained right-wing for the most part), but from their opinions regarding social and civic issues (Gitelman and Goldstein, 2001; Horowitz, 1994; Fein, 1995; Al-Haj and Leshem, 2000).

3. *On the subject of state and religion*: most of the immigrants defined themselves as secular Jews, and some of them claimed to be atheists. This may be because they were cut off from traditional Judaism during the Soviet period and experienced a high rate of intermarriage (Gitelman and Goldstein, 2001; Goldstein and Gitelman, 2004). Even those immigrants defined as Jews by the Rabbinate, many of whom would like to draw closer to Jewish culture and tradition, do not identify with Jewish orthodoxy (and ultra-orthodoxy in particular), which represents most of the religious population of Israel. This is especially the case relative to immigrants who are the product of mixed marriages and who account for a high proportion of those immigrants who arrived from 2000 on. Nevertheless, quite a large number of immigrants in this group are traditional Jews (mainly those of non-Ashkenazi origin).

The analysis shows that most of the immigrants, primarily those originating from the European republics, do not support the religious parties (including Mafdal) and regard themselves as secular. However, such issues as state and religion, civic issues, and public transport on the Sabbath take only third place in their order of priorities, after security and employment (Goldstein and Gitelman, 2004). The immigrants who came to Israel in 1996–1999, and especially those who arrived from 2000 on, are the exception, indicated by their clear support for Shinui in the 2003 election. This support is linked to the fact that these groups comprise a large proportion of immigrants not defined as Jews by the Rabbinate. Predictably, the greatest support among the immigrants from the former USSR for the religious parties (especially Shas) came from the non-Ashkenazi groups.

4. *The support for the sectoral parties* displayed by the immigrants from the former USSR was quite high. This declined in the 2003 election (mainly for Israel Ba'Aliya, after which the party ceased to exist), but in the 2006 election support for Avigdor Lieberman's Israel Beiteinu party greatly increased. Support for the sectoral parties was strongest among the immigrants who arrived in Israel between 1992 and 1999. It was weaker among those in the 1989–1991 group, whose absorption within Israeli society went more smoothly than that of the other groups, as well as among those who arrived from 2000 on, most of whom supported the general Israeli parties (Shinui in 2003 and Kadima in 2006). Support for the sectoral parties was highest among the Ashkenazi immigrants, and markedly less among those originating from the Caucasus and Bukhara.

The support for the sectoral parties displayed by the Russian "man in the street" is explained not only by absorption and language difficulties, but also because the political views of the veteran Israeli parties were not always suited to those of most of the immigrants, or only in part. The parties of the left—Labor and Meretz—repelled many immigrants because of their positions on peace and security, even though the immigrants to a great extent approved of their position on state and religion and sometimes on social issues as well. To some extent this also applied to the parties of the center, such as Shinui and Kadima. The parties of the extreme right—Moledet, and National Front when it had not merged with Israel Beiteinu—were not supported by the immigrants because of their position on religion. This applied moreover to the religious parties. While the Likud movement, which is a secular, right-wing party, attracted considerable numbers of immigrants from the former USSR, it also repelled many of them because of its Thatcherist approach to economic and social issues, including the reduction of support for science, education, and welfare.

5. It is difficult to predict the future electoral behavior of the immigrants from the former USSR. It depends to a great extent on political and economic developments in Israel in the coming years. The continuation of economic growth and the amelioration of the immigrants' situation could affect their support for the current government to some extent, but their lack of appropriate representation in Ehud Olmert's government as well as cuts in the resources required to meet their needs, could serve to augment their support for the sectoral parties during the next election. Security and political factors, like the results of the Second Lebanon War, the threat to Israel from Syria and Iran, as well as terrorist attacks, could cause them to increase their support for Likud and other right-wing parties.

Notes

1. "1999 Elections: Results of Voting for the Fifteenth Knesset and Prime Minister," *Maariv*, May 19, 1999; "2001 Prime Ministerial Elections: All the Results," *Yediot Aharonot*, February 8, 2001; "2003 Elections: All the Results," *Yediot Aharonot*, January 30, 2003; "2006 Elections: Real Results," *Maariv*, March 30, 2006.
2. The survey was published on the *2006 elections* channel of *zahav.ru*, the popular Russian-language Israeli portal http://israel2006.zahav.ru.
3. *Ibid.*
4. *Ibid.*
5. This group is defined as "from 2000 on," because of the changes in the periods of immigration; in the 2003 election immigrants who had arrived in the 2000–2002 period were taken into consideration, while in the 2006 election immigrants who had arrived in the 2000–2005 were considered. Immigrants who arrived in the 2003–2005 period have not been assigned to a separate group because of their low number (table 3, below).
6. Data from the database of the *Hebrew University of Jerusalem*, http://isdc.huji. ac.il.

References

Al-Haj, Majid, and Eliezer Leshem. 2000. *Immigrants from the Former Soviet Union in Israel: Ten Years Later.* A Research Report, Haifa: University of Haifa, 55–63.

Bick, Etta. 1998. "Sectarian Party Politics in Israel: Case of Yisrael Ba'Aliya, The Russian Immigrant Party." In Daniel Elazar and Shmuel Sandler, eds. *Israel at the Polls, 1996.* London: Frank Cass, 121–148.

Central Bureau of Statistics. 1993. *The Results of the Elections for the 13ᵗʰ Knesset,* Jerusalem, CBS [Hebrew].

Central Bureau of Statistics. 1995. *The Population of Immigrants of the Former USSR, 1990–1992: Demographic Trends,* Jerusalem, CBS [Hebrew].

Central Bureau of Statistics. 1997. *The Results of the Elections for the 14ʰ Knesset,* Jerusalem, CBS [Hebrew].

Central Bureau of Statistics. 1998. *The Population of Immigrants of the Former USSR, 1995: Demographic Trends* Jerusalem, CBS [Hebrew].

Central Bureau of Statistics. 2000. *The Population of Immigrants of the Former USSR, 1998: Demographic Trends* Jerusalem, CBS [Hebrew].

Central Bureau of Statistics. 2001. *Immigration into Israel, 1999,* Jerusalem, CBS [Hebrew].

Central Bureau of Statistics. 2004. *The Population of Immigrants of the Former USSR, Selected Data, 2000–2001* (Compilation 11/2004), Jerusalem, CBS [Hebrew, published in Internet only].

---- http://www.cbs.gov.il/publications/USSR/intussrh.pdf

Central Bureau of Statistics and Ministry of the Interior. 1997. *The Local Authorities in Israel, 1995: Physical Data,* Jerusalem, CBS and Ministry of the Interior [Hebrew].

Diskin, Abraham. 1988. *Elections and Voters in Israel.* Tel Aviv: Am Oved Publishers [Hebrew].

Fein, Aharon. 1995. "Voting Trends of Recent Immigrants from the Former Soviet Union." In: Asher Arian and Michal Shamir, eds. *The Elections in Israel 1992.* Albany: SUNY Press, 161–173.

Gitelman, Zvi, and Ken Goldstein. 2001. "The Russian Revolution in Israeli Politics." In Asher Arian and Michal Shamir, eds. *The Elections in Israel 1999.* Albany: SUNY Press, 203-232 [Hebrew].

Goldstein, Ken and Zvi Gitelman. 2004. "From 'Russians' to Israelis?" In Asher Arian and Michal Shamir, eds. *The Elections in Israel, 2003*. Jerusalem: Israel Democracy Institute, 349-369 [Hebrew].

Horowitz, Tamar. 1994. "The Influence of Soviet Political Culture on Immigrant Voters in Israel: The Election of 1992." *Jews in Eastern Europe* 1(23): 5–22.

Horowitz, Tamar. 1999. "Ideology, Identity, and Frustration as Factors Affecting Voting Patterns of Immigrants from the Former USSR." In Asher Arian and Michal Shamir, eds. *The Elections in Israel 1996*, Jerusalem: Israel Democracy Institute, 145-170 [Hebrew].

Katz, Ze'ev. 2000. "The Immigrants from the Former USSR in Israel's Political Life: the 1990s." In Ludmila Dimarsky-Tziegelman, ed. *The Jews of the USSR in Transition*, 4(19): 145–157 [Hebrew].

Khanin, Vladimir. 2001. "Israeli 'Russian' Parties and the New Immigrant Vote." In Daniel Elazar and M. Ben Mollov, eds. *Israel at the Polls, 1999*, London: Frank Cass, pp. 101–134.

----. 2005. "The Israeli 'Russian' Community and Immigrant Party Politics in 2003 Elections." In Shmuel Sandler, M. Ben Mollov, and Jonathan Ryhhold, eds. *Israel at the Polls, 2003*, London: Routledge, 146–180.

Lochery. Neill. 2006. "The Impact of the Soviet Aliyah on the Middle East Peace Process, 1988–2005." *East European Jewish Affairs* 36(1): 1–30.

Ministry of Immigrant Absorption. 2000. *Immigrants by Area of Residence in the Ministry of the Interior, Immigration Between 1.1.1989 and 31.12.1999*. Jerusalem: Ministry of Immigrant Absorption, Information Systems Department [Hebrew].

----. 2001. *Immigrants by Area of Residence in the Ministry of the Interior, Immigration Between 1.1.1989 and 31.12.2000*. Jerusalem: Ministry of Immigrant Absorption, Information Systems Department [Hebrew].

----. 2003. *Distribution of Immigrants who Immigrated to Israel Between 1.1.1989 and 31.12.2002 by Area of Residence, Relative to Total Population in Area of Residence*. Jerusalem: Ministry of Immigrant Absorption, Information Systems Department [Hebrew].

----. 2006. *Distribution of Immigrants who Immigrated to Israel Between 1.1.1989 and 31.12.2005 by Area of Residence, Relative to Number of Immigrants in Area of Residence*. Jerusalem: Ministry of Immigrant Absorption, Information Systems Department [Hebrew].

Reich, Bernard, Meyrav Wurmser, and Noah Dropkin. 1995. "Playing Politics in Moscow and Jerusalem: Soviet Jewish Immigrants and the 1992 Knesset Elections." In Daniel Elazar and Shmuel Sandler, eds. *Israel at the Polls, 1992*, London: Frank Cass, 127–156.

Weiss, Shevah. 1997. "An Analysis of Voting Among Immigrants from the Former USSR." In David Prital, ed. *The Jews of the USSR in Transition* 3(18): 233–245 [Hebrew].

1990s Immigrants from the FSU in Israeli Elections 2006: The Fulfillment of the Political Dreams of Post-Soviet Man?

Michael Philippov

The electoral behavior of immigrants from the former USSR who arrived in Israel in the 1990s has impacted critically on election results in Israel. In 2006 the immigrants accounted for 16 percent of the electorate (all those with the right to vote) in Israel, and they were responsible for the election of approximately 19 of the 120 Knesset members. The importance of the "Russian" vote was previously demonstrated in the 1992 election. The voting pattern of these immigrants, indicating their slight preference for the political bloc of the left, was the deciding factor that year in the shift of power from the parties of the right to those on the left. The immigrants' vote also had a significant effect on the composition of the Knesset and on the prime ministerial election in subsequent years. In 1996, for example, the immigrants' voting pattern differed from that of the rest of Israel's electorate: only 30 percent of the immigrants voted for Shimon Peres in contrast to 70 percent for Binyamin Netanyahu (Horowitz, 2003). Netanyahu defeated Peres by a small margin (only a few percentage points), with the immigrant vote determining the election results in 1996 as well.

The immigrant vote is therefore important, and has the ability to grant any of the parties an advantage over their competitors, and even unseat the ruling party in Israel. Therefore the political behavior of immigrants from the former USSR who arrived in Israel in the 1990s has aroused considerable interest, with research focusing mainly on the rationale behind immigrant voting patterns. The immigrants came from a country whose regime differed from that of Israel, and most of them underwent a unique process of political socialization in their country of origin. The immigrants' political views can best be described as "Soviet Man" (*Homo Sovieticus*), depicting an individual relatively unskilled in coping with democratic society (Horowitz, 1996, 2003; Horowitz and Leshem, 1998; Gitelman, 1995). The cultural uniqueness of Soviet Man occupies an important place in the worldview of individuals originating from the former USSR now living all over the world. The collective Soviet memory, the poverty, the educational content in institutions of education and higher education, the official propaganda, and the social structure of the former USSR helped to create an exceptional political outlook among its citizens, and one which impacts on their electoral behavior. This worldview is characterized by weak democratic values, authoritarian tendencies, and a low level of trust in political effectiveness, in other words, skepticism as to the ability of citizens to influence politics (Reisinger et al., 1994; White et al., 1997; Carnaghan, 2001; Colton and MacFaul, 2001).

The political culture of Soviet Man continues to be evident even after a prolonged stay in Israel. The Israeli debate on the political and cultural values of immigrants from the former USSR began in the 1970s, when their keen interest in strong leadership, which alone could solve the country's problems, was first identified (Gitelman, 1982, 308). The immigrants also bring their own unique attitude to territory and territorial concessions. They come from a country of vast proportions and are used to the traditional Russian expanses, and many of them refuse to agree to any territorial concessions (Gitelman, 1977, 1982; Goldstein and Gitelman, 2004). They also demonstrate a stereotypical pattern of thinking and a negative attitude toward the Arab minority in Israel. This negative attitude is not unique to them. After arriving in Israel they quickly learn that prejudices against Arabs are acceptable among Israelis (Gitelman, 1995), and they view the Arabs as a hostile group. This behavior pattern is known as the "Amalek Complex" (Feldman, 2003) and in the literature dealing with post-Soviet culture it is called the "Enemy Complex" (Heller, 1988; Gozman and Shestopal, 1996; Levada, 2000; Gudkov, 2004). Another characteristic of immigrants from the former USSR is their demand that the authorities deal with issues of security before attempting to tackle any and all other political problems. Other Israelis, however, focus less on security (Goldstein and Gitelman, 2004). The immigrants' confidence in political effectiveness is lower than that of the rest of the Israeli public. Like the Soviet citizens of Russia in the early 1990s, the immigrants maintain a view that citizens are unable to influence politics (Horowitz, 1996).

The research hypothesis presented here is that the cultural characteristics and political views of the immigrants living in Israel impacted on the "Russian vote" in the 2006 election. To examine this contention, the attitudes of immigrants regarding various issues are compared to those of the general Israeli electorate. The data were gathered by researchers at the Israel Democratic Institute (IDI) between 2003 and 2006, within the framework of the project on the "Israel Democracy Index," by means of telephone surveys and election polls (undertaken in 2006). The respondents were a representative sample of the adult Israeli population. Table 1 below gives the number of participants in the surveys on which this study is based. Immigrants who came in the 1970s, and who account for only 3 percent of the sample are included in the category of "other Jews." The responses of Arab citizens were not included in this study.

The researchers decided not to isolate the Haredi and orthodox sectors in the sample but to include them in the category of "other Israeli Jews," even though immigrants arriving in the 1990s constitute a sector that is overwhelmingly secular. In other words, the attitudes of the immigrants are analyzed relative to those of the rest of the Jewish population without restricting the research group to secular Jews only. The study, therefore, seeks to compare the unique attitudes of the immigrants with those of the general Jewish population of Israel, and not only with those of secular Jews who account for only 40 percent of the Jewish population (i.e., those who defined themselves as "secular").

The Vote and the Political Tendencies of
Immigrants in Contrast to Other Israeli Jews

Twenty-two percent of the Israeli public voted for the Kadima party headed by Ehud Olmert in the election for the Seventeenth Knesset, held on March 28, 2006; 15.1 percent voted for the Labor party headed by Amir Peretz; 9.5 percent voted for Shas under the leadership of Eli Yishai; 9 percent voted for Likud, headed by Binyamin Netanyahu; and 9 percent voted for Israel Beitenu, headed by Avigdor Lieberman. The rest of the votes were divided among the seven other parties (see figure 1, below). The votes were divided differently in the immigrant sector. Approximately four months prior to the election, in December 2005, the Kadima party led by Ariel Sharon seemed destined to win the immigrants' votes and obtain 34.3 percent of the vote. After January 2006, when it became clear that Sharon would not be Kadima's leader in the election that he had initiated, there was a decline in the immigrants' support for his party. In the last three months prior to the election Kadima lost approximately one fifth of the immigrants' votes (see figure 2, below).

A few days before the election the immigrants' votes were divided among three parties—Israel Beiteinu, Kadima, and Likud—with a slight advantage to Lieberman, the chairman of Israel Beiteinu, over his rivals (among the im-

Table 1
Number of Participants in Study

Date of survey	No. of 1990s immigrants in survey	No. of other Jews in survey
April 2003	196	853
April 2004	194	799
March 2005	287	1,477
December 2005	130	768
February 2006	191	787
March 2006	311	1,319
April 2006	239	991

migrants who had already decided for whom to vote): Israel Beiteinu obtained 47 percent of the immigrants' votes; Kadima, received 28.1 percent; and Likud gained 15.4 percent. As in most elections, the parties on the left obtained fewer of the immigrants' votes in the 2006 election as well, with Labor and Meretz together receiving only 2 percent of these votes, compared with 3.6 percent in the previous election (Horowitz, 2003). The results of the survey undertaken in April 2006 show that Avigdor Lieberman's party obtained over 57 percent of the immigrants' votes, while their support for Kadima and Likud decreased to 21 and 10 percent respectively. Most of the immigrants who were undecided, as well as those who had declared in the past that they would vote for Kadima, voted for Israel Beiteinu on election day. Among the rest of the Jewish population Israel Beiteinu received only 3 percent of the votes.

An analysis of the demographic characteristics of voters from the Russian sector demonstrates that differences in education, gender, age, and the amount of time since their immigration to Israel impact minimally on their voting patterns. No significant difference was found relative to levels of education between immigrants who voted for Israel Beiteinu, Kadima, or Likud; there was no appreciable difference between male and female immigrants, and no correlation between the immigrants' age and their voting pattern or between the length of time since their immigration and their vote. Furthermore, the voting pattern of immigrants arriving in Israel between 1989 and 1991 appears to be similar to that of those arriving after them.

Taking into account the lack of differences on the statistical level, the deeper discussion should therefore focus on why, after Sharon's illness, 20 percent of the immigrants abandoned Kadima and almost two-thirds of them, irrespective of gender, age, or length of time in Israel, shifted to the political right and voted for Avigdor Lieberman's Israel Beiteinu party, which is not particularly popular among the rest of Israel's Jewish population. The explanation for this could stem from the differences in the political views of the immigrants and those of the rest of the Jewish electorate.

Figure 1
The Vote for the Seventeenth Knesset in the 2006 Election

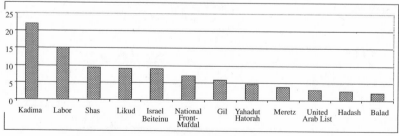

SOURCE: The Knesset Website, www.knesset.gov.il

Figure 2
Changes in Voter Preferences Prior to the 2006 Election among
1990s Immigrants

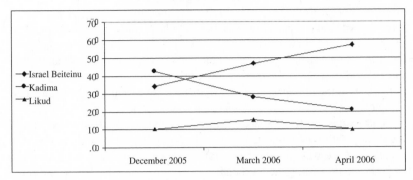

SOURCE: Based on Israel National Election Studies (INES) data (http://isdc.huji.
ac.il/ehold.shtml).

There is a strong correlation in Israel between how individuals vote and their position on the political spectrum. In the last thirty years there has also been a strong correlation between an individual's political-security outlook and his or her vote (Arian et al., 2003). The views of most immigrants are located at the center of the political map (46 percent) and on its right (48 percent), with very little support for the left (see figure 3, below), so that the location of the immigrants along the political spectrum is different from the rest of the Jewish electorate. This might explain the difference between the voting patterns of the two sectors. Of particular interest is the fact that the immigrants appear to completely ignore the political left: 94 percent of them locate themselves at its center or to the right of it. This does not seem to be a transient phenomenon. From the 1996 election until 2006 the parties of the left have not succeeded in gaining the support of the immigrant sector. The parties of the left obtained 11.7 percent of the immigrant vote in the 1996 election, 15 percent in 1999, and only 3.6 percent in 2003. This has been explained ideologically in that most of the immigrants subscribe to hawkish views on peace and security, and these are reflected in their vote for the parties of the right and their location on the right-hand side of the political spectrum (Horowitz, 2003). The immigrants' vote in 2006 can also be explained by their location between the two political extremes. They voted for the center party (Kadima) as well as for those on the right (Likud and Israel Beiteinu).

The differences in the political tendencies of the general Jewish electorate can also be explained by differences in ethnic origin. In contrast to a population of Ashkenazi origin, those of Sephardi origin tend to favor the right over the left (Shamir and Arian, 1999). Within the framework of this study comparisons were made among three groups: (i) immigrants who arrived in the 1990s; (ii) Israelis with a father who was born in a North African country (individuals of Sephardi origin); and (iii) Israelis with a father who was born in Europe, America, or South Africa (individuals of Ashkenazi origin). The tendency of immigrants to withhold support from the political left was found to be stronger than that of the other two ethnic groups (figure 4, below). On a scale of 1 to 10 (0 = left, 10 = right) the immigrants' grade was 6.03 (SD = 1.6), while that of the group of Sephardi origin was 6.28 (SD = 2.5), and that of the group of Ashkenazi origin was 5.47 (SD = 2.3). As the figure shows, two features distinguish the political preferences of the immigrants: their low distribution around the mean and their extremely limited presence on the left-hand side of the political spectrum.

Another substantial difference between the immigrants and the rest of Israel's Jewish population is connected with their economic inclination. Eighty-one percent of those who voted for the parties of the left (Labor and Meretz) in the 2006 elections supported a socialist economic system for Israel, and some of them supported the left because of their economic and political tendencies. However, most of the immigrants who came in the 1990s preferred the capitalistic approach to a socialist one (see figure 5, below), and it is therefore not surprising that only a few of them voted for the parties with a socialist background in 2006.

The current research has taken into account the fact that some of the immigrants might have openly opposed the socialist approach because of negative associations for them with this term. But even when participants in the study were asked whether the state should intervene in the workplace to provide employment, thereby assuring a reasonable standard of living for all citizens, the immigrants approved of government intervention to a lesser extent than the rest of the Jewish population (54 percent of the immigrants compared with 65

Figure 3
Distribution Between Political Left and Right of Immigrants and the Rest of the Jewish Electorate, March 2006 (percentage)

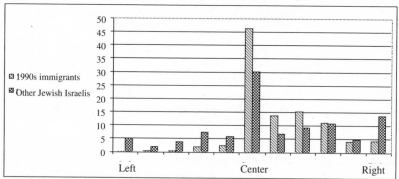

SOURCE: Based on Israel National Election Studies (INES) data (http://isdc.huji. ac.il/ehold.shtml).

Figure 4
Left and Right Affiliation of Immigrants, Population of Sephardi Origin, and
Population of Ashkenazi Origin, March 2006 (percentage)

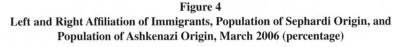

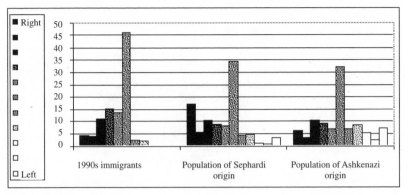

SOURCE: Based on Israel National Election Studies (INES) data (http://isdc.huji. ac.il/ehold.shtml).

percent of the general Jewish population). The capitalist tendencies of a large part of the immigrants can therefore be assumed to be stronger than those of the general Jewish population in Israel.

The switch from Sharon to Lieberman: the Desire for a Strong Leader

A large part of the immigrant population changed their preferences as to which party to vote for in the 2006 election in the months leading up to election day. Approximately one fifth of the immigrants decided to vote for Israel Beiteinu after Ariel Sharon's illness, and only then did their support for Kadima begin to decline. Sharon was popular on an unprecedented scale among the immigrants throughout his period as prime minister. To understand their admiration and unqualified support it is important to examine their attitude to him during the implementation of the disengagement plan. Our research demonstrates that the immigrants who opposed the plan or refrained from supporting it continued to offer approval and display affection for Sharon. In June 2005, a few weeks before the disengagement plan was put into effect, the immigrants' general endorsement of Sharon was far greater than that of the rest of the Jewish population, with the immigrants' grade in support of Sharon standing at 6.22 (SD = 2.42) out of 10 (1 = hatred or revulsion, 10 = support or adoration), while that of the rest of the Jewish population in Israel (p < 0.001) was 5.44 (SD = 2.88). Only 7 percent of the immigrant population which "strongly opposed" the disengagement process defined its attitude to the prime minister as "hatred or revulsion" (a grade of 1). Among the rest of the Jewish population which was strongly opposed to the disengagement plan, 32 percent hated or rejected

Figure 5
Preference for Economic Approach, March 2006 (percentage)

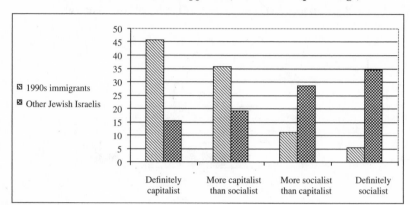

SOURCE: Based on Israel National Election Studies (INES) data (http://isdc.huji. ac.il/ehold.shtml).

Sharon. These findings are consistent with the continued trust placed in Sharon by the immigrants in his last three years as prime minister. As figure 6 below shows, during those years most of the immigrants trusted him to a greater extent than the rest of the Jewish population in Israel.

Sharon came under considerable criticism during his second term as prime minister for allegedly acting contrary to the will of the people, preventing a referendum, and trampling on Israeli democracy. This censure did not harm his image among the immigrants. On the contrary, among that electorate which for years had preferred a strong leader rather than laws and debate, Sharon's determination aroused spontaneous admiration and support. Figure 7 below shows the extent of the immigrants' agreement with the idea that a strong leader can benefit the country more than "all kinds of laws and debate." As the figure shows, in the last three years that Sharon was in office, their support for this idea was consistent.

This finding concurs with the conclusions reached by Gitelman (1982) relative to immigrants who arrived in Israel in the 1970s as well as with those of research studies conducted in contemporary Russian society on the political culture of Soviet Man. The need to contend with a complex modern society which cannot be changed appears to find expression among individuals originating from the former USSR as loyalty to a strong leader and an "omnipotent" government. In the traditional Russian dream the "strong czar" protects his people from enemies both within and outside the country, looks after the individual citizen, and resolves national problems with speed, determination, and efficiency. Only a strong leader can defeat enemies threatening to conquer the homeland. When a survey question in contemporary Russia asks who is the most

Figure 6
Extent of Confidence in Ariel Sharon ("Complete Confidence"
and "Partial Confidence," percentage)

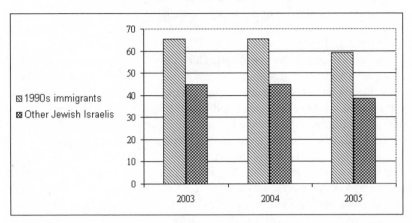

SOURCE: Based on Guttman Center (Israel Democracy Institute) data (http://www. idi.org.il).

Figure 7
"Strong Leaders Can Benefit the Country More Than All the Laws and Debates"
("Agree" and "Strongly Agree," percentage)

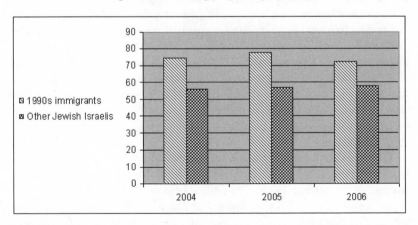

SOURCE: Based on Guttman Center (Israel Democracy Institute) data (http://www. idi.org.il).

famous Russian historical personage, the leading figure is Peter the Great, the strongest and most resolute leader in Russia's history (Levada, 2001). While the Russians do not express clear authoritarian attitudes, they believe that the ideal ruler is first and foremost one who is able to take care of every aspect of the state, just as a capable landlord would (Reisinger et al., 1994; Carnaghan, 2001; Levada, 2000).

The voters' attitude to the party leader in the 2006 election was decisive. Those who supported Kadima preferred Olmert to all the other candidates. The same applied to Netanyahu among those who supported Likud, as well as to Peretz among those who supported Labor. Similarly, the immigrants' broad support for the principle of strong and resolute leadership significantly impacted on the decision to vote for Israel Beiteinu rather than Kadima. The qualities of a strong leader, which were important to the immigrants, did not mesh with their image of Olmert. This tendency was expressed in a survey undertaken in March 2006, in which only 14.5 percent of the immigrants believed that Olmert possessed "leadership qualities." Only 4 percent of those who voted for Lieberman's party agreed with that statement. Olmert's weak image as a leader was one of the main reasons why the "Russian vote" abandoned Kadima. Lieberman was viewed as a stronger and more resolute leader than Olmert. Lieberman's image in the Hebrew press and the Russian media was that of a strong, unyielding, and uncompromising leader. Immigrants from the former USSR prefer these qualities, believing that only someone with these qualities is capable of bringing stability to the country. Even while lacking the tools for assessing the correlation between Lieberman's image and that of a strong leader, it is possible to examine the immigrants' general approval ratings of politicians. In a poll undertaken before the 2006 election, when immigrants were asked to grade their support for Lieberman on a scale of 1 to 10 (1 = hate, 10 = admire), 23 percent gave Lieberman a grade of less than 5, compared with 54 percent of the general Jewish population in Israel. Among the general Jewish population 25 percent even defined their attitude to Lieberman as "hatred" (1 on the scale), as opposed to 5 percent of the immigrants. Figure 8 below shows the mean grades reflecting the attitudes of the two sectors to politicians prior to the 2006 election.

The figure shows that if Sharon had not been hospitalized at that time, he would have competed successfully with Lieberman's considerable popularity among the immigrants. In a survey undertaken before the election, 90 percent of the immigrants graded their attitude to Sharon as five or more, compared with 73 percent of the rest of the Jewish population. Olmert did not have much chance of gaining the immigrants' support, and only 20 percent gave him a grade of more than five, with most of them favoring either Lieberman or Sharon. Even among those immigrants who voted for Kadima, Olmert's grade was a modest 6.4, while it was 7.6 among the general Jewish population that voted for Kadima (p < 0.001).

About one fifth of the immigrants voted for Kadima in the election and there were three main reasons for this. First, Kadima's list included several politicians, such as Marina Solodkin, who could attract some of the immigrants' votes. Second, the fact that the Kadima party had been established by Ariel Sharon, the immigrants' favored leader, could not be ignored. Some of them may have regarded Kadima as Sharon's political testament, and voted for it even though they knew that Sharon would not return to politics. An article by journalist Lily Galili, appearing in *Haaretz* approximately two months prior to the election, after it had become clear that Sharon would not be participating in it, describes the story of a Labor party activist who contacted large numbers of immigrants in an attempt to persuade them to vote for Amir Peretz. "Some of them replied that they intended to vote for Sharon. It was still Sharon. It was almost mystical."[1] The third reason for the immigrant vote for Kadima related to the differences in the political stance of immigrants who voted for Kadima and those who voted for Israel Beiteinu. Those who supported Avigdor Lieberman appeared to be more hawkish and right-wing than those who voted for Kadima. The average grade given by Kadima supporters on a scale of 1 to 10 (0 = left, 10 = right) was 5.5, and that given by Israel Beiteinu supporters was 6.4 (p < 0.001).

The Security Position of Israel Beiteinu and the Russian Electorate

Israel Beiteinu, under the leadership of Avigdor Lieberman, garnered most of the immigrant vote in the 2006 election. The party's official website reads: "Israel Beiteinu is the home of the Jewish state and security."[2] Most of the salient topics included in the party's platform are linked, one way or another,

Figure 8
Attitudes of 1990s Immigrants to Politicians, March 2006
(1 = Rejection/Hatred, 10 = Support/Adoration; mean grades)

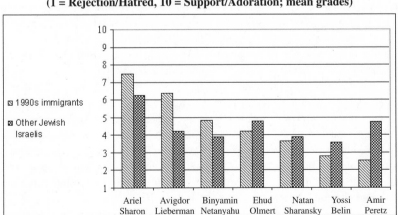

SOURCE: Based on Israel National Election Studies (INES) data (http://isdc.huji. ac.il/ehold.shtml).

with the expression "the security of the state of Israel." The very first page of the party's manifesto displays a large heading which reads: "The Background to the Program: the Threats to Israel," with a list underneath detailing the threats: the Arab countries, Palestinian terrorism, the regional dimension, both near and far, and the demographic threat. Lieberman's political program in the 2006 election was more focused on security than ever before. An additional element was the promise to combat the crime wave then prevalent throughout Israel. The issue of the war on crime was expressed more intensely only on the party's Russian-language website. This may have been merely a coincidence, but it is also possible that this was deliberately directed at the needs of the immigrants from the former USSR. Lieberman promised to make the battle against crime "the number one target of the government of Israel," and the word "security," which appeared on the party's Hebrew-language website, was replaced with "security and public order" in the Russian version. In every interview Lieberman stressed his plan to be appointed minister of internal security, restoring personal security to Israel's citizens.

It was not by coincidence that Lieberman focused on this issue, which the immigrants who arrived in the 1990s regard as "Israel's most important problem," namely, the individual's sense of security. In a survey undertaken in 2006, 58 percent of the immigrants reported that the issue of security influenced the way they voted, while in the rest of the Jewish population the figure was only 20 percent. This is not surprising in light of the fact that the election was held in a relatively calm security atmosphere, with no major terror attacks. The annual surveys examining the demands which Israelis make of the government also demonstrated that security concerns occupy a prominent position among the immigrants while other subjects are mentioned less often. Before the 2006 election the immigrants demanded that the government deal primarily with security issues (see figure 9, below). A cross-section of immigrants who voted for Lieberman, and immigrants who voted for Kadima, showed that 58 percent of the former and only 42 percent of the latter regarded security as the main issue in Israel. The immigrants who voted for Lieberman were more sensitive to the subject of security than those who voted for Kadima.

With the exception of security problems, the immigrants who participated in the survey found it difficult to pinpoint any of Israel's other problems. Only a handful were prepared to explain their choice and describe any aspect of "security," such as, "the Arab-Israel conflict," "terrorism," or "crime." Most preferred to use the more general term "security" to denote the main problem confronting the government. They have subscribed to this view since 2003 (Goldstein and Gitelman, 2003). The rest of the Jewish electorate however, assigned greater importance to economic, political, and social issues, and to education. The immigrants did not feel that the government should attend primarily to the specific problems of the Russian sector, such as pensions, civil marriage, or employment.

Figure 9
"What is the Most Important Problem the Government Needs to Address?"
March 2006 (percent)

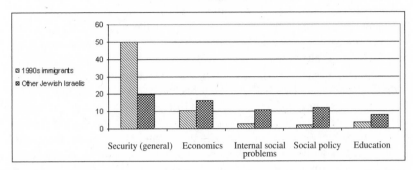

SOURCE: Based on Israel National Election Studies (INES) data (http://isdc.huji. ac.il/ehold.shtml).

There is further proof of the importance attached by the immigrants to issues of security. In a survey undertaken in March 2006, 80 percent of the immigrants agreed with the sentence: "The government should invest more money in the defense budget," while only 51 percent of the rest of the Jewish population agreed with this statement. When the participants were asked which principle they would prefer if there was a conflict between "obeying the law" and "maintaining security," only 15 percent of the immigrants chose obeying the law, as compared with 24 percent of Israel's general population ($p < 0.005$). Those immigrants who support Lieberman tend to prefer "security" over "law" to a greater extent than those voting for Kadima, with 42 percent of those who support Kadima preferring the middle option ("it depends on the situation"), 42 percent of those who vote for Lieberman preferring "security," and only 18 percent convinced that law is the most important factor. The overall impression was that among immigrants who support Lieberman, the mention of terms such as "law" and "security" does not engender any hesitation, and they hold stronger views relative to those issues than immigrants who vote for Kadima.

Like the citizens of Russia (Lapin, 2004; Gozman and Shestopal, 1996), the "Russian" immigrants also have a deep mistrust of the institutions of law, which results in a lack of a sense of security in their daily life. Only 42 percent of the immigrants in 2004 reported that they trusted the Israeli police, while in the general Israeli population 72 percent reported that they did. This proportion fell in 2006 in both sectors, with 24 percent of immigrants and 47 percent of the rest of the Jewish population in Israel stating that they trusted the police.

In light of the detailed results presented above, the issue of security as defined by Lieberman, altering its narrow definition as "the war on terror" to a wider one of "the war on terror and crime," was compatible with the wishes of immigrants who came from the former USSR in the 1990s. The deployment of terms like "public order" is precise and seems to be in accord with the post-Soviet consciousness of the immigrant sector, which regards "security and order" as a supreme political value. Only a minority of the immigrants trusts the Israeli police, and therefore Lieberman's promise to seek the appointment of minister of internal security seemed appropriate to the mood of the "Russian" electorate on the eve of the election.

The importance attached by the immigrants to security does not derive solely from the situation in Israel. Throughout his history, Soviet Man has suffered from a lack of security as well as a sense of being unable to trust the authorities responsible for enforcing the law. Individuals born in the former USSR never trusted the Soviet or Russian police, and the yearning for a regime that would restore order and security to the country has been at the center of public debate there since the 1980s. Ever since then demands have been made in modern Russia to employ force in restoring order to the disintegrating state. These demands have been made not only by veteran citizens who yearn for Stalin but also by young people with a liberal orientation socialized during the period of Perestroika and who claim to support human rights and basic democratic values. Young people demand that the authorities restore order and individual security to citizens by force, and restore a police presence to the streets as well. They view demonstrations of strength by the authorities as a sign of genuine and efficient government (Lapin, 2004; Gozman and Shestopal, 1996).

The Territorial Exchange Plan

With the approach of the 2006 election, Israel Beiteinu renewed its platform and publicity campaign. It was not yet content to merely promise "to restore order to Israel's streets" but also presented Lieberman's new program of "the exchange of territory and population." This time Lieberman did not only advocate combating terrorism but he also promoted the idea of exchanging land, under the slogan "Disengagement from Um-al-Fahm." Within the framework of this concept Lieberman proposed that blocs of Jewish settlement, such as Ma'aleh Adumim and Ariel, should be pronounced part of the State of Israel, and in return the area with the largest Arab population, Um-al-Fahm,[3] should be transferred to the Palestinian Authority. This plan appears to have been popular with the immigrants for three reasons.

First, the slogan, "Disengagement from Um-al-Fahm" reflects the solution to the Arab problem mentioned by immigrants in surveys. In the March 2006 survey, 81 percent of the immigrants supported the idea that the government should encourage Arabs to emigrate from Israel, while only 56 percent of the rest of the Jewish population in Israel subscribed to this view. Sixty-nine percent of the immigrants who voted for Lieberman strongly supported the idea of encouraging Arabs to emigrate from Israel, compared with only 44 percent of the immigrants who voted for Kadima.

Second, making territorial concessions and shedding the image that "only the wall is to the right of him" could only aid Lieberman and his party, since a minority of the immigrants defined themselves as being on the extreme right politically (4 percent, compared with 14 percent of the general Jewish population in Israel). Lieberman's readiness to reach some kind of territorial compromise could shift his image among the immigrants toward the center-right, where most of the sector's electorate is situated. Lieberman's plan also represented a substitute for the solution to the demographic problem proposed by Kadima in the one-sided convergence plan. Kadima's plan stipulated that Israel would have to relinquish territory without receiving any in return. Therefore, those who supported Lieberman opposed the convergence plan. Only 9 percent of those who voted for Lieberman thought that giving territory back did not imperil Israel's security, while 32 percent of those who voted for Kadima agreed with that statement. Unlike the convergence plan, Lieberman's plan included the exchange of territory rather than relinquishing territory and receiving nothing in return. This corresponded with the political view of the immigrants who had opposed making territorial concessions while receiving nothing in return since the 1970s.

Third, the plan to exchange territory is extreme. If executed, it will completely alter Israel's demographic and political situation, and possibly because it is so extreme it might even gain support among the immigrants who arrived in the 1990s. It is necessary to take into account one of the characteristics of the immigrants from the former USSR—their support for extreme measures because of their lack of trust in political effectiveness. Researchers who have studied the elections in Russia claim that part of the post-Soviet electorate prefers to vote for parties that promise dramatic and extreme changes, thereby bringing them into the political arena and altering the *status quo*. The extreme vote takes place because individuals feel that only at election time do they possess any real power to influence government policy, whereas this is not the case in daily life. The low level of belief in political effectiveness makes it easier to vote for an extreme party; the individual does not take responsibility for the possible extreme outcome as a result of his or her vote but rather regards the election as a fascinating game (Levada, 2000).

Changes in voters' attitudes have also been studied in Israel. The immigrants' attitudes changed after the 1992 election. Their lack of belief in the ability of an individual to influence politics was replaced by a sense of electoral self-confidence (Horowitz, 2003), while in 2006, 45 percent of the immigrants reported that they could not exert any influence on government policy, compared with 33 percent in the rest of the Jewish population in Israel. Only 47 percent of them disagreed strongly with the statement "It doesn't matter what I vote for because it doesn't alter the situation," compared with 22 percent of the rest of the Jewish population in Israel. Like the citizens of modern Russia, the immigrants have no faith in their ability to influence government policy in daily life, while at the same time acknowledging an awareness of their electoral power. These patterns of thought may well encourage immigrants from the former USSR to choose extreme ways of altering the current reality.

The Enemy Complex and the Citizenship Law

Israel Beiteinu's political platform after the 2003 election included a new citizenship law. This was another significant innovation in Avigdor Lieberman's political program. The principles of the law were simple: every citizen over sixteen would have to swear allegiance to the State of Israel, its flag, and its declaration of independence. Anyone refusing to do this would lose the right to vote and run for elective office.[4]

Adding a new citizenship law to his political agenda paved the way for Lieberman into the hearts of many immigrants. According to that law, anyone who did not accept the basic principles of the State of Israel would not be able to benefit in full from the rights of a citizen. This meant that Lieberman's citizenship law offered individuals over the age of sixteen the option of choosing between fully belonging to the State of Israel and opposing it. He thereby eliminated a situation where Arab citizens could have full citizenship without also subscribing to the State's basic principles.

This law conforms to the main features of the underlying psychology of Soviet political culture—the Enemy Complex. Individuals born in the former USSR are accustomed to living with the conceptual approach wherein they are the defenders of a fortress surrounded by enemies. This leads to a worldview with a division of the world into "the good guys" and "the bad guys," "us'" and "them." Many generations of those born in the former USSR became accustomed to that dichotomous and simplistic division. Sometimes it is convenient for Soviet Man to know exactly who his enemy is, as that enables him to justify most of the difficulties in his life, repress self-criticism, and overcome the sense of failure often experienced by citizens living in a non-democratic regime with no rule of law. The Enemy Complex even enables those born in the former USSR to create a national identity, as hatred toward a shared enemy offers the individual a sense of belonging with a larger group. The subjective feeling derived from a life surrounded by enemies causes some of those born in the former USSR to develop an extreme sensitivity to danger, and they view the enemy as a threatening figure devoid of the human characteristics which distinguishes the group of "us" (Heller, 1988; Gozman and Shestopal, 1996; Gudkov, 2004; Levada, 2000).

The guidelines to Lieberman's citizenship law suit the immigrants' worldview. The immigrants' attitude to the Arabs in general, and Israeli Arabs in particular, is characterized by the symptoms of the Enemy Complex—fear and a complete lack of trust. Surveys show that the sense of threat from the Arab population felt by the immigrants is particularly strong, and greater than that of the rest of Israel's Jewish population. Seventy-seven percent of the immigrants believe that the Israeli Arabs represent a threat to Israel's security, compared with 61 percent of the rest of the Jewish Israeli population (based on a survey conducted in June 2005). There were also differences between the views of the immigrants and those of the rest of the Jewish population as to the general threat that Arabs constitute to Israel. In an opinion poll taken prior to the 2005 election, 59 percent of the immigrants agreed that the ultimate intention of the Arabs was "to conquer the State of Israel and annihilate a large part of its population," while only 38.5 percent of the general Jewish population endorsed that statement. That poll also found that 59 percent of the immigrants "are very afraid of being injured by Arabs in daily life," while only 23 percent of the rest of the Jewish population concurred. When the immigrant respondents were further divided into those supporting Kadima and those favoring Israel Beiteinu, it was found that the latter feared "the Arab danger" more than the former. Eighty-four percent of those who supported Lieberman (Israel Beiteinu) and 75 percent of those who supported Kadima felt that the Arabs' true intention was not to liberate the areas that had been occupied in 1967 but to conquer all of Israel and destroy a significant portion of its population. Sixty-six percent of Lieberman's supporters were afraid of being injured by Arabs in their daily life, compared with 56 percent of Kadima supporters.

The assumption that a large proportion of the immigrant population is poor, uses public transport, and shops at open markets is a commonly held view of the Israeli media, with the ensuing assumption that the immigrants are therefore more exposed to terrorist attacks than the general Israeli population (Goldstein and Gitelman, 2004). This assumption might explain the high level of anxiety regarding terrorist attacks found among the immigrants, although terrorist attacks are equally as likely to occur in more upscale locations, which are exposed to terror attacks no less than on public transportation or at open-air markets. As a result, those well-to-do segments of the population who frequent restaurants, attend plays, or use airplanes to travel abroad, may also suffer from terrorist attacks. In short, the immigrants' fear of terrorist attacks does not stem solely from their socio-economic situation and their increased exposure to attacks in their daily life but also from a Soviet mind-set like the Enemy Complex.

The Information Bubble in the Immigrant Sector

There was a marked difference in the 2006 election between the immigrants' voting pattern and that of the rest of the Jewish population of Israel, not only as a result of the political values they brought with them from their country of origin but also because of the information bubble they currently live in. Most of the immigrants who had come from the former USSR in the 1990s were still obtaining information about what was happening in Israel in 2006 from Russian-language channels of communication (see figure 10, below). Only 2 percent viewed television channels broadcast from their country of origin. Most preferred Israeli channels, such as Israel Plus and the international Russian-language channel RTVi, also transmitted from Israel. But outside the Russian sector the debate about political issues relied on information obtained from the Hebrew-language press and television media. The political debate in each sector was therefore based on different sources of information, which may explain the differences in the outlooks of the two sectors.

Political discourse in Israel is not always linked only with the communications media. People often discuss politics, and the social environment can impact on an individual's political views. It would appear that the immigrants do not often discuss politics with the veterans and that each sector keeps to itself. Ninety-three percent of the immigrants stated that they talked about politics with their friends. It is important to note that the close friends of 76 percent of the immigrants are comprised of other immigrants from the former USSR, with only 24 percent of the close friends of immigrants belonging to groups other than those of immigrants from the former USSR who immigrated, like them, in the 1990s (see figure 10, below).

Each year an increasing number of young immigrants join the electorate, and these youngsters possess a better command of Hebrew than their parents. As figure 11 below shows, immigrants who came from the former USSR in the 1990s, and are less than forty years old, are more exposed to the press, television, and conversations with friends in Hebrew than the general population of immigrants (figure 11, below).

Figure 10
Preferences of 1990s Immigrants for Communications Media and Friends ("Who are your closest friends?" "Which newspaper do you read?" "On which TV channel do you usually watch the news?"), March 2006 (percentage)

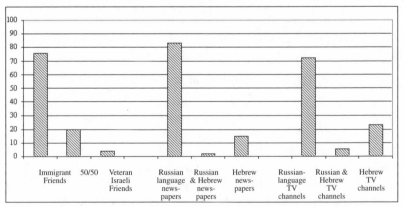

SOURCE: Based on Israel National Election Studies (INES) data (http://isdc.huji. ac.il/ehold.shtml).

Figure 11
Preferences of 1990s Immigrants for Communications Media and Friends;
Sample of Immigrants Aged 40 or Less ("Who are your closest friends?"
"Which newspaper do you read?" "On which TV channel do you usually
watch the news?"), March 2006 (percentage)

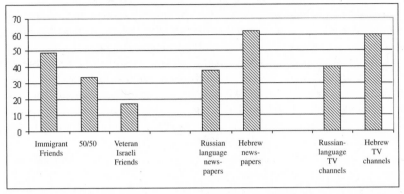

SOURCE: Based on Israel National Election Studies (INES) data (http://isdc.huji.ac.il/ehold.shtml).

Conclusion

Seventeen years after the influx of immigrants from the former USSR to Israel began, such sentiments as the yearning for a strong leader, for order and security, and the Enemy Complex still play an important role in the political outlook of those immigrants. Future research on the subject may help to understand the "mystery of the Russian soul," and thereby avoid the surprises to which Israeli society is subject at almost every election. The strategic advisors of some of the parties appear to have unraveled that mystery: the image of Avigdor Lieberman in the 2006 election was molded perfectly to suit the immigrants and most of their post-Soviet dreams—a strong leader addressing Israel's security problems, promising to put an end to neglect in the realm of internal security, and offering a clear-cut path for contending with enemies of the state. Lieberman stressed his ability to restore order to the country by measures which, while extreme, were supposedly also quick and highly efficient. As a result, over 50 percent of the immigrants supported his party's platform. The immigrants who voted for Kadima, however, were less affected by certain Soviet values, including the Enemy Complex and the attachment to order and security. It may well be that the extent of adherence to a post-Soviet culture may be responsible for the variance in voting patterns in the immigrant sector.

Cultural and Soviet values seem to find expression in attitudes that have influenced Israeli politics for many years. Despite the fact that the immigrant vote changes from one election to another, over the years it is possible to discern some similarities between their voting patterns. Most of the immigrants who came to Israel from the former USSR tended to vote for a strong leader who would convince them that he could bring law and order to the country. If immigrants' preferences over the years are reviewed—Yitzhak Rabin in 1992, Binyamin Netanyahu in 1996, Ehud Barak in 1999, and Ariel Sharon in 2001—in every election the immigrants invariably preferred someone who could present himself as being a stronger leader than his rivals. Ehud Barak, competing against Netanyahu in 1999, endeavored to reinforce his image among the immigrants as someone who was strong and forceful with his book, *Ehud Barak: Number One Soldier*, which was translated into Russian and distributed free of charge by his party activists. Israel Ba'Aliya also established its image as a strong and powerful party in 1996 (Horowitz, 2003), by pledging to "redesign the priorities at the Ministry of the Interior" and used Soviet-style slogans (M.V. D. Pod Nash Kontrol!) (The Ministry of the Interior—under our control!). Prior to the 2001 election, the BBC's correspondent in Israel reported that the right-wing vote of the immigrants appeared to be completely predictable given the fact that those who had immigrated in the 1990s had been educated in the Soviet fighting spirit of never surrendering to the enemy, especially when dealing with a small country like Israel.[5]

But it would be too simplistic to state that the immigrants voted for the right in general and Lieberman in particular only because they had been educated in the former USSR that a leader should be authoritative, that the world is divided into friends and enemies, and that on no account should any inch of the homeland be relinquished. Some research studies (Shestopal, 1997; Levada, 2000) affirm that post-Soviet culture is not homogeneous but full of internal contradictions resulting from later periods. Democratic and authoritarian values intermingle with the consciousness of the citizens of the former USSR in ways that often seem strange and illogical. Adherence to one particular value often depends on what is more convenient for the individual in a concrete situation. Post-Soviet Man can support a strong, authoritarian, and all-powerful regime while at the same time opposing any restriction of freedom of speech because that combination appears attractive and convenient to him. It would therefore be correct to say that the political situation of Israel Beiteinu, which provides unequivocal solutions to complex political problems, encourages immigrants to rely conveniently on classic Soviet values, but this should not be taken to mean that all the political views of the immigrants who came to Israel in the 1990s are a direct result of Soviet political socialization.

The discussion of the immigrant vote in the elections should not be limited to the political values established in the former USSR, as the crystallization of attitudes among the Russian sector in Israel is a fairly complex process, and Russian political culture plays a limited role in this process. Within the framework of the political socialization of the immigrants in Israel, it is important to address such issues as the role of Israel's Russian-language media as an agent of socialization. The ongoing failure of the parties of the left in the "Russian" sector may be connected directly with the hostile and even vicious image accorded these parties by the "Russian" media. The discussion of the sectoral vote is still topical, and even though the purely ethnic party Israel Ba'Aliya has been removed from the Israeli political scene, Israel Beiteinu cannot be seen as its natural successor. Most of the issues that Lieberman's party focused on were general-national issues rather than sectoral, and his plan concurs with the wishes of most of the immigrants.

I will refrain from making long-term predictions as there is no way of knowing which party will benefit most from the immigrants' cultural background in the next elections, and which leader will best adapt his agenda to the mind-set of immigrants from the former USSR in Israel. Lieberman accomplished this in 2006, but the survey indicates that he is not the only individual to gain the admiration of the immigrants. Binyamin Netanyahu also won relatively widespread support in the immigrant sector. After the 2006 election Lieberman will need to justify his image as a strong leader with a security agenda as a minister. His future image may also depend on the extent to which he succeeds in proving that he actually is a strong leader as well as on his actions in his new position as a minister in the government.

The shift in the immigrants' media consumption is also likely to affect the change in their voting patterns in the future, and there may be substantial differences between the political cultures of the older immigrants and the younger generation of immigrants who have grown up in Israel. Goldstein and Gitelman (2004) have mentioned that the younger generation of immigrants from the former USSR has a different political outlook than that of its parents. It cannot, however, be taken for granted that the younger generation of immigrants will be completely free of their parents' patterns of political thought. For example, modern-day Russia demonstrates that Soviet values manage to survive, and some are transmitted from one generation to the next. The present research study has not demonstrated that there are inter-generational differences in political views and voting patterns even though the younger generation of immigrants obtains political information from Hebrew and other non-Russian sources.

In view of the findings of this study it should be noted that the immigrants who arrived in Israel in the 1990s have considerable electoral power, accounting for nineteen Knesset seats. These dimensions attest to the power of this group of voters to change the political balance of power in Israel, to place new ideas on the parliamentary agenda, and to eventually change the country's direction of development. Therefore it is important to understand which values and cultural systems motivate the "Russian" electorate in Israel in the 2000s. This is an important subject which should be placed on the public agenda. Future research should be focused on such topics as the immigrants' historical memory, the democratic and non-democratic values of the former USSR natives, and their impact on the formation of attitudes in Israeli politics.

Notes

1. Lily Galili, "The Immigrants Consider How to Vote. 10 Seats in Search of a Home," *Haaretz*, January 19, 2006.http://www.haaretz.co.il/hasite/pages/ShArt. jhtml?itemNo=672570&contrassID=1
2. www.beytenu.org.il
3. Ibid.
4. Ibid.
5. Gary Reznikovsky, "The Russians in Israel Yearn to be a Big Power."

References

Arian, Asher, David Nahmias, Doron Navot, and Daniel Shani. 2003. *Democracy in Israel: Progress Report 2003, The Democracy Index Project.* Jerusalem: Israel Democracy Institute [Hebrew].

Carnaghan, Ellen, 2001. "Thinking about Democracy: Interviews with Russian Citizens." *Slavic Review* 60(2): 336–366.

Colton, Timothy J. and Michael McFaul. 2001. *Are Russians Undemocratic? Working Paper* 20, Carnegie: Carnegie Endowment for International Peace.

Gitelman, Zvi. 1977. "Soviet Political Culture: Insights from Jewish Emigres." *Soviet Studies* 29(4): 543–564.

------. 1982. *Becoming Israeli*, New York: Praeger Publishers.

------. 1995. *Immigration and Identity: The Resettlement and Impact of SovietImmigrants on Israeli Politics and Society, A Research Report,* Los Angeles: Wilstein Institute.

Goldstein, Ken, and Zvi Gitelman. 2004. "From 'Russians' to Israelis?" In Asher Arian and Michal Shamir, eds. *The Elections in Israel 2003.* New York: SUNY Press, 245-260.

Heller, Mikhail. 1988. *Cogs in the Wheel: The Formation of Soviet Man,* New York: Alfred A. Knopf.

Horowitz, Tamar. 2003. "The Increasing Political Power of Immigrants from the Soviet Union in Israel: From Passive Citizenship to Active Citizenship." *International Migration* 41(1): 45–71.

------. 1996. *Between Three Political Cultures: the Immigrants from the Former USSR in Israel.* Jerusalem: The Hebrew University of Jerusalem [Hebrew].

------, and Eliezer Leshem. 1998. "Immigrants from the Former USSR in Israel's Cultural Domain," in Moshe Sicron and Elazar Leshem, eds. *A Portrait of Immigration: the Process of Integration of Immigrants from the Former USSR 1990–1995.* Jerusalem: Magnes Press [Hebrew].

Lapin, Nikolay I. 2004. "How the Citizens of Russia Feel and What They are Striving for." *Russian Social Science Review* 6(6): 4–21.

Levada, Yuri A. 2000. "Soviet Man Ten Years Later, 1989–1999." *Russian Social Science Review* 41(1): 4–28.

Reisinger, William M., Arthur H. Miller, Vicki L. Hesli, and Kristen H. Maher. 1994. "Political Values in Russia, Ukraine and Lithuania: Sources and Implications for Democracy." *British Journal of Political Science* 24(2): 183–223.

Shamir, Michal, and Asher Arian, 1999. "Collective Identity and Electoral Competition in Israel." *The American Political Science Review* 93(2): 265–277.

Shestopal, Elena B. 1997. "The Prospects of Democracy in Russian's Minds." *Russian Social Science Review* 38(5): 4–30.

White, Stephen, Richard Rose, and Ian McAllister. 1997. *How Russia Votes,* Chatham, NJ: Chatham House Publishers, Inc.

Гозман, Леонид Я., и Елена Б. Шестопал, 1996. Политическая психология, Ростов на Дону: Феникс. (Gozman, Leonid and Elena B. Shestopal. 1996. Political Psychology)

Гудков, Лев, 2004. Негативная идентичность: Статьи 1997–2002 годов, Москва: Новое литературное обозрение, ВЦИОМ-А. (Gudkov, Lev. 2004. Negative Identity: Articles 1997–2000)

Левада, Юрий А., 2000. От мнений к пониманию: Социологические очерки 1993–2000, Москва: Московская школа политических исследований. (Levada, Yuri A. 2001 From Opinions to Understanding: Sociological Articles 1993 -2000)

Резниковский, Гари, «Русским» в Израиле обидно за державу, 1 февраля 2001 (Reznikovsky, Gary. 2001. The Russians in Israel Yearn to be a Big Power, http://news. bbc.co.uk)

Фельдман, Элиэзер, 2003. Русский Израиль: между двух полюсов, Москва: Маркет ДС, Академическая серия. (Feldman, Eliezer. 2003. Russian Israel: Between Two Extremes)

The Arab Minority in Israel and the Seventeenth Knesset Elections: The Beginning of a New Era?[1]

Elie Rekhess

1. Introduction

This article addresses the question of whether the voting patterns of Arabs in Israel—reflected in the results of Arab sector voting in the elections to the Seventeenth Knesset—attest to an essential shift in the nature of the political activity of the Arab minority, or whether the patterns of the past remain relevant for the 2006 elections.

Voting pattern characteristics are discussed below in the context of the current changes affecting the Arab minority in Israel in three areas: politics, national identity, and socio-economic conditions.

In the sphere of politics, the article discusses the ongoing exclusion of the Arab population from the political system, particularly, those unwritten principles and procedures that render ineffective the representation of Arabs in the executive and the political arena, and their impact on their voting patterns. These effects are manifest in the ineffectiveness of Arab representation in the Knesset, the trust crisis between Arab Knesset Members and their voting public, and factionalism within Arab politics preventing the formation of a united front.

In the sphere of national identity, the article examines national-religious changes which are reshaping the processes of "Palestinization" and "Israelization" for Israeli Arabs. These developments are manifest on several levels: the debate centering on the nature of the state and on propositions for alternatives models; the coalescing self-identity of this group as a national minority possessing collective rights; the initiation of a debate on "the 1948 files"; the growing strength of the Islamic trend; and the changing patterns of public protest. These factors have left a clear imprint on party politics in Arab society.

Concerning the socio-economic sphere, the article reviews the increasing frustration of the Arab population in light of the growing disparity between Jews and Arabs (manifest in land shortages, a lack of infrastructure and industrialization, and economic stagnation), the government's incompetence in dealing with the socio-economic needs of the Arab public, and the its enduring policy of discrimination and deprivation toward this population.

In the discussion below, we examine how these developments are reflected in the seventeenth Knesset elections, and discuss the significance of typical voting patterns within Arab society (Cohen, 2006; Ghanem and Ozacky-Lazar, 1999, 2001; Kaufman and Israeli, 1999; Jamal, 2002; Neuberger, 1996, 1998; Rouhana et al., 2003, 2004), focusing on three perspectives: political parties, election results, and voters. The issue of political participation is discussed extensively, in view of the far-reaching and significant developments that occurred in this area.

2. Political Parties

Two Arab parties competed for the votes of the Arab and Druze population in the 2006 elections: The National Democratic Assembly (NDA, "Balad") and the joint list of the United Arab List and the Arab Movement for Change (UAL-AMC). The UAL comprised the Arab Democratic Party (ADP, "Mada") and the Southern Faction of the Islamic Movement. A joint Jewish-Arab party, the Democratic Front for Peace and Equality (DFPE, "Hadash") was also a contender in these elections. Other parties participating in the election in the Arab sector were Zionist-Jewish parties, primarily Labor, Kadima, Meretz-Yahad, Shas, and Likud.

NDA was headed by the team that led the party in the 2003 elections: Dr. Azmi Bishara, Dr. Jamal Zahalka, and Wasil Taha.[2] The party's platform primarily focused on the national and civil rights of the Israeli Arabs. The party called to transform the State of Israel into a state "of all its citizens," equalize the civil rights of Arabs and Jews, recognize the Israeli-Palestinians as a national minority entitled to the minority rights stipulated in UN declarations, and recognize the right of the Palestinian public in Israel to establish an autonomous administration to handle with their unique affairs, chief among them education. The land issue received special emphasis: NDA demanded to cease all expropriation of land, grant recognition to unrecognized Arab villages, and resolve the issue of the "internal refugees," including their right to return to their ruined villages, and finally, it called to promote initiatives to establish new Arab settlements on state land.[3]

UAL-AMC and DFPE lists underwent fundamental changes since the previous elections. The collaboration between DFPE and AMC, Dr. Ahmad Tibi's party, collapsed following a bitter disagreement between the partners over the order of the candidates on the joint ticket. Following this rift, the DFPE council, for internal-party reasons, chose Knesset Member Muhammad Barakeh to head the party, with Dr. Hanna Swaid in second place, replacing Knesset Member Issam Makhoul, while assigning a Jewish candidate, Dov Khenin, to third place, which had been occupied in the 2003 elections by AMC leader, MK Ahmad Tibi. Tibi was slated for the fourth place, which was not certain to be won, and when DFPE refused to accede to Tibi's demand to reinstate him in third place, he dissolved the partnership with DFPE and allied himself with UAL.

The DFPE thus entered the elections as an independent ticket with no partners.[4] The first places on the ticket were assigned to two Arab candidates and one Jewish candidate.[5] Loyal to its socialist outlook, the party platform stressed the struggle for social rights and welfare issues (protecting the standard of living and working conditions of workers, raising the minimum wage, combating unemployment, supporting national pension legislation, ensuring equal opportunities, and promoting health, education, accommodation, welfare, cultural and sports services). A separate section of the manifesto was devoted to equal rights for the Arab population (recognition as a national minority, cessation of land expropriations and the demolition of houses; enactment of the Basic Laws: Human Rights legislature; combating ethnic discrimination; affirmative action and equalization of budgets; industrialization; and issues concerning the Muslim waqf). The party platform also demanded the promotion of peace between Israel and the Palestinians.[6]

UAL-AMC was transformed: The party's ticket was headed by Sheikh Ibrahim Sarsur, a member of the Southern Faction of the Islamic Movement who replaced MK Abd Al-Malik Dehamshe. Second on its ticket was MK Ahmad Tibi, ADP's representative MK Talab A-Sana was third, Abbas Zakur of the Islamic Movement was fourth, and Salman Abu Ahmad, another representative of the Islamic Movement was fifth.[7]

Like the platforms of the other Arab parties, UAL-AMC's manifesto focused on the issue of the Palestinians and peace, and the status of Israel's Arab citizens, demanding that they be recognized as a national minority. The party, which stressed the need for Israel to be a democratic country, a country of "all its citizens," called to amend the "racist Law of Return." UAL-AMC also emphasized those issues highlighted by the other Arab parties: land, construction and housing, national insurance, welfare and health, and education and teaching.[8]

The platform propounded by UAL-AMC was unique in its demand to liberate Islamic waqf property (religious endowments), which was a reflection of the dominant position of the Islamic Movement in the party. In addition to the call to restore administration of waqf property to the Muslims, the platform called to support the Supreme Council of the Muslims in Israel, founded in 2001, and grant judicial independence to the Shari'a courts.[9]

One Druze and three Arab candidates appeared on the Labor party ticket: Nadia Hilu in 15th place (as the women's representative), MK Ghaleb Majadle in nineteenth place, Shakib Shannan, a Druze, in twentieth place, and Hasib Abud, a Christian, in twenty-ninth place.

The Labor party platform included a section on "the Arab citizens of Israel," containing a general statement on the need to introduce fundamental changes in government policy, with an emphasis on complete equality between Arab and Jewish citizens. According to the party platform, the state should reduce the disparities in education, employment, industry, infrastructure, health, welfare, and social services.[10]

The party's election campaign focused on three main issues: the first was its commitment to improve the situation of Arabs in Israel by increasing the special budgets for the Arab sector and mixed Arab-Jewish towns, establishing centers of technology-intensive industry, especially for women,[11] ending the discrimination against Arab municipalities, and resolving obstacles to the employment of Arab academics.[12] The second issue reflected the party's desire to address the trust crisis of its Arab supporters, that grew particularly strong during Ehud Barak's term as Prime Minister (when the events of October 2000 took place), through a commitment to change its previous policies and receive guidance from a new, younger leadership.[13] Third was the issue of the Arab parties themselves, which the Labor party criticized, claiming that they had no accomplishment they could point to in improving the conditions of the Arab population.

Meretz-Yahad placed its Arab candidate, Issawi Freij of Kfar Qassem, in seventh place on its ticket. Issues concerning Arab citizens were given more space in this party's manifesto than in that of any other Zionist party. The party acknowledged the unique nature of the Arab national minority in the Jewish state, and pledged to enable it to fulfill and express its own culture and language. The party also promised to work toward several goals: the immediate implementation of the Or Commission recommendations; the formulation of a comprehensive program of infrastructure development; approval of zoning plans; granting town status to Arab villages; increasing the integration of Arab citizens in business ventures and investments; granting recognition to unauthorized Arab villages; transferring the waqf to Muslim administration; and permitting Biram and Ikrit deportees to return to their homes.[14] Special attention was devoted to Arab education: the party called to establish an independent department in the Ministry of Education, modify the educational curriculum by introducing a program that became known as "Darwish instead of Tchernichovsky," and cease the "shameful" intervention by the Security Services in appointments and curricular decision of the Arab schools.[15]

Kadima's activities among the Arab population focused on the figure of Deputy Minister of Education, MK Majalli Wahbee, who headed the party's "non-Jewish sector" campaign. At the start of the election campaign, the party negotiated with several prominent figures in the Arab sector, most of them municipal leaders. However, when the list of candidates was concluded, not a single Arab had been placed in the first forty spots, possibly because of fears that this would discourage support by potential Jewish voters. Wahbee, who was in the eighteenth position, claimed to be representing the entire Arab population, but his statements failed to win public trust. As election day drew nearer, the heads of Arab municipalities whose names had been mentioned as possible candidates for Kadima's ticket hastened to dissociate themselves from the party.[16] Harsh criticism was directed at MK Ruhama Avraham, who during a visit to Qalansawa, remarked, "Those Arabs who vote (for Kadima) will benefit from unmatched priority, preference, and government support."[17]

The platform of the Shas party reflected its patronage status and benefactor of the Arab sector when the party was in power. Party leader, MK Eli Yishai, and the individual responsible for the Arab sector, David Azulai, repeatedly pledged the party's commitment to action, especially in the area of social welfare.[18]

The issue of women's participation in the elections for the Seventeenth Knesset underscored the gap between awareness of the needs of Arab women and their actual incorporation into the political arena. The Arab parties devoted large sections of their platforms to the status of women: in section 7 of its platform, DFPE pledged to "guarantee equality for women in every sphere," including enactment of a Basic Law: Equality of Women; guarantee work for unemployed women; fully enforce laws against domestic violence; increase women's representation and reinforce their status in all local authorities and institutions. In section 9 of its manifesto, UAL-AMC promised to improve the status of women in all areas of life, specifically: end discrimination, establish day-care centers, prevent violence, and promote family unification legislation. In section 6 of its manifesto, NDA pledged to work to achieve equality for women and protection of women's rights.[19]

Arab political activists spoke extensively about the need to bring Arab women into politics, but despite numerous declarations and statements, little was done in practice. However, although the Arab parties continued to exclude women from achievable positions on their tickets, some shift in the parties' awareness of this issue nevertheless became apparent in the 2006 elections, as female activists made considerable efforts to break through the barrier of gender-based exclusion. Not a single female candidate was placed in any of the first ten positions of the UAL-AMC ticket, [20] but several women in NDA and DFPE did compete for a winnable position. Hanin Zuabi, a member of NDA's political council and the director of I'lam, the Palestinian media center in Israel,[21] was a contender for the third spot on the party's ticket, but was unsuccessful. Inas Oda Haj was given the unrealistic ninth place on the NDA ticket.

The most intense battles were fought in DFPE, where five women played a prominent role: Aida Touma-Suleiman, Manal Shalabi, Attorney Taghreed Shabita, Abir Kobti, and Khulud Badawi.[22] Aida Touma-Suleiman, a veteran activist, withdrew from the contest for second place in favor of MK Issam Makhoul and Dr. Hanna Swaid, apparently in an attempt to secure the election of the latter.[23] Rising to the challenge, Tira resident Taghreed Shabita competed for first place against the front runner, MK Muhammad Barakeh, and won an impressive 35 percent of the votes (Shabita, 2003). In another spirited campaign, Manal Shalabi competed for fourth place against Dr. Afu Aghbariya from Umm Al-Fahm and was supported by 40 percent of the DFPE council members.[24] Shalabi was eventually awarded the fifth spot on the DFPE ticket, while Dr. Edna Zaritzky-Toledano was placed in tenth place.[25]

Hussniya Jabara, the first Arab woman ever elected to the Knesset in 1999 represented left-wing Zionist party, Meretz. In 2006, another Arab woman, Nadia Hilu of Jaffa, was elected to the Knesset after being given the fifteenth spot on the Labor party ticket. However, she was placed in a realistic position as a representative of women rather than a representative of the Arab population per se.

Thus, no real change in women's participation occurred in 2006, and the trend to marginalize women, which had already been discussed by Rouhana, Saleh, and Sultany (2003; 39–41), persisted. Nonetheless, there was evidence of a growing appreciation of the need to assign places for women.[26]

The election threshold was a cause of concern for the Arab parties. Although all eventually reached the threshold, their success was more than slightly due to the national turnout in Israel. The low turnout in the Jewish sector acted in their favor. A higher turnout of Jewish voters would have increased the threshold of representation, adversely affecting the Arab parties, which were certainly aware of the danger.

Already at an early stage of the election campaign, Arab parties were alarmed by the fear of failing to obtain a sufficient number of votes for representation in the Knesset.[27] Apparently believing that the Zionist parties posed the greatest danger to them, the Arab parties conducted a vigorous campaign to prevent votes from draining to Zionist parties. Their fears may have originated in the expectations of the Arab public, fed at an early stage in the campaign by the Labor party—whose leader, Amir Peretz, "promised the moon and the stars" to the Arab sector—and by Kadima's negotiations with a large number of Arab leaders, concerning the allocation of a realistic spot on the party's ticket to an Arab candidate.

In any case, while the internal disputes between DFPE and NDA, or between UAL-AMC and the others, did not disappear, they subsided to some extent, as all the parties worked to exert moral pressure on voters to remain loyal to the nationalist cause and not vote for "the Zionists." The Arab Knesset Members spoke effusively on this point: "We must foil the schemes of the Zionist parties and prevent them…from stealing our votes. A vote for the Zionist parties is immoral and illegitimate" (MK Jamal Zahalka);[28] "There are those who are trying to restore the plague of the Zionist parties to our villages" (MK Azmi Bishara);[29] "Do not forget that Sharon, Hanegbi, and Olmert were the ones who slaughtered our people and who are Judaizing the Galilee" (MK Ahmad Tibi);[30] "The Zionists are appropriating our land, killing our sons, and destroying our homes, and do not hesitate to accuse the victim" (MK Muhammad Barakeh).[31]

Election propaganda was mobilized to promote this effort. NDA, for example, published a sarcastic election poster, modeled on a wanted ad by a Zionist party seeking an Arab candidate with thick skin, with a sense of inferiority, willingness to submit to oppressors and the capacity to tolerate racism; "knowledge of Arabic not necessary," the ad said.[32] "If your vote is Zionist, who are you?"

an NDA election slogan asked. "If you vote for Zionism, you are putting a Jewish MK in the Knesset," stated another slogan. One of NDA's most popular sketches depicted a camel dawdling along and saying: "They say I should vote for a Zionist party. No way! I'm a camel, not an ass!"[33]

The "Arab" parties' fear of the "Zionist" parties may have been justified at the start of the election campaign, but the election campaign against these parties continued in full force even as the prestige of Labor and Kadima in the Arab sector declined as time went by. In their campaign, the Arab parties adopted a sophisticated strategy that condemned voting for Zionist parties and simultaneously attempted to tarnish the reputation of the establishment, claiming that it had committed the "original sin" and was responsible for all the hardship and misery of the Arab society in Israel. Up to the final minutes of election day, the Arab parties made a concerted effort to encourage voters to go to the polling booth.[34] Some people mocked the Arab parties, noting the paradox of a situation in which loyal representatives of the Palestinian-national factions preached against the Zionist parties but did everything they could "to return to the Knesset—the holy of holies of Zionism and the symbol of the revival of the Jewish people."[35]

In terms of political cohesion the political behavior of Arabs in Israel was characterized by fragmentation and factionalism (Cohen, 2006; 177–180), the source of the fluctuations which have repeatedly traumatized the Arab political system from one election campaign to the next. Since the early 1980s, voices have called to unite the ranks and establish a united Arab bloc to stand for election as a solid, cohesive entity able to amass Arab votes. The object was to prevent fragmentation and a subsequent loss of votes by establishing a single grouping of Arab Knesset Members that might achieve twelve seats, allowing the parties to leverage their influence in the foci of decision making.

The issue of joining forces assumed special significance in the seventeenth Knesset elections in view of the fact that the election threshold was raised to 2 percent. The equation was clear: forming a united party would decisively remove the sword hanging over the heads of the independent Arab parties and guarantee proper representation to the Arab public in the Knesset.

The Arab public continued to express its yearning and unreserved support for internal cohesion. A poll conducted by Tel Aviv University in late November 2005 indicated that 60 percent of voters would vote for a united Arab party. When respondents were asked to state the factors behind Arab politicians' failure to unite, 50 percent cited personal interests rather than ideological differences as the main cause. Another 34 percent believed that the reason was disagreement over candidates' order on the united ticket. Combining these categories, 84 percent of the interviewees believed that one of these two factors was the main cause of disunity. Only 10 percent of the interviewees felt that the disunity was grounded in ideology.[36]

Reverberations of the disappointment resulting from the failure to establish internal cohesion were also audible in public discourse. The call for unity became "a worn-out slogan, reflecting the political bankruptcy of some of the forces and factions active in the Arab arena," accused Zuheir Andreus, editor of the Israeli-Arab paper, *Kul Al-Arab*.[37] Dr. Muhammad Amara, a lecturer at Bar-Ilan University, joined in the criticism, claiming that the Arab parties knew fragmentation would lead to meager Arab representation in national politics yet nonetheless failed to achieve the desired unity. The result, he said, was an increase in the number of Arabs who doubted the value of electoral participation: "If our political participation is very limited, why should we participate at all?" he concluded.[38]

The aspirations of the Arab public fell on deaf ears. The possibility of forming a united front was discussed at the beginning of the election campaign, but it soon became apparent that these attempts were doomed to fail. Three separate lists ran for election. In addition, the "National Arab Party," led by Muhammad Kan'an, and the "Progressive National Alliance" party, headed by Hashim Mahameed, both negotiated with the existing parties, but ultimately found themselves out of game entirely. MK Ahmad Tibi also negotiated: initially he fought to retain his status within the alliance with DFPE, and only when he realized he would have to relinquish his place in favor of a Jewish candidate, he surprised everyone by partnering with *UAL*. Such actions, not unlike a game of "musical chairs," contributed to the public contempt directed toward the issue of unification.

3. Election Results

As previously mentioned, the Arab parties as well as the single Arab-Jewish party crossed the election threshold and gained representation in the Knesset. NDA retained its former strength: it received 71,299 votes in 2003, and 72,066 in 2006, an increase of 767 votes (a 1 percent increase). Its share of the total votes for the three major parties representing the Arab population (NDA, DFPE, and UAL-AMC) declined from 30.9 percent in 2003 to 28.4 percent in 2006 (see table 1 below). Nationally, (excluding the mixed towns), the party won 20.2 percent of the Arab-Druze votes in 2006, compared with 20.9 percent in 2003 (see table 2 below). NDA needed a vote-allocation agreement with DFPE to secure a third representative.

DFPE lost 7,727 votes, and fell from 93,819 votes in 2003 to 86,092 in 2006, an 8.3 percent decline. Its relative share of the votes for the three major parties declined from 40.6 percent in 2003 to 34 percent in 2006. Nationally, DFPE dropped from 28.3 percent in 2003 to 23.2 percent in 2006. It nevertheless gained three Knesset seats, proving that a Jewish candidate on the ticket did not deter Arab voters, and that the appeal of an Arab-Jewish ticket was still valid. Indeed, DFPE—containing the core of Maki (The Israeli Communist Party) veterans—once again proved its organizational power.

UAL-AMC—the successful combination of ADP, the Islamic Movement (Southern Faction), and AMC—secured a significant achievement. Its voting base rose from 65,551 in 2003 to 94,786 in 2006, an imposing 44.6 percent increase. Nationally, its share rose from 20 percent of the total vote in 2003 to 27.8 percent in 2006, and it sent four representatives to the Knesset. The success of UAL-AMC stemmed from its message of unity, an ideal which the Arab public longed to realize, as well as from the regional focus of its operations in the Triangle. Its success also reflected the growing dominance of the Islamic Movement.

Table 1
The Distribution of Votes Between UAL-AMC, DFPE, and
NDA in the 2003 and 2006 Elections

Party	2003 elections		2006 elections	
	Votes	%	Votes	%
UAL-AMC	65,551	28.4	94,786	37.5
DFPE	93,819	40.7	86,092	34.0
NDA	71,299	30.9	72,066	28.5

SOURCE: Based on data from the Knesset website: http://www.knesset.gov.il/elections17/heb/cec/CecIndex.asp

Note: data does not include votes of Arabs residing in towns with mixed Jewish-Arab population.

Table 2
Results of the Elections in the Arab and Druze Sectors in the 2003 and 2006
Elections (percent)

Party	2003 elections	2006 elections
UAL-AMC	20.0	27.4
DFPE	28.3	24.3
NDA	20.9	20.2
Labor	8.8	12.8
Kadima	–	6.8
Shas	3.6	2.9
Meretz	4.8	2.8
Likud	4.1	0.9
Religious parties and others	9.5	1.9

SOURCE: Based on data from the Knesset website: http://www.knesset.gov.il/elections17/heb/cec/CecIndex.asp

Note: the figures do not include the votes of Arabs residing in towns with mixed Jewish-Arab population.

Smaller political parties also participated in the 2006 elections. "The Progressive National Alliance," headed by former Knesset Member, Hashim Mahameed was one such party. Initially, Mahameed sent signals to DFPE, NDA, and the southern faction of the Islamic Movement, proposing collaboration based on the votes he believed he would gain (in the 2003 election he received 20,571 votes but failed to reach the election threshold). After his overtures were rejected and his hopes of standing for election on a joint ticket were dashed, Mahameed announced that he would run on an independent ticket. In the end, however, he dropped out of the race and encouraged his supporters to vote for NDA.[39]

Another party that entered the political fray was the "Arab National Party," headed by the former ADP Knesset Member, Muhammad Hassan Kan'an. Its leader held talks with NDA, with the Islamic Movement, and with Hashim Mahameed, but eventually he, too, dropped out of the race.[40] Another group which competed, receiving 3,692 votes, was the "Democratic Action Organization" (Da'am), headed by Asmaa Aghbariya.[41]

The success of the Arab parties contrasts with the limited achievements of the Zionist parties. At the outset of the election campaign, considerable credit was given to Labor and Kadima. According to one survey undertaken at the end of November 2005, Labor, under the leadership of Peretz, was expected to win 33 percent of the votes of the Arab sector (compared with 8.8 percent in 2003) and Kadima—10.7 percent.[42] These figures reflected the high expectations held by sections of the Arab public of Amir Peretz, who promised to promote negotiations with the Palestinians, implement an egalitarian policy regarding the Arabs in Israel, include them in the government coalition, and even to appoint an Arab minister. Kadima, on the other hand, negotiated intensively with several Arab leaders, primarily from the municipal sector, on their placement in realistic positions on the party ticket.

However, as election day approached, the Arab public became disenchanted. In 2003 Amir Peretz's Am Ehad party received 6.5 percent of the votes of the Arab population (excluding residents of mixed Jewish-Arab towns). Labor successfully increased its support in the 2006 elections and won 12.8 percent of the Arab vote, compared with 8.8 percent in 2003. The combined votes of Am Ehad and Labor in the 2003 election amounted to 15 percent of the Arab vote, and therefore the 12.8 percent won by Labor, headed by Peretz in 2006, reflected a decline.

The proportion of votes for Kadima was also relatively small—6.8 percent—while Likud plummeted to an unprecedented low of 0.9 percent. Presumably, a large part of the votes it received in 2003 (4.1 percent) shifted to Kadima in 2006.

Meretz-Yahad lost almost half the votes it had obtained in 2003. The share of the votes captured by the party dropped from 4.8 percent in 2003 to 2.8 percent in 2006. The party's Arab candidate, Issawi Freij claimed that his placement as number seven on the ticket, which reflected the deep fissure in trust between Arab voters and the Jewish leftist parties, had adverse repercussions on voting.[43]

The total outcome of these developments was that the Zionist-Jewish parties lost about 3 percent of their support among Arab voters, who switched to the Arab parties. The ratio of 69:31 percent which prevailed in 2003 shifted to 72:28 percent in 2006.

This outcome highlighted the growing strength of the Arab and the Jewish-Arab blocs in the Knesset at the expense of the bloc supporting the Zionist lists. In 1965, for example, the Zionist parties and their affiliated minority lists won 78.4 percent of the Arab vote, while 23.1 percent of votes went to Maki or the New Communist List (Rakah). In 1973, the Zionist parties and their supporting minority lists won 62.8 percent of the vote, while Rakah obtained 36.9 percent. The balance shifted only in 1977: the Zionist and minorities parties received only 46.6 percent of the vote, while Rakah won 50.6 percent (Neuberger, 1998; 121).

In the final analysis, total Arab representation in the Knesset remained unchanged: the Seventeenth Knesset has nine Arab Knesset Members in Arab and joint Arab-Jewish parties: four in UAL-AMC (Sheikh Ibrahim, Sarsur Abdullah, Dr. Ahmad Tibi, Talab A-Sana, and Sheikh Abbas Zakur), three in NDA (Dr. Azmi Bishara, Dr. Jamal Zahalka, and Wasil Taha), two in DFPE (Muhammad Barakeh and Dr. Hanna Swaid; the third MK is a Jew, Dov Khenin). There are also three Arab and Druze MKs in Jewish-Zionist parties: two in Labor (Nadia Hilu and Ghaleb Majadle), and a Druze MK (Majalli Wahbee) in Kadima, totaling twelve Arab Knesset Members, similar to their total number in the previous Knesset.

To sum up, election results in the Arab and Druze sectors show no indication of any fundamental shift. In the competition between the Arab parties (including DFPE) and the Zionist parties, the former increased their strength, but there was no change in the internal Arab political structure as a whole. NDA, DFPE, and UAL-AMC no doubt heaved a sigh of relief when they crossed the election threshold, but voters were critical, and there was no sense of victory or triumph among the Arab population when election results were published. On

Table 3
Distribution of Arab Votes for Arab and Zionist-Jewish Parties in the 2003 and 2006 Elections (percent)

Parties	2003 elections	2006 elections
Arab	69	72
Jewish-Zionist	31	28

SOURCE: Based on data from the Knesset website: http://www.knesset.gov.il/elections17/heb/cec/CecIndex.asp

Table 4
Number of Arab and Druze Knesset Members in Parties, 1992–2006

	1992	1996	1999	2003	2006
DFPE	2 + 1*	2 + 1	2 + 1	2	2 + 1
NDA		2	1	3	3
UAL		4	5	2	3
ADP	2				
AMC			1	1	1
Labor	3	3	2	2	2
Likud	1		1	2	
Kadima					1
Meretz	1	1	1		
Total	9 + 1	12 + 1	13 + 1	12	12 + 1

* Two Arab and one Jewish Knesset Members SOURCE: Based on data from the Knesset website: http://www.knesset.gov.il/elections17/heb/cec/CecIndex.asp

the contrary, many spoke of defeat and failure. Wadi' Awawda, for example, mocked the parties' self-declared achievements, which he defined as "no more than a feeble attempt to sweep their mistakes under the rug."[44] Lutfi Mashour similarly commented "These elections cannot be considered a success but rather a complete failure and a tangible danger [because] over 40 percent of Arabs did not vote.... The fact that they abstained from voting is a clear strong-minded declaration of disillusionment with our representatives in the Knesset."[45]

4. Voting Patterns

Geographical region and locale both had a significant impact on election results. Benjamin Neuberger (1998: 130–131; see also Cohen, 2006; 195–199) discusses the "the local boy" phenomenon in his book, and the role of the "personal factor" in voting. If a candidate in a given locale represents one of the parties, it is reasonable to assume that this party will gain more votes than the others. For example, the dramatic drop in support for Labor in Sakhnin, from 33 percent in 1981 to 10 percent in 1984, is explained by the village's protest over the elimination of their local candidate, Hamad Khalaile, from the party's ticket. Another example is provided by the 1992 election, when Iksal resident Abd Al-Wahab Darawshe headed ADP. Forty-four percent of the vote in that village was for ADP, whereas on the national level the party received 15 percent of the vote.

This phenomenon recurred in the 2006 elections, as indicated by the voting results in the southern and central areas of the Triangle, shown in Table 5, below.

Table 5
Results of the Arab Vote in the 2006 Elections in the Southern and Central Triangle, Compared with the Vote on the National Level (percent)

	UAL AMC	DFPE	NDA	Labor	Kadima	Meretz
Triangle	41.9	18.0	20.7	8.4	3.1	6.0
National	27.4	24.3	20.2	12.8	6.8	2.8

SOURCE: Based on data from the Knesset website: http://www.knesset.gov.il/elections17/heb/cec/CecIndex.asp

Locales examined: Kfar Qassem, Kfar Bara, Jaljuliya, Taibeh, Tira, Qalansawa, Baqa Al-Gharbiya, Jatt, Kfar Qara, Arara-'Ara.

UAL-AMC received considerable support in the Triangle area, especially from its southern sections, where two of its leaders, Sheikh Ibrahim Sarsur (Kfar Qassem) and Dr. Ahmad Tibi (Taibeh) reside. UAL-AMC gained considerable strength in 2006 in areas in the Triangle where it had been weak in the 2003 election. This is evident from voting data for Baka Al-Gharbiya: in 2003 UAL received 9 percent, and in 2006 32.1 percent. NDA, on the other hand, received 40.9 percent there in 2003, and 26.9 percent in 2006.

Table 6
The "Local Boy" Vote

	2003		2006		
	Total votes for ticket	Share of votes for ticket of all valid votes	Total votes for ticket	Share of votes for ticket of all valid votes	Percentage change in total voters for ticket
Umm Al-Fahm (DFPE candidate)	1,922	15.5%	7,044	57.3%	336 +
Taibeh (UAL-AMC candidate)	2,263	20.3%	6,080	51.4%	268 +
Kfar Qassem (UAL-AMC candidate)	1,510	23.8%	4,000	52.5%	264 +

SOURCE: Knesset website:
http://www.knesset.gov.il/elections16/heb/results/CitiesName.asp
http://www.knesset.gov.il/elections17/heb/results/Result17.xls

Umm Al-Fahm is another clear example of the "local boy" phenomenon. DFPE obtained the overwhelming majority of votes in the town because one of its local residents, Dr. Afu Aghbariya,[46] was in the fourth spot on its ticket. It won 7,044 votes, compared with 1,922 in 2003 (an increase of 366 percent). The same happened in Ahmad Tibi's town of Taibeh: the number of votes for UAL-AMC rose from 2,263 in 2003 to 6,080 in 2006 (a 268 percent increase), and in Kfar Qassem (Sarsur's home town) the vote increased from 1,510 to 4,000 (a 264 percent increase).

What is distinctive about the sectoral or religious-ethnic vote is that among certain population groups, parties gain a share that is significantly higher or lower than national shares. The Bedouin, for example, traditionally voted for the ruling party, while the Druze, many of whom serve in the defense forces, tend to vote for Zionist parties, especially Likud (see Neuberger, 1996: 14–16; Cohen, 2006: 199–200, 206–211). Table 7 below shows the voting pattern of the Bedouin in the South.

In 2006, the Bedouin vote was characterized by massive support for UAL-AMC. Compared with the achievements of ADP-UAL in 1996, UAL ticket lost 9 percent of its support, although the Bedouin of the South still expressed

Table 7
Distribution of Votes of Bedouin in the South in Four Elections,
1996–2006 (percent)

	UAL	UAL AMC	NDA	DFPE	Kadima	Labor	Likud	Meretz
1996	64.3	–	–	2.3	–	14.9	1.5	5.1
1999	54.3	–	6.2	4.3	–	9.7	0.9	7.2
2003	28.8	–	8.1	7.3	–	5.0	1.6	2.8
2006	–	55.7	10.5	7.2	8.2	10.9	0.7	1.0

SOURCE: The data for the 1996 and 1999 elections are taken from Ghanem and Ozacky-Lazar, 1999, p. 45; the data for the 2003 election are from the Knesset website: http://www.knesset.gov.il/elections16/heb/results/CitiesName.asp
The data for the 2006 election are from the Knesset website: http://www.knesset.gov.il/elections17/heb/results/Result17.xls

The data for the 2003 and 2006 elections is based on the Bedouin vote in the permanent Bedouin settlements (Rahat, Tel-Sheva, Lakia, Hura, Segev-Shalom, Ksafia, and Ar'ara in the Negev) and on the vote of the scattered Bedouin tribes: Abu-Korinat, Abu-Juway'ad, Abu-Rubay'a, Abu-Rukayk, Al-Atrash, Al-Asad, Al-A'asam, Janabib, Huwashla, Al-Huzail, Mas'udin Al-Azazma, Nasasra, Al-Sayyed, Al-Atawna, Al-Uqbi, Kabua, Kudeirat Al-Sana, Qawa'in, Tarabin Al-Sana, Qasr A-Sirr (2006 only), Darijat (2006 only), Umm Batin (2006 only).

noticeable support for the Islamic Movement (Southern Faction) and AMC: together these parties garnered 55.7 percent of the Bedouin vote. This achievement stemmed from the strong influence of the Islamic Movement in the southern region, as well as from the fact that MK Talab A-Sana comes from this area. The success of the UAL-AMC ticket among the Bedouin is even more pronounced when compared with its achievements in other sectors: only 2.3 percent of the Druze vote, as described below, and 27.4 percent of the national vote.

Concurrently, NDA and DFPE gained a sizeable share of the votes of the Bedouin in the South—a total of 17.7 percent, compared with 10.5 percent in 1999, reflecting a strengthening nationalist element.

Compared with the Bedouin, data for the Druze vote indicate that the tendency of this group to vote for Zionist parties is stronger than its tendency to vote for Arab parties, and in this respect there has been no change over time (see Table 8, below). Kadima garnered considerable support among the Druze in 2006, gaining 21.9 percent of the vote thanks to the spirited efforts of MK Majalli Wahbee. Support for Kadima came at the expense of Likud, whose share dropped from 12.2 percent to 2.2 percent. Support for Labor also increased from 19.8 to 30.8 percent, but the Druze representative, Shakib Shannan, who was given the twentieth spot, was not elected to the Knesset.

The Arab parties performed poorly in the Druze community: UAL-AMC gained 2.3 percent of the vote, DFPE 6.1 percent, while *NDA* soared to 9.3 percent. This has been attributed to the efforts of MK Azmi Bishara, who intervened on behalf of the Druze when he visited Syria.

Table 8
Distribution of the Druze Vote in Four Elections, 1996–2006 (percent)

	UAL	UAL-AMC	DFPE	NDA	Labor	Likud	Kadima	Meretz	Shas	Yisrael Beitenu
1996	5.1	–	14.3	–	40.3	11.7	–	12.1	4.2	–
1999	2.9	–	5.3	6.1	24.5	8.3	–	4.8	10.3	–
2003	3.0	–	4.5	4.8	19.8	12.2	–	2.4	12.4	3.2
2006	–	2.3	6.1	9.3	30.8	2.2	21.9	2.2	10.4	5.1

SOURCE: The data for the 1996 and 1999 elections are taken from Ghanem and Ozacky-Lazar, 1999, p. 45; the data for the 2003 election are from the Knesset website: http://www.knesset.gov.il/elections16/heb/results/CitiesName.asp
The data for the 2006 election are from the Knesset website: http://www.knesset.gov.il/elections17/heb/results/Result17.xls
Figures for the 2003 and 2006 elections summarize the Druze vote in the following settlements: Yanuah-Jatt, Sajur, Buq'ata, Julis, Mas'ada, Yarka, Beit Jann, Majdal Shams, Daliyat Al-Carmel, Hurfeish, Kisra-Samiya, Pequi'in (Buqai'a), Usfiya, Meghar.

5. Participation in the Elections

Election turnout of the Arab public was a major issue of concern in the 2006 election. Scholarly literature has dealt extensively with this subject (Cohen, 2006: 171–177; Jamal, 2002; Kaufman and Israeli, 1999: 114–115, 124–127). Neuberger (1998: 118–119) noted the inverse correlation that characterizes Arab society in Israel: contrary to the theory according to which democratic societies are expected to show a high correlation between modernization and

Table 9
Voting Rates in Knesset Elections, 1949–2006

Election year	Arab population	Total population
1949 (First Knesset)	69.3	86.9
1951 (Second Knesset)	85.5	75.1
1955 (Third Knesset)	91.0	82.8
1959 (Fourth Knesset)	88.9	81.6
1961 (Fifth Knesset)	85.5	83.0
1965 (Sixth Knesset)	87.8	83.0
1969 (Seventh Knesset)	82.0	81.7
1973 (Eighth Knesset)	80.0	78.6
1977 (Ninth Knesset)	75.0	79.2
1981 (Tenth Knesset)	69.7	78.5
1984 (Eleventh Knesset)	73.7	78.8
1988 (Twelfth Knesset)	73.9	79.7
1992 (Thirteenth Knesset)	69.7	77.4
1996 (Fourteenth Knesset)	77.0	79.3
1999 (Fifteenth Knesset)	75.0	78.7
2003 (Sixteenth Knesset)	62.0	68.9
2006 (Seventeenth Knesset)	56.3	63.2

SOURCE: The data for the elections between 1949 and 1992 (from the First to the Thirteenth Knesset) were taken from: Neuberger, 1996: p.3; the data for the 1996 elections (the Fourteenth Knesset) were taken from: Kaufman and Israeli, 1999, p. 126; the data for the 1999 elections (the Fifteenth Knesset) were taken from Ghanem and Ozacky-Lazar, 2001, p. 190; the data for the 2003 elections (the Sixteenth Knesset) were taken from Rouhana et al., 2003, pp. 18, 329; the data for the 2006 elections (the Seventeenth Knesset) are based on the government services and information portal:
http://www.first.gov.il/FirstGov/TopNav/Elections/EresultElections/EEElection17
and on the Knesset website:
http://www.knesset.gov.il/elections17/heb/history/PercentVotes.htm
http://www.knesset.gov.il/elections17/heb/results/Main_Result.asp

voting rates, the voting rate of Arabs in Israel was high when modernization was low: ranging from 91 percent (in 1955) to 80 percent (in 1973). Possible explanations for this are the relative backwardness of Arab society, fear of the authorities (the military government), and the mobilizing power of the clans.

The situation changed radically in subsequent years: as the level of education and the standard of living rose, voting rates declined due to heightened national-political consciousness and a sense of alienation from the state.

Only 56.3 percent, or slightly more than half of all Arab voters participated in the elections for the Seventeenth Knesset in 2006, reflecting a 6 percent decline compared to the 2003 voting rate.[47] It has already been pointed out that this is the most significant outcome of this election and, as defined by As'ad Ghanem, "an unprecedented historic turning-point."[48] Others regarded the boycott of the Knesset elections as a "mark of shame on the face of Israeli democracy, the first indication of the Arabs' lack of trust in the Knesset, a knife-thrust into the legitimacy of the (Zionist-Israeli) establishment, and an expression of disgust and anger by the Arab public."[49]

This drop in voter turnout is part of an ongoing trend: continuously from 1996, there has been a 21 percent decline in the voting rate of the Arab population in Knesset elections.

The final results of the elections in the Arab sector might divert attention from the drop in voter rate, as the achievements themselves seem impressive: all the Arab parties crossed the election threshold rather easily, gained entry to the Knesset, and representation rates did not fall during this period. However, scratching the surface of these election results reveals a different situation. The study of the declining voting rate requires a distinction between "abstaining from participating" and "boycotting." We first turn to examine the behavior and the reasons of the public that chose not to vote.

Rouhana et al. (2003: 90) maintain that in Arab society, an individual who refrains from voting actually reflects the normalization of relations with the state. They claim that voters prefer not to go to the polling booth for reasons unrelated to collective political efforts, but rather are based on their personal desire to abstain from participation in any political activity, including voting. To a great extent, non-participation of Arabs reflected indifference, weariness, and disinterest. Moreover, the decline in the Arab voting rate is not unconnected to the trend that characterized Israeli society as a whole (the national voting rate fell from 67.8 percent in 2003 to 63.2 percent in 2006).[50]

Another reason for low voter turnout was voters' disillusionment with the Arab leadership. The low voting rate signified the Arab public's protest against the Arab Knesset Members for their incompetence and inability to engender any real change in their lives (Cohen, 2006: 109–113; Ghanem [forthcoming] Jamal, 2002). Zuheir Andreus provided an accurate analysis of the mood that dominated the elections when he wrote that the Arab MKs exploited rather than defended the interests of the Arab public. Andreus claimed that the election results proved decisively that the gap between the leaders and the man in the street was widening.[51] Others went even further, maintaining that the Arab Knesset Members were, consciously or not, implementing the policy of the establishment by obstructing any approach that advocated active resistance.[52]

Another critical comment, and one which had been made in the past, was that the Arab Knesset Members neglected the campaign to improve the socio-economic conditions in favor of the national-Palestinian issue. This call was also expanded to include accusations of neglect in both spheres—everyday problems and national issues. The national struggle of the Arab Knesset Members was defined by Majid Al-Haj as a "televised struggle, a campaign conducted by digital and electronic means." He adds: "There are people whose job it is to go from one channel to another to be interviewed... It's far harder, however, to say, for example, I achieved A, B, and C on civic matters regarding legislation for greater equality" (Al-Haj, forthcoming).

The Arab Knesset Members are in fact among the most active parliamentary representatives. Some of them head the list of MKs submitting questions and motions to the agenda (Rekhess & Navot, 2006: 155–157).[53] The government coalition often needed the Arab parties' support, as with the election of the President of State, for example. But this does not alter the basic truth: Arab politicians are consistently excluded from the center of decision-making. No Arab party has ever been invited to join the coalition. As MK Ahmad Tibi noted on one occasion, "We did not even have the privilege of being able to refuse."

Nevertheless, in the 2006 election there seemed to be a strong feeling among part of the Arab public that the somewhat overused claim of "exclusion"—though recognized and acknowledged—was inadequate in explaining the MKs failure to engender socio-economic change. In other words, the Arab public yearns for change and a solution to its current dead-end situation.

The discontent with the parties also contributed to the decline in voter turnout of the Arab sector. The election campaign was characterized by a sense of disenchantment of party politics. "The parties have become hostage to their need to remain in the arena through the Knesset, and in return, refrain from any escalation in the methods of [our] struggle," was the criticism leveled by the Popular Committee for the Boycott of the Elections.[54] Many voters voiced the faults [of the Arab MKs]: the declining role of party ideology, the inefficient conduct, their lack of contacts with the grass-roots, the lack of regular activity in the regional branches or regular committee meetings, the failure of party leaders to visit the grass-roots on a regular basis, and the fact that the parties failed to adapt to the changing reality. Many condemned the use of tricks or publicity gimmicks and the appeal to the Arab populace from the television stations of Beirut or Doha. "What is needed is a special strategy," Al-Haj complained to the Arab political leadership, "to stop reacting and adopt an informed, weighed outlook [...] instead of merely using the fax and e-mail to issue declarations of condemnation."[55]

An extremely significant factor in the decline in the voting rate appears to have been the Arab population's response to the call to boycott the election. This was not a new phenomenon (Haidar, forthcoming),[56] but seems to have gathered considerable momentum in 2006. The campaign against the election was led by the Popular Committee for the Boycott of the Election, headed by Raja Aghbariya of the Sons of the Village Movement, Umm Al-Fahm branch, Attorney Wakim Wakim, head of the Association for the Defense of the Rights of the Internal Displaced Persons, and Dr. As'ad Ghanem, head of the Department of Government and Political Thought, Haifa University.

The Committee presented a detailed doctrine justifying non-participation in the elections, and by calling for the establishment of a separate parliament for Arabs in Israel, it proposed an institutional alternative.[57] The opposition to participation in the election was based primarily on "the principled national basis" which, according to the Committee, required that Arabs refrain from supporting the legitimacy of the Knesset as the representative of the state "which was founded on the ruins of our nation."[58] On a practical level, the Committee's leaders claimed that participating in the Knesset elections was futile, standing for Knesset elections was a wasted effort, and sixty years of Arab presence in the Knesset had produced no results: according to Raja Aghbariya, the appropriation of land continued, and the struggle for equality remained an empty slogan while Jewish racism intensified.[59] The Committee's leaders proposed setting up a "Higher National Council" and an Arab parliament in Israel, claiming that these institutions, as an alternative to participation in the Knesset, could be built on the foundation of the Supreme Follow-up Committee and in the framework of institutional (not territorial) autonomy of the Arabs of Israel.[60]

Another group behind the initiative to boycott the elections, albeit one that played an indirect role, was the Northern Faction of the Islamic movement, whose categorical opposition to participation in the elections had been known for some time (Neuberger, 1998: 117; Rekhess, 2000: 280–281).[61] While the leaders of the Northern Faction did not call explicitly for the boycott of the election, leaving this to individual choice, they reiterated the movement's position of opposition to such participation on the grounds of principle.[62] The head of the movement, Sheikh Ra'id Salah, said quite clearly that the Knesset was no more than an ineffective opposition platform, adding that his movement would not support any Arab candidate or ticket.[63] The movement's spokesman and mayor of Umm Al-Fahm, Sheikh Hashim Abd Al-Rahman, announced at the outset of the campaign: "The lack of Arab representation in the Knesset is no tragedy."[64] On the eve of the election, however, he declared that he intended to vote in line with the movement's current policy of neutrality and in contrast to former party policy.[65] He did in fact vote, but observers felt that this demonstrative act did not bring a massive stream of Islamic Movement supporters to the election booths, and was intended primarily to forestall accusations of causing the Arab parties to fail to cross the election threshold.[66]

Along with the analysis of the reasons for the poor turnout, an examination of the factors encouraging Arabs in Israel to vote in the elections is also warranted. Rouhana et al. (2003:92–94) employ three theories to explain the phenomenon: (a) the theory of modernization, which links the rise in voting rates to improved standard of living and education levels; (b) the theory of institutional structure, by which the structure of the institutions and the political processes in the country (such as the right to vote, the system of voting, the laws determining the rules regarding political parties, their registration and funding) determine the level of participation; (c) the agency theory, which stresses the encouragement of political participation by typical mobilization agencies (parties, movements, professional unions, religious movements, etc.). Ghanem and Ozacky-Lazar (2001) explained Arab electoral behavior based on the model of the national minority crisis in an ethnic state, and Jamal (2002) described electoral participation as an expression of communality.

Ten factors can account for the continued participation of Arabs in Israel in the game of parliamentary politics. Some are longstanding, while others have only recently coalesced.

1. A factor that is mentioned extensively in the scholarly literature is traditional clan-based loyalty or tribalism. This loyalty exerts pressure on members of a family, a clan, or a tribe to vote for the preferred candidate or party.
2. Localism or regional affiliation—this factor has been mentioned above.
3. Party loyalty—there are large groups of members and supporters who, together with their relatives, are loyal to a party. Despite the changes in party politics, these groups have remained steadfast in their loyalty to, and willingness to make sacrifices for, their parties. This attitude is typical of supporters of the Communist party and members of the Islamic Movement, for example.
4. Loyalty to the ruling establishment—this applies to individuals close to the establishment, those who are employed by government ministries or benefit from official favors. These voters are expected to vote for the ruling and Zionist parties which are likely to form the government.
5. Belief in the democratic process—this factor is more value-based and represents one aspect of the "Israelization" process. The process is grounded in the confidence that it is appropriate and advisable to influence the country's decision-making process despite the resulting cognitive dissonance, namely, acknowledgement of the limitations of Arab parliamentary representation. This factor is the result of a developing civic political consciousness among the Arabs of Israel, and its impact can be expected to increase as civic consciousness grows.
6. The identity vote, in which considerable importance is ascribed to the national Palestinian-Arab affiliation (Rouhana et al., 2003: 68). This motif figured prominently in the election campaigns of NDA and DFPE, and it was also evident in its religious connotations in the achievements of the Southern Faction of the Islamic Movement.[67]

7. The protest vote—this factor reflects the belief in the power of Arab repre-sentation in the Knesset and its effectiveness as a platform of protest. About a week before the elections, fifty leading public figures made an emotional call to the public to go to the polling booths, and in their written declaration, signatories stressed what might happen if voters refrained from voting: this would "undermine our representation as a national minority and diminish our political presence in the public arena."[68]

8. Another factor is the aspiration for inclusion and integration, which has been described by Neuberger, Ra'anan Cohen, and others. This factor remains valid today, and defines voting as an internal and external sign of belonging to Israeli society. This trend has developed since the Oslo Accords, engen-dering a synthesis between "Israelization" and "Palestinization," i.e., the feeling that Arabs are an integral part of Israel, and that is the reason for their participation in its institutions. This "Israelization" has been ascribed national-Palestinian content (Rekhess, 2002), in which abstaining from voting signals voluntary exclusion and a challenge to the state, thereby validating the criticisms leveled at the Arab population for being disloyal and separatist.

9. *Civic consciousness*—Rouhana et al. (2003: 101) have expanded on this concept at length, claiming that "most Arab citizens take their citizenship very seriously. Sending representatives to the Knesset, even if their influence is limited, is an expression of the civic connection (which the Arab citizen knows is unequal) of the Palestinian community in Israel to the state and its institutions."

10. Fear and apprehension of the implications of not voting—this factor also seems to affect the Arab public. In the context of the animated public debate on land exchange and transfer of sections of the Triangle to Palestinian con-trol, and in view of the entry of Yisrael Beiteinu, led by Avigdor Lieberman, into the political game, voting appears to be an expression of defiance, and a declaration—"We are here to stay!"

6. Conclusion

Can the elections for the Seventeenth Knesset be seen as a turning-point? The answer to this is complex and ambiguous. In some areas there was no real change or shift. Women's participation and representation in Arab politics has remained marginal, notwithstanding the growing involvement of women activ-ists and the increasing awareness of Arab parties to include women. This trend presumably will grow as women's struggle to attain appropriate representation becomes more intensive in the forthcoming elections.

Voting trends have also remained unchanged. Support for the Arab parties (NDA, Ra-am-AMC) and the joint Jewish-Arab party (DFPE) has grown to 72 percent of Arab voters (compared with 69 percent in the 2003 elections), but the basic structure of this support remains without change, apart from internal shifts in party composition. What is notable, however, is the success of the UAL-AMC bloc, which has become the foremost political stream among Israel's Arabs.

The religious-ethnic factor and the geographical base—the influence of region and locale—also continue to make their mark on voting patterns. This was evident in the 2006 elections in the tendency of the Druze population to vote for Zionist parties, in the ascendancy of the Islamic stream, expressed in the increased support for UAL-AMC in the Triangle and among the Bedouin in the south, and in the link between competing Knesset Members' area of origin and the number of votes they received. Furthermore, there are weighty factors that continue to encourage active involvement in the parliamentary life of the State of Israel, whose principal expression is voting in the Knesset elections.

Concurrently, it is possibly justified to speak of powerful changes which have shaken Arab politics. These found expression largely in debates over participation in the elections and the failure to achieve political unity. The elections for the Seventeenth Knesset, which were characterized by anxiety relating to the election threshold and the declining voting rate, clearly underscore the national-political changes in the Arab society in Israel.

The 1990s marked the beginning of a new era in the relations between Jews and Arabs in Israel. Developments in the political process between Israel and the Arab world, and the emerging peace negotiations between Israel and the Palestinians, weakened the external aspect of "Palestinization" insofar as attachment to the PLO and the Palestinians in the Territories were concerned. Israel's recognition of the PLO and the legitimate right of the Palestinians for self-determination, as well as the establishment of the Palestinian Authority, reflected a partial realization of the Palestinian-national aspirations of the Arabs of Israel, as these had been formulated in the 1970s and 1980s.

Notably, a unique synthesis emerged between Israelization and Palestinization, as a result of which the Arab national platform gradually refocused on internal issues pertaining to the legal status of the Arab-Palestinians within Israel as a national minority (Rekhess, 2002). No longer viewed by the Arabs in Israel as elements in a zero-sum game, the boundaries dividing the Israeli and Arab-Palestinian components in the national identity of the Arabs in Israel became blurred.

The results of the elections to the Seventeenth Knesset point to two contrasting trends in Arab society in Israel. Participation in the elections attests to the stability of the Israeli component of the political worldview of Arabs in Israel. At the same time, other sections of the Arab public Israel sought to establish an alternative political system of local, independent, elected Palestinian national institutions inside Israel. This latter trend reflects the increased strength of Palestinian sentiments, but—as stated—this element of their identity became focused inward to the local context.

The Islamic Movement's views have gained in strength and cannot be ignored. Its actions are taking place simultaneously in two opposing directions: on the one hand, there is the Southern Faction's demonstrative participation in the political process, to the point of its spearheading the UAL-AMC party, and on the other, the principled opposition of the Northern Faction, inspired by the rigid religious doctrine.

Also to be noted are the fragmentation and factionalism that illustrate the inherent weakness of the Arab political system. The 2006 election demonstrated that Arab society is not yet ready for the type of deep-seated internal reconciliation and unification that could considerably increase its strength. This further undermines the status of Arab politicians and the political system in the eyes of the public. If Arab politics fail to achieve internal unity and shatters the dreams of those who seek to form a united ticket; if Arab Knesset Members are unable to prove that they can change the socio-economic situation; if the parties limit themselves to a merely virtual presence—it is reasonable to assume that the Knesset will become less and less attractive to the Arabs in Israel. Perhaps only the sword of Damocles—in the form of the impending decision to raise the election threshold—can compel the Arab parties to join forces.

The possible withdrawal of the Arabs from the Knesset will undoubtedly affect Jewish-Arab relations in Israel, impacting the very foundation of the country's democratic regime. There is of course the likelihood that the Zionist parties will become the chief representatives of Arabs in Israel, but based on their conduct to date, this possibility does not seem likely. Another possible outcome is that alternative frameworks will develop to fill the void, namely, national institutions such as the Follow-Up Committee and the National Committee for the Heads of the Arab Local Authorities, extra-parliamentary movements such as the Islamic Movement, whose Northern Faction is cultivating the concept of an "self-made community" (*Al-Mujtama Al-Issami*), groups seeking to establish a representative Arab parliament, and civic welfare organizations, such as the non-governmental organizations, amongst them Adalah, Mossawa, Ittijah, and others.

Notes

1. This article is based on a lecture given by the author at Tel Aviv University on June 14, 2006 in the framework of a day-long conference on *The Arabs in Israel and the Elections to the Seventeenth Knesset: The Beginning of a New Era?* The conference was initiated by the Konrad Adenauer Program for Jewish-Arab Cooperation at the Moshe Dayan Center. The author would like to thank Mr. Arik Rudnitzky for his work on gathering and processing the data.

2. The subsequent candidates on the ticket were: Sa'id Nafa', Jum'a Al-Zabarga, Haj Abd Al-Rahim Fukara, Mahasen Rabuss, Mazen Ghanaim, Inas Oda Haj, Fuad Sultani. *NDA party website*: http://www.NDA.org/index.php?id=21 In general, names of Arab political figures follow the transliteration appearing on the Knesset website.

3. · For the main points of NDA's platform, see *NDA party website*: http://www.NDA.org/index.php?id=162

4. At one stage negotiations were conducted between DFPE and NDA, but they broke down. Secretary of NDA, Awad Abd Al-Fattah, noted that his party was prepared to relinquish the first place to DFPE provided NDA had three representatives in the

first five places, but DFPE refused. See remarks made by the NDA party secretary, *Al-Sinara*, February 5, 2006. www.assennara.net

5. The subsequent six spots were assigned to: Dr. Afu Aghbaria, Yusuf Al-Atawna, Mannal Shalabi, Dakhil Abu-Zaid, Dr. Abdullah Abu-M'aruf, Yishai Menuhin, and Dr. Edna Zaritskey-Toledano. DFPE *party website*: http://www.DFPE.org.il/index. html

6. For details of DFPE's manifesto, see the *DFPE party website*: http://www.DFPE. org.il/matza.html

7. The candidates for the next five places were: Bassel Darawshe (ADP), Yusuf Shahin (AMC), Mahmud Muwassi (ADP), Dr. Hassan Abu-Hajla (AMC), and Sheikh Yusuf Fadili (Islamic Movement). *Al-Meathaq website*: http://al-methaq. net/akhbar/?safha=Sh%2526aid%253D512 Oral communication by Kifah Abd Al-Halim, parliamentary assistant to MK Ahmad Tibi.

8. *Ibid*; and information obtained verbally from Muhammad Zabidat, journalist on *Al-Meathaq*, the newspaper of the southern faction of the Islamic Movement.

9. *Ibid*.

10. For the main points of the Labor party's manifesto, see the *Labor party website*: http://www.avoda2006.org.il/workingforyou.asp?cc=0113

11. See remarks made by Amir Peretz, *Al-Sinara*, March 10, 2006; *Al-Sinara website* (note 4 above), March 19, 2006.

12. See remarks made by Avishai Braverman, *Panorama*, January 13, 2006.

13. *Kul Al-Arab*, January 20, 2006.

14. Manifesto of the Meretz-Yahad party, *Meretz-Yahad party website*: http://www. myparty.org.il/elections/maza.php?id=18

15. *Kul Al-Arab website*, February 17, 2006, www.kul-alarab.com

16. *Al-Sinara*, January 27, 2006. See, for example, the reservations expressed by the head of the Kfar Bara local authority, Ayoub Aas, *ibid.*, February 17, 2006.

17. *Kul Al-Arab*, February 10, 2006.

18. *Kul Al-Arab*, February 24, 2006. *Al-Sinara*, February 24, 2006

19. *DFPE* manifesto: *DFPE party website* (note 5 above). *NDA* manifesto; *NDA party website* (note 2 above). UAL-AMC manifesto; *Al-Meathaq website* (note 6 above), and oral communications with Kifah Abd Al-Halim, the parliamentary assistant of MK Ahmad Tibi, and with Muhammad Zabidat, journalist on *Al-Meathaq*, the newspaper of the southern faction of the Islamic Movement.

20. See interview with Suzanne Asadi a twenty-five-year-old social worker and member of the Islamic Movement who has an M.A. degree from the Hebrew University of Jerusalem, with Salwa Alinat. "I am not waiting for men to give me a seat, but fighting for my seat myself." *Mahsom*, January 18, 2006. http://www.mahsom. com/article.php?id=2234.

21. Hannin Zuabi has a B.A. in Philosophy and Psychology from Haifa University and an M.A. from the Hebrew University of Jerusalem. See interview with her, *ibid*.

22. Khulud Badawi, a member of the DFPE council, was chairperson of the Association of Arab Students in Israel. Abir Kobti has a B.A. in Economics and Accounting from Haifa University and works as spokesperson and media advisor at the Mossawa Center. She is a political activist and a feminist. See the article by Abir Kobti, "Where Is the Woman Arab Knesset Member?" *ynet*, December 4, 2005. http://www.ynet.co.il/articles/0.7340.L-3178936.00.html

23. See Alinat (note 19 above), and remarks made by Uri Bitan on the subject: Mannal Shalabi, "Permit Me to Introduce Myself," *Green-Red Blog*, March 3, 2006. http://www.dovblog.org/blog/15

24. Shalabi has a B.A. in Social Work and is currently completing a degree in Gender Studies at Bar-Ilan University; she has been active in the Communist party since

childhood and is a member of the party's institutions. She is also active in the feminist organizations of the Arab population. See Alinat (note 20 above). Shalabi conducted a lively public campaign, involving extensive utilization of the Internet. See, for example, 'Mannal Shalabi,' *Asimon*, February 12, 2006. http://www.asimon. co.il/ArticlePage.aspx?AID=1836&AcatID=97

25. Asmaa Aghbariya headed the Workers Party, Democratic Action Organization (Da'am).

26. Compare Ora Herzog, "The Men Will Continue to Rule," *Maariv*, March 28, 2006.

27. See, for example, comments by MK Muhammad Barakeh, who claimed that abstaining from voting was tantamount to voting to support the demand for a population exchange (*Kul Al-Arab*, January 6, 2006). See also the remarks of MK Jamal Zahalka that the polls indicating that NDA would not pass the election threshold were biased (*Al-Sinara*, January 20, 2006). NDA's election slogan was "Citizenship is a right and voting is an obligation" (*Fasl Al-Maqal*, January 27, 2006).

28. *Kul Al-Arab*, December 23, 2005.

29. *Ibid.*, February 17, 2006.

30. *Ibid.*

31. *Ibid.*, February 24, 2006.

32. *Fasl Al-Maqal*, February 17, 2006.

33. See the response of Yossi Beilin, Meretz chairman , to the sketch: "If a Jewish party were to say that...they would be called racists," *Haaretz*, March 15, 2006.

34. See remarks by the candidate in fourth place of the UAL-AMC ticket about the fact that it was necessary to be properly prepared for the next elections "so that we won't need loudspeakers" (*Kul Al-Arab*, March 31, 2006).

35. *Al-Sinara*, April 7, 2006.

36. See Rekhess, 2005: http://www.dayan.org/kapjac/files/Survey2006.ppt

37. *Kul Al-Arab*, November 25, 2005.

38. *Ibid.*, January 6, 2006.

39. *Ibid.*, December 30, 2005, January 6, 2006. *Al-Sinara*, 1 February 17, 2006. *Kul Al-Arab website* (see note 15 above), March 16, 2006. According to Al-Sinara, many of Mahameed's supporters in Umm Al-Fahm preferred to disregard his advice and voted for DFPE. The fourth candidate on the *Balam* ticket, Dr. Afu Aghbariya, was from that town. *Al-Sinara website* (note 4 above), March 13, 2006.

40. *Al-Sinara*, January 20, 2006, January 27, 2006, February 3, 2006, February 17, 2006. *Kul Al-Arab*, March 10, 2006.

41. Together with Aghbariya, the ticket included Mustafa Abu Hashab from the village of Manda, Wafa Tiara from the village of Kara, and Osnat Bar-Or from Pardes Hanna; *Panorama*, February 17, 2006.

42. See note 36 above.

43. *Panorama*, January 20, 2006.

44. *Kul Al-Arab*, May 5, 2006.

45. Lutfi Mashour's column, "The Failure: A Fait Accompli," *Al-Sinara*, March 31, 2006.

46. See the article by Yoav Stern, "Umm al-Fahm: 2006 Elections," *Haaretz*, March 28, 2006.

47. It has been claimed that the actual voting rate was even lower. There is evidence that votes were falsified in Tamra and Majd Al-Kurum, with double votes, vote-buying, and bribes in the form of gasoline vouchers. See *Maariv*, April 5, 2006, *Kul Al-Arab*, June 5, 2006.

48. *Kul Al-Arab*, May 5, 2006.

49. Remarks made by Muhammad Muhsin Watad regarding the low voting rate in the Triangle. *Kul Al-Arab*, March 31, 2006. Contrasted with the comments made by Zuheir Andreus, according to whom the boycott was a central element of the elections, *Kul Al-Arab*, November 25, 2005.
50. See editorial, "Indifference Reigns," *Kul Al-Arab*, March 31, 2006.
51. *Kul Al-Arab*, November 25, 2005, March 30, 2006.
52. See the remarks made by Raja Aghbariya to Ali Waqad, "The Organization of the Arab Sector," "Boycott the elections and establish our own parliament." *ynet*, February 21, 2006. http://www.ynet.co.il/articles/1.7340.L-3219297.00.html.
53. In the Sixteenth Knesset, Abd Al-Malik Dehamshe was the MK who made the most speeches (233); Muhammad Barakeh was the MK who submitted the greatest number of motions for the agenda (77); Dehamshe, Jamal Zahalka, Wasil Taha and Ahmad Tibi attended 97, 90, 86 and 85 percent of the Knesset sittings, respectively. Tibi submitted four proposals for bills in the Sixteenth Knesset (*Al-Sinara*, December 23, 2005).
54. "Public announcement by the Popular Committee for the Boycott of the Elections," February 14, 2006: http://mokata3a_48.tripod.com.
55. *Kul Al-Arab*, May 12, 2006.
56. For further elucidation, see Sa'abna, 2004.
57. See note 54 above.
58. *Ibid*. See note 55.
59. See note 52 above.
60. *Ibid*. and the article by As'ad Ghanem, "Electing a National Council and the Knesset Elections," *Kul Al-Arab*, December 23, 2005, and interview with Raja Aghbariya, *Makor Rishon*, March 10, 2006. See note 53.
61. The Northern Faction opposed participation in the election fearing that this would be considered recognition of the State of Israel, and as far as it was concerned there was in any case no point in taking part in parliamentary politics as the Arab parties had not achieved anything for the Arab public.
62. See the remarks made on the subject by Sheikh Kamal Khatib, deputy head of the Northern Faction; *Panorama*, January 13, 2006.
63. *Kul Al-Arab website* (note 15 above), June 30, 2006; *Kul Al-Arab*, December 30, 2005.
64. *Panorama*, December 2, 2005. See note 15.
65. *Kul Al-Arab website* (note 15 above), March 16, 2006.
66. *Haaretz*, March 29, 2006; *The Jerusalem Post*, March 30, 2006. See note 15.
67. See comments on this subject by Ibrahim Sarsur: "The government here should be Muslim, headed by a Caliphate." Subsequently, he and other representatives explained that this did not mean that Israel should disappear. See *Kul Al-Arab*, February 17, 2006; *ynet*, February 15, 2006. http://www.ynet.co.il/articles/0,7340,L-3216531,00.html.
68. "Declaration against Boycotting the Elections," March 21, 2006 (personal communication to the author). See also the remarks made by Attorney Rafiq Jabareen, who emphasized the importance of the Knesset, defining it as "an arena where we can have our say and try to prevent disasters such as the transfer, which extreme right-wing Jewish groups…are calling for." *Panorama*, January 6, 2006.

References

Al-Haj, Majd (forthcoming). "Voting Trends of Israeli Arabs in the Knesset Elections" in Elie Rekhess (ed.), *The Arab Minority in Israel and the Elections for the Seventeenth*

Knesset, Tel Aviv, Tel Aviv University, Konrad Adenauer Program for Jewish-Arab Cooperation (Hebrew).

Cohen, Ra'anan. 2006. *Strangers at Home: Arabs, Jews and the State of Israel*, Tel Aviv, Diunon (Hebrew).

Ghanem, As'ad (forthcoming). "The Leadership Crisis and Possible Alternatives," in Elie Rekhess (ed.), *The Arab Minority in Israel and the Elections for the Seventeenth Knesset*, Tel Aviv, Tel Aviv University, Konrad Adenauer Program for Jewish-Arab Cooperation (Hebrew).

Ghanem, As'ad and Sarah Ozacky-Lazar. 1999. *The Arab Vote in the Elections to the 15th Knesset*, Givat Haviva; Peace Studies Institute (Hebrew).

———. 2001. "Israel as an Ethnic Democracy: the Test of the Arab Vote in the Elections to the 15th Knesset," in Asher Arian and Michal Shamir (eds.), *The Elections in Israel—1999*, Jerusalem, The Israel Democracy Institute, pp. 171–202 (Hebrew).

Haidar, Aziz (forthcoming). "The Boycott of the Elections by the Arab Public: A Perspective of a Decade (1996–2006)," in Elie Rekhess (ed.), *The Arab Minority in Israel and the Elections for the Seventeenth Knesset*, Tel Aviv, Tel Aviv University, Konrad Adenauer Program for Jewish-Arab Cooperation (Hebrew).

Jamal, Amal. 2002. "Abstinence as Participation: the Vagaries of Arab Politics in Israel," in Asher Arian and Michal Shamir (eds.), *The Elections in Israel—2001*, Jerusalem, The Israel Democracy Institute, pp. 57–100 (Hebrew).

Kaufman, Ilana and Rachel Israeli. 1999. "The Odd Group Out: the Arab-Palestinian Vote in the 1996 Elections," in Asher Arian and Michal Shamir (eds.), *The Elections in Israel—1996*, Jerusalem, The Israel Democracy Institute, pp. 107–148 (Hebrew).

Neuberger, Benjamin. 1996. *The Knesset Elections Among the Arab and Druze Public*, Tel Aviv, Tel Aviv University, Program for the Study of Arab Politics in Israel, information pages and content no. 3 (Hebrew).

———. 1998. *The Arab Minority in Israel: Alienation and Integration*, Tel Aviv, Open University (Hebrew).

Rekhess, Elie. 2000. "The Islamic Movement in Israel and its Connection with Political Islam in the Territories," in Ruth Gabizon and Dafna Hacker (eds.), The Jewish-Arab Rift: A Reader, Jerusalem, The Israel Democracy Institute, pp. 271–296 (Hebrew).

———. 2002. "The Arabs in Israel Following the Oslo Process: Localization of the National Struggle," *Hamizrah Hehadash* (vol. XLIII), pp. 275–304 (Hebrew).

———. 2005. *The Arab Vote in the Next Knesset Elections: Results of a Public Opinion Poll*, Tel Aviv, Tel Aviv University, Konrad Adenauer Program for Jewish-Arab Cooperation (Hebrew).

——— and Doron Navot. 2006. "Egalitarian Policy and the Politics of the Arabs in Israel: Pragmatic and Paradigmatic Constraints," in Shlomo Hasson and Michael Karayani (eds.), *Arabs in Israel: Barriers to Equality*, Jerusalem, Floersheimer Institute for Policy Studies, pp. 141–162.

Rouhana, Nadim, Nabil Saleh, and Nimer Sultany. 2004. "Voting Without Voice: About the Vote of the Palestinian Minority in the 16th Knesset Elections," in Asher Arian and Michal Shamir (eds.), *The Elections in Israel—2003*, Jerusalem, The Israel Democracy Institute, pp. 215–243.

Sa'abni, Amid. 2004. *The Reasons for the Boycott of the Elections by Arab Citizens of Israel*, Haifa, Mada Al-Carmel (Arabic).

Shabita, Taghreed. 2003. "Fourth in Line," *Eretz Aheret* 16, pp. 25–27 (Hebrew).

(

Part 3

The Politics of the Elections

Candidate Selection in Israel:
Between the One, the Few, and the Many

Gideon Rahat[1]

Many dramatic political developments took place during Israel's general elections in 2006. Within the inter-party electoral arena, these included the significant decline in voter turnout, the fragmentation of the right, and the historical success of Kadima becoming the largest party and attaining a pivotal position on Israel's political map. But what about developments within the parties themselves, in the intra-party arena of candidate selection? Were they significant, and what can we learn from them? This chapter aims to analyze recent developments in candidate selection methods in Israel and to examine their impact on the continuing problem of women's under-representation.

In most established democracies, voters can influence (at least potentially) the personal composition of parliament. In Israel, with its rigid, closed list electoral system, the individual composition of the Knesset remains solely in the hands of the political parties. The political parties have complete autonomy in deciding how their candidates will be selected. A single leader can select and rank all of his or her party's candidates; hundreds of delegates can vote and decide the candidate list; or the aggregation of the individual choices of tens of thousands of party members can be the determining factor. Indeed, parties are influenced by their surrounding environment when they choose their candidate selection methods – from their immediate competitive inter-party arena (e.g., imitation of other parties' seeming success stories) and from the general normative, cultural, and institutional framework. Ultimately however, after calculating the benefits and rewards of adopting various kinds of candidate selection methods from both partisan and sub-partisan perspectives (i.e., factional, personal), each party decides which candidate selection method it wishes to employ (Barnea and Rahat, 2007).

The first part of this chapter analyzes the main developments in candidate selection methods, focusing on the levels of inclusiveness of the selectorates—the bodies selecting the candidates. The selectorate may be highly exclusive (e.g., a single leader or a nominating committee composed of a few party leaders and/or apparatchiks); moderately inclusive (a party agency whose members were selected by a larger group of party members); or highly inclusive (party members or even party supporters). The analysis identifies a seemingly transient decline in the participatory aspect of party democracy, expressed by the adoption of more exclusive selectorates; a clear trend of the largest parties to avoid selection by party agencies, preferring either more exclusive selectorates (e.g., the party leader) or more inclusive ones (party members); a widening of the range of the selectorates used by the largest parties, extending from the extremely exclusive, composed of a single leader, to the highly inclusive selectorate of party members; and a tendency to entrust a single selectorate with candidate selection rather than involving several in the selection process.

The second part of the chapter examines the impact of the developments in candidate selection methods on women's representation just prior to the 2006 elections. The use of a highly proportional electoral system ensures that Israeli democracy is truly representative in many respects. However, women's representation in Israel remains low, especially in comparison to countries which have similar proportional representation (PR) electoral systems. An opportunity to significantly boost women's representation presented itself in 2006, when the leaders of several parties were to determine the composition and rank of their party lists (Rahat and Hazan, 2001). The analysis highlights this missed opportunity to significantly increase women's representation.

Developments in Candidate Selection in Israel

Candidate selection methods can be defined according to several distinct dimensions: candidacy requirements; the type of selectorate; the level of centralization; and the appointment/voting system in use (Rahat and Hazan, 2001). However, the main aspect—especially within the Israeli context, on which this study focuses—is the selectorate (Barnea and Rahat, 2007). Israeli parties employed a variety of selectorates: the highly exclusive nominating committees; the moderately inclusive party agencies; and the highly inclusive selectorates comprised of party members. Democratization in candidate selection is evident "…when the selectorate that is adopted following a reform of the candidate selection method is more inclusive than the previous one" (Rahat and Hazan, 2001: 309). Similarly, a reverse trend could be identified when the selectorate that is adopted following reform of the candidate selection method is less inclusive than the previous one.

The major developments in the levels of inclusiveness of the selectorates of the largest parties in Israel are presented in figure 1. It makes sense to relate to the group of the largest parties' selectorates because they represent the way the incumbent parties that dominate the scene select their representatives. Each white point indicates the inclusiveness of the selectorates of the six largest parties (or party factions, when the selectorates were kept separate within parties that were undergoing a process of unification) in any given outgoing Knesset.[2] The inclusiveness of each party selectorate was estimated on the basis of a thirteen-point scale. Zero indicates that a highly exclusive selectorate comprised of a few individuals (e.g., a nominating committee), or even a single leader, was completely autonomous in determining the composition and rank of the candidate list; six signifies that a selected party agency (e.g., a central committee), a wider selectorate, was autonomous in determining the composition and rank of the candidate list; twelve connotes that party members, the most inclusive

Figure 1
Israeli Parties' Selectorates—1949-2006*

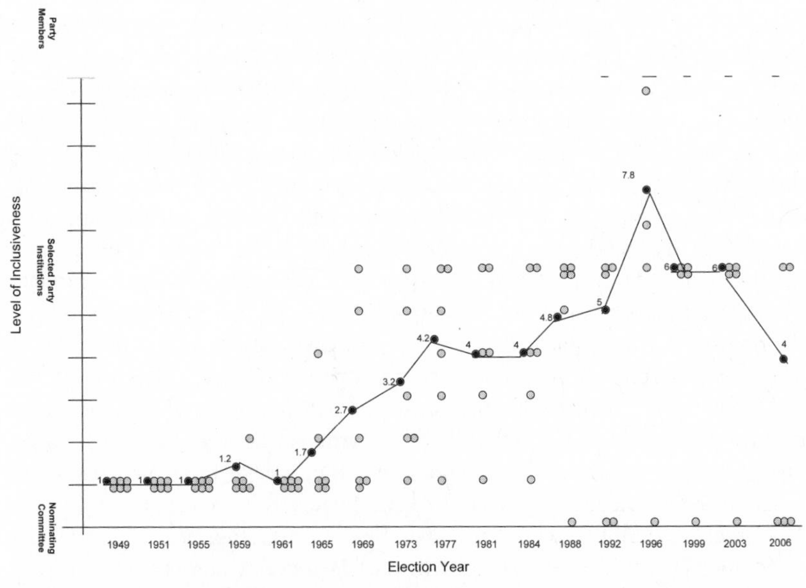

* Updated from Barnea and Rahat (forthcoming).

The figure relates to the selectorates of the following parties (or factions within parties or parties within party alliances): Mapai (1949-1973); Mapam (1949-1965, 1981-1988); Herut (1949-1988); General Zionists (1949-1961); Hapoel HaMizrachi (1949-1955); Progressive Party (1949, 1951); Maki (1955); National Religious Party (1959-1999, 2006); Achdut Ha'avoda (1959-1973); Liberal Party (1965-1988); Rafi (1969-1973); Labor (1977-2006); Independent Liberal Party (1977); Hadash (1977-1981, 1999); Agudat Yisrael (1984, 1992); HaTehiya (1988); Shas (1992-2006); Ratz (1992, 1996); Likud (1992-2006); Tzomet (1996); Yisrael Ba'aliya (1999, 2003); Meretz (2003); Shinui (2003, 2006); Kadima (2006).

selectorate ever used in Israeli national politics, determined the composition and rank of the candidate list (Barnea and Rahat, 2007). The spaces between these pure types enable us to identify instances in which more than one selectorate was involved in candidate selection, and to convey the relative influence of each.[3] The black points represent the average level of inclusiveness of the six largest parties' selectorates for each election year. The black line connecting these points represents the overall developments in the levels of inclusiveness of candidate selection methods over the years.

In order to analyze current developments, it would be helpful to first look at the historical development of candidate selection methods in Israel, as represented in figure 1. The history of the development of candidate selection methods in Israel could have been told, up to 1996, as the story of an (almost) linear development of democratization. This story covers almost all parties, with the exception of the ultra-orthodox parties, which have demonstrated resistance to the democratization trend and remained loyal to their highly exclusive selectorates (councils of rabbis). The 1950s were characterized by the use of nominating committees. These were small committees composed of party leaders, sometimes working in cooperation with representatives of other elements within the party—party functionaries, representatives of social groups, and the heads of important party branches (Brichta 1977). The candidate lists designed by these committees were often submitted for en-bloc ratification of a party agency (typically the central committee). Between 1961 and 1977 we witnessed a trend toward democratization, expressed by an increase in the involvement and influence of selected party agencies (e.g., central committees) in the selection process. There was not much change in the 1977-1984 period; the dominant role of party agencies in most cases seems to be consolidated. There were significant developments in the period between 1988-1996, from one election to the next. The most dramatic developments of 1988 and 1992 occurred in Labor, one of the two major parties at the time. In 1988, Labor, one of the last parties to use a nominating committee as the main selectorate, transferred the selection of most of its candidates to its central committee. In 1992, Labor continued with its democratization, adopting party primaries for selecting its party leader and candidate list.[4] Democratization reached its peak in 1996, when the four largest parties of the Thirteenth Knesset—Labor, Likud, Meretz and Tzomet—gave their members a role in candidate selection.[5] In the 1999 and 2003 elections, parties returned to selecting their candidates by party agencies; only Labor retained the primaries method.[6]

The white points in figure 1 above the year 2006 represent the selectorates of the six largest parties in the outgoing Sixteenth Knesset: Likud, Labor, Kadima, Shas, Shinui, and the National Religious Party (NRP). Labor continued to select all of its candidates through the party primaries and was therefore assigned twelve. The NRP and Likud were assigned six. In both cases the central committee was the selectorate. Kadima, Shas and Shinui (actually the largest splinter group of Shinui that established the Hetz party) were assigned a zero. In Kadima, a single leader—Ehud Olmert—appointed the candidate list. In Shas, a group of four rabbis—the Council of Sages, headed by Rabbi Ovadia Yosef—appointed (as always) the candidates for the Knesset list. In Shinui, the selection process began in the central committee, but the defeat of MK (Member of Knesset) Avraham Poraz in his bid for the second spot on the list led to a split. Only two MKs remained in Shinui, while nine MKs established a new party (Hetz) and divided the positions at the top of the list among themselves.[7]

A look at the average point in 2006 indicates a sharp decline in inclusiveness, from six to four. A look at the spread of the cases points to the increase in the range of the selectorates in use. Highly exclusive selectorates are no longer (as they were for the last two decades) the realm of the ultra-orthodox parties. Within the wider range, however, there is a lower rather than higher diversity. Since 1999, the largest Israeli parties refrained from involving more than a single selectorate in candidate selection. These three distinct phenomena—the decline in inclusiveness, the widening of the range of selectorates, and the drop in their diversity—will be examined in the following three sub-sections.

Decline in Inclusiveness

Table 1 presents the number and ratio of MKs selected prior to the last four elections by one of three kinds of selectorates: the highly exclusive selectorates of party leader/non-selected party agency; the moderately inclusive selectorate of selected party agency (or, in the case of new parties, a group of tens or hundreds of the party's founders); and the highly inclusive selectorate of party members. In those cases when more than one selectorate was involved, the table refers to the dominant selectorate.

It is apparent that since the peak in inclusiveness of 1996 there was a decline in the inclusiveness of the selectorates. This decline was expressed in the nixing of party primaries already in 1999; only Labor has employed primaries since then. In 2006, we witness the abandoning of selected party agencies. A majority of MKs (55 percent) owe their selection to either a single leader or to a non-selected party agency: the MKs of the largest party, Kadima, and those of the successful Yisrael Beiteinu owe their selection to Ehud Olmert and Avigdor Lieberman, respectively. To these we should add the eighteen MKs from the ultra-orthodox parties (Shas, Agudat Yisrael, and Degel Hatora) who were selected by councils of rabbis, and the surprising Pensioners party (7 MKs) whose list was composed through informal deliberations among a few of its leaders. Most other (smaller) parties continued to employ party agencies.

The general trend of democratization, of the increase in inclusiveness of party selectorates that Israel experienced up to 1996, was similar to the general trend found in many other established democracies (Bille, 2001; Caul-Kittilson and Scarrow, 2003; Scarrow, Webb, and Farrel, 2000). Reverse trends in specific countries are also not an unknown phenomenon. Parties in Belgium

Table 1
The selectorates that selected MKs to the 14th-17th Knessets (1996-2006)

Knesset	Party leader/ non-selected party agency	Selected party agency	Party members	Unknown	Total
14 (1996)	16 (13%)	42 (35%)	62 (52%)	0 (0%)	120
15 (1999)	42 (35%)	55 (46%)	22 (18%)	1 (1%)	120
16 (2003)	25 (21%)	69 (58%)	19 (16%)	7 (6%)	120
17 (2006)	66 (55%)	33 (28%)	20 (17%)	1 (1%)	120

and the Netherlands adopted more exclusive selectorates when they wanted to gain control over the composition of their lists, thus ensuring a balanced representation of various groups within the parties. This was also an important motive for the adoption of less inclusive candidate selection methods in Israel in 1999 (Rahat, 2002). Parties that are built around a leader who is also highly influential in candidate selection is a phenomenon which is not unique to Israel. Sylvio Berlusconi's Forza Italia resembles Kadima in this respect (Hopkin and Paolucci, 1999). The leader's influence in candidate selection in extreme right-wing European parties—such as those in Norway (Valen, Narud, and Skare, 2002), Denmark (Pedersen, 2002) and Italy (Gallagher, Laver and Mair, 2001)—may be viewed as a similar phenomenon to that of Lieberman in Yisrael Beiteinu.

It can be argued that the retreat from inclusiveness is a temporary phenomenon stemming from circumstantial factors. Kadima can claim that as a new party it did not have the time needed to organize a proper selection method; indeed, Kadima promised that selection by the party leader was a one-time occurrence and that it would conduct primaries before the next elections. Likud also decided to hold primaries before the next elections, rather than relying on its central committee. Thus, in the run-up to the next elections we may witness another peak of democratization rather than a continuing decline (or a consolidation of methods that are of highly exclusive selectorates).

It is clear, however, that the range of choice of legitimate methods has widened: there were times when new parties attempted to demonstrate a certain level of inclusiveness: the Democratic Movement for Change (DMC)—a new party in 1977—was actually the first to conduct party primaries in Israel. The Third Way and Gesher, established prior to the 1996 elections, when the primaries trend peaked, used their founders' committees to select their candidates. While these were not selected party agencies, and in the case of Gesher it was certainly a pre-determined show, they still symbolized the attempt by a new party to use a relatively wide selectorate.

The "shameless" use of exclusive methods in 2006 is not a new phenomenon; already in 1999 parties dared to use more exclusive methods (Rahat, 2001). This transpired because the 1996 elections disproved the myth of a correlation between the expansion of the selectorate and electoral success. The three parties that employed primaries at that time saw their representation decline, while other parties, where the candidates were named by a selected party institution or through appointment by highly exclusive selectorates, managed to maintain or even increase their strength in the Knesset. The problems caused by party primaries were also apparent after 1996, especially regarding party cohesion and the designation of a balanced representative list. The parties also understood that there is little demand for primaries, and that most voters were not frustrated participants simply waiting for their chance to take part in candidate selection, but rather passive consumers of personal and partisan labels reflecting identities and issues.

The story of Shinui's candidate selection is illustrative here. When Shinui left the umbrella party of Meretz in 1999, it determined its candidate list partly through selection by its central committee (positions #2, #3) and partly through a kind of nominating committee (positions #1, #4, #5, #6). Prior to 2003, the central committee selected the candidates. In 2006, the central committee began selecting the candidates. However, after a newcomer defeated the incumbent Avraham Poraz in his bid for the second position, most competitors and selectors left the scene: Nine MKs established a new party list (Hetz); two joined Likud; one joined Yisrael Beiteinu; and only two MKs remained in Shinui. Thus, even the leaders of the self-acclaimed anti-corruption party did not view the rules of candidate selection as obligating when they failed to produce certain results. Personal composition was preferred over respect for the rules of the game, even by the self-acclaimed champions of liberal democracy.

What was especially striking in 2006 was the use of the single leader as a selector. In the 1950s, the larger parties attempted to legitimize their use of nominating committees by involving broader selectorates. Their central committees usually ratified the compositions of the nomination committees as well as the proposed list. There were occasions when the central committees asked the nomination committees to reconsider their proposals, or suggested their own corrections (Brichta, 1977). In 2006, a single leader often had the first and final word. In conclusion, as far as the large parties are concerned, the selectorates that were in use by some of them in 2006 were the most exclusive in Israel's history.

The adoption of selectorates of a single leader may signify what the adoption of more inclusive selectorates—which made personal competition more explicit—signified in the past, that is, the personalization of politics (Rahat and Sheafer, 2007). A selectorate of a single leader is the pure type of a personalized method. Its adoption (even temporal) indicates that we may witness an era (a worrisome one) in which personalization is not restricted by democratic convention.

An additional explanation of the decline in inclusiveness relates to inter-party competition. The frequent changes in candidate selection methods since 1977, usually toward the expanding of the selectorates, were ignited by the competitiveness that characterized the bipolar party system. The parties reformed the candidate selection procedures in an attempt to improve their image and gain some leverage in the close competition between right and left in general and Labor and Likud in particular (Barnea and Rahat, 2007). A decrease in competitiveness in the 2003 and 2006 elections—elections in which the victory of Likud (2003) and Kadima (2006) were clear from the start—may have further neutralized, or at least decreased, pressures for demonstrating a democratic facade.

It is still too early to claim that the use of primaries to improve the party image has completely disappeared. Likud—motivated by electoral considerations—reformed its candidate selection method during its election campaign, promising to use party primaries in the next elections. This was clearly a desperate last-minute attempt by Binyamin Netanyahu to rescue Likud from an electoral defeat. As Goldberg (1994: 43) states, because it cannot demonstrate responsiveness by implementing certain policies or through legislation, "The internal life of the party becomes one of the single arenas in which an opposition party can actively compete with a governing party."

Current developments, and the prospects of widespread use of primaries before the next elections, imply that the long-term trend is not toward either inclusiveness or exclusiveness. Rather, there seems to be a move by the large parties away from candidate selection through selected party agencies. This may be interpreted as the consolidation of the cartel party model, in which the "party in government" achieves its dominancy over the party organization by transforming candidate selection away from selected party agencies (Katz and Mair, 1995). While the party elite would like to be in full control of candidate selection, the use of a highly exclusive selectorate is not likely to be perceived as legitimate, especially in the long run. It thus seems reasonable to prefer selection by the large, unstable, non-committed atomistic crowd of passive members to the small, relatively stable, committed and attentive group of party activists (Katz, 2001).

The behavior of members of the Likud central committee ignited the move to expropriate candidate selection from the selected party agencies. The conflict between Prime Minister Ariel Sharon and his opponents within Likud created a clear rift between the party in government and the party organization. The opponents of the Israel-Gaza disengagement plan focused their pressure on Likud because of its pivotal position—only a rebellion from within the party could have blocked the move. Sharon tried to bypass the party central committee, where the majority seemed to reject the plan, by conducting a poll among all Likud members. While Sharon then failed in the members' poll, in which about 60 percent voted against the disengagement plan, he continued with his plans, portraying himself as the trustee of Israeli citizens, rather than merely the delegate of Likud party members. Majority support across the political map, evident in opinion polls, helped Sharon and his supporters to execute the move in the face of intra-party rejection. The coverage and interpretation by most of the media of the conflict between the party in government and the party organization helped to create a poor image for the central committee. The central committee was now perceived as a corrupt institution comprised of self-interested people, or as a body controlled by extremists, led by Moshe Feiglin, the leader of the extreme right Jewish Leadership group. This was clearly a victory for Sharon's spin doctors, as the real threat to the prime minister was not the minority Jewish Leadership group or the corrupt who could be (and were) bought, but rather those who insisted that he stick to the Likud manifesto and to the 2003 campaign promises. In sum, the negative image that the Likud central committee earned for itself clearly led its offshoot Kadima to avoid constructing such a selectorate; caused Likud to promise to employ party members in the next elections; and most likely convinced most members of the Labor party central committee to reject an initiative to transform selection to a similar selectorate.

A Wider Range

If the range of possibilities considered legitimate in several previous elections extended from the moderately inclusive selected party agencies to the highly inclusive party primaries, in 2006 the range stretched from the highly exclusive selectorate of a party leader to the highly inclusive party primaries. The use of a highly exclusive selectorate was no longer limited to the ultra-orthodox parties, as was the case over the last two decades. Furthermore, a single leader is actually a more exclusive selectorate than even the councils of rabbis, or the nominating committees used in the past.

The range of party selectorates that are concurrently in use is broad not only in comparison to Israel's past, but also from a cross-national perspective. As far as we can conclude from studies of candidate selection methods in other countries, Israel is among the countries in which the widest range of possible selectorates is used, if not the one with the widest range.[8]

Three factors explain the wide range of selectorates—from the highly exclusive selection by the party leader to the highly inclusive party primaries—that are (and were) in use in Israel. First, there is a dearth of legal provisions regarding candidate selection methods. The electoral law and the Parties Law—adopted in Israel in 1992—do not address the issue of candidate selection methods.[9] Parties are not legally bound to adopt any specific kind of candidate selection method in preparing their lists of candidates, nor does the law define a range of possible options. Indeed, in countries where laws oblige (US states), partly oblige (Finland), encourage (Norway until 2002), or restrict (Germany) the range of possible candidate selection options (and in particular, parties' choice of selectorates), we witness a relatively limited variety of selection methods.

It is fascinating to note, as figure 2 demonstrates, that all fifty states in the U.S. have legislated the use of a relatively small variety of candidate selection methods. In the U.S., party supporters are permitted to take part in the selection of candidates for congress in all cases, and the differences between the states pertain to the relatively narrow range of the rules of registration as a party supporter: from one year before the primaries to no need for prior registration as a party supporter. Israel, on the other hand, spans a much wider range: from a single leader to party primaries. However, in most established democracies there is no legislation on candidate selection methods that binds or limits the parties' choice (Muller and Sieberer, 2006). This leads us to look for additional explanations for the wide range of methods that are in use in Israel.[10]

The institutional setting in which parties act in Israel is also one that allows for variance in candidate selection methods. While in other established democracies parties compete within electoral districts and thus have to take into consideration the interests of the party organization at the constituency level (and calculate it with other interests, such as the sufficient representation of women, minorities, etc.), the use of a single nationwide constituency system in Israel assures the dominance of the national level and its autonomy in determining the nature of the candidate selection method. In addition, the use of a closed list system offers the parties a broader space in which to maneuver than in more personalized electoral systems.

Israeli society is also very heterogeneous, and many socio-political cleavages are reflected in the party system, resulting in many parties representing different political sub-cultures (Kimmerling, 1999). Each sub-culture has its own menu of legitimate methods. The importance of the political sub-culture is particularly evident in the case of the ultra-orthodox parties which use their religious authority (councils of rabbis) to select candidates. Their selection method reflects adherence to traditional authority with most other parties often retaining predetermined formal procedures—in Weberian terms, they adhere to

Figure 2
The Range of Selectorates in Use in Israel and the US—A Comparison

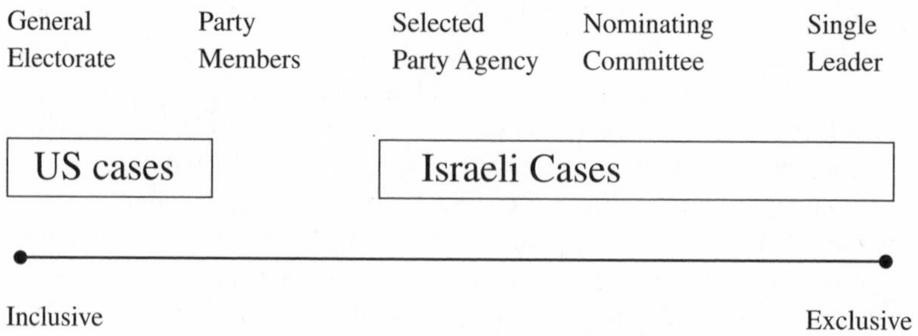

General Electorate	Party Members	Selected Party Agency	Nominating Committee	Single Leader

US cases	Israeli Cases

Inclusive   Exclusive

Source: Based on Rahat and Hazan (2001).

a legal-rational authority. It is reasonable, however, to suggest that the influence of political sub-culture is also apparent in the candidate selection methods in use in other sectarian parties, such as the Arab and the new immigrant parties. Even if each sub-culture does not develop a typical candidate selection method of its own, Israeli parties are more resilient than those in more homogenous societies to the contingency effect, to pressures to imitate other parties.

In summation, the lack of legislation concerning candidate selection methods, the freedom that the electoral system affords the parties with their choice of selection methods, and the existence of many political sub-cultures, side by side, all explain the wide range of selectorates used by parties in Israel.

Less Diversity

From 1959 to the 1980s, nomination committees and selected party agencies were both involved simultaneously in the selection of candidates in many parties (the 1-5 range in figure 1). This combination was at times implemented by using multi-stage methods, whereby one selectorate was used to screen the candidates (to create a short list) and the other ranked them. In other cases, some candidates were selected by one kind of selectorate while the others were selected by another kind. In 1996, some parties used multi-stage processes involving both their members and their selected party agencies (the 7-11 range in figure 1). Since 1999, the large parties, presented in figure 1, refrained from involving more than a single selectorate in candidate selection.

The use of single selectorates is a puzzling phenomenon, not only from a domestic historical perspective, but also in the context of the politics of reform and from a cross-national perspective as well. In the case of the politics of reform we would expect candidate selection methods to reflect compromises among several intra-party actors. A likely result of pressure for reform would be that of adding a selectorate, of sharing power, rather than a complete surrender of power to a single selectorate. Not surprisingly, candidate selection in the Labor and Conservative parties in the U.K. follows this trajectory of development. Democratization in Labor meant adding party members to the selection process in which more exclusive selectorates were already involved. No reform was needed in the Conservative party. There was, however, a change in the role of the members from ratifying candidates chosen by selected party agencies to choosing among a few candidates after screening by the selected party agencies (Norris and Lovenduski, 1995). In many other cases of candidate selection in established democracies, several selectorates are involved in the selection process (Gallagher and Marsh, 1988; Narud, Pedersen, and Valen, 2002).

There is also a democratic–systemic logic in involving several selectorates in the process. Spreading power among several selectorates may enable the creation of a mini-system of checks and balances, and a set of relatively balanced behavioral incentives for those who are selected (Diskin, 2006; Nissim, 2006; Rahat, 2006). If candidate selection methods involving several selectorates were used in Israel in the past, and are in use in many established democracies, and appear as well to be a logical result of a compromised reform, and are justified from a systemic democratic point of view, why did they then disappear from the Israeli menu in the last three elections?[11]

The question of who is served by the use of a single selectorate might lead to an explanation of this phenomenon. Incumbent MKs appear to benefit from debate over candidate selection methods which is limited to the either/or format. Only empirical research will verify the notion that incumbents are likely to enjoy less success in multi-stage candidate selection processes. But it is plausible that they tend to prefer a simple system to a complex one. An MK seeking to ensure his or her re-selection would prefer a system with a single selectorate, one whose interests and positions s/he can clearly identify and address. The use of several selectorates may place candidates for reselection under multiple and sometimes conflicting pressures.

Women's Representation and Candidate Selection:
2006 as a Missed Opportunity

An impressive body of political science literature deals with the issue of women's representation in parliament, especially with the recent trend of women's higher parliamentary numbers in established democracies (for recent publications see Caul-Kittilson, 2006; Dahlerup, 2006; Mateo-Diaz, 2005). Figure 3 presents the rate of women's representation in the Knesset after each election as well as the average rate of representation of women in established democracies with PR electoral systems for each decade. Israel is compared to democracies with PR systems because it was found that there is a significant positive relationship between the use of PR electoral systems and women's representation (Caul-Kittilson, 2006). Figure 3 demonstrates that for half a century (1949-1999) women's representation in Israel remained at more or less the same level, while at the same time in other PR democracies it significantly increased, especially from the 1970s on. Furthermore, Israel, which boasted a relatively high rate of women's representation in the 1950s, became one of the last in this respect among established democracies employing PR electoral systems, even though women's parliamentary numbers did rise following the 1999 and 2003 elections (see also McAllister and Studlar, 2002).

Less-inclusive candidate selection methods give leaders an opportunity to control the composition of their list, and create a balanced list in terms of gender representation. An analysis of women's representation in the two largest parties in Israel from 1949 to 2003 revealed that the more exclusive selectorates produced comparatively more representative lists. The nominating committees of the 1950s placed a relatively high number of women on the candidate lists in comparison to parties in other democracies of the same era. However, while women's representation in other democracies increased over the years, in Israel it froze and even declined. This occurred as the inclusiveness of the

Figure 3
Women's Representation in Israel and in PR Democracies, 1950-2003

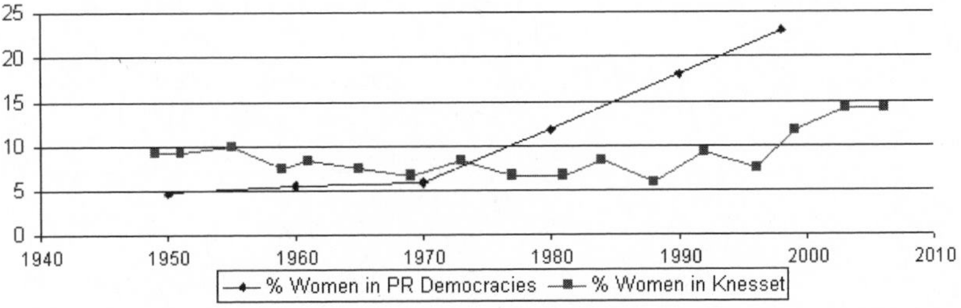

Source: PR democracies from Matland, 1998.
Data on the representation of women in the Knesset relate to women's representation immediately following the elections. Data taken from http://www.knesset.gov.il/mk/eng/mkmain_eng.asp.

selectorates increased (up to 1996). Only after 1996, when a reverse trend in the development of candidate selection methods was apparent, did we witness a boost in the representation of women (Rahat and Hazan, 2005). It can then be expected that those parties that adopted highly exclusive selectorates might still have served the overall democratic cause by composing more representative lists. The adoption of highly exclusive selectorates in 2006 created a special opportunity to improve women's representation in the Knesset.

But was exclusiveness exploited to produce a more representative outcome? Did those (non-ultra orthodox) employing highly exclusive selectorates enhance women's representation? Did those leaders who selected their party lists exploit their status and behave like "enlightened dictators"?[12]

The fact that only seventeen women were elected to the Seventeenth Knesset (14.2 percent), the same number as in previous elections, seems to imply that this anticipation failed. However, it is necessary to examine the party level and clarify the possible linkage between types of selectorates and women's representation in the 2006 elections.

Table 2 compares levels of women's representation among the parties, and presents the totals for three kinds of selectorates: the highly exclusive party leader/non-selected party agency; the moderately inclusive selected party agency; and the highly inclusive selectorate of party members. It tallies the number of women in each party list (separating alliances for the sake of comparison of the distinct selectorates) in the safe positions, before and after the activation of the representation correction mechanisms.

A look at table 2 reveals that, as anticipated, the most exclusive selectorates produced the highest representation for women (23.4 percent). However, in contrast to this expectation, primaries yielded higher representation for women than selected party agencies, even prior to the activation of the representation

Table 2
The number of women in safe positions, 2006*

Party	Selectorate	Number of women in safe positions before the activation of the correction mechanism	Number of women in safe positions on the candidate list
Kadima	Leader	11/44	11/44
Yisrael Beiteinu	Leader	0/3	0/3
	Total exclusive selectorates	**11/47 (23.4%)**	**11/47(23.4%)**
Renewed Religious Zionism	Secretariat	0/2	0/2
Tkuma	Central committee	0/2	0/2
Moledet	Party council	0/2	0/2
ADP	A selectorate composed of 501 delegates	0/1	0/1
Ta'al	Conference	0/1	0/1
Hadash	Central committee	0/3	0/3
Balad	Party conference	0/3	0/3
NRP (Mafdal)	Central Committee	1/4	1/4
Meretz	Conference	1/5	1/5
Likud	Central Committee	1/14	1/16
	Total Moderately Exclusive selectorates	3/37 (8.1%)	3/39(7.7%)
Labor	Party Members	2/11**	5/22
	Total Inclusive Selectorates	**2/11 (18.2%)**	**5/22 (22.7%)**
Total		**16/95 (16.8%)**	**19/108 (17.6%)**

* The number of safe positions is determined by the number of seats the party won in previous elections. The results of the last Dahaf opinion polls (published in Yediot Aharonot), which were conducted prior to the selection of the candidates, were used for splintered parties (for Kadima, January 27, 2006; for Likud, January 6, 2006).

The table excludes parties with no women on their candidate lists (the ultra-orthodox Shas and Yahadut Hatora).

** Relates to the results of the voting for the national list only.

correction mechanisms (18.2 percent against 8.1 percent). It is evident that the level of inclusiveness of the party selectorate is not the sole determinant of the rate of women's representation. The low representation of women in the group of parties that selected their candidates through selected party agencies in comparison to the relatively higher rate in Labor can be explained as a result of their rootedness in a more traditional community (the "Arab" parties) or their right wing inclination. In order to withstand the influence of the selectorate type there is a need for control of party ideology.

However, for current purposes it is sufficient to focus on the performance of the highly exclusive selectorates; did the party leaders use their position and, as "enlightened dictators" exploit them to enhance the representation of women? A rate of 23.4 percent of women's representation for the highly exclusive selectorates (table 2) is far from impressive. It is indeed high for Israeli parties, but not particularly high for a large non-sectarian party like Kadima. And it is low in comparison to women's representation in most of the parliaments in established democracies with a PR electoral system (http://www.ipu.org/wmn-e/classif.htm).

An alternative venue for examining women's representation is to study their share among non-incumbents, thereby neutralizing incumbency as an explanation for the under-representation of women. In other words, under-representation among new aspirants cannot claim to reflect the old traditional order.[13] Only five women (25 percent) won positions among Kadima's first twenty non-incumbents. Olmert did not exploit the opportunity presented him to wield his power and enhance women's representation. There were only two women in the list of sixteen candidates submitted by the Pensioner's party (#7, #10). Avigdor Lieberman used his authority in Yisrael Beiteinu to place women in positions that were attainable thanks to his electoral success (#5, #7, #11). This is indeed an impressive rate for an extreme right-wing party. For the sake of comparison, the first woman to appear in the Ichud Leumi-NRP alliance was given the #10 position. However, women's representation was still higher in the left-wing Zionist parties. Meretz had four women up to the eleventh position; Labor had five up to the seventeenth position, which was perceived as safe even before the elections. The last two parties used relatively inclusive candidate selection methods, making it more difficult to ensure women's representation. Meretz used the party conference, composed of about 1,000 members, while Labor used primaries, in which about 65,000 of its members took an active part. Furthermore, these parties employed special mechanisms to ensure what they determined to be a minimal level of women's representation. This comparison makes the failure of the supposedly "enlightened dictators" to exploit their position as (women) candidate makers even more apparent.

Kadima and the Pensioners party (and to some extent Yisrael Beiteinu, unless expectations are limited in the case of extreme right parties) missed an opportunity to significantly enhance women's representation. In the coming elections their incumbents will compete for the positions that were considered "open" in the 2006 elections. Experience teaches us that they are most likely to capture them, thus maintaining the state of women's representation at the same level. Even if these parties adopt representation correction mechanisms, they are likely to reflect current rates of representation rather than any improvements. Incumbent men tend to consent to adopt quotas for women that do not threaten their own status. These quotas reflect the status quo when relating to safe positions (i.e., positions held by the party in the current Knesset) and are more generous when applied to marginal and unsafe positions; those positions for which new aspirants usually compete among themselves.

Conclusions

As with inter-party politics, Israeli intra-party politics demonstrates high levels of instability. The 2006 candidate selection methods, as demonstrated earlier in this chapter, were indeed characterized by signifying a further retreat from democratization (which peaked in 1996). It is likely that this is a temporal phenomenon, and we may even witness the most inclusive candidate selection in Israel's history before the next elections. The trend is not in opposition to (participatory) party democracy but rather against using selected party agencies (in those parties that view themselves as governing parties). While the range of candidate selection methods in use is wider than ever, it is apparent that parties restrict their choice to a limited menu of selectorates: either a single leader, a selected party agency, or party members, but not a combination of them. Several analyses point to this aspect as an important part of the problem with candidate selection in Israel, inasmuch as the solution for many problems related to them can be found by integrating several selectorates within the candidate selection process (Diskin, 2006; Nissim, 2006; Rahat, 2006).

Can democracy reconcile the fact that a few leaders decide who will staff more than half of the seats in their parliament? These elections teach that personalization of politics does not necessarily lead to the democratization of candidate selection methods. Another, perhaps purer version of personalization—more so than primaries that make the personal intra-party contest highly prominent—is to put all the eggs in the basket of a single party leader. Parties shamelessly adopted exclusive candidate selection methods, thereby explicitly ignoring the public image of the primaries as the more democratic system. It also means that they were prepared to replace a ritual of mass participation, perceived as democratic, with less democratic and non-democratic rituals (Aronoff, 2000). But did democracy really suffer, beyond the participatory and the symbolic aspects? After all, inclusiveness does not equal democracy, and democracy is not limited to intra-party participation. Parties, unlike states, are not obligated to allow for universal participation, especially because they provide the individual with the option to exit (unlike states), that is, to leave and join another party, or establish a new one.[14]

But parties could have compensated for exclusiveness—for adopting methods that do not fulfill the symbolic and participatory elements of democracy—by enhancing representation. Their leaders could exploit their control of the composition of their candidate lists to enhance the representation of women. Unfortunately, as the second part of the chapter demonstrates, Israel concluded this election with the same rate of women's representation in the previous Knesset, seventeen MKs (14.2 percent). From its position as a leading country in terms of women's representation in parliament, Israel has become a country with one of the lowest rates of women's representation among established democracies employing list-PR electoral systems.

There is a trend in democracies to widen participation in candidate selection, and at the same time to somewhat limit the selectors' choice to achieve higher representation for women (Norris, 2006). Israel seems to be participating in the first aspect, and although since 1996 we have witnessed second thoughts concerning democratization, these in themselves are reasonable if we take into consideration some of the negative aspects that resulted from the adoption of party primaries (Rahat and Sher-Hadar, 1999). The problem is one of ignoring the possibility of adopting multi-stage processes, and not of democratization or a retreat from it. As to the second aspect, that of enhancing women's representation, Israel indeed witnessed an increase in the 1999 and 2003 elections, yet missed an opportunity to make much progress in 2006. Women's representation in Israel lags behind most PR-established democracies.

Notes

1. Thanks to Shlomit Barnea and Naomi Himein-Raisch for their wise comments and to Lisa Perlman for her help in editing.
2. The size of the party/party factions was determined according to the results of the previous elections (except, obviously, for the first elections of 1949), because the candidate selection method is determined before the general elections.
3. For example, a score of ten meant that party members determined the rank of the candidates in the party candidate list, but that their choice was somewhat limited because the party agency screened the candidates and presented the members with a short list. This gave the party agency a significant role in the process, but party members were still the most influential selectorate because they made the final decision concerning the position (safe, marginal, or unsafe) of the candidates.
4. The first party to use party primaries in Israel was the Democratic Movement for Change, in 1977.
5. In Labor and Likud, members were the exclusive selectors; in Meretz, party members were the dominant selectorate; in Tzomet, party members were given a very limited role (Hazan, 1997; Rahat and Sher-Hadar, 1999).
6. Leadership selection also became more inclusive over the years. However, in their case, we do not witness a reverse trend, and the large parties stick to party primaries as a mechanism for leadership selection (Kenig, 2006).
7. Seven Shinui MKs occupied the first seven positions on the Hetz list while an additional two, that retired voluntarily from partisan politics, among them chairman Tommy Lapid, were allotted the closing positions as a demonstration of their support for the new party list.

8. Compare to the cases described, for example, in Gallagher and Marsh, 1988; Narud, Pedersen and Valen, 2002.
9. The Party Law does, however, dedicate a chapter to the regulation of the financing of candidate selection campaigns within the parties. On the attempt to regulate the financing of intra-party campaigns, see Hofnung, 1996; 2006.
10. Since the 1990s, several countries have adopted constitutional amendments and laws that oblige parties to present a minimal share of candidates from each gender (Htun, 2004). Such rules influence parties in the design of their candidate selection methods, but still leave them with a wide range of choices. For example, through the adoption of quotas, parties can assure women's representation using any kind of selectorate.
11. In Meretz—which does not appear in figure 1 because it was the seventh largest party in the Sixteenth Knesset—a small screening committee and the party conference (a selected party agency) were involved in candidate selection.
12. While the fulfillment of other kinds of claims for representation, that are usually more specific to certain parties (e.g., in terms of ethnicity, interest group affiliation) may also be of interest for the study of representation, women's representation is the best focal point as it is an issue shared by most parties (save for the ultra-orthodox). Moreover, the need to respond to claims for other kinds of representation and for those of women do not need to conflict: women can be young or old, employees or employers, affiliated with the Jewish majority or the Arab minority, and so on.
13. In the case of Kadima, Olmert "owed" those incumbents who defected from their parties and joined Kadima, sometimes bringing with them their share of party finances and also contributing to the image of the party as a centrist, or "middle" party.
14. For a discussion of the issue of intra-party democracy, see Mersel, 2006.

References

Aronoff, Myron Joel. 2000. "The Americanization of Israeli Politics and Realignment of the Party System." *Israel Studies* 5 (1): 92-127.

Barnea, Shlomit and Gideon Rahat. 2007. "Reforming Candidate Selection Methods: A Three-Level Approach." *Party Politics* 13(3): 375-394.

Bille, Lars. 2001. "Democratizing a Democratic Procedure: Myth or Reality? Candidate Selection in Western European Parties 1960-90." *Party Politics* 7 (3): 363-380.

Brichta, Avraham. 1977. *Democracy and Elections.* Tel Aviv: Am Oved. [Hebrew]

Caul-Kittilson, Miki. 2006. *Challenging Parties, Changing Parliaments: Women and Elected Office in Contemporary Western Europe.* Columbus: Ohio University Press.

------, and Susan E. Scarrow. 2003. "Political Parties and the Rhetoric and Realities of Democratization." In Bruce E. Cain, Russell J. Dalton, and Susan Scarrow, eds. *Democracy Transformed? Expanding Political Opportunities in Advanced Industrial Democracies.* Oxford, Oxford University Press, 59-80.

Dahlerup, Drude, ed. 2006. *Women, Quotas and Politics.* New York: Routledge.

Diskin, Avraham. 2006. "Candidate Selection in Knesset Elections: Dilemma and Several Possible Solutions." In Gideon Rahat (ed.), *Candidate Selection in Israel: Reality and Ideal.* Tel Aviv: Sapir Institute, 124-129 [Hebrew].

Gallagher, Michael, Michael Laver, and Peter Mair. 2001. *Representative Government in Modern Europe.* Third Edition. Boston: McGraw-Hill.

------, and Michael Marsh. 1988. *Candidate Selection in Comparative Perspective: The Secret Garden of Politics.* London: Sage.

Goldberg, Giora. 1994. *The Israeli Voter, 1992.* Jerusalem: Magnes Press [Hebrew].

Hazan, Reuven Y. 1997. "The 1996 Intra-Party Elections in Israel: Adopting Party Primaries." *Electoral Studies* 16 (1): 95-103.

Hofnung, Menachem. 1996. "The Public Purse and the Private Campaign: Political Finance in Israel." *Journal of Law and Society* 23 (1): 132-148.

------. 2006. "Financing Internal Party Races in non-Majoritarian Political Systems: Lessons from the Israeli Experience." *Election Law Journal* 5 (4): 372-383.

Hopkin, Jonathan and Caterina Paolucci. 1999. "The Business Firm Model of Party Organization: Cases from Spain and Italy." *European Journal of Political Research* 35: 307-339.

http://www.ipu.org/wmn-e/classif.htm. IDEA, "Women in National Parliaments," August 5, 2007.

http://www.knesset.gov.il/mk/eng/mkmain_eng.asp. The Knesset, "Knesset Members by Knesset, August 5, 2007.

Htun, Mala. 2004. "Is Gender Like Ethnicity? The Political Representation of Identity Groups," *Perspectives on Politics* 2 (3): 439-458.

Katz, Richard S. 2001. "The Problems of Candidate Selection and Models of Party Democracy." *Party Politics* 7 (3): 277-296.

------, and Peter Mair. 1995. "Changing Models of Party Organization and Party Democracy: The Emergence of the Cartel Party." *Party Politics* 1 (1): 5-28.

Kenig, Ofer. 2006. "Selection and Dismissal of Party Leaders: Israel in Comparative Perspective." In Gideon Rahat, ed. *Candidate Selection in Israel: Reality and Ideal.* Tel Aviv: Sapir Institute, 37-58 [Hebrew].

Kimmerling, Baruch, 1999. "Elections as a Battleground over Collective Identity." In Asher Arian and Michal Shamir, eds. *The Elections in Israel 1996.* Albany: State University of New York Press, 27-44.

Mateo Diaz, Mercedes. 2005. *Representing Women? Female Legislators in West European Parliaments.* Colchester: European Consortium for Political Research.

Matland, Richard E. 1998. "Enhancing Women's Political Participation: Legislative Recruitment and Electoral Systems." In Azza Karam, ed. *Women in Politics: Beyond Numbers.* Stockholm: International Institute for Democracy and Electoral Assistance.

McAllister, Ian and Donley T. Studlar. 2002. "Electoral Systems and Women's Representation: A Long-Term Perspective." *Representation* 39 (1): 3-14.

Mersel, Yigal. 2006. "The Dissolution of Political Parties: The Problem of Internal Democracy," *International Journal of Constitutional Law* 4 (1):84-113

Muller, Wolfgang C. and Ulrich Sieberer. 2006. "Party Law." In Richard S. Katz and William Crotty, eds. *Handbook of Party Politics.* London: Sage, 435-445.

Narud, Hanne Marthe, Mogens N. Pedersen, and Henry Valen, eds. 2002. *Party Sovereignty and Citizen Control: Selecting Candidates for Parliamentary Elections in Denmark, Finland, Iceland and Norway.* Odense: University Press of Southern Denmark.

Nissim, Moshe. 2006. "Can the Deterioration be Stopped." In Gideon Rahat, ed. *Candidate Selection in Israel: Reality and Ideal.* Tel Aviv: Sapir Institute, 132-136 [Hebrew].

Norris, Pippa. 2006. "Recruitment." In Richard S. Katz and William J. Crotty, eds. *Handbook of Party Politics.* London: Sage, 89-108.

------, and Joni Lovenduski. 1995. *Political Recruitment: Gender, Race and Class in the British Parliament.* Cambridge: Cambridge University Press.

Pedersen, Mogens N. 2002. "Denmark: The Interplay of Nominations and Election in Danish Politics." In Hanne Marthe Narud, Mogens N. Pedersen, and Henry Valen, eds. *Party Sovereignty and Citizen Control: Selecting Candidates for Parliamentary*

Elections in Denmark, Finland, Iceland and Norway. Odense: University Press of Southern Denmark, 29-61.

Rahat, Gideon. 2002. "Candidate Selection in a Sea of Changes: Unsuccessfully Trying to Adapt?" In Asher Arian and Michal Shamir, eds. *The Elections in Israel—1999*. New York: State University of New York Press, 245-268.

------. 2006. "How Should the Parties Select their Candidates to the Knesset? A Proposal for a Three-Stage Method." In idem, ed. *Candidate Selection in Israel: Reality and Ideal*. Tel Aviv: Sapir Institute, 138-149 [Hebrew].

------, and Reuven Y. Hazan. 2001. "Candidate Selection Methods: An Analytical Framework." *Party Politics* 7 (3): 297-322.

------. 2005. "On the Difference Between Democracy Within Parties and Democracy Within States: The Uneasy Relationship Between Participation, Competition and Representation." Presented at the workshop on Democracy and Political Parties, European Consortium for Political Research, University of Granada, Spain, 15-19 April.

------, and Tamir Sheafer. 2007. "The Personalization(s) of Politics: Israel 1949-2003," *Political Communication* 24 (1): 65-80.

------, and Neta Sher-Hadar. 1999. "The 1996 Party Primaries and Their Political Consequences." In Asher Arian and Michal Shamir, eds. *The Elections in Israel 1996*. New York: State University of New York Press, 241-268.

Scarrow, Suzan S., Paul Webb, and David M. Farrell. 2000. "From Social Integration to Electoral Contestation: The Changing Distribution of Power Within Political Parties." In Russell J. Dalton and Martin P. Wattenberg, eds. *Parties Without Partisans: Political Change in Advanced Industrial Democracies*. Oxford: Oxford University Press, 129-153.

Valen, Henry, Hanne Marthe Narud, and Audun Skare. 2002. "Norway: Party Dominance and Decentralized Decision-Making." In Hanne Marthe Narud, Mogens N. Pedersen, and Henry Valen, eds. *Party Sovereignty and Citizen Control: Selecting Candidates for Parliamentary Elections in Denmark, Finland, Iceland and Norway*. Odense: University Press of Southern Denmark, 169-215.

Party Strategy in the 2006 Elections: Kadima, Likud, and Labor

Jonathan Mendilow

I. Introduction

Electoral campaigns provide rare moments of clarity wherein underlying social and political processes converge and coalesce. They simultaneously put to test elite understandings of these processes and the policy packages prescribed in response to them. The leadership team and party lines chosen often depend on the preferences of the electorate. Citizens however do not enjoy complete freedom of choice. The candidates and platforms they vote for are contingent on the alternatives presented to them. One may expect a degree of consistency in party offerings over time. Nevertheless, within the bounds set by their programs, past performance, and electoral base, parties must select key campaign issues and put forward public policies which respond to current needs. An analysis of the considerations governing their choices, and how they are presented to voters, can provide important insights into individual contests as well as to the general nature of elections as the defining institutions of democracy. The Knesset elections of 2006 constituted a uniquely interesting case for such an analysis, in light of the profound change in Israel's political landscape engendered by the emergence of Kadima as a center party commanding significantly wider support than either of the erstwhile contenders for power, Likud and Labor. This chapter focuses on the strategy adopted by the three competitors as they confronted the possibility that for the first time in Israeli history neither Likud nor Labor would serve as the mainstay of an incoming government coalition.

Before embarking on the analysis itself we should reflect on some methodological questions. For the student of party strategy, the discontinuities that marked the 2006 political landscape hamper the effectiveness of drawing on earlier studies of Israeli elections for research questions and hypotheses. Analyzing broad models of party strategy would seem to be more efficacious. Three such commonly cited models define political parties relative to their primary goals, structures, and link to the electorate as representatives, ideological advocates, and vote maximizers. Each of these models has contributed significantly to the comparative study of competitive party behavior, yet to date insufficient effort has been invested in interrelating them within a unified schemata. The following chapter will endeavor to do so in hopes that in addition to achieving greater clarity, we may also be able to identify some improbable postulates resulting from their isolation.

The concept of political parties being representative of the voting public harks back to the earliest scholarship on party behavior. The underlying assumption was that parties are "specialized interest aggregation structures" of specific publics (Almond and Powell, 1978: 205–6). By linking local, ethnic, cultural, or socio-economic groups to "the larger political world," they act, on the one hand, as specialized group associations and as "organizers of electorates and governments at the national level" on the other (Price, 1984: 111–12). Leaders and activists tend to think of themselves as representatives, endeavoring to act on behalf of their constituents (Kirkpatrick, 1997: 281; Muller and Strom, 1999), thereby inhibiting the strategic maneuverability of these parties. Their programs express the group's interests, and electoral campaigns are opportunities to appeal to deep rooted attachments, reinforced by a call to action. This confers relatively high levels of continuity on the parties because shifts in group identities and interests are often gradual. Consequently the choice of strategy is determined by forces over which the parties have little control. Nor are they expected to modify their stands in mid-campaign in response to shifting circumstances and electoral preferences.

This also holds true for ideological advocates, but for different reasons. Such parties focus on the manner in which social and political realities ought to be constructed. The principles they espouse and the issue positions they adopt are determined with little regard to voters' opinions (Kessel, 1980: 66). In this model, leaders and activists view themselves as representatives of the party and its ideology, rather than of the electorate. At times referred to as "missionary parties", these actors are concerned primarily with the role ideas play in shaping social interactions and they seek to convert the public to their particular visions (e.g. Duverger, 1995). They thereby "represent themselves as instruments of social change" (Lipset, 1981: 239) as determined by their worldviews. Ideologies are likely to undergo modifications in reaction to shifts in the underlying socio-political realities, and because of the need to devise "operative ideologies" (Seliger, 1976). Nevertheless, consistency is of paramount importance, and these parties are unlikely to abruptly shift strategies.

Vote maximizing parties, in contrast, are driven by the desire to attain or retain political power, and policy stances are viewed first and foremost as a means to this end. As rational agents, such contenders are expected to adopt positions which contribute to electoral victory (e.g.; Enelow and Hinich, 1984; Shepsle, 1991). In Downs' words (1957: 20), such parties "formulate policies in order to win elections, rather than win elections in order to formulate policies." It follows that such parties can easily alter their positions, or revise their policy promises to adapt to changing situations and attract additional supporters.[1] They may also skirt ideological commitments, relying instead on what Kirchheimer (1966) called "catch all tactics" to appeal to the widest electorates possible.

Models are presented in an attempt to reduce complexity. Nevertheless, the treatment of representation, ideological advocacy, and vote maximizing as stark options among which parties must choose, simplifies complexities beyond the point of effectiveness. Referring to models of party organization, William Wright (1971: 8) cautioned that "parties need not be treated in dichotomous, polarized ("either-or") terms; ... basic party models should be viewed as end points of a continuum along which specific parties range." Extending his statement to include the choice of electoral strategy necessitates taking into account these three modes of behavior as options which are not mutually exclusive. We should therefore expect that most parties will combine objectives and strategies, and present a mix to the electorate, although the proportions will most likely vary. The three models can be more readily understood as representing points of a triangle defining three continua, to which I shall refer as the "party goal triangle" (see figure 1). Parties position themselves on any two legs of the triangle, and their locations define the boundaries of their electoral activity. This allows us to avoid the view, shared by the three models discussed above, of parties as "static" entities whose goals are set and whose strategies are determined individually by their leaders. In reality, environmental factors like changes in the rules of the game or the structure of the competition, shifting circumstances, and the behavior of adversaries all impact on the choices and necessitate prioritization. The end result is that party behavior is not necessarily consistent throughout all campaigns, and locations along the legs of the party goal triangle need not be fixed even within the same campaign. Shifts can be expected to occur along the two legs that the party occupies, but in extreme cases it is conceivable that the parties might exchange one of the legs altogether.

In either case, the location of parties along the legs of the party goal triangle reflects decisions made by authorized individuals. Difficulties in addressing leadership roles in determining party strategy constitute another "cost" of the separation between the representation, ideological advocacy, and vote maximizing models. Whereas the first two tend to downplay the role of leadership, the third exaggerates it. In the former, leaders are constrained by exogenous factors over which they have little control, whether they are group interests or ideological demands. In the latter, leaders function as autonomous rational actors, weighing the efficacy of various options and reaching decisions. Parties however, do not campaign solely on what they represent, nor do they accord equal weight to all the elements of their platform. Even those parties positioning themselves close to the representation or ideological advocacy polls of the party goal triangle must select and prioritize issues and determine how they are to be presented. Vote maximizers, for their part, are bound by such factors as party traditions, the interests of the electoral base, or the internal balance of power among leaders and factions.

If strategic decisions are not made under the same constraints, what factors should the analyst consider to achieve a better understanding of this process? The history and values of leaders and parties may predispose them to accept or reject specific options. Nevertheless, strategic decisions are deliberative acts shaped substantially by their context. To study them it is necessary to take the institutional environment into account. Among the factors that should be included are:

a. *The rules of the electoral game and the structure of the competition.* Neither rules, nor the structure of the competition, are neutral arbiters. By defining the stakes, available resources, the "pulls of the system," and the methods of converting votes into seats, they present opportunities and dangers that must be taken into account.

b. *The public and the party's concerns that the party could feasibly target.* Even parties positioning themselves close to the vote maximizing point must assess the interests of various public groups, so that promises that win over the greatest number of votes can be made and unnecessary mistakes avoided.

c. *The strengths, weaknesses and courses of action of parties potentially competing for that public.* In an interdependent environment, outcomes are achieved as a result of the interaction of choices taken by the participants. Parties therefore must assess the decisions made by the contenders, along with their possible outcomes.

But there is an additional environment to consider. An added "price" incurred by the treatment of the party models in isolation is the consideration of parties as unitary, cohesive actors. This is common in much of the research on political party behavior. As Laver (1999: 9–10) points out, parties are treated "as if each ... had a single brain. At best, the party is seen ... as a sort of insect hive, comprising physically distinct individuals but working intellectually to a single coherent design." Most parties, however, are complex organizations whose internal dynamics play an essential role in shaping the mix among the objectives pursued, and constrain the choice of strategies employed to attain them. Among the intra-institutional factors impacting on strategic decisions are the following:

a. *Competing elites and their pressure potential.* One of the most important dimensions of electoral competitions is the ability of the contenders to manipulate voter perception. Party unity facilitates the simultaneous transmission of two images: leadership authority and team cohesion. In addition to any resultant perceptual damage, party disunity may impair the ability to convey a coherent message, or alternately lead to its dilution through a series of compromises.

b. *The resources (money, in-kind resources, manpower) upon which the party strategy relies.* In a word defined by scarcity, funding is invariably limited, while virtually all promotional activities entail expense. Resource allocation and its attendant prioritization are therefore critical components of strategic and operational campaign decisions. Targeting specific publics, and choosing the means by which to communicate with these groups, obviously impacts on the content of the campaigns (Mendilow, 1992).

Figure 1

The Party Goal Triangle

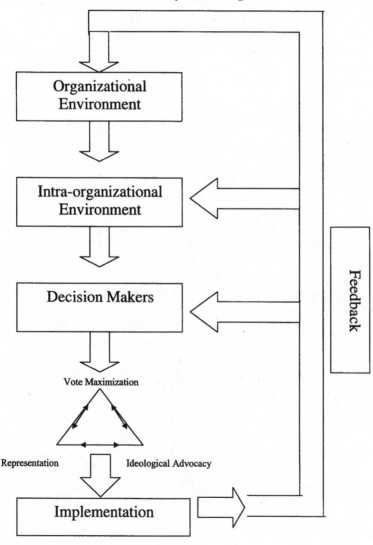

Finally, we must consider party reactions to the dynamic flow of events and public opinion. Party competition is an ongoing process in which each side attempts to shift environmental factors to its own advantage. The capacity to detect the reactions to such efforts both by the party and its rivals is in itself a valuable asset, and political parties invest heavily in public opinion surveys, focus groups, daily trackings, and other techniques of information collection. Shifts in public opinion, or changes in circumstances, are likely to result in adjustments or even strategic shifts in the middle of a campaign.

The ensuing section can be divided into three parts. The examination of the main rival's strategy in the 2006 contest begins with a brief examination of organizational and intra-organizational factors. The reciprocal impact of these factors is then approached in an attempt to understand the strategy of Likud, Labor, and Kadima within the dynamic context of the campaign up to the last three weeks of operation. And finally, the chapter will focus on the last and most intensive part of the competition, with particular attention given to campaign television advertising.

II. The Organizational and Intra-Organizational Environments

The famous maxim "There is nothing permanent except change" resonates strongly for students of the recent Israeli elections. The decade preceding the 2006 Knesset contest witnessed no less than four national polls, each one resulting in wide-ranging fluctuations in the fortunes of the main parties. Up until the mid-1990s the country experienced only two turnover elections (1977 and 1992), yet all Knesset elections since then have resulted in power shifts (though that of 2003 merely confirmed the Likud's victory in the 2001 special Prime Ministerial ballot, and was therefore an electoral turnover only as against the previous parliamentary election of 1999). What partly obscured this volatility was the preservation of patterns established in the 1970s. The most conspicuous of these patterns was the battle for power between two coalitions, the center-right and the center-left, each of which comprised a larger party (Likud and Labor respectively) with its more ideological satellites. Neither camp however was able to form a government on its own. Consequently, another persistent pattern was the victor's dependence on coalition partners: several smaller parties, or a left-right "national unity coalition" in which the two large parties joined forces. The 1980s experienced successive governments of the latter type, and this pattern was repeated in the elections of 2001–3 and 2004–5. The formation of Kadima was designed to bring about the erosion of these patterns and facilitate the birth of a new party system. The widespread expectation that it would achieve its goals formed the basis of its decisions as well as those of its main rivals.[2]

A brief description of Kadima's origins might help to clarify some of the issues. The elections for the Sixteenth Knesset resulted in a crushing defeat for Israel's Labor party, and a momentous victory for the Likud. The former lost over 20 percent of its Knesset representation; the latter doubled it to become, for the first time in Israel's history, twice as strong as its adversary. Predictably, there were critics who viewed the results as presaging a new era of Likud domination.[3] However, the interpretation of the electoral outcome as a reflection of a rightward trend in public opinion failed to detect the true twist of the campaign: Likud was able to adopt a vote-maximizing strategy because Sharon forcibly moved it to the center of the left-right ideological continuum, aligning it with public opinion which overwhelmingly supported territorial accommodation with the Palestinians, an Israeli-Palestinian "separation," and a Palestinian state as the inevitable resolution of the conflict. In contrast to previous contests, the electorate was not asked to choose between the opposing views of the left and the right, and it was this that frustrated Labor's attempt to center its campaign on a peace plan which would force Likud to defend a party platform unpopular with an overwhelming majority of Israelis. The transmutation of the moderate left's main platforms into territory shared by the main contestants, enabled Sharon to focus voter attention on his unrelenting plea for national unity and on the personal aspects of the contest between himself, as an experienced centrist incumbent, and Mitzna as a relatively young and unknown novice (Mendilow, 2005).

The success of this campaign was greater than meets the eye. The victor acquired a pivotal position within a fragmented system, opposed only by its radical right and left. The division however, permeated Likud itself. Sharon's acceptance of a two-state solution to the Palestinian problem as "a reasonable, pragmatic and practicable one, that offers a real opportunity to achieve an agreement" (Sharon, 2002), contradicted party ideology, as well as the resolutions of its governing bodies. Similarly, his embrace of the popular call for construction of a "defensive fence" separating the West Bank from Israel proper was also unaligned with the party line. Sparring with party leaders preceded the campaign itself (e.g., *Haaretz*, December 23, 2002; Shifer, 2002), but became especially venomous after Sharon decided to embark on his disengagement plan in late 2004. His detractors within the party felt that he "betrayed the spirit and soul of the Likud." The following year was characterized by repeated efforts of the so-called Likud rebels to bring down what they considered a "legal but illegitimate government" (www.info.co.uk/am/publishs/article9976.shtml. 11 January 2005), and attempts to steer the party away from the direction set by its chairman. The central position of Sharon and his camp was further accentuated when Labor entered the coalition as a counterweight to the right-wing faction within Likud. The impasse created by Labor's decision to leave the coalition, and Sharon's wish to lead the country unshackled by party hawks, led him to bolt Likud and establish his own party. Kadima was designed to turn his personal popularity, and the pivotal position of his camp within the party system as a whole, into the basis for a strong center party that would constitute the core of any possible coalition. The enlistment of former Labor chairman and peace prize Laureate Shimon Peres, as well as other Labor and independent MKs, emphasized the nature of the new party as a meeting point for the center left and center right. Pre-election polls consistently predicted a significant Kadima victory over both the truncated Likud and Labor, and helped to create the perception that Kadima's success was a foregone conclusion. This was further strengthened in the aftermath of Sharon's debilitating stroke, less than three months before voting day, when Kadima defied initial predictions that Sharon's absence at the helm would weaken party loyalty (see e.g., Verter et al., 2006). The party united around the successor, and polls continued to register the support of a large plurality of voters even after the shock lessened. By the start of the campaign in late January it became clear that, barring any unexpected occurrences, the chances of Likud or Labor rebounding, thereby enabling them to prevent the restructuring of the party system, were slim.

An examination of Israel's first party system enables a fuller appreciation of the potential effects of what took place in 2006. Kadima lacked both the ideological and cultural attributes of Mapai's domination:[4] its identification "with an epoch…its doctrines, ideas, methods, [and] style" (Duverger, 1967: 308–9). Nor did Kadima enjoy the institutional dimension of Mapai's supremacy, its leadership of the Jewish Agency, the Histadrut (Labor Federation), and the local authorities. Yet Mapai's longevity in office was also a result of its plurality of votes, its position at the center of the ideological map, and the absence of any cohesive opposition. This enabled Mapai to bargain effectively with the smaller parties on its platforms in forming governments, so that election results merely determined which of these parties it would choose as coalition partners (usually one from its right, one from its left, along with a religious party).

The predicament of the former ruling parties in 2006 may be illustrated by Likud's attempt to form a pre-election preventative bloc with Labor, thus thwarting Kadima's plan to deprive them of power, and the dismal failure of this attempt.[5] The general expectation of a Kadima victory also explains the small parties' espousal of the strategy successfully employed under the direct and separate election of the prime minister. Tommy Lapid, for instance, could thus claim on behalf of Hetz at the beginning of the 2006 TV campaign that "these elections are really over. We already know the results more or less. What is the importance of who will be Kadima's thirty-fifth member of Knesset? What is now needed is that the secular public will vote its secular interest" (Israel Broadcasting Authority, Channel Two, March 7, 2006). The feeling that the dye had been cast can also account for Labor's attempt, approximately two weeks before election day, to prove its determination to fulfill electoral promises by conducting what amounted to coalition negotiations with Kadima in the media. It demanded the finance ministry, rejected coalitional partnership with Yisrael Beiteinu, and insisted on the passing of a series of laws, including the raising of the minimum wage to $1000 and the institution of a universal pension plan (e.g., *Yediot Aharonot*, March 17; *Jerusalem Post*, March 22, 2006).

The elections, however, were not over before election day. The distribution of Knesset seats and the composition of the incoming coalition still hung in the balance, and the structure of the competition actually became more complex. What substituted the focal point of earlier competitions—the stand-off between right and left—may best be described as a triangle: the top point representing Kadima, with the two other points representing Labor and Likud. The strategic objective of Kadima was to maintain the electoral support predicted by the polls until election day so as to be able to form a durable, stable coalition. This presented a significant challenge, as Kadima was still a skeleton of a party lacking a framework of activists, traditions, or even an elaborately detailed program. Yet it was precisely these deficiencies that freed it from dependence on any social, economic, or political sector whose needs and interests might warrant special consideration. As a new and large party, devoid of institutions such as primaries that might afford opportunities for mass participation, it was free to extend its appeal to the entire public save for the extreme right, the extreme left, and the religious sectors. Likud and Labor, on the other hand, sought to recapture past supporters who had drifted to Kadima and to attract the large number of undecided voters. Both therefore found themselves directing much of their appeal to their core constituencies. Each one attempted to hamper Kadima's ability to establish a government coalition. Likud toyed with the idea of heading a bloc of right wing and religious parties that would be sufficiently large to prevent the establishment of a Kadima–Labor government; Labor sought to prevent Kadima from joining forces with the right wing parties and to maximize its share of the government pie.

However, an essential part of the picture were the secondary struggles conducted by both these parties. Having experienced a prolonged in-house conflict and party split, Likud found itself in a precarious position. Falling below a critical number of Knesset seats could jeopardize its privileged position as the largest party of the right, and erode its credibility as a potential ruling party in future elections. This engendered an in-house struggle in which Likud sought not only to arrest any rightward hemorrhaging but to lure away voters inclining toward its right wing competitors/allies. Labor likewise attempted to broaden its electoral hunting grounds—not so much to the Meretz electorate[6] but rather toward low income Sephardim who were for the most part off-limits to them after Likud won their allegiance in the 1970s. These voters were also courted by Shas and generated a three-way contest between Likud, Shas, and Labor. This can be attributed to a shift in the Labor agenda, with the ousting of Shimon Peres as Labor party Chairman by Amir Peretz, a Moroccan born Israeli who became the first Sephardi to head either the Labor or the Likud party during elections. To better appreciate this development, we must focus on the role of leadership in the elections rather than the structure of the political contest and the targeted public sectors.

Every campaign is waged with the previous election in mind. Even when the match takes place on a realigned playing field, parties tend to return to what they believe worked in the past and avoid what brought about failure. Likewise, voters' past experiences shape expectations that in turn serve as a prism through which the contest can be understood. The result is the tendency of modes of competition to become ingrained and, like all other institutions, become embedded in and interact with their social and historical contexts. As noted by Grofman et al. (1999: 2), the result is that "seemingly identical electoral rules may give rise to very different types of outcomes in different political settings." This may explain the residues of the law for the direct election of the prime minister, which was first instituted in Israel in 1996. In combining the parliamentary and presidential systems by separating the direct and personal prime ministerial vote from the simultaneous list-based proportional Knesset elections, it constituted a unique experiment.[7] It was also a short-lived one, and was repealed five years later. Nevertheless, its effects were so entrenched that nullifying this change was not sufficient to eradicate them. The most significant of these effects was the focusing of the campaign on the prime ministerial candidates, along with the expectation that the victor's authority would be a result of his agenda, and the personal support of large segments of the population. The former reflected the fact that under the double ballot system it was the electoral strength of the candidate rather than that of his party that determined who would win office. The reliance of the party on its candidate was further accentuated by the growing weakness of the major parties, engendered by the desertion of supporters who combined the ballot for the candidate of a national party with a Knesset vote for a party representing a specific interest. This weakness enabled the candidates to run on their personality and foreign policy and defense agendas, and insured their continued autonomy from both the Knesset and their own parties.

The same phenomenon was repeated in the 2003 elections. Both the Likud and Labor campaigns were conducted, in the words of Labor Secretary General Ophir Pines-Paz, as "one man crusades," and in both "most of the party's MKs worked much harder in their own primaries than in the general elections" (Less, 2003). This may be due, at least in part, to a lack of party unity. As mentioned above, the new line adopted by Sharon brought about disputes with top party leaders, and much of what Mitzna articulated on the issues of peace and security was unacceptable to all but a narrow group of supporters. The Likud also suffered the consequences of vote rigging scandals in the primaries. It demoralized the grassroots and clung to the party throughout the campaign, whereas Sharon himself remained a highly popular veteran leader for whom polls forecast a sweeping victory. Labor found itself, of necessity, playing to the general public's expectations, as revealed in both polls and focus groups. "The repeal [of the direct prime ministerial elections] had not filtered into public consciousness," explained a senior Mitzna advisor, and so "the electorate focused on leadership. Mitzna for it was an 'unidentified object.' Not to advertise him would have been suicidal" (Baltiansky, 2003). Both Sharon's attempt to establish independence from Likud and govern on the basis of his overwhelming popular support and the establishment of Kadima were to a degree a continuation of the same patterns.

As the countdown towards the 2006 elections began, it became clear that the three-way competition between Kadima, Likud, and Labor would to a large extent focus on the three candidates vying for the top position: Olmert, Netanyahu, and Peretz. Similarly it was evident that each of the three leaders suffered from political handicaps and that each was therefore a ready target for the others. Consequently, all three faced the same strategic need: to reach the finishing line as credible leaders, with unique policy visions and proficiency in dealing with the country's problems.

Unlike the other two candidates, who were not then widely known and relatively untested in the uppermost government echelons, Netanyahu's problem could be located in his recent performance as finance minister. Despite pundits' skepticism at his boast of an invitation to serve as Italy's finance minister, he was widely considered to have been successful in his post. However, during his tenure the country experienced austerity budgets and massive cutbacks in education, health, and social welfare spending. The simultaneous adoption of free market policies favoring the well-to-do severely polarized Israeli society, resulting in a deep feeling of resentment among the low income and lower middle class populations, precisely the strata on which Likud relied for its core support.

Peretz, on the other hand, was well positioned to attract these very same voters, and to satisfy what Labor strategists perceived as a growing public concern over socio-economic issues. His background as a member of a family sent to live in a transit camp upon arrival from Morocco, and as a resident of a poor, peripheral Southern town, along with his lack of higher education and his career as a trade union leader, enabled him to present himself as an authentic voice of the "have-nots." These same attributes however, also contributed to a widespread image of Peretz as someone lacking the gravitas necessary for premiership. His background could potentially alienate the Ashkenazi middle and upper middle class Labor electoral base. The problem was particularly noticeable in the million strong Russian sector. In 2003 this sector gave Labor a mere 5 percent of its vote, and surveys revealed that personal support for Peretz was almost nonexistent. These obstacles were further highlighted with the creation of Kadima and the defection of Peres. In the first poll following the accession of Peretz to the chairmanship, the party achieved impressive gains, reaching a high of twenty-eight MKs. But by early January 2006 the polls predicted a decrease to sixteen MKs, a loss of over 40 percent.

Olmert, for his part, enjoyed the "home court" advantage of incumbency. Most electoral contests are to some extent based on a retrospective assessment of those in office. The fact that Olmert succeeded the prime minister within an ongoing administration and before the campaign began in earnest, identified him both with Sharon and his policies in the mind of the voter. But it was precisely the tacit comparison with Sharon that became the source of Olmert's vulnerability. Despite a political career stretching over dozens of years, service in several governments, and being the first Likud mayor of Jerusalem, he never held any of the prominent ministries and did not gain widespread public popularity. The differences between Olmert and Sharon regarding the issues of security, peace, and war were especially damaging. Sharon was one of Israel's most famous generals and his legacy implied the replication of the successful Gaza model of "separation" in the more sensitive West Bank. Yet the closest Olmert had come to policy-making in such spheres was his membership (1981–8) in the Knesset Foreign Affairs and Security committee. As an untried figure, stepping into Sharon's shoes was a major challenge, and it was clear that the opposing parties would attempt to capitalize on this issue. Here too the Russians served as the canary in the mine. Sharon brought his overwhelming popularity in this sector to Kadima. Yet immediately after his sudden illness, polls registered a mass return among the Russians to Likud (Galili, 2005).

The combination of candidate–centered campaigns and flawed candidates magnified the importance of the intra-organizational factors, particularly party unity, and Likud was worse off than its rivals. In part, this reflected the heightened competition whereby a loss of Knesset seats was considered inevitable. As Speaker of the Knesset Rivlin stated upon the Likud split, "the Likud is likely to find itself in the opposition for years" (*Haaretz*, November 22, 2005).[8] Yet the tensions between Silvan Shalom and his faction, and Netanyahu and his supporters, ran deeper and spilled over into the public realm. As soon as the campaign began, Shalom referred to Netanyahu's loss of credibility as a prime minister and his defeat in 1999 by noting that the public "has not found a new Bibi" (Shalom, 2006). A week following the publication of the initial party slogans, a "senior Likud official" reiterated this statement and expressed the concern that "the campaign is an informational tragedy, the party isn't finding its line, the strategy isn't working ... the mood in the Likud is gloomy, and the MKs and ministers aren't cooperating with the campaign" (*Haaretz*, February 5, 2006).[9] Such tactical disagreements persisted throughout the campaign,[10] but there were also substantive disputes that affected the party's message. The party's foreign and defense program was published just a few days before the ballot, due to a debate over the mention of the road map.[11] As we shall see, this hindered Likud from presenting peace policies as alternatives to the Kadima plan it had attacked.

If Labor was spared this internal bickering it was in part because the central figures who could have led the opposition preferred "exit" over "voice" (Hirschman, 1970) even before the campaign began. The bolting of Peres and his associates to Kadima is a case in point, but no less important is the departure of Labor's last Prime Minister, Ehud Barak from the party leadership. Acrimonious clashes between Barak and Peretz came to the fore immediately following the party primaries, but Barak's decision to take a prolonged hiatus abroad prevented any possible escalation. Upon his return[12] he attended party rallies, criticizing both Peretz and the conduct of the campaign. His call to vote for the party "despite its deep internal divisions" (*Jerusalem Post*, March 13, 2006) drew media attention to these disagreements. But the fact that such incidents occurred only before the campaign began and toward its end, and the fact that Barak did not attempt to galvanize his backers, muted the impact of these incidents. The relative unity of the party was also due to the party message. Peretz's chairmanship was greeted by media reports of anonymous complaints by party ministers that the new party leader's dovish stands constituted "an embarrassment" (e.g., *Haaretz*, November 15, 2005). This could have been alarming, especially recalling the events of 2003, when rifts over Mitzna's foreign policy proposals hindered Labor's efforts to present a coherent message on the central campaign issue (Mendilow, 2005: 57–9). But the change of priorities from defense to the socio-economic sphere, and the narrowing of the gaps between Labor and Kadima following Hamas' rise to power, significantly reduced this risk.

Kadima, for its part, was restricted mainly to its top leaders, many of whom had little in common apart from loyalty to Sharon and his agenda. As one commentator noted, "this is scarcely a party. It is a corporation" (C. Verter, 2006). One might have expected disorder and disarray, especially after Sharon's sudden departure. But the absence of unanimity and the lack of institutional frameworks and procedures mitigated against such an eventuality. Lacking any common denominators other than on security related matters, the party focused on these issues, and until late in the campaign had not developed these ideas much beyond Sharon's initial presentation. On the other hand, Kadima's bylaws delegated the authority to draw the party's Knesset list to Sharon. This authority was in turn assumed by Olmert, and this in turn obviated power struggles akin to those that plagued Likud. Some friction was unavoidable. Peres criticized his party's "convergence" plan. "I am not part of the group rushing to advocate unilateral withdrawals," he declared. "If the Palestinians want peace, we'll enter negotiations based on the road map, and if they turn to terror, we'll use force against them" (*Haaretz*, April 5, 2006). But such disagreements did not result in factional strife. Compared to the turmoil in Likud, Kadima managed to present an impressive image of unity, and this became one of its important selling points in the TV ad campaign.

The one relatively level, if not slightly tilted in Likud's favor, playing field was that of resource availability. Israeli parties rely almost entirely on state funding, with private contributions typically accounting for only 1 percent to 2 percent of their electoral budgets.[13] Subsidies are allocated for "current party expenditures," and in election years for campaign costs based on the numbers in the outgoing Knesset.[14] Parties receive 60 percent of their funding before the campaigns begin. Accounts are then settled after the elections relative to the outcome of the election. A similar method is used for the allotment of free TV and radio broadcasting time. Regardless of size, each party receives a fixed share, in addition to units of time multiplied by the size of its numbers in the outgoing Knesset. The money and broadcasting time received by the party reflects its past electoral performance. Likud doubled its numbers in 2003, thereby entitling it to relatively large supplements to the electoral grants it received before the election, as well as an enlarged off-election year funding. The loss of sixteen MKs to Kadima substantially reduced the grant for the 2006 elections, though it was still a higher sum than Labor's (roughly 16.94 million shekels to 14.82 million shekels respectively). If Labor was the poorest of the three rivals, it was not because of its reduced government funding. The Labor party incurred large debts prior to the 2003 campaign as a result of poor performance in earlier contests, and the significant losses it suffered in 2003 considerably worsened the situation (Mendilow, 2003: 118–19). The impact on its decision-making ability was noticeable. In view of their severe economic constraints, and the meager support in the Russian sector, its American strategists suggested shutting down its immigrant campaign headquarters (Galili, 2006 A). The suggestion was rebuffed, but Labor's campaign in the Russian sector was late in starting and was allocated a mere 1.5 million NIS (in contrast to Likud's six and Kadima's four million). Of the three major competitors, Kadima received the smallest amount (approximately 12 million NIS) as an allowance for the sixteen Likud and two independent MKs that joined them (the three Labor MKs who switched party allegiance were not counted because the law recognizes as a Knesset faction only a number equal to or greater than a third of their original party) but it was debt free. The budget of all three parties was much higher: in Kadima's case some 40–45 million NIS.[15] All three needed to borrow from commercial banks, with Kadima borrowing the largest sums. Its lead in the polls, however, facilitated bank approval of its loan applications.

Kadima's disadvantage was that by the time the campaign was in full swing it had only managed to establish a small number of branches and could therefore only rely on a smaller cadre of unpaid activists. By mid-March its enrollment efforts netted only some 10,000 card-carrying members (*Yediot Aharonot*, March 16, 2006). Likud and Labor, in contrast, were parties with abundant registered members, branches spread all over the country, and party institutions leading all the way to the office of Chairman. Membership has gradually declined over the years. Since the 1990s few branches have been active in off-election seasons, with few members attending their activities. In effect, the two parties have progressively come to resemble the American model of cadre parties (Goldberg: 130-57). Nevertheless, the existence of an identifiable pool of potential volunteers, as well as detailed lists of likely supporters who could be contacted, was a valuable asset. Equally important, both parties had mayors and office holders in local and professional associations who could be counted on to use their positions to further the party's interests. These assets confronted Labor and Likud with the necessity of arriving at strategic decisions that Kadima was not forced to make. Reliance on grassroots organizations and party branch operations can help in building support among core constituencies, as well as reducing dependence on capital-intensive methods of advertising and "getting out the vote." However, effective use of such resources demands a programmatic approach that will serve as the glue to bind and energize the membership. In terms of the party goal triangle, this entails a move towards ideological advocacy and /or representation, with the attendant costs in terms of vote maximizing. This is obviously not an "either/or" question but one of trade-offs. Both Likud and Labor attempted to reach out to their members, but this did not result in any appreciable programmatic shifts. The reason will become clearer once we examine the interactions among all the factors considered above within the dynamic context of the campaign.

III. The Early Campaign, January–February 2006

The principal element of all campaign strategies is creating a message that will capture audience attention and votes. This is where the contestants are liable to be drawn in conflicting directions as presented by the points of the party goal triangle. This is perhaps true of all competitors in democratic elections, and it impacted on both Labor and Kadima. Likud, however, was considerably worse off, and the strains were particularity evident during the first part of the campaign.

The choice of message involves the prior identification of the target public and its needs. This usually consists of party stalwarts, defectors who altered their choice due to shifts in their basic positions, or perceived failures in the performance of a party whom they nevertheless continue to identify with, as well as cohorts of close parties who could be persuaded to move to an adjacent ideological field. There are also the uncommitted and undecided. The former may switch votes from one election to the next; the latter vacillates between specific parties. Both Likud and Labor strategists based their calculations on unusually large numbers of undecided voters, or defectors to Kadima who could still switch back to Labor or Likud. The core party constituency also included many who were vulnerable to Kadima's appeal, and therefore special attention needed to be lavished on protecting the home field. The two parties differed in that Labor, as noted earlier, believed it could extend its reach to include Likud and Shas voters. Likud strategists, on the other hand, realized that the party would need to limit its appeal to voters of the right, especially within its own constituency, to potential defectors to Kadima as well as the undecided among these two groups.

This could seemingly simplify Likud's quest for an effective message. After 1967, the territorial issue, and especially the settlements, defined the ideological differences between right and left. In campaigns fought under the double ballot system, this fault line was progressively blurred. It reflected the fact that victory in the prime ministerial contest was contingent on the candidates' ability to extend their support to all but the extreme groups. As noted above, the lingering effects persisted in 2003, with the additional shift in Sharon's posture. The result in 1996 and 1999 was a disparity between the campaigns conducted by the candidates and the more ideological campaigns conducted at the party level. In 2001 the contest was restricted to the prime ministerial level, but after the 2003 vote, hidden tensions erupted and eventually led to the succession of Sharon and his followers. In the wake of the traumatic "disengagement" and subsequent party split, one could have anticipated the release of the pent-up pressures and a return to the ideological style of the "good old days." Events "on the ground" seemed to indicate this eventuality. Even before the campaign began, clashes erupted in the Hebron market between Jewish squatters and Israeli security forces who attempted to serve them with eviction orders. Tensions also increased as the evacuation date of the illegal settlement in Amona, slated for the end of January, neared. The opening salvos of the campaign seemed to confirm the move toward an ideological stance. The party's first slogan was "Kadima [in Hebrew, Onwards] to the 1967 lines"; Netanyahu warned in his Herzliya conference speech against a return to pre-Six Day War borders, and Likud's reaction to Peretz's address at the same conference was that it "proved that Labor and Kadima are Siamese twins proffering up…withdrawals from Judea, Samaria and the Jordan Valley" (*Maariv*, January 25, 2006; *Haaretz*, January 23, 2006).

And yet, disengagement continued to enjoy widespread popularity, with many party leaders (including Silvan Shalom and Netanyahu himself until a week before implementation) supporting it with their vote. In the campaign several of them attempted to justify their position, but their explanations focused on procedural issues,[16] thus making it difficult to marshal a principled argument against withdrawal. Likewise, the first meeting of the program committee, on January 16, witnessed a debate over the inclusion of the "road map" that the government had accepted in principle. More importantly, the adoption of a hard-line ideological approach would have guaranteed an electoral disaster. The electoral need was to appeal to erstwhile supporters who were considering a switch to Kadima, and to those who had already switched party affiliation. Both had abandoned traditional party positions, and efforts to bring them back into the fold were liable to backfire. Losing all but the ideologically faithful, Likud would be reduced to a medium-sized protest party, eclipsed by the more credible and consistent National Union. Such fears explain the demand, especially among Shalom's supporters, that Likud draw up a persuasive peace plan: "the burden of proof is on Likud and Netanyahu to demonstrate that they have a plan for Israelis to have a peaceful future. A plan will come sooner rather than later" (*The Washington Times,* January 18, 2006). Such a strategic option, however, would have been no less dangerous. Apart from the question of credibility, it was liable to throw the party into disarray and raised the risk of massive desertions to the competing parties of the right, Yisrael Beiteinu, and the National Union.

The solution arrived at was to avoid ideology altogether, and attempt instead to ignite the party spirit with a "sizzling" campaign capitalizing on widespread concerns about the uncertain security future. This was already apparent in Netanyahu's Herzliya speech. The existing route of the separation fence, he argued, would place Israel's international airport and the roads to Jerusalem in danger, and would reward and facilitate terrorism. No alternative was offered, however, other than a return to the original route which was rejected by the Supreme Court in June 2004 (*Maariv*, January 25, 2006). A day later Israel was shocked by Hamas's victory in the Palestinian parliamentary election. This facilitated another line of attack—the accusation that Kadima was at fault and that its "unilateral withdrawal rewarded Hamas terror." Furthermore, "Labor and Kadima are scheming an additional unilateral withdrawal from the West Bank, and this reflects complete blindness to reality. Olmert and Kadima are establishing a Hamas terror state that will be an Iranian offshoot only a few kilometers from Israeli population centers" (*Haaretz*, January 27, 2006). This argument enabled Likud to present itself as the bulwark against terror in the words of its slogan, "Likud–strong against Hamas." This argument was sharply delineated for the Russian sector by comparing the rise of Hamas and that of Nazism.[17] This was further bolstered by singling Olmert out as inept and unworthy of leading a nation confronting a looming crisis. The first Internet Likud spot (February 9, 2006) presented an ominous march of Hamas fighters, and invited the viewer to wonder whether Olmert was equal to the challenge. Other attacks (February 16, 2006) drew on ideological echoes: for example, pictures of mounted police charging into the crowd of settlers at Amona with the statement "it is not the horses, or the police, or the soldiers. It is Olmert. Olmert is insensitive and irresponsible. He should not be given a state [to govern]."

This strategy was open to question. Would the accusations of a Labor (the "old enemy")–Kadima secret scheme stick, especially when the latter party had not yet put forward a plan for an additional withdrawal? Would the effort to run against Hamas prove credible? In 1996 Netanyahu ran successfully against Arafat (and Peres), and Likud's most effective spot depicted Arafat and Peres descending the stairs hand in hand. But Olmert enjoyed right-wing credentials and could not be accused of any personal contacts with Hamas. Nor was it certain that Internet and billboard advertising would arouse a somnolent campaign. Polls and daily trackings conducted throughout early February confirmed that the message failed to rally the undecided, or even the party membership, to the cause. However, without the ability to come up with positive party positions on the issues of security and peace, this game plan was viewed as the least objectionable option.

Strategists enjoy a fair amount of leeway, but in order to be successful they must respond to the questions uppermost in voter's minds. In a contest held not long after some half a million Israelis were listed as living below the poverty line, the state of the economy and the society belonged to that category of issues. Likud's economic platform was presented in early February. It contained a detailed list of economic reforms, designed to appeal to all sectors of the population. These, Netanyahu argued, constituted a direct continuation of the guiding principles he had followed as finance minister. Some, like the accelerated tax cuts, or the continued privatization of public services, were designed to ensure continued economic growth. Others involved welfare reform, including free daycare for families under a given income level, higher allowances for senior citizens, and grants for residents of public housing. These would be paid for by the money secured through continued growth. In effect, this was a "trickle-down economics" program that rested on Netanyahu's credibility as the architect of the economy's impressive expansion, coupled with a promise to use the fruits of this expansion to mitigate the policies which had propelled it. Polls and focus groups continued to demonstrate that resentment among potential Likud voters persisted, and Netanyahu's explanations were not convincing. Most respondents also regarded his electoral promises, especially to terminate poverty within three years,[18] as insincere and unrealistic. In short, it was clear that this message did not help the party, and could even be considered counterproductive by drawing attention to Netanyahu's "soft underbelly." It was impossible to forgo socio-economic issues, if only because that would concede this sphere to the competitors. Nevertheless, it was clear that there was no alternative but to rely on the party's negative stand on foreign and defense issues as the centerpiece of the campaign.

By the second half of February a new opportunity seemed to have presented itself. At the beginning of the month Kadima was stable in the polls despite the Hamas victory, the violence in Amona, and the Kassam rockets fired from Gaza. Surveys conducted revealed a downward trajectory and growing doubts as to whether Olmert was qualified to be prime minister.[19] The primary cause was corruption charges that began to be leveled at Kadima. On February 14, the Tel Aviv District Court meted out a severe punishment to Omri Sharon for filing false reports dealing with his father's 1999 electoral campaign. A week later the state comptroller announced an inquiry into Olmert's sale of his Jerusalem home to a Jewish American billionaire for $2.7 million. However, this did not bring about a breakthrough for Likud or Labor. Most of the voters leaving Kadima joined the undecided. One reason was the seeming parallel between Kadima and Likud. Along with Omri Sharon being one of its members in 1999, roughly at about the time of his sentencing, Likud MK Naomi Blumenthal was convicted for the vote-buying scandal that haunted the party since the December 2002 primaries. The conclusion drawn was that Likud's chances hinged on its ability to present a "rejuvenated party," one that could compare favorably with the tarnished Kadima. On February 21, Netanyahu called for transferring the selection of the party's electoral list from the Central Committee to open primaries, where all party members had a vote. A full quarter of the Kadima membership were contemplating a return to the Likud fold, he declared, and it would be this anti-corruption reform that would increase Likud's strength by no less than six MKs. On March 1, the Central Committee passed the decision to demote itself, and a "renewed Likud" came into being. Yet polls failed to register the expected momentum. By the beginning of the campaign's last three weeks Likud seemed to reach the point where it was relying only on Kadima's deepening woes and on its own advantage as a mass party in the last minute "get out the vote" drive.

Labor conducted a campaign that was diametrically opposed to that of Likud. Peretz's assumption of the Chairmanship meant, as we have noted, that the party was required to shift the weight of its message from peace and security to social and economic questions. In adopting this issue it moved along the legs of the triangle, away from the vote maximizing positions (that Peres would probably have had to adopt) toward the representational and ideological polls. This played to the new chairman's strengths, but in equal measure reflected the difficulty of constructing an effective security related message. Labor's foreign policy and security program, presented on January 17, included the traditional principles of two states for two nations, the immediate completion of the separation fence, and a war against terrorism. It also pledged that a Labor led government would hold onto the large settlement blocks and to Jerusalem as the country's "eternal capital." All this, however, was virtually indistinguishable from Kadima's positions. If there was any difference, it lay in the latter's endorsement of unilateral withdrawal, as against Labor's call for direct negotiations. Yet Sharon urged (at least semantically) negotiations, a position repeated in Olmert's Herzliya speech, whereas Labor did not rule out unilateral separation should it become clear that Israel had no partner for peace. The rise of Hamas brought the parties even closer together. This was made clear in Peretz's Knesset statement (January 26, 2006): "we will not conduct negotiations with an organization that does not recognize Israel's right to exist. If we have to, we will implement unilateral moves." In February, Peretz still voiced a "preference to holding negotiations and using unilateralism as a last resort," and in early March he met with PA Chairman Abbas and issued a joint declaration in favor of continued negotiations (*Haaretz*, March 11, 2006). Nevertheless, Peretz was forced to admit that "Labor's voters realize that there's no difference [between Labor and Kadima] on the diplomatic side. There's no doubt that the socio-economic realm...will determine this election" (*Ibid*).

In a party where socio-economic issues were rarely discussed with any passion, placing them at the top of the agenda constituted a noteworthy ideological turn that was liable to exacerbate the alienation of the party's middle class and Ashkenazi base. The recruitment into the party's upper echelon of Avishai Braverman, President of Ben Gurion University and one of the country's most respected economists, was calculated to offset this risk. Widely assumed to be the top candidate for a senior economic ministry, should the party join the incoming coalition, he was well-suited to lend Labor's socio-economic ideas academic credibility and to introduce them to its traditional electorate. In substantive terms, a set of social-democratic measures were put forth, including increasing the minimum wage and old age allowances, guaranteed pensions, and a concerted effort to bring about a "fairly distributed economic growth" (*Haaretz*, January 22, 2006). Other pledges were geared toward the middle class party base, e.g., support of enterprises, or the granting of student loans to be returned only after entering the workforce with an average, or above average earned monthly salary. These proposals were presented as integral and mutually supportive elements of a single vision, and it was to this concept that Braverman referred when he spoke of "the revolution Amir Peretz and I are determined to bring about" (*Yediot Aharonot*, December 1, 2006). Once again the Russian sector pointed to the potential: polls showed that over 50 percent of the Russian speaking respondents voiced support of Labor's socio-economic platform, irrespective of their dislike of Peretz and suspicions of his "socialist" past (Galili, 2006).[20]

A related question concerned the desirability of negative campaigning. Direct attacks against Likud were ruled out from the start. The social agenda itself achieved that effect, whereas attacks on the foreign and defense front could only prove harmful when directed at a public which had supported Likud in previous elections. As for Kadima, polls conducted in the early phases of the campaign showed that criticism of the popular Sharon would be ineffective. The conclusion drawn was that the party should concentrate on promoting its program and leadership. In the wake of Sharon's illness there were party advisers who recommended staying the course. Olmert, they pointed out, was not associated in the public mind with the hardships of the Netanyahu period, and negative campaigning would unnecessarily dilute the party message. There was however, widespread criticism of an anemic campaign that failed to pick up momentum. In late January, Peretz singled Olmert out as the impediment to increasing the minimum wage and social security payments, and accused him of planning university tuition hikes (*Haaretz*, January 22-23, 2006). Some three weeks later the party's nation-wide campaign was inaugurated under the slogan "Olmert will divide Israel's rich and poor."

Omri Sharon's sentence strengthened those[21] who urged a more aggressive line of attack. Labor formed an anti-corruption committee, which defined the elections as a referendum on "democracy and the rule of law" (*Haaretz*, February 14, 2006). What followed was a short, venomous exchange. The assault on Kadima was met with unspecified accusations of corruption scandals involving the Histadrut. These seemed to be substantiated soon after, when a lawsuit was brought against Peretz for allegedly dismissing a high-ranking Histadrut official who refused to use his position to further the interests of One Nation, Peretz's party at the time. Labor returned fire by accusing Kadima of masterminding a smear campaign, and launched a new slogan—"corrupt Kadima, we're sick of you." For its part, Kadima demanded "an explanation in court about as to who took over the Labor Party via the Histadrut" (*Haaretz,* February 19, 2006). Focus groups and daily trackings revealed to both sides that each stood to lose should the mutual recriminations continue. Kadima campaign director, Reuven Adler, circulated a directive ordering an end to all personal attacks on Peretz, and an undeclared truce came into effect. By early March, Labor had returned to positions that were closer to the ideological and representational points of the party goal triangle. From this position it confronted the challenge of retaining the loyalty of its supporters despite Peretz's chairmanship[22] while reaching out across the socio-economic divide to the traditional Likud and Shas base.

Beyond the impact of attacks and counter-attacks on party strategy, what took place between Labor and Kadima illustrates the latter's growing concern about the scandals and their effects. From its inception Kadima was a "one dimensional" party, designed to win parliamentary backing for its founder's defense and foreign policy ideas. Although it did come up in late February with a socio-economic program,[23] this clearly played a minor role. On the other hand, throughout January and February, the party did not feel the need to adopt a missionary style or to elaborate its positions. Public opinion polls indicated that a majority of Israelis supported these positions and that the party was expected to win approximately forty Knesset seats. A "dormant" campaign made it difficult for the truncated Likud to galvanize its public, and reinforced the perception of Kadima as the forerunner. It also facilitated a change of guard at the helm. By adopting a low profile and avoiding a partisan tone Olmert was able to "ease" gradually into the Prime Minister's shoes. The outbreak of the corruption issues and Kadima's flagging numbers at the polls raised the question as to whether the party could afford not to modify its strategy. Several advisers cautioned against any move that would enable Likud to heat up the campaign, rally the troops, and engender Kadima losses. Olmert himself, as well as other strategic advisers, argued that staying the course would entail a progressively heavier price, and that to prevent this loss the party should seize control of the agenda. This would most likely cause shifts in the polls, since many of the undecided would move their support to either Likud or Kadima. Surveys showed, however, that Kadima enjoyed a large advantage, and that this would probably be augmented by undecided voters vacillating between itself and Labor.

Two days before the beginning of the TV campaign, the debate came to an abrupt end. Channel 10 released documents and excerpts from Omri Sharon's calendar. They detailed his involvement in a large number of political appointments during his father's tenure. Moreover, many of these appointments were arranged through the offices of Olmert and other prominent Kadima leaders. The Labor party reacted by calling this "a moral and political earthquake," and even Likud announced that all its corrupt members had left to Kadima and that "no honest person can identify with a movement that has values like these" (israelnationalnews.com downloaded September 25, 2006). On Friday, March 10, Israeli newspapers published interviews with Olmert, in which he articulated the "convergence plan." Kadima thereby moved along the vote maximizing/ideological advocacy leg of the party goal triangle. This, along with the beginning of the party's TV broadcasts, inaugurated the campaign's final phase.

IV. The Final Phase, March 10-27

If Kadima successfully took control of the agenda, it was in no small measure because the "conversion" plan provided Likud with a concrete target against which it could position itself. There was an almost palpable sense of relief: "It was not clear what these elections were about, and now it is obvious that there is an unmistakable choice to be made" (*Haaretz*, March 12, 2006). On the following TV broadcast, Netanyahu declared the elections to be a referendum on "Olmert's plan for another disengagement that would hand territory to Hamas without getting anything in return" (Israel Broadcasting Authority, Channel 2, March 11, 2006). Netanyahu also pledged that Likud would not enter into any coalition that is attempting to implement the "great withdrawal." This served several purposes. It highlighted the differences between Likud and Kadima, and diluted the relevance of the socio-economic issues. It also lent credibility to the claim that Likud was the only opposition capable of preventing withdrawal, and therefore deserves the votes of all those who view themselves as right-wing. This assertion had until now only been made in the Russian sector, where Lieberman enjoyed tremendous popularity. Likud's advisors decided to pursue an indirect attack by claiming that any voter interested in a strong Yisrael Beiteinu should cast a vote for Netanyahu. Likud now felt free to extend the call to all and sundry: "Whoever intends to vote for one of the small parties, it is as if he is giving his vote to Kadima … We call upon all the voters of the national camp to cast only one vote that could prevent the big withdrawal" (Israel Broadcasting Authority, March 12, 2006).

At the same time, Netanyahu initiated contacts with Labor, Yisrael Beiteinu, and Shas in hopes of consolidating a preventative anti-Kadima bloc. It is unclear to this writer whether the assumption was that this would reach the media. Be it as it may, as noted earlier, the contacts were leaked and denounced by all concerned, including Yisrael Beiteinu and Shas. This tacitly proved Netanyahu's point: that voters who gave these parties their ballots were liable to find their representatives side by side with the hated Labor in a Kadima-led coalition. The final party message in the TV campaign explicated this assertion and added the innuendo of a left wing plot. Following the depiction of the almost legendary hero, Begin, calling on the public to vote only Mahal (the Likud acronym), the allegation was made that "Olmert and the Left seek to destroy Likud. They know that only it can bring together the National camp and form an electoral alternative. Hence they do not care who the public votes for—Shas, Lieberman or National Union—as long as it is not Likud. Without the Likud all's lost." This was followed by a direct attack on Yisrael Beiteinu. Left-wing supporters on the party's electoral list were exposed, and the public was warned against

Table 1
Content Analysis of Electoral Appeals Appearing on Israeli Television,
March 7–26, 2006, and January 8–25, 2003 (in brackets)
in percentage of net advertising time

Contents of Appeal	Likud	Labor	Kadima
Building up the image of party leaders	17.5 (54.5)	38.0 (66.1)	39.2
Strong Team	1.2 (0)	20.0 (0)	25.65
Party past achievements and positive traits	7.5 (0)	2.5 (0)	8.4
Call to vote for the party	11.1 (3.7)	1.0 (3.7)	7.3
Top candidate's achievements in system management	12.0 (2.1)	30.0 (3.0)	1.1
Stand on controversial domestic issues (economic priorities, etc.)	0.0 (0)	19.0 (3.3)	0.0
Stands on controversial foreign/defense issues (borders, negotiations with Palestinians, etc.)	0.0 (3.0)	0 (2.8)	6.4
General non-controversial issues (democracy, defense of country, etc.)	3.3 (14.5)	25.2 (11.8)	32.4
Total Positive	**52.7**	**135.7**	**120.6**
Criticism of main candidates on grounds of corruption, failures in system management or credibility. Capital case letters refer to the target of attack: O = Olmert, P = Peretz, N = Netanyahu	20.6 (18.5) P = 0; O = 20.6	2.50 (5.5) O = 2.5; N = 2.8	28.5 P = 7.2; N = 21.3
Criticism of main adversaries' positions (foreign or domestic issues)	7.7 (7.1)	1.5 (7.5)	0.7
Criticism of rivals other than main adversaries	2.1 (5.0)	1.0 (0)	0.0
Warning of what a government led by the adversaries could bring	17.5 (8.5)	0.0 (3.7)	0.0
Threats confronting the state of Israel	6.6 (0)	0.0 (0)	0.0
Total Negative	61.5 (39.1)	5.0 (16.7)	29.2
Others	7.9 (4.2)	10.8 (10.3)	8.1
N	6762 (2934)	4940 (3390)	2905

NOTES: The data appearing in the table were generated according to the following procedures: (a) the television campaign appeals were videotaped; (b) party jingles and time devoted to broadcasting acronyms were deducted; (c) party presentations were reviewed independently by two panelists and divided into content segments; (d) each segment was timed and categorized by two panelists according to a pre-prepared list of content appeals; (e) in cases of disagreement, the author served as a judge; (f) where all three failed to include the broadcast time under any of the content items, it was listed under "Others"; (g) because each broadcasting second may contain more than one of the content items, the total percent of content items to broadcasting time does not equal 100; (h) each broadcast was divided into seconds and each broadcast was rounded to the nearest whole minute. Percentages were rounded to the nearest 0.5 percent.

Lieberman's intention to join a left-wing coalition: "if you wanted Right, you will get Left [and] an express [journey] towards the Great Withdrawal" (Israel Broadcasting Authority, Channel 2, March 26, 2006).

These shifts were not accompanied by any positive message, and Likud did not swerve from the substantive course it had charted from the beginning. Table 1 demonstrates a remarkably negative campaign, not only in comparison to its rivals but also to its own prior performance. A content item found only in 2006 is "threats confronting the state of Israel," and 6.6 percent of the party's TV time was devoted to raising the viewer's anxiety by portraying catastrophes threatening the state. The connection between this and the election was not always made clear, but it seemed to have been a warning against what was likely to take place should the nation be led by an unworthy leader like Olmert. Conspicuous in their absence were the items listed under "stands on controversial issues." In 2003, Sharon ignored domestic issues and the change in his defense and foreign policy position was reflected in the party's high score in the general non-controversial category (14.5 percent). In 2006, the party avoided ideological positions on foreign defense policies as well, while rejecting the basic positions adopted by the mainstream. As a result, there was a rise in the warnings of the consequences of a government led by others (17.5 percent) without offering any commensurate positive content. In terms of the party goal triangle, the party persisted in its move away from the ideological and representation points, and toward the vote maximization end of both legs.

Labor likewise did not present any last minute surprises. Table 1 indicates an overwhelmingly positive campaign focusing on ideological appeals. This is apparent not only when compared to its rivals but also to itself in 2003. Then, too, the party was more positive and ideological than its main competitor. Yet in terms of the party goal triangle, it occupied a position considerably closer to the vote maximizing point than to ideological advocacy (on the one leg), or representation (on the other). In 2006 the party migrated to positions that were significantly closer to the two latter points. This, however, was restricted to domestic issues. Foreign and defense issues were virtually ignored, thereby rendering Labor a "one-dimensional party."

If there was a change in the party's strategy, it related to a question "in the air" since the beginning of the campaign: should Labor campaign for the premiership, or as a potential member of a Kadima-led coalition? It was felt that the latter option (see, e.g., *Haaretz,* March 13, 2006) might dampen activist enthusiasm and provide an incentive for the undecided to jump ship and vote for Kadima. Others pointed to public opinion surveys taken in January, demonstrating that less than 10 percent of the electorate believed Labor would lead the incoming coalition. Even among Labor voters the number barely reached 25 percent. More than 60 percent of the general electorate (58 percent in Labor) believed that Kadima would be the next ruling party (*Haaretz,* January 26, 2006). Disregarding such figures risked a loss of credibility. Conveying the message that a strong

Labor is needed in the government to stave off the entry of right-wing parties to the coalition, and to influence its socio-economic policies was both more believable and effective.[24] Despite Peretz's resistance (e.g., *Yediot Aharonot*, March 16, 2006) this line was adopted with growing frequency in rallies and telephone contacts with the membership (Hassan, 2006).[25] In the final days of the campaign, Peretz himself seemed to have accepted the verdict, as evidenced by his aforementioned threat not to join a coalition that included Yisrael Beiteinu, or in his attempt to secure the finance ministry as well as other portfolios in the Kadima-led government. Labor's last TV broadcast recycled one of the party's more creative spots. An off-screen narrator listed the common concerns about Peretz's fitness for the top post (he comes from a small provincial town, he was a trade union leader, he lacks formal education, and his English is "funny"), and at the end, the outlines of Ben Gurion's face appeared on screen. It was a last-ditch plea to cast a vote for Peretz as prime minister.

Table 1 demonstrates that Kadima also emphasized positive messages. Apart from enhancing the image of its leaders (39.2 percent), the most prominent item in its ad campaign was the response to Likud's fear-inducing scenarios. The ads repeatedly stressed Israel's military strength, as well as assuring that a Kadima government would continue to retaliate forcefully against terrorism. This was reinforced with ads attacking Netanyahu (21.3 percent) as an untrustworthy, fear-mongering leader. There was also an indirect response to the allegation that Kadima was a mere collection of individuals with little in common, destined to follow the dismal career trajectory of parties like the DMC, Center Party, or Shinui, all of which disintegrated after a short-lived success—25.45 percent of the allotted broadcast time focused on the Kadima team, with special emphasis on its cohesiveness. The party however, did devote 6.4 percent of the time to clarifying and legitimizing the demographic and territorial rationale behind its foreign policy and security program. With zero percent controversy over socio-economic issues, it was, like Labor, a one-dimensional party. It positioned itself, however, much closer to the vote maximizing point, and its appeals in the final days of the campaign highlight the main reason: as the forerunner, it presented itself as a "party for all" and sought a broad range of support, enabling it to fulfill a vision shared by most of the voting public. In the final ad, voters were reminded that Begin and Rabin were able to become "great prime ministers" because they were backed by large parties. Kadima, as their successor, likewise needed masses of voters "who would enable it to reach peace, the end of terrorism, and a strong and healthy economy." The fact that the speaker was Peres, Rabin's partner who now acknowledged the greatness of Begin, was in itself part of the message. The ad ended with Sharon's plea to all who believed in his ideas to join the party he founded so that "the big revolution that started in the Gaza withdrawal would continue."

In the end, none of the three rivals achieved their aims. Following their final ads, a spokesman on behalf of Hetz reiterated Tommy Lapid's message offered at the beginning of the campaign. Most voters, he stated, support the conversion plan. But precisely because the result is so obvious, "an additional vote to Olmert and Kadima is a waste. To bring in Hetz to the Knesset is a success." He, too, was to be disappointed.

V. Conclusion

In the opening section of this chapter I noted the tendency in the literature to view the models of the party separately; as representative, ideological advocate, and vote maximizer. One result of this approach was the assumption of partisan consistency. Parties may alter their approach following electoral shocks, leadership change, or any significant alterations in circumstances which might propel them from one model to another. However, barring these dramatic circumstances, most scholars persistently treat parties as "static" entities, with set goals and autonomously determined strategies, with insufficient attention paid to the effects of the intra-organizational environment on party strategy. Electoral studies tended therefore to concentrate almost exclusively on party responses to their environment. Vote maximizing parties were expected to determine their positions based on their evaluation of the distribution of public opinion; other parties were expected to possess arsenals of fundamental positions, which could serve as baselines to be adjusted and employed in response to changing conditions, and the rival strengths and weaknesses of competing parties.

As presented earlier, the viewing of representation, ideological advocacy, and vote maximization as simultaneous, rather than mutually exclusive party goals, may allow for a more complex understanding of the dynamics involved in determining and carrying out party strategy. The three goals may be regarded as constituting the points of a single triangle, along the legs of which parties move in an attempt to achieve the best possible balance between their goals. This assumption leads in turn to the supposition that parties are not necessarily consistent between, or even within, campaigns. This is evident in the behavior of the three main rivals during the 2006 elections. A comparison of the previous performance of Likud and Labor demonstrates that the former moved toward the vote maximizing point of the triangle, while the latter moved towards its ideological advocacy and representation points. Shortly before the end of the campaign, Kadima also shifted toward the ideological point, but to a far lesser extent. In some measure, these modifications were in response to stimuli from the organizational environment. The change in the structure of the competition, the residual effects of the semi-presidential contest for the premiership, the strengths and the weaknesses of the opponents, and the corruption issue which surfaced—all impacted on the campaign. However, personal leadership decisions also played a significant role in the changes initiated, and it was the shift in Labor that precipitated the elections. The leaders were not simply rational actors. Each was constrained by their party's history, program, and electoral base. Parties are also multifaceted organizations, with internal dynamics playing an essential role in shaping their competitive behavior. Even the new Kadima dealt with these limits, as its leaders were identified with public stands and needed to take into account the effect on the targeted public. Moreover, all parties had to make choices relative to the feedback received from the environment, and on their hypotheses as to what factors would influence various constituencies and rival counter-moves. The convergence of all these factors contributed not only to change, but also to the absence of change. This was most evident in Likud, where constituency needs, previous programs, positions taken by the leaders under different circumstances, and a lack of internal cohesion led to inaction even in the face of a looming electoral calamity. It was also evident in the "one dimensionality" of Labor and Kadima. Parties that find an issue too dangerous or difficult to deal with can decide to ignore it altogether. Especially when voters' priorities were at stake, the one dimensionality of the parties in question was not a result of "forgetfulness," but of a deliberate strategy aiming at shifting attention to more rewarding spheres.

The frameworks for analysis that I have employed by no means answer all the inquiries raised about party strategy. I have not moved away, for instance, from spatial analysis, and there is still a need to examine the reciprocal relationships among the various issue dimensions in which parties may operate. Nevertheless, I have attempted to demonstrate how interconnections among the factors shaping the party message and mode of delivery ended with a battle between two one-dimensional parties, and one that resorted to avoiding all substantive responses to the questions that occupied the voter's minds. This, in turn, created an "autistic" campaign. The rivals did not address one another, but attempted to talk past each other, and this may have added to the sense that the electorate was not offered any real choice. Along with the focus on flawed leaders, and the widespread feeling that the results were a foregone conclusion, the strategy adopted by the parties may have contributed to a lackluster campaign and low turnout. From this vantage point, the 2006 elections constituted a failure of Israeli democracy.

Notes

1. This elasticity encouraged theorists to consider rational vote maximizing behaviors under differing systems. Thus, if vote maximizing serves the goal of gaining or retaining power, then in single districts, parties may attach the greatest importance to maximizing pluralities rather than votes (Hinich and Ordshook, 1970).
2. Such expectations explain why the possibility that Sharon would bolt the Likud and team up with other leaders to present a new party was popularly dubbed "the Big Bang."
3. For academic assessment of this type see, e.g., Ephraim Ya'ar (forthcoming) "Towards the Third Era of Israeli Democracy." The first era was of Mapai domination, followed by the era of left–right equilibrium that had terminated in the ascendance of the Right into dominance as of the elections of 2003. For a survey of journalistic interpretations see Susser, 2003.
4. For the application of the thesis to the Israeli context see Goldberg, 1992, pp. 23–28; Aronoff, 1990; Arian, 1974.

5. The anti-Kadima bloc was also to include Israel Beitenu. Both prospective partners refused the overtures and leaked the story to the media. Kadima promptly denounced what it defined as a coalition of "election-robbers." See the *Jerusalem Post*, April 14, 2006; *Maariv*, March 17, 2006; *Haaretz*, March 18, 2006; Verter, 2006 B. The claim that "Kadima is the new Mapai" has in fact been made by Haim Ramon. See news.walla.co.il. March 10, 2006.

6. Some in-camp competition was, however, inevitable though not necessarily intended. Thus in mid-February 100 of the 1,000 strong Meretz convention members announced that they were joining Labor because "Meretz has been neglecting social issues as of late and has been dealing only with the Geneva Initiative." Smadar Aharoni, Quoted in *Haaretz*, February 15, 2006.

7. The parliamentary and the presidential methods themselves are too well known to warrant any analysis here. Suffice it to say that in parliamentary systems a prime minister is expected to win power courtesy of his party, and his mission is to pursue the agenda set by it. In the Presidential system, the chief executive gains his authority directly from the electorate on the strength of his qualifications, and bears ultimate responsibility to it. One is hard put to imagine systems that apply either scheme in its pure form. Voters usually bring the party leadership into consideration and hence even in parliamentary systems parties are expected to rely on their leadership in their bid to attract electoral support. On the other hand, presidential candidates must secure the electoral base supplied by the party faithful, while the separation of powers renders presidents dependent on, and limited by, the powers of the separately elected legislators. Even so, the Israeli hybrid stood out because it was based on the simultaneous conduct of two elections, one parliamentary and the other semi-presidential. As Ottolenghi (2002) points out, the concept of direct election of a prime minister whose government would depend on parliamentary confidence was not a novelty, having been offered by French and Italian scholars. It was put into practice however only at the local level. Israel itself used direct elections for city mayors since 1977.

8. One example is the tension between the Likud ex-ministers and Netanyahu. One of the main causes for this was his demand that they resign from the government on the eve of the primaries. This deprived them of the ability to bolster support for themselves and their followers in the central committee. The result was a relatively poor showing for all but Silvan Shalom, who was guaranteed the second place in the Knesset candidate list.

9. Netanyahu and Shalom did agree however to conduct a joint campaign tour. Shalom nevertheless rejected the offer to head the campaign headquarters and insisted instead on managing his own personal campaign command center.

10. An example from the latter part of the campaign was the public criticism of Netanyahu's declaration that Likud will not join a government that would carry out the Kadima "conversion plan." He "shot the Likud in the foot," argued Shalom. "The Likud voters want it in office and hence will vote for Leiberman who stated that he will join Olmert's coalition." *Yediot Aharonot*, March 16, 2006.

11. MK Landau opposed mention of the road map whereas Shalom demanded it. The compromise was the statement that "when a Palestinian government comes to power, that would recognize Israel and disavow terror, negotiations would resume in keeping with agreements Israel had signed, including the road map and Israel's fourteen reservations to it." The Likud Electoral Program, April, 2006.

12. Barak made an earlier appearance at the campaign kick off convention in Jerusalem, but he left before the event itself had gotten under way, and associates explained that he simply popped in to "meet old friends."

13. This is one of the consequences of the 1994 amendment to the Israeli Party Finance Law (updated in 2005) that set a relatively low ceiling and restricted the allowable donors to individuals who are eligible to cast a vote. For an analysis see Hfung, 2005.

14. Each party is entitled to a yearly funding unit multiplied by its number of seats for "current activities," and an additional unit in an election year. In addition, every party represented in the Knesset receives one yearly "current activity" unit and an election unit for campaign expenditures. Each party also receives 10 minutes of free TV time and 3 minutes per Knesset member (25 and 6 minutes radio time respectively).

15. I would like to thank Menachem Hofnung for sharing his assessment with me. Interview conducted April 15, 2006.

16. See e.g., Avishai Zohar, interview with Limor Livnat, *Maariv*, March 23, 2006. What persuaded her to vote for the withdrawal was Sharon's unfulfilled promise to implement it in three phases with government votes affirming each one.

17. E.g., the *Only Facts* pamphlet published in mid-February and Natan Sharansky's interview on RTVI.

18. I would like to express my thanks to Zvi Barzel and anonymous Likud officials who were ready to discuss the information with me.

19. See e.g., Globes–Smith surveys, February 9 and February 23, 2006. The first predicted 40 Kadima seats and 52 percent view Olmert as suitable for the prime ministership. The second predicted 38-9 Kadima seats and only 40 percent convinced in Olmert's suitability. In the Russian sector this was even worse, with intentions to vote Kadima falling from about a third to little over a quarter of the voters. See Galili 2006 B.

20. Peretz's suggestion that he himself would head the immigrant campaign headquarters may testify to his optimistic belief in the party's ability to cut across ethnic lines. He was quickly dissuaded. The decision was made to conduct a Russian campaign, but to restrict the direct involvement of the party Chairman to media interviews.

21. Among them Peretz himself. In his words, "the connection between capital and [the Kadima] government constitutes one of the greatest dangers facing Israel." Quoted in Marcus, 2006.

22. Even so, *Haaretz*-Channel 10 poll showed that under former Shin Bet director, Ami Ayalon, Labor results could improve (20 to 26 MK s) at the expense of Kadima and Meretz (*Haaretz*, March 2, 2006).

23. Most of the clauses were indistinguishable from ideas brought forward by Labor and may have been intended to obviate its accusations, e.g., the call for student loan programs, for a safety net that would include increasing the National Insurance payments for the elderly, or for a "negative income tax." Others included ideas that were not expected to give rise to much disagreement, e.g., reduction of the number of foreign workers, or improving the transportation links between the center and the periphery. More interesting were clauses intended to help the party in the Russian sector: civil marriages and burials. For obvious reasons, these were not mentioned outside their intended audience.

24. Thus, a poll conducted at the end of February revealed that Netanyahu and Olmert had in fact received the same high grade on the "corruption index" and that even 13 percent of Kadima's vote believed Olmert is either "corrupt" or "very corrupt" (*Maariv*, March 5, 2006).

25. It was also pointed out that such a policy could also serve to deflect doubts concerning Peretz's inexperience and lack of formal education. See e.g., Eldar, 2006.

References

Arian, Asher. 1974. "The Dominant Party System: A Neglected Model of Democratic Stability." *Journal of Politics* 36 (August): 592-614.

Aronoff, Myron. 1990. "Israel Under Labor and the Likud: The Role of Dominance Considered." In T. J. Pempel, ed. *Uncommon Democracies: The One Party Dominant Regimes*. Ithaca: Cornell University Press, 260-281.

Baltiansky, Gadi. 2003. Interview conducted 24 July.

Downs, Anthony. 1957. *An Economic Theory of Democracy*. New York: Harper Collins.

Duverger, Maurice. 1967. *Political Parties: Their Organization and Activity in the Modern State*. Barbara North and Robert North, Trans. London: Methuen.

Eldar, Akiva. 2006. "The Problem with Peretz." *Haaretz*, 16 March.

Enelow, James and Melvin Hinich. 1984. *The Spatial Theory of Voting—An Introduction* Cambridge: Cambridge University Press.

Galili, Lily. 2006. "To Them, He's the Other." *Haaretz*, 10 March.

------. 2005. "The Russian Agenda." *Haaretz*, 25 November.

Goldberg, Giora. 1992. *Political Parties in Israel: From Mass Parties to Electoral Parties*. Tel Aviv: Ramot.

Grofman, Bernard, et al. 1999. *Elections in Japan, Korea and Taiwan Under the Single Non-Transferable Vote: The Comparative Study of an Embedded Institution*. Ann Arbor: The University of Michigan Press.

Hasson, Nir. 2006. "Peretz Admits Labor Aiming Only for Second Place," *Haaretz*, 17 March.

Hinich, Melvin and Peter Ordeshook. 1970. "Plurality Maximization vs. Vote Maximization: A Spatial Analysis with Variable Participation." *American Political Science Review*, 64: 772-791.

Hirschman, Albert. 1970. *Exit, Voice and Loyalty: Responses to Decline in Firms, Organizations, and States*. Cambridge, MA: Harvard University Press.

Hofnung, Menachem. 2005. "Israel." In Thomas D. Grant, ed. *Lobbying, Government Relations and Campaign Finance Worldwide: Navigating the Laws, Regulations and Practices of National Regimes*. New York: Oceana   Publications, 261-279.

Kessel, John. 1980. *Presidential Campaign Politics*. Homewood, Ill: Dorsey Press.

Kirchheimer, Otto. 1966. "The Transformation of the West European Party System." In Joseph La Palombara and Myron Weiner, eds. *Political Parties and Political Development*. Princeton: Princeton University Press.

Kirkpatrick, Jeane. 1997. *The New Presidential Elite: Men and Women in National Politics*. New York: Russell Sage.

Laver, Michael. 1999. "Divided Parties, Divided Government." *Legislative Studies Quarterly* 24: 5-29.

Less, Amira. "Labor Presents: The Debacle." *Yediot Aharonot Weekend Supplement*. 31 January.

Marcus, Yoel. 2006. "Not a Banana Republic." *Haaretz*, 10 February.

Mendilow, Jonathan. 2005. "Uniqueness and Similarities in the Study of Israeli Parties: the Case of the 2003 Elections." *Israel Studies Forum*, 20 (summer):49-69.

------. 2003. "Public Campaign Funding and Party System Change: The Israeli Experience." *Israel Studies Forum* 19 (fall): 115-122.

------. 1992. "Public Party Funding and Party Transformation in Multi-Party Systems." *Comparative Political Studies* 25 (April): 90-117.

Muller, Wolfgang and Kaare Strom. 1999. *Policy, Office, or Votes? How Political Parties in Western Europe Make Hard Decisions*. New York: Cambridge University Press.

Ottolenghi, Emanuel. 2002. "Israel's Direct Elections System and the (Not so) Unforesee-able Consequences of Electoral Reform." *Israel Studies Forum* 18. (Fall): 88-116.

Price, David. 1984. *Bringing Back the Parties*. Washington, DC: CQ Press.

Richardson, Bradley. 1991. "European Party Loyalties Revisited." *American Political Science Review* 85: 751-775.

Schickler, Eric, and Donald Green. 1997. "The Stability of Party Identification in Western Democracies." *Comparative Political Studies* 30: 450-483.

Seliger, Martin. 1976. *Ideology and Politics*. New York: Free Press.

Shalom, Silvan. 2006. "At Home Interview with Silvan Shalom." *Yediot Ahronot*. 17 January.

Sharon, Ariel. 2002. "Speech by Prime Minister Ariel Sharon at the Herzliya Confer-ence," 4 December. www.mf.gov.il/mfa/go.asp?MFAH)mty0. Downloaded 25 February 2003.

Shepsle, Kenneth. 1991. *Models of Multiparty Electoral Competition*. New York: Harwood.

Shifer, Shimon. 2002. "What Do They Want From My Children." *Yediot Aharonot*, Weekend Supplement, 20 December, 2002.

Susser, Leslie. 2003. "Signs of Historical Power Shift Seen in Labor Party's Loss." *NJJN*, 11 February.

Verter, Yossi, et al. 2006. "Haaretz Analysts: Political Scenarios in a Post-Sharon Era." *Haaretz*, 5 January.

------. 2006 B. "The Day After—Already?" *Haaretz*, 16 April.

------. 2006 C. "He's In the Hot Seat," *Haaretz*, 30 February.

Wright, William. 1971. "Theory." In William Wright, ed. *A Comparative Study of Party Organization*. Columbus, OH: Charles E. Merrill, 3-16.

Patronage and the 2006 Elections

Doron Navot[1]

Introduction

Recent years have witnessed a change in Israeli discourse with regard to party patronage and political appointments. Political appointments have been described as a threat to Israeli society,[2] and have become synonymous with political corruption (Goldberg, 2004: 3). In addition, for the first time in Israel, a former minister is standing trial for his involvement in political appointments.[3] This chapter aims to clarify the influence of patronage on the current political discourse, and to examine the extent to which patronage influenced the 2006 elections.

This chapter will claim that an increase in patronage took place only in the last five years and that it may be temporary and limited in scope; the increase is the unintended and unpredicted by-product of political changes that occurred during the 1990s, and of the hybrid electoral system used in Israel between 1996 and 2001. Furthermore, the use of patronage helped Ariel Sharon to be elected Likud chairman, but prevented him from effectively promoting the disengagement plan. Thus, patronage encouraged the split in the ruling party [Likud] and contributed to the establishment of a new party, Kadima, and may have also contributed to its own demise.

The chapter is organized as follows: the subsequent section presents the analytical framework of the research and the third section describes the methodology employed. The fourth section attempts to estimate the extent of patronage in Israel from 1984 on, followed by a critical analysis of patronage development in Israel, and culminating in the 2006 elections. In the fifth and final section, I will summarize the main arguments presented and briefly discuss possible future developments regarding patronage in Israel.

Analytical Framework

Patronage is a theory-laden concept. The phenomenon has been analyzed from several perspectives and has many different definitions (see Blondel, 2002; James, 2006; Kopecky & Mair, 2006; Piattoni, 2001; Warner, 1997; Weingrod,

1968). The following analysis will combine the "New Historical Institutional Approach" with a materialistic analysis of politics. [4]

For the purposes of this chapter, patronage is defined as an exchange in which politicians or public officials selectively distribute governmental assets as a means of gaining political power. Examples of such behavior include giving party members an unfair advantage in public tenders, selecting them for public positions, or helping the son of a party member to be placed in an undemanding job in the army in order to obtain the father's political support, especially during intra-party contests (see also Blondel, 2002: 241).

There is no comprehensive theory of patronage (Blondel, 2002). It is understood that patronage is used to provide selective incentives to encourage participation in party activities and to mobilize political support (Panebianco, 1988). There also appears to be a causal link between the developmental stage of bureaucracy and that of political appointments. More specifically, in cases where the bureaucratic system has had more time to establish itself before the formation of political parties in particular, and the democratic system overall, we anticipate finding fewer instances of political appointments (Shefter, 1994). We still however, lack data and research offering a comprehensive view of patronage in contemporary political systems (Kopecky and Mair, 2006).

I do not presume to offer a full-fledged theory for the development of patronage patterns, or for "the rise and fall of patronage regimes." [5]I will, however, attempt to place the phenomenon within a wider political context and offer a preliminary model describing its progression. Using this model, I will attempt to form some empirical conjectures with regard to the development of this phenomenon.

I suggest viewing the interest politicians may have in using patronage as a derivative of their need to mobilize the support of people lacking any evident economic power. Ironically, the use of patronage may indicate that the public still has some power. It attests to the existence of real competition between politicians for the support of citizens and groups devoid of financial capital (compare to Piattoni, 2001), in a world where parties and politicians are less and less dependent on public involvement and party participation, and tend to cooperate with one another, thereby forming a type of cartel (Blyth and Katz, 2005).

The ability to execute patronage-type interactions stems from the "blind eye" turned by "gate keepers" (such as the Civil Service Commission, the media and the economic elite), actors that should demonstrate an inherent interest in opposing this phenomenon.[6] Given the significant power these actors wield, in situations where patronage is successfully employed on a large scale, it is important to ascertain their more particular interests.

To fully understand the incentive structure and reciprocal relations between the various actors mentioned above, we must first appreciate the changes and transformations that globalization processes have brought about, and are still engendering, to the nature of politics worldwide. The first effect of globalization necessary to understanding patronage patterns is the privatization of the public sector and the concurrent downsizing of functions fulfilled by the state (Ram, 2005; Shafir and Peled, 2002). On the one hand, small government, privatized corporations, and reduced civil service leave less room for patronage. The ideology underlying the privatization process depicts political appointments as yet another example of the inefficiency of public service. On the other hand, by permitting at least some public authorities to remain under somewhat lax supervision, the privatization process itself creates localized opportunities for corruption and the distribution of public goods in an attempt to promote private and party interests (Meny, 1996; Rose-Ackerman, 1996).

A second globalization phenomenon is the adoption of institutional arrangements that may weaken the link between parties and their constituents (Blyth and Katz, 2005; Katz and Mair, 1995).[7] Some view this process as a "parties' crisis" (Mair, Muller, and Plasser, 2004: 8-12). This process influences patronage in two opposite directions. As politicians become less dependent on active support from ordinary citizens,[8] they have fewer incentives to use patronage. However, when politicians do need political support, they find it much harder to elicit this support. In such situations, the importance of selective, individual incentives is amplified, resulting perhaps in a significant, although localized, increase in patronage usage.

Globalization also encourages the expansion of judicial supervision to include the political and party spheres. Tighter judicial supervision lessens the ability to use patronage as it includes, among other things, the adoption of more stringent criteria for appointments and therefore reduces the ability to nominate inept cronies.

These globalization phenomena amplify the influence of "liberal discourse"[9] while also strengthening criticism of semi-corrupt political phenomena like patronage (see also Kitschelt, 2000a: 863, 869; 2000b: 163-164; Naim, 1995). Moreover, the media, at least partially controlled by the business elite,[10] have an inherent interest in exposing and censuring occurrences of patronage. Reports of inappropriate governmental actions, strongly emphasizing their sensational and dramatic aspects, provide entertainment geared toward boosting newspaper sales and increasing the ratings of news programs. Media owners also appear to have an inherent need to restrain public officials, thereby preventing a situation from developing in which these officials are no longer dependent on the active support of the business elite. The media's interest in exposing patronage will therefore act as a negative incentive for politicians to use it.

Most of the actors mentioned thus far have a strong interest in the battle to reduce patronage patterns. Patronage causes the political process to become less predictable and controllable, leading to uncertainty in the markets and slowing down the country's attempts to integrate itself into the new global order. While globalization does create new opportunities for patronage, it does in the long run contribute to a significant reduction in the use of such practices.

There is, however, a strong possibility that the use of patronage will increase before significant political changes can be realized. This increase can be explained by two factors: first, the weakening connection between the party and its constituents makes it much more difficult to mobilize support for new policies. Despite recent changes, governments today still require democratic legitimization of their policy initiatives. When a policy coincides with the structural interests of the business elite and the media, they may choose to turn a blind eye to an increase in patronage that provides a modicum of public support to enable the implementation of the policy in question (see also Kitschelt, 2000a, 2000b); second, despite the many changes brought about by globalization over the past few years, public officials still wield a considerable amount of power. Politicians can on occasion initiate personnel changes among the "gate keepers." In the long run, the business elite and progressive governmental norms can be expected to maintain the upper hand, but in the short term, these circumstances may lead to an increase in patronage.

Research Design, Methodology and Data Sources

There is no scientifically accurate way to examine the range of patronage patterns. It is difficult to follow the trail of personal motivations leading to a public official's deeds and choices. However these cannot be ignored, as patronage is defined as such when the choice is predicated on a personal, political aim.[11] This difficulty is not purely epistemological in nature; ministers who know that some of their political appointments are illegitimate not only attempt to mask their true intentions, but in fact go to great pains to depict themselves as having acted in the public's interest. [12]In addition, many patronage patterns resemble legitimate governmental exchanges. It is necessary therefore to focus on one pattern, or on a limited number of patterns, which will, using factual evidence, allow us to substantiate the appropriateness of the public officials' conduct without having to delve into their subconscious or subjective beliefs.

The extent and volume of political appointments may be used as an empirical measurement of patronage.[13] To address the difficulties mentioned above, an illegitimate political appointment will be defined here as any nomination process in which at least one administrative flaw can be proven, and in which a person, or a crony or relative of that person, who wields significant influence over a party's candidate list, was nominated.

This definition contains several drawbacks. It does not include political appointments devoid of procedural flaws, although the existence of these flaws is not a prerequisite for political appointments to be defined as illegitimate. This definition also lacks any reference to the motivation for the appointment, thereby permitting the inclusion of nominations that were not executed for the purpose of individual political gain, and therefore should not be considered political (see also Dery, 1993: 51-62). Despite these apparent shortcomings, the appointment of an individual with potential influence over the political future of a minister to a job where political identity does not impact on performance, is most likely the result of the minister's wish to promote personal political interests. [14]A large proportion of the appointments in this study belong to the latter category. I therefore find the definition to be justifiable.

The State Comptroller's reports and the Appointments Committee,[15] established in response to the sixth amendment (1993) to the Government Corporations Act of 1975,[16] were used to determine the extent of political patronage as defined above in the public service. The State Comptroller's reports included quantitative information regarding political appointments in government corporations, statutory authorities, and the civil service.[17] The appointments are classified according to a number of parameters: government (identified by the party of the PM), political identity of the appointee, nature of the position (junior, middle management, senior; civil service or other public function); and the specific flaws in the appointment (see table 1). Because of the nature of nomination arrangements in the Defense, Foreign Affairs, Treasury and Justice Departments, as well as in local authorities, findings regarding them were not included in this study.[18] Regarding the Appointments Committee, its data are based on questionnaires administered to candidates for senior positions in government corporations.[19]

It is important to note that the Comptroller's reports, as well as the data from the Appointments Committee, do not lack for issues touching on validity and trustworthiness. In light of the presumption of legitimacy that governmental institutions enjoy,[20] the Comptroller's wish to avoid unjustified harm to the institutions under review, and the need to maintain credibility, the State Comptroller's office tends to refrain from dealing with political appointments unless an unequivocal procedural flaw is discovered. In addition, the Comptroller tends to focus mainly on appointments of party members, even though the extent, and therefore the importance, of these appointments has decreased in recent years. Finally, the Comptroller does not possess a methodical system to determine the extent of political appointments. In fact, it is not at all clear how governmental bodies are selected for review by the Comptroller (see Barzilai and Nachmias, 1998). It is important to note that the appointments committee does not authenticate the answers. The Committee's role is to check political affinity and determine whether a specific appointment requires special qualifications, but it has no definition for political affinity on which to base such a determination, nor does it have any formal, objective criteria for formulating such a definition.[21] As a result, the Committee often relies solely on the subjective opinions of its members.[22]

Another problem stems from the fact that both the State Comptroller and the Appointments Committee have increased the demand for appointments that can be considered above reproach.[23] Thus the Comptroller may view nominations that in past reports were ignored by dint of their classification as illegitimate political appointments. In other words, an increase in the amount of political appointments may be a by-product of changes in the perception of the Comptroller's role rather than a change in the empirical data.[24] There is only partial information available on political appointments in government corporations between 1989 and 1990, and the data that does exist was extracted from the Comptroller's reports. There is also no publicly accessible information on such appointments between 1991 and 1997. However, because complete date for 1999-2005 is available from the Appointments Committee, reasonable estimates of the extent of political appointments to senior positions in government corporations can be made, and changing trends examined, in spite of the incomplete data.

One final caveat: although the legal principles underlying public appointments dictated by law are identical for all public bodies, there are in fact many differences in the processes and in how they are overseen. While there is an explicit legal obligation to appoint by tender (unless the position in question is a low-rank),[25] this obligation does not apply to government corporations or statutory authorities. External supervision of public service appointments is performed by the Civil Service Commission. Overseeing government corporations is the responsibility of the Appointments Committee and there is little, if any, supervision of appointments by statutory authorities. It is therefore easier to appoint cronies to positions in government corporations (in the lower-than-director echelons) and statutory authorities than to civil service, tender-based, positions. The next section describes the political developments in the period under discussion.

Findings

Figure 1 shows a significant drop in political appointments of directors, chairs of boards and CEOs in 1999, compared to the findings reported by the State Comptroller in 1988 and 1990 (no data is available for the years 1991-1998). Additionally, even when politically-affiliated nominees to those positions were appointed, they possessed more professional skills relevant to the position. In other words, since the amendment to the Government Companies Act was enacted in 1993 (Barak-Erez, 2002: 623), the number of appointments of inept party members has dramatically decreased.

In the civil service the trend is more complicated (see table 1). The Comptroller's reports from the mid-1980s to the beginning of the 1990s demonstrate an average of ten per year or forty political appointments for each four-year tenure. The annual average during the Rabin, Netanyahu, and Barak administrations was three to six—half that of their predecessors. During the Sharon governments, however, there were more than four times that number, almost tripling the higher rates of the 1980s.

Critical Analysis of Patronage Development in Israel

Prior to analyzing the findings using the framework offered in this article, I would like to refer to a number of arguments sometimes used to explain pa-

Figure 1
Politically-Affiliated Senior Level Appointments in Government Companies, as a Percentage of Total Appointments, 1988-2005

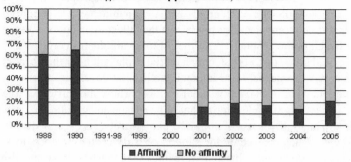

Table 1
Nature and Extent of Political Appointments in the Public Sector according to the State Comptroller's Reports, 1984-2005[26]

	Public Service and Nomination Level						Nomination Flaw				
	Government Companies Statutory Authority			Civil Service			(a)	(b)	(c)	(d)	Total
	J[27]	MM[2]	S[2]	J[2]	MM[2]	S[2]					
11th Knesset (rotation)	2	6	12	4	9	6	14	6	6	7	39
12th Knesset Shamir	1	6	3	5	25	-	13	5	3	3	40
13th Knesset Rabin	1	8	2		5	2	7	3	2	-	18
14th Knesset Netanyahu	-	1	3	-	9	4	5	-	5	3	17[28]
15th Knesset (I) Barak	-	4	5	-	-	-	4	-	-	-	9
15th Knesset (II) Sharon	-	-	-	11	42	-	5	11	11	1 + 3[29]	53
16th Knesset Sharon	16	3	1	-	4	4	-	1	6	4	28[30]

Flaws:

(a): Lack of qualifications or experience.

(b): Position was "invented"—A job that was created even though it is apparent that the function is superfluous.

(c): Extraordinary remunerations, including payment for services not rendered.

(d): Miscellaneous (including hiring in a government corporation as a "bribe" of the political echelon; hiring an employee with a bad conduct track record; an illegal deal with the union to approve the nomination; an employee forging tenders).

tronage and political appointments. The first such explanation, popular among legal experts, gatekeepers and publicists, is that political appointments are the result of a "loss of shame" plaguing the Israeli public arena.[31] They argue that the appointments are also a by-product of the "illegal-ism culture" entrenched in the Israeli political sphere.[32] Neither of these arguments corresponds to the findings and they offer, at best, only a partial explanation for the phenomenon. Alternately, it is argued that the internal election system employed until recently by Likud, in which 2,500 party center members chose the party's Knesset candidate list, is a significant determinant of patronage and corruption. According to this explanation, the use of political appointments has expanded because of the ministers' dependence on the support of party center members to attain a realistic place on the list. Ministers were forced to show favoritism and distribute public goods to the members, including appointments to public positions, in order to enlist the center members' support.[33]

In arguing that politicians have lost their sense of shame, the assumption is that politicians are omnipotent. In fact, public officials must act within a legal framework. They are also strongly influenced by external pressures and the interests of the media and the business elite. Even if politicians were without shame, they are still restricted by external forces not covered by the "loss of shame" argument, thereby invalidating this as being the sole reason for the phenomenon. These arguments also imply that Israel's public service sector has been irreparably corrupted, while the data implies the existence of a much more complicated reality and actually shows significant improvement in the nomination process for certain types of positions. If loss of shame has indeed infected the entire public arena, and is the influential factor it is depicted to be, then the decrease in appointments at the end of the 1990s is difficult to explain or understand. Those who accept this theory seem to view political appointments as shameful by definition, ignoring the possibility that public officials often cannot survive in the political arena without appointing their cronies to public positions. In fact, the exaggerated focus placed on the concept of shame obscures the true factors contributing to the phenomenon of patronage. This can be analogous to a description of rummaging through garbage in search of food as something shameful, whereas the real shame lies in adopting policies that drive citizens to such poverty that they are forced to rummage through garbage to survive.

The "illegal-ism culture" can be criticized from a slightly different angle. If an instrumental attitude to the law is a critical component of Israeli culture as well as a factor contributing to the increase in patronage, why have political appointments to senior positions in government companies decreased? How can we explain the decrease in illegal political appointments in the civil service throughout the 1990s? How does this argument coincide with the increasing influence of the Appointments Committee or the pro-active sentencing policy of the Supreme Court?

A more reasonable and important claim is that the internal election system employed by Likud impacted on the extent of the patronage. However, this is also only a partial explanation and one that needs to be fine-tuned. For example, the explanation does not attribute any importance to the gatekeepers even though their policies had a marked influence on the extent of appointments. Furthermore, it does not correspond with the restraint the Sharon administration demonstrated vis-à-vis appointments to senior positions in government companies, nor to the lack of success of Likud ministers in their attempt to annul the amendment to the Government Companies Act, which significantly limited political appointments to those companies, or to the fact that few ministers have attempted to have the amendment annulled. [34]

In the next section I shall attempt to provide an alternative analysis for the changes in the scope of political appointments from 1984 to 2005.

The Decline in Political Appointments in the 1990s

A number of developments in the late 1980s impacted on the extent of political appointments. On the one hand, these developments contributed to the decline in patronage in the 1990s. On the other hand, they hastened a change in the election and governing systems, engendering a rise in political appointments at the turn of the millennium.

In December 1987, the outbreak of the Intifada encouraged the business elite to support peace and reconciliation initiatives, and to urge the Labor party to increase its efforts at establishing political relations with the Palestinians. This trend increased with the collapse of the Soviet Union and expanding globalization (Ram, 2005; Shafir and Peled, 2002). But the Intifada also brought about a strong reaction against the peace process in the Jewish population in Israel. In the 1988 election to the Twelfth Knesset, Likud won the largest number of seats (forty) and, together with the religious wing, held sixty-five seats in the house. The opposition held only fifty-five seats. The Likud-Labor government led by Yitzhak Shamir formed at the end of 1988 supported its Prime Minister's hawkish line and rejected Shimon Peres' conciliatory initiative to resolve the Israeli-Palestinian conflict. Peres, as acting prime minister, worked tirelessly to win back his position of leadership in the government. In March 1990, he led a no-confidence vote against his own government in the Knesset. The government lost the vote, becoming a transitional government. However, due to political wheeling-dealing, Peres was unable to recruit enough support to form a new coalition and in June 1990, Shamir once again headed a government, this time without Labor's participation (Korn, 1994: 227-46).

The political confusion of the first half of 1990 led to a number of changes in the political system and in the parties themselves, which in turn impacted on political appointments. The political fiasco enraged the public and encouraged the "gate keepers" to take a firmer stand against dirty politics in general, and specifically against political appointments. As part of the new policy, Attorney

General Yosef Harish issued strict directives limiting the ministers' authority to appoint party center members to government directorates unless they were qualified for the position.[35] Peres' political shenanigans, which were soon named the "dirty trick," also led the Labor party to adopt a partisan primaries system for electing both the party leadership and choosing the Knesset candidate list. This was an attempt to repair the damage to the party's public image. [36]

In comparison to the previous system employed by the Labor Party, of party center members selecting the list, the partisan primaries system created fewer incentives for political appointments by Knesset nominees. Though the partisan primaries system demands that Knesset member hopefuls mobilize the support of people who may ask for public appointments in exchange for their vote, there was no longer a need to try to win the trust of a few hundred party center members (Hazan, 1997a; Hofnung, 1996; Rahat, 2002; Rahat and Sher-Hadar, 1999).[37]

However, the political fiasco of the first half of 1990 also triggered the change in prime-ministerial and Knesset elections (Doron and Kay, 1995: 307; Hazan, 1996: 27-28; Hermann, 1995; Roniger, 1994: 176). As will be demonstrated below, this new system unintentionally contributed to a rise in political appointments.

The second Rabin Government, elected in 1992, was in office in the period between the passage of the Direct Prime-Ministerial Elections Act in 1992 and its subsequent implementation in 1996. During that time there was a significant decrease in political appointments. This was due to several factors. First, the partisan primaries system reduced the ministerial demand for appointments. Second, the amendment to the Government Companies Act of 1975 (see above) reduced the supply of these appointments. The amendment was a product of the liberalization process and of the government's attempt to help the executive branch adjust to a new global order. Third, an extremely pro-active Supreme Court, led by Chief Justice Aharon Barak, blocked inappropriate appointments.[38] The Court's policy itself was also the result of liberalization trends in Israel.[39] An additional factor was the appointment, in 1994, of Professor Yitzhak Galnoor, an expert in public administration, as Civil Service Commissioner. Appointing a professional to this position might also be a by-product of liberalization processes. Galnoor raised the aptitude requirements for positions of trust and fought against political appointments (State Comptroller, 1997: 839-840). In the spirit of these developments, in July of that year, the government decided to establish a committee formulating clear standards and regulations for the appointment of tender-free positions. [40]

In May 1996, as an expression of the Jewish public's rejection of the "Oslo accords," and perhaps partly in response to Peres' reelection as leader of the Labor party, Netanyahu won the first direct prime-ministerial elections held in Israel.

The data show that during the Netanyahu administration (June 1996-July 1999), the extent of political appointments was small. It is also possible that a mild decrease in political appointments in government companies began during that period. In view of the dominant role that the liberal ethic played in the Israeli public sphere at the time, and in light of the fact that in 1993 Likud also adopted the partisan primaries system,[41] the decrease in political appointments is understandable. There is also evidence that, for similar reasons, the short-lived Barak government (July 1999-March 2001) also used political appointments sparingly when compared to their use in the 1980s.

The Rise in Use of Political Appointments in the Sharon Era

The growth in the number of political appointments in the early 2000s can be traced back to the second half of the 1990s. The implementation of the direct prime-ministerial election reform, in May 1996 and again in 1999, resulted in a variety of unexpected and undesirable consequences. Primary among these was the weakening of the large parties and the strengthening of the small ones (see Doron and Kay, 1995: 316; Hazan, 1996, 1997b; Nachmias and Sened, 1999). Most significant to the discussion at hand is the growing conflict between the prime minister and his party elite, a result of the partisan primaries and the new governing system.[42] This new system forced the major parties to elect a leader capable of attracting at least 40 percent of the voters. It was difficult to locate a leader like this within the parties themselves inasmuch as identity with a known party automatically alienated at least some of the voters. In addition, developments in mass communication induced the parties to reach out for a leader with strong media appeal. The party elite was then obliged to choose leaders likely to deliver an electoral victory, at the expense of the ability to trust, or even work with, the individual chosen. The new leaders did not necessarily possess the skills required for establishing working relations with politicians. The system also encouraged nominees to disassociate themselves from the party in order to win over large groups of voters, making it necessary to redirect resources from the party campaign to the candidate's campaign.[43]

The intra-party conflict, exacerbated by the direct election system, encouraged Netanyahu to cancel the partisan primaries system for determining the party's Knesset candidate list, and to adopt a new version of the "party center" system in November 1997.[44] The change in the candidate selection method was designed to weaken those Likud leaders who drew their political pull from the wider membership, rather than from the party center, or from those who were affiliated with Netanyahu himself. The change would eventually make it easier to replace "inconvenient" leaders. Netanyahu knew that members of the party center were eager to punish those ministers and Knesset members, like Dan Meridor, who, from the operative point of view, had ignored them ever since the Netanyahu government was sworn in.[45] At the same time, the change was intended to strengthen Netanyahu's position in Likud; he was very popular with the party center, having filled party institutions with his cronies from the day he was elected chair of the center (Moshkovitz, 2002). The change in the candidate selection method probably affected the ministers' behavior toward the last year of the Netanyahu administration.[46] This change was one of the major factors contributing to the increase in political appointments during the first Sharon government in 2001, as will be clarified below.

It is important to note that canceling the partisan primaries and adopting the new center system was in direct contradiction to the inherent interests of the party leaders. They would have preferred to weaken party institutions, as these inhibited the leaders' ability to increase their independence from the party. The change also countered adjustments that parties in other parts of the world were undergoing at the time (Mair et al., 2004). The underlying reality accounting for this anomaly is the political crisis in Israel in the late 1980s and the beginning of the 1990s, and the worsening of the crisis resulting from a method that was adopted in an attempt to prevent it.

Another development during Netanyahu's term, which impacted on political appointments in the new millennium, was the dismissal of Civil Service Commissioner Yitzhak Galnoor and replacing him with Shmuel Hollander. This was intended to facilitate the promotion of government reforms including many political appointments (Arian, Nachmias, and Amir, 2002: 142). It is likely that, if relations between Netanyahu and the left wing, including parts of the establishment and the media, who held Rabin in high esteem (and accused Netanyahu of stirring up the violent public mood prior to the assassination), had not been as poor as they were (Peri, 2000: 44), he would have avoided implementing some of the procedures he initiated during his first year in office. But the conflict was intense, and Netanyahu believed, perhaps justifiably, that he was being unfairly harassed. Whether or not these speculations are true, Hollander, who was still Civil Service Commissioner at the time this chapter was written, had a much more tolerant attitude than his predecessor toward political appointments.[47] His lenient policy resulted in many manifestations that became more apparent during the Sharon era.[48]

The rise in the use of political appointments during the first Sharon government was a result, among other things, of the change in Likud's internal election system and the penetration of opportunists into the Likud party center as a result of the loosening of the link between the public and the political system. It is important, however, to note not only the new system's contribution to the demand for appointments, but also to the supply factor. A minister may wish to appoint his cronies to a position, but for this to become a reality, it is necessary to understand how the gatekeepers' policy affected the implementation of appointments, and, more importantly, the role that liberalization played in the process.

Though the State Comptroller paid close attention to political appointments in the first Sharon government, due to the retrospective nature of the Comptroller's work, information about political appointments was only collected after Sharon's first term had ended, when the extent of appointments in the Environmental

Protection Ministry became common knowledge. Elyakim Rubinstein, appointed Attorney General in April 1997, consistently avoided prosecution of public officials involved in inappropriate actions unless there was enough solid enough evidence for an indictment.[49] The Treasury Ministry elite, one of the most powerful gatekeepers and the forerunner of economic liberalization, were never overly bothered by political appointments.[50] They did not view the phenomenon as harmful, and in fact had an inherent interest against fighting junior level political appointments. While junior level appointments had no affect on the liberalization that the ministry was promoting, acting against them might have prompted some government ministers to change the Government Companies Act, thereby increasing the extent of political appointments to positions on much higher levels. These changes would have increased the influence of elected public officials over economic policy. To avoid this, the Treasury Ministry, in accordance with its "laissez faire" policy, simply needed to refrain from interfering on the lower levels.[51] Moreover, in contradiction with its authority and the civil service directive, the Treasury Ministry "allowed" ministers to hire employees through manpower companies (State Comptroller, 2004). This policy coincided with the ministry's attempts to privatize and reduce the size of public service. The Civil Service Commissioner did not supervise these appointments and thus facilitated their abuse in service of political goals.

Another factor affecting the extent of political appointments was the ongoing rivalry between Prime Minister Sharon and Binyamin Netanyahu. Netanyahu was an influential figure with party center members during Sharon's term.[52] This prompted Sharon to recruit thousands of new party members before the general elections for the party leadership in December 2002.[53] These new members could both increase Sharon's chances of winning the party leadership, and elect different delegates to the party convention that would choose the list of Knesset nominees (which, unlike the party leadership, was elected by the party center, not the rank and file). The most effective way to recruit that many people in so short a time was to use "vote-contractors" who could deliver the goods. The "vote-contractors" were aware of the forecasts predicting a Likud landslide in the next election, and were equally aware of the skyrocketing demand for the services they could provide any of the incumbent Likud ministers or nominees. Not surprisingly, the "vote-contractors" demanded quid-pro-quo for their services: the demand for political appointments soared together with the ministers' tendency to appoint cronies to public positions (Hofnung, 2005: 75).

The Effects of Patronage on the Structure of the Party System

On the eve of the internal elections for Likud's candidate list for the Sixteenth Knesset (the 2003 election), Tzachi Hanegbi declared, "Whenever I could offer any of our members a job befitting his skills, I asked him to submit an application." [54]

Although Hanegbi's statement seems to affirm the "loss of shame" argument, I would like to suggest a different explanation. It is more likely that the statement was the outcome of the tough competition in Likud at the time. Hanegbi believed that the most effective way to ensure a high place on the party's candidate list was by establishing the image of a public official who could be trusted to make political appointments in the future. Creating such an image increased the chances that center members who had not yet benefited from his help would vote for him with the anticipation that they would benefit from his pro-party policy in the future.

The massive number of political appointments involving Hanegbi, and his public statements in support of the practice, won him first place in the Likud's internal elections in December 2002. But his statements also led to a thorough examination of the appointments by the State Comptroller, leading eventually not only to the publication of a critical report on the matter, but also to the deployment and implementation of a much tougher gate keeping policy against patronage.

In light of the report, Menny Mazuz, the newly appointed attorney general, directed the police to open a criminal investigation against Hanegbi. He also instructed Hanegbi, who was then Internal Security Minister, to suspend himself from the position. Two months later, the Attorney General issued a directive limiting the jurisdiction of government ministers in terms of their ability to grant the requests of members of an electing body or of "vote-contractors."[55] One month later, the Civil Service Commissioner and the Attorney General ordered an inter-office team to examine the Comptroller's findings on appointments in the Environmental Protection Ministry.[56] The team compiled a set of operative recommendations, accepted by the Commissioner and the Attorney General in May 2005. Many of these recommendations have been implemented by the Civil Service Commission.[57]

Another factor that may have led to a reduction in patronage was its lack of effectiveness in mobilizing support for Sharon's political initiative. In fact, it had quite the opposite effect and helped Sharon's opponents to strengthen their struggle against him.

Sharon announced his "Disengagement Plan" toward the end of 2003. Despite the fact that the plan was in direct contradiction to the party platform and its campaign promises,[58] had Sharon's stance in Likud been strong, he might have won the party's support for his scheme. However, even as prime minister, Sharon did not wield much power in Likud and his plan irritated many Likud operatives.

In an attempt to appease the opposition from within, Sharon declared on the Knesset floor that he would subject the proposal to a Likud referendum and respect the decision of the party.[59] However, contrary to Sharon's expectations, Likud rejected his political initiative. Some of those who had joined the party at the end of 2002 were no longer party members at the time of the referendum,[60] participation in the referendum was low, and the field was left wide open to Sharon's opponents.

It is not uncommon for self-interest-driven players, like those who joined Likud to promote their own interests, to be free riders and defect at any time. Political appointments resulted in yet another ramification that was in opposition to Sharon's interest. Party membership was based almost solely on various types of patronage, rather than on ideological coherence or leadership and persuasion, creating a situation where some Likud ministers cultivated their own power centers and were no longer dependent on loyalty to Sharon (compare to: Warner, 1997: 542-543). A good example is Israel Katz, the agriculture minister and to a lesser degree, Danny Naveh, the minister of health. Both used their job appointments to develop their party strength, and both often openly opposed the prime minister's policies.[61]

Eventually, the lack of effectiveness of political appointments in promoting the "Disengagement Plan," the negative image they imparted to Likud, and the high price some of those involved in patronage were beginning to pay, as well as Sharon's inability to establish leadership of the Likud without patronage, led to his decision to abandon Likud and create the new party, Kadima.

The massive use of party patronage by Ariel Sharon and his son Omri, on the one hand, and Sharon's dissociation from the Likud on the other, created a paradoxical situation whereby, during the 2006 election campaign, both Kadima and Likud accused each other of corruption and patronage during the previous government's term of office (see chapters by Weimann et al. and Jonathan Mendilow, here). Following the revelation of Omri's private diaries, in which the massive amount of political appointments made by Omri on behalf of his father was exposed, Ehud Olmert absurdly claimed, that "we formed Kadima because we were tired of all that business, because we wanted a different kind of politics, we wanted to disassociate ourselves from the Likud central committee. So Omri called me a few times over the years, so what?" (Mualem, 2006).

It is highly likely that the majority of voters knew that both Likud, and the politicians who created Kadima, were equally responsible for the corruption in Israeli politics in recent years. This realization was probably among the reasons for the low voter turnout in the 2006 elections.

Summary

In this chapter I argued that the use of patronage and political appointments was diminishing, and that increases in the phenomenon were temporary and would probably be followed by a significant reduction. More concretely, if the judicial elite, the business elite, and any number of politicians had known what shape the direct election reform would take, they probably would not have supported its adoption in 1992, and the rise of the "patronage regime" of the early 2000s would have been avoided.

This claim is based on the theoretical assumption that liberalization weakens the parties and their ability to use illegal means to gain power and influence. Each deviation from this pattern is limited in scope, and temporary, and might be the result of political misunderstanding on the part of the power elite, or of a specific need to mobilize public support for the promotion of new policies.

The findings presented here confirm this assumption, and stand in contrast to current political discourse.

The 2006 elections exposed the Janus face of party patronage and its limitations. On the one hand, political appointments enabled politicians and public employees to be elected to the top of Likud's list and establish their standing, and also enabled Ariel Sharon to win the internal party elections. They therefore contributed indirectly to the electoral success of the Likud in 2003. On the other hand, patronage empowered Sharon's rivals within the party, and lessened support for the disengagement plan (Caspit, 2006; Lam, 2006). Patronage also damaged the image and reputation of Likud and its electoral potential. Sharon was left without any basis for remaining in the party he had established thirty years earlier. In other words, the establishment of Kadima was intended to enable Sharon, not only to be elected, but also to rule.

The research exposed two additional phenomena. It is clear that the use of patronage was not aimed at controlling policy, but at gaining power within the parties. Israel differs in this matter from other industrialized countries where a tendency toward politicization of the bureaucracy elite has recently become apparent (Peters and Pierre, 2004). Patronage has also proven to be a useful instrument for gaining power, but less useful in promoting policy changes, especially radical ones. In the long run, patronage appears to be a menace to political parties, as Warner (1997) claimed.

In conclusion, Kadima's establishment, with its undemocratic institutions, is a natural substitute for the Likud corruption that existed in the early 2000s, as a result of party patronage. Kadima, like the earlier use of party patronage, represents the lack of will—or lack of power—of Israel's most powerful politician to promote his agenda through an organization with relatively recognizable democratic features: the political party.

In accepting this claim, Kadima can be viewed not only as a mirror image of party patronage, but also as a clear expression of the severe crisis, which the Israeli party system is currently undergoing. On a more abstract level, Kadima is a manifestation of the weakened role of political parties as a link between the public and the decision makers, and does not bode well for the future prospects of political parties.

The new organization that Sharon established may have been able to provide what patronage could not, i.e., public support for territorial changes in the region. Unfortunately, because the prime minister had a stroke in January 2006, Kadima's performance will probably give more support to the claim of those who believe that there is no such thing as democracy beyond political parties.

Notes

1. I would like to thank Dr. Danny Korn, Dr. Gideon Rahat, Shoshi Breiner, and an anonymous reader for their helpful comments. I would also like to thank Noga Isaacson and Gila Haimovic for their help with the translation and editing.

2. An example can be found in the Comptroller's speech at the 2006 Annual Bar Convention during which he argued that political appointments are "A cancer in the heart of the Israeli nation," *Orech Hadin*, 61 (June 2006), 21, 48-49.

3. On September 25, 2006, MK Tzachi Hanegbi, who, at the time this article is being written, is chair of the Knesset Foreign Affairs & Defense Committee, was indicted. The indictment refers to the period of time when Hanegbi served as minister of Environmental Protection, between March 2001 and January 2003. Hanegbi was accused of having abused his power by executing forty-nine different illegal political appointments, as well as deceit and breach of confidence, election bribery and an attempt to influence the vote of Likud members. He was also accused of perjury and giving false evidence (*Haaretz*, September 26, 2006, p. 4). For more information on the appointments, see State Comptroller (2004).

4. For more information on these research perspectives see Hall and Taylor (1996: 936-942).

5. James (2006) first introduced the concept of a "patronage regime." The importance of the concept was emphasized in Pempel (1999: 19-41), and was used by Shafir and Peled (2002) in their seminal work to analyze citizenship in Israel.

6. For more on institutional interest to stump patronage, see Kitschel (2000a: 163-164).

7. Alternately, we can view it as bureaucratization of political life and turning the state into a corporation, led by economic and administrative logic only. This development was predicted by Max Weber (Wolin, 2004: 581-606). For instances of this phenomenon in Israel, see Galnoor (2004).

8. An example of the reduction in the party's dependency upon the public is public funding of party electoral campaigns and ongoing activities. As a result of public funding, parties rely less on membership fees and contributions. See also Hofnung (1996); Katz and Mair (1995).

9. The liberal discourse emphasizes citizenship rights, in particular civil rights and the need to constrain government power to ensure loyal, reasonable, and fair service to the public as a whole.

10. As former Vice President Al Gore said in August 2006: In many countries media control was being consolidated in the hands of a few businessmen and women or politicians [http://abcnews.go.com/International/wireStory?id=2363650].

11. Itzhak Zamir, one of the strongest and most perspicacious opponents of political appointments, attributes such high importance to motivation in political appointments that he believes that "the fault is in the thought itself, not the deed" (Zamir, 1991: 149).

12. In many respects, many political appointments cannot be identified by measuring the quality of the appointees and their conduct in executing their jobs. A public official is likely to nominate a highly qualified individual to a public position, but for political reasons. Alternately, a minister may appoint an incompetent fool to a position from which he or she can cause incredible damage to the public good without there being any illicit private intent. Moreover, the public good is defined differently by different people. Without a sweeping consensus as to what defines public interest , and what constitutes harm to such interest, it is difficult to prove that a nomination goes against the public good or to conclude that the appointing minister was acting with illicit intent in mind (see also Stark, 2000: 119-123). Given

this reality, it is not uncommon, except in instances when politicians leave explicit evidence as to their state of mind (such as private diaries) or a direct statement of motive, for the public to remain in the dark as to the motives. According to the Comptroller's report, in which, for the first time, a separate chapter was dedicated to political appointments, "Ordinarily, we cannot find, in the documents of a reviewed governmental body, evidence which explicitly indicates that a nominee was chosen for irrelevant personal political reasons, nor do we expect to find such evidence. Instead, we look for evidence of attempts to disguise such motives" (State Comptroller, 1989: 627).

13. For the rationale underlying this methodology, see also Kopecky and Mair (2006.)

14. For example, when a minister appoints his cronies to technical-administrative positions, such as head of the Substance Control department in the Environmental Protection Ministry, a junior clerk in the Social Security Institute, or as a head of department in the Ports and Trains Bureau, he or she is more likely to be doing so due to private political interests. It is difficult to see how political kinship is relevant to any of these positions.

15. I received the information (for a fee) from Ms. Noga Kadush, secretary of the Appointments Committee, according to the Free Information Act.

16. The amendment to the Government Companies (Appointments) Law, 1993 requires minimal qualifications for executive positions in government companies. The law also stipulates the establishment of an Appointments Committee, charged with examining whether the candidates meet the qualifications for executive positions in government companies. If the candidates have personal, business, or political associations with any government minister they need to have special qualifications, otherwise the Committee would disqualify the appointment. See Government Corporations (Amendment no. 6) (Appointments) Act, 1993, sections 18b-18c.

17. The data was extracted from the annual Comptroller's report (State Comptroller, 1987), in which, for the first time, political appointments were mentioned, and all the reports that followed.

18. In each of these departments or governmental agencies, there is a unique procedure, rendering it inadequate for an examination of the extent of political appointments. Many of the Defense Department's procedures are confidential and cannot be reviewed by the public. By the very nature of its work, the ministry marches to a different drummer where appointments are concerned. For instance, the extent of nominations without tender is much higher than in any other ministries. As a rule, inappropriate nominations in the Treasury and Justice Departments are almost never the result of political interests but rather an expression of the closed ranks of the economic and legal elites, not of patronage. The situation in the Foreign Affairs Ministry is almost exactly the opposite: in this ministry, special arrangements for political appointments are enshrined in law, which makes it increasingly difficult to track any changes in patterns of political appointments. Finally, it should be noted that political appointments in local authorities, while crucial to the exploration of the issue at hand, as they may shed light on the patronage phenomenon, are also linked, at least in part, to structural changes in the authorities themselves, and the manner in which authority heads fortify their position within the authority.

19. Candidates for senior positions such as Chair or CEO of a Board of Directors of a governmental corporation or a statutory authority are asked, among other things, to report any connection or political affinity they may have to government ministers.

20. According to Israeli common law, governmental authorities are considered to be operating within the legal restrictions set by the legislator, that is to say that a

minister's appointments are considered to be lawful and devoid of irrelevant consideration, including any considerations of his or her personal political well being. Anyone who wishes to claim the contrary must provide evidence for such a claim. See also Zamir (1991: 149).

21. The courts and the attorney general's guidelines have also failed to provide an exact definition for "political affinity." For important verdicts that dealt with defining and identifying political appointments, see Israeli Supreme Court Decision (ISCD) 4566/90, *David Dekel v. Minister of Finance and others*, p. 28; ISCD 154/98, *The New General Workers Union v. Government of Israel*, p. 111; ISCD 932/99, *The Movement for Quality Government in Israel v. Chair of the Appointments Committee and others*, p. 784. The attorney general's opinion on the issue of political appointments can be extrapolated from Directive 6,500 of February 2006, which replaced all previous guidelines on the issue of appointments to government corporations and public authorities.

22. I participated in a discussion initiated by Attorney Tana Spnitz, chair of the Appointments Committee, held at the Center for Ethics in Jerusalem in September 2006, dedicated to defining political affinity. In response to my question, Ms. Spnitz clarified that no definition has been set to date and that members of the committee do not have a list of situations according to which they determine such affinity.

23. In its early years, when the Committee's jurisdiction was not yet clearly established, it adopted a rather temperate policy (for more, see State Comptroller, 1998). However, since 1999, the Committee espoused a much stricter approach, the results of which can be observed in the data presented here. This change in policy can be attributed to Ehud Barak's prime-ministerial victory, to a personnel change on the Committee, and to a ground-breaking Supreme Court verdict that determined that "a nominee affiliated to a minister fulfills the 'special qualifications' clause only if the weight of those special qualities is so overwhelming, and their contribution to society so great, that they justify the risk of appointing him in spite of his connections to a government Minister. In any case, adequate qualifications to fulfill the position must be extraordinary and rare." See HCJ 932/99, *The Movement for Quality of Government in Israel v. Chair of the Appointments Committee and Others*, p. 784.

24. It seems that the Comptroller's office has been gradually toughening its demands regarding the propriety of appointments. For example, in Report no. 48, specific appointments to trust positions were criticized because some of the nominees did not have academic degrees, although at the time the law did not demand this, and despite the fact that the Civil Service Commissioner did not view academic education as a prerequisite for such positions.

25. Civil Service Act (Appointments) 1959, articles 19 and 22.

26. Not including nominations in the Treasury, Justice, Foreign Affairs and Defense Ministries; boards of directors of government companies (Directors, Chairs, and CEOs) unless stated otherwise. The data in this table were taken from the annual State Comptroller's reports (beginning with report no. 37 where the first reference to inappropriate appointments was made) and three special reports published on the subject of illegitimate appointments (political and inappropriate appointments in the Environment Protection Ministry, inappropriate appointments in Magen David Adom, and political appointments in the Small and Medium Enterprises Authority).

27. J = Junior, MM = Middle Management, S=Senior

28. Not including two appointments which were mentioned in the reports: CEO of the Good Housing association and CEO of Amidar as the table does not include CEO appointments at all.

29. Three of the employees received complaints about their poor job performance.
30. Not including reported appointments: Chair of the Games and Gaming commission, CEO of the Plant Production & Marketing Board, CEO of Magen David Adom.
31. For example, see Doron Rosenblum's opinion article in which he complained about "the reign of a culture predicated on the shameless *nouveau riche*"(*Haaretz*, April 16, 1998, p. B1); Also, see the interview with former Justice and State Comptroller, Eliezer Goldberg, on the eve of his retirement (*Haaretz, The Marker*, November 25, 2005, p. 10), an interview with former Justice, at the time Deputy President of the Supreme Court, Mishael Cheshin (*Haaretz*, November 25, 2005, p. A18), and an article by Amnon Dankner and Dan Margalit in *Maariv*, May 17, 2005.
32. For example, see former Justice Itzhak Zamir (*Haaretz, The Marker*, January 18, 2006, p. 26); see also Negbi (2004) and Sprinzak (1986).
33. For example, see an interview with former Judge Or Strozman, who presided as head of the Likud Election Committee (*Orech Hadin*, 33 (November 2002), 36-44).
34. For example, P/591, a private bill proposed by MKs Gilad Erdan, Daniel Benlulu, Inbal Gavrieli, and Michael Girolovski (May 12, 2003), calling for cancellation of the special skills and increased experience requirements for the appointment of directors with political affinity. Also P/3239, Government Corporation Act (Amendment), canceling the special skills and increased experience requirements for the appointment of directors, a bill proposed on February 21, 2005. At the time of this writing, a professional committee—the Committee for the Appointment and Review of Senior Positions Promoting Policy in the Civil Service, created in accordance with government Decision 3560 on April 19, 2006—is still deliberating the criteria for appointments to such positions.
35. See the attorney general's Directive 28.016 to the Government, January 1991.
36. The partisan primaries system, which was fairly popular in the US at the time, provided the party that adopted it with an instant veneer of democratic values and progress. No less important is the fact that the new system helped oust Peres from his position as Chair of the Labor party—the most powerful man in the party at the time. Peres' defeat, and Yitzhak Rabin's election in his stead, was also considered to be a good move for Labor's ambition to further the peace process, as Peres' chances of leading the Labor party to a victory at the polls were considered slim at the time, while Rabin was believed to be able to break the "structural advantage" that the right wing enjoyed at the time (Doron and Kay, 1995).
37. Large union leaders' "vote-contracts," local authority heads, and large party branch heads could all help to recruit tens of thousands of voters, enough to cause a significant change in elections in which the number of voters could reach 300,000.
38. See: HCJ 6177/92, *Eisenberg v. Minister of Housing and Construction*, 47(2) P.D. 229; HCJ 3094/93 *The Movement for Quality of Government in Israel v. The Israeli Government*, 47(5) P.D. 404; HCJ4267/93 , *Amitai—Citizens for Clean Government v. Prime Minister of Israel*, 47(5) P.D. 441.
39. For the connection between economic liberalization and the courts' policy, see also Shafir and Peled (2002: 301-316).
40. Government Decision No. 3644 of 24.7.1994.
41. Until November 1997, the Likud ministers operated under the assumption that this would also be the system under which the next internal election would be held.
42. In this system, senior party member have little incentive to cultivate close connections with the party leader or members of the party center as they would not be those who decide the fate of their political careers; the rank and file would. See also Rahat and Sher-Hadar (1999).

43. The double vote meant that the big parties had to split their organizational effort and financial resources between the prime-ministerial campaign and the Knesset campaign. Even worse for the big parties, party leaders had the incentive to isolate themselves from their own parties to make themselves more appealing to the average voter. For more on the conflict between the party leader and the party elite caused by the electoral reform, see Doron (2002).
44. The party chair was still elected using the partisan primaries system.
45. Ministers were, at least in theory, less worried about maintaining a close relationship with party center members as they mistakenly assumed that the party rank and file would be determining their political future, not the center members. This is how Moshe Dolgin, one of the Booth 28 men who were promoting the move to cancel the primaries, interpreted the situation in an interview with me on July 13, 2006. See also Rahat (2002: 248, 258).
46. See Gidi Weitz and Yuval Karni "The Bosses," *Yediot Aharonot*, February 20, 2004, p. 19; Hanna Kim's report, "Bibi's Babushka," *Haaretz*, September 18, 1998, p. B3.
47. For instance, compare Hollander's statement about the skills necessary to man trust positions in ministerial chambers with that of ousted commissioner Galnoor (State Comptroller, 1997: 840).
48. For instance, by not setting clear guidelines for the appointment of aides and advisors in ministerial chambers, given the de-facto growth in the number of such appointments (see State Comptroller, 2005: 5-37). Or by silently accepting hiring practices which included extensive use of manpower companies in direct violation of regulations (see State Comptroller, 2004: 33, 37; 2006: 39-60). Or by allowing ministries to hire individuals on a regular basis before a tender was issued (see State Comptroller, 2006a: 247-274).
49. It is also possible that political appointments took a back seat to the many corruption practices which the attorney general had to deal with at the time. As mentioned, the Civil Service Commissioner, Shmuel Hollander, did not put the full weight of his office behind the battle against political appointments.
50. According to Yuval Rechalvski, who headed the Wages and Labor Accord Unit between 1999 and 2005, and participated in the senior level discussions in the ministry. The information was given to me during an interview on March 27, 2006.
51. Fighting appointments, which had little to no affect on the privatization and liberalization reforms, could have come with an undesirable price tag as far as the Treasury ministry was concerned. Ensuring high professional nomination standards could reinforce the civil service and as a result weaken the justification for subordinating other ministries' economic accountants to the Treasury ministry. This possibility was suggested to me, off the record, by an interviewee who was under the impression that the Treasury ministry was not interested in improving the quality of the civil service.
52. Netanyahu's standing with the Likud members and party center members before the big party census in the second half of 2002 can be seen from the party center's vote in May 2002, against creating a Palestinian state.
53. In June 2002, the Likud counted 92,000 registered members. Two months later, by the end of July 2002, when the members' list closed in preparation for the convention of delegates and internal party leader elections (in October), there were 304,770 registered members. That is, more than 200,000 members joined the party just before the internal elections.
54. The statement also appears in the State Comptroller, 2004: 13.
55. See Directive no. 1.1708, October 24, 2004, titled "Limitation On Handling Requests From Members Of Electing Bodies By Public Officials."

56. See "Recommendations of the Inter-Office Team to Examine the Findings of the State Comptroller's Report on Political and Inappropriate Appointments in the Environment Protection Ministry," submitted on April 14, 2004.
57. This determination is based on interviews with senior members of the Civil Service Commission's legal department and the follow-up reports on the execution of the team's recommendations which were given to me in July 2006.
58. Even though Sharon declared during the election campaign that Israel would be forced to make painful concessions, the Likud platform rejected the idea of a unilateral move. The objection to such a move was one of the differences between the Likud and Labor platforms. See also HJC: 1661/05 *The Gaza Beach Local Authority v. Israeli Knesset*, June 2005 (not yet published).
59. See his Knesset speech on April 22, 2004. Available at http://www.pmo.gov.il/PMO/Archive/ Speeches/2004/04/Speeches9389.htm.
60. In April 2004, when the party referendum on the Disengagement Plan was held, the Likud had 193,190 registered members. Less than two years earlier, the number was 304,770 (This information was provided by Mr. Alex Glassman, head of the computing department in the Likud). It is therefore very likely that 100,000 people, who had very little real connection to the party, registered as members for the sole purpose of influencing the party center and leadership elections.
61. Details of political appointments in the Agriculture ministry when Israel Katz presided as its minister can be found in the State Comptroller's Annual Report (2005: 655-692); Details on political appointments during Danny Naveh's tenure in the Health ministry can be found in a special report that published about appointments in Magen David Adom (State Comptroller, 2006b).

References

Arian, Asher, David Nachmias, and Ruth Amir. 2002. *Executive Governance in Israel.* New York: Palgrave.

Barak-Erez, Daphne. 2002. "Judicial Review of Politics: The Israeli Case." *Journal of Law and Society* 29(4): 611-631.

Barzilai, Gad, and David Nachmias. 1998. *Accountability: The Comptroller General.* Jerusalem: The Israel Democracy Institute.

Blondel, Jean. 2002. "Party Government, Patronage, and Party Decline in Western Europe." In Richard Gunther, Jose Ramon Montero and Juan J. Linz, eds. *Political Parties: Old Concepts and New Challenges.* Oxford: Oxford University Press, 233-256.

Blyth, Mark, and Richard Katz. 2005. "From Catch-all Politics to Cartelisation: The Political Economy of the Cartel Party." *West European Politics,* 28(1): 33-60.

Caspit, B. 2006. "One Mandate More Than Bibi." *Maariv Weekend Magazine,* 31 March.

Dery, David. 1993. *Politics and Civil Service Appointments.* Tel-Aviv: The Israel Democracy Institute [Hebrew].

Doron, Gideon. 2002. "Barak, One—One Israel, Zero, Or, How Labor Won the Prime Ministerial Race and Lost the Knesset Elections." In Asher Arian and Michal Shamir, eds. *The Elections in Israel 1999.* Albany, NY: SUNY, 179-196.

Doron, Gideon, and Barry Kay. 1995. "Reforming Israel's Voting Schemes." In Asher Arian and Michal Shamir, eds. *The Elections in Israel 1992.* Albany, NY: SUNY, 299-320.

Galnoor, Itzhak. 2004. "The Judicialization of Public Life in Israel." *Mishpat U'Mimshal* 7(1): 355-380 [Hebrew].

Goldberg, Eliezer. 2004. *Political Appointments* [Hebrew]. 3 November. Retrieved 3 October, 2006, from http://www.mevaker.gov.il/serve/content.

Hall, Peter A., and Rosemary C.R. Taylor. 1996. "Political Science and the Three New Institutionalisms." *Political Studies* 44: 936-957.

Hazan, Reuven. 1996. "Presidential Parliamentarism: Direct Popular Election of the Prime Minister, Israel's New Electoral and Political System." *Electoral Studies* 15(1): 21-37.

------. 1997a. "The 1996 Intra-Party Elections in Israel: Adopting Party Primaries." *Electoral Studies* 16(1): 95-103.

------. 1997b. "Executive-Legislative Relations in an Era of Accelerated Reform: Reshaping Government in Israel." *Legislative Studies Quarterly, 22*(3): 329-350.

Hermann, Tamar. 1995. "The Rise of Instrumental Voting: The Campaign for Political Reform." In Asher Arian and Michal Shamir, eds. *The Elections in Israel 1992*. Albany, NY: SUNY, 275-298.

Hofnung, Menachem. 1996. "The Public Purse and the Private Campaign: Political Finance in Israel." *Journal of Law and Society*, 23(1): 132-148.

------. 2005. "Fat Parties-Lean Candidates: Funding Israeli Internal Party Contests." In Asher Arian and Michal Shamir, eds. *The Elections in Israel—2003*. New Brunswick, NJ: Transaction Publishers, pp. 63-84.

James, Scott C. 2006. "Patronage Regimes and American Party Development from 'The Age of Jackson' to the Progressive Era." *British Journal of Political Science* 36(1): 39-60.

Katz, Richard S., and Peter Mair. 1995. "Changing Models of Party Organization and Party Democracy: The Emergence of the Cartel Party." *Party Politics* 1: 5-28.

Kitschelt, Herbert. 2000a. "Citizens, Politicians, and Party Cartelization: Political Representation and State Failure in Post-Industrial Democracies." *European Journal of Political Research* 37(2): 149-179.

------. 2000b. "Linkages between Citizens and Politicians in Democratic Polities." *Comparative Political Studies* 33(6-7): 845-879.

Kopecky, Petr, and Peter Mair. 2006. "Political Parties and Patronage in Contemporary Democracies: An Introduction." Paper presented at the Workshop on Political Parties and Patronage, ECPR, Nicosia.

Korn, Dan. 1994. *Time in Grey*. Haifa: Zmora Bitan [Hebrew].

Lam, Amira. 2006. Real Politic. *Yediot Aharonot, 7 Days Magazine*, 31 March.

Mair, Peter. 2005. *Democracy Beyond Parties* (Paper 05-06). Center for the Study of Democracy.

Mair, Peter, Wolfgang C. Muller, and Fritz Plasser. 2004. "Introduction: Electoral Challenges and Party Responses." In Peter Mair, Wolfgang C. Muller, and Fritz Plasser, eds. *Political Parties and Electoral Change*. London: Sage.

Meny, Yves. 1996. "'Fin de siecle' Corruption: Change, Crisis, and Shifting Values." *International Social Science Journal* 48(3): 309-320.

Moshkovitz, Yaffa. 2002. *Party Organizational Changes as Outcome of Changes in the General Political System: The Likud Party*. Unpublished doctoral dissertation, Bar-Ilan University [Hebrew].

Mualem, Mazal. 2006. Kadima seeks to distance itself from Omri. *Haaretz*, 7 March.

Nachmias, David, and Itai Sened. 1999. "The Bias of Pluralism: The Redistributive Effects of the New Electoral Law." In Asher Arian and Michal Shamir, eds. *The Elections in Israel 1996*. Albany, NY: SUNY, 269-294.

Naim, Moses. 1995. "The Corruption Eruption." *Brown Journal of World Affairs* 2: 245-261.

Negbi, M. 2004. *We Were Like Sodom: On the Slope from a Law-Abiding Country to a Banana Republic*. Tel Aviv: Keter [Hebrew].

Panebianco, Angelo. 1988. *Political Parties: Organization and Power*. Cambridge: Cambridge University Press.

Pempel, T.J. 1999. *Regime Shift: Comparative Dynamic of Japanese Political Economy*. Ithaca: Cornell University Press.

Peri, Yoram. 2000. "The Assassination: Causes, Meaning, Outcomes." In Yoram Peri, ed. *The Assassination of Yitzhak Rabin*. Stanford, CA: Stanford University Press, 25-62.

Peters, B. Guy and Jan Pierre. 2004. "Conclusion: Political Control in a Managerialist World." In B. Guy Peters and Jon Pierre, eds. *Politicization of the Civil Service in Comparative Perspective*. London: Routledge, 283-290.

Piattoni, Simona, ed. 2001. *Clientelism, Interests, and Democratic Representation*. Cambridge: Cambridge University Press.

Rahat, Gideon. 2002. "Candidate Selection in a Sea of Changes: Unsuccessfully Trying to Adapt." In Asher Arian and Michal Shamir, eds. *The Elections in Israel 1999*. Albany, NY: SUNY, 245-268.

Rahat, Gideon and Neta Sher-Hadar. 1999. "The 1996 Party Primaries and Their Political Consequences." In Asher Arian and Michal Shamir, eds. *The Elections in Israel 1996*. Albany, NY: SUNY, 241-268.

Ram, Uri. 2005. *The Globalization of Israel: McWorld in Tel Aviv, Jihad in Jerusalem*. Tel Aviv: Resling [Hebrew].

Roniger, Luis. 1994. "Images of Clientelism and Realities of Patronage in Israel." In Luis Roniger and Ayse Gunes-Ayata, eds. *Democracy, Clientelism, and Civil Society*. Boulder, CO: Lynne Rienner, 167-180.

Rose-Ackerman, Susan. 1996. "Democracy and 'Grand' Corruption." *International Social Science Journal* 48(3): 365-380.

Shafir, Gershon and Yoav Peled. 2002. *Being Israeli: The Dynamics of Multiple Citizenship*. Cambridge: Cambridge University Press.

Shefter, Martin. 1994. *Political Parties and the State: The American Historical Experience*. Princeton, NJ: Princeton University Press.

Sprinzak, Ehud. 1986. *Every Man Whatsoever His Own Eyes: Illegalism in Israeli Society*. Tel Aviv: Sifriat Poalim [Hebrew].

Stark, Andrew. 2000. *Conflict of Interest in American Public Life*. Cambridge, MA: Harvard University Press.

State Comptroller. 1987. *Annual Report No. 37*. Jerusalem: The State Comptroller [Hebrew].

State Comptroller. 1989. *Annual Report No. 39 for 1988 and the 1987 Financial Year*. Jerusalem: The State Comptroller [Hebrew].

State Comptroller. 1997. *Annual Report No. 47*. Jerusalem: The State Comptroller [Hebrew].

State Comptroller. 1998. *Report on the Appointment of Directors on Behalf of the State to Government Companies*. Jerusalem: The State Comptroller [Hebrew].

State Comptroller. 2004. *Report on Political Appointments and Inappropriate Appointments in the Environment Ministry*. Jerusalem: The State Comptroller [Hebrew].

State Comptroller. 2005. *Annual Report No. 55b*. Jerusalem: The State Comptroller [Hebrew].

State Comptroller. 2006a. *Annual Report No. 56b*. Jerusalem: The State Comptroller [Hebrew].

State Comptroller. 2006b. *Special Report on Appointments in Magen David Adom*. Jerusalem: The State Comptroller [Hebrew].

Warner, Carolyn M. 1997. "Political Parties and the Opportunity Costs of Patronage." *Party Politics* 3(4): 533-548.

Weingrod, Alex. 1968. "Patrons, Patronage, and Political Parties." *Comparative Studies in Society and History* 10(4): 377-400.

Wolin, Sheldon S. 2004. *Politics and Vision: Continuity and Innovation in Western Political Thought* (2nd ed.). Princeton, NJ: Princeton University Press.

Zamir, Itzhak. 1991. "Political Appointments in Judicial Review." *Mishpatim* 21(1): 145-159 [Hebrew].

Part 4

Political Communication

Media Coverage of the 2006 Campaign: The Needs and Attitudes of the Public vis-à-vis the Functioning of the News Media

Gabriel Weimann, Yariv Tsfati, Tamir Sheafer

Introduction

A democratic system is based on the participation of its citizens in the political process. Apathy on the part of citizens, their alienation from the political process, and mistrust of their political representatives constitute a dangerous corruption of any democratic regime. One of the accepted indices for assessing the extent of political involvement is voter turnout. Israel's voter turnout rate in past Knesset elections reached high levels, placing Israel at the forefront of countries with high voter participation rates (in all eight election campaigns between 1949 and 1969 this rate exceeded 80 percent). With time, however, there has been a steady decline in this rate: in the elections for the Sixteenth Knesset in 2003 the voter turnout rate was only 67.8 percent (and only 63.2 percent in the prime ministerial election in 2001). The 2006 general election marked a low point, with a turnout of only 63.5 percent. This decline is not unique to Israel; there has been a steady drop in voting rates in many Western democracies, averaging slightly more than 1 percent from one election campaign to the next. The lowest point among Western democracies was reached in established democracies, such as Switzerland and the U.S., where voter turnout rates have fallen to around 54 percent. This drastic decline arouses concern, signaling a rise in the political alienation felt by citizens and the undermining of the essential infrastructure of participatory democracies.

The erosion of voter participation can be ascribed to several factors, including the politicians themselves. A sense of loathing in response to the perception of the dishonesty that envelops politics and politicians has exacerbated feelings of alienation and indifference. The Sixteenth Knesset, with its display of members arraigned, interrogated, tried, and under suspicion of dishonesty, as well as the many scandals involving duplicate voting, bribery, and corruption, undoubtedly helped to erode political participation. However, other factors, such as the news media, should have been able to mitigate the sense of alienation and apathy, bringing people closer to the system and increasing their involvement in it.

In a democratic system the news media's function includes several important and essential roles, among them, transmitting information, serving as a bridge between the general public and its elected representatives, and augmenting the public's involvement in the political process. The news media, however, tend to be overly critical, sarcastic, and cynical, leading the public to recoil from politics. Thus, the news media may facilitate the creation of a cycle of cynicism, culminating in complete alienation from politics and politicians, with quiescent non-participation in the political process. The effect of the news media is felt even more strongly during elections, when citizens must decide which of the parties, individuals, and manifestos presented to them are best suited to their expectations and the path they want the country and society to take. In the modern world it is the news media that constitute the intermediary between voters and candidates, acting as purveyors of essential information between the public and its leaders. At election time, however, the task of the news media is not confined to serving as an intermediary between candidates and voters; their role is also one of molding the agenda of public discourse, aiding voters in making considered electoral choices, providing information about the candidates, the parties, and the platforms, and interpreting information about how the candidates have functioned in the past.

This study focuses on an analysis of media coverage of the 2006 election campaign and compares the viewpoint of the Israeli public (as indicated by a survey of attitudes and expectations of media coverage during the election campaign) with the actual situation (as indicated by an analysis of television coverage of the campaign and party political broadcasts). This is the first study of its kind to be undertaken in Israel, contrasting the needs of the public with media response, or lack of it, and examining public criticism relative to actual data on the coverage insofar as it relates to quality, fairness, and reliability.

Criticism of Election Coverage

Several studies have demonstrated that most voters have two main sources of information in an election campaign. The first and also the most widespread and significant source is media coverage, incorporating both news reports and commentary. The second is political party broadcasts, especially those on television (Kaid and Holtz-Bacha, 1995). However, considerable criticism has been leveled against media coverage of elections in Israel and in other countries, focusing on the quality, fairness, and reliability of this coverage.

The Quality of Media Coverage

Does the coverage provide essential and important information? Does it respond to the public's needs at a time when voters have to consider the various options and make a choice? Relative to political party broadcasts, news coverage should be of better quality and offer more information, but it also tends to focus to an inordinate extent on such issues as campaign strategy and propaganda rather than on political topics (Just et al., 1996; Norris, 1998). There are those who feel that media coverage of an election campaign focuses on its "horse-race" aspects: personal competition, popularity polls, and predictions of losers and winners (Joslyn, 1990; Wolfsfeld, 1995). But election propaganda can highlight political issues and serve as a venue for "civic education," enabling voters to become acquainted with the candidates and examine their plans and vision. Moreover, political party broadcasts can raise issues and increase involvement in the political process as well as place subjects on the agenda for public debate. Nevertheless, because of the aggressive and negative nature of modern election propaganda, the quality of media coverage and political discourse may be damaged. This might deter political involvement, engendering distaste toward those who do engage in this activity. Some studies have shown that negative campaigns tend to harm the quality of political discourse, reduce the number of voters on election day, and polarize the political camps (Ansolabehere and Iyengar, 1995). A recent study undertaken in the U.K. and the U.S. found that media coverage of political campaigns contribute to public apathy on political issues (Lewis and Wahl-Jorgensen, 2003).

The Extent of Fairness or Bias in Coverage of Candidates

Accusations of the news media's political-ideological bias come from several sources. Politicians from parties on the right consistently make these criticisms, mainly during election campaigns. For example, in the final stages of the 1999 campaign, the prime minister, Binyamin Netanyahu, accused "the media" of being biased in favor of the One Israel party and the left. In a famous speech featured prominently in the news media, Netanyahu asserted that "the media" and their journalists "were afraid" that Likud and the right would be victorious. A similar event took place in the 2003 elections. After the news media published investigations into a loan that the prime minister, Ariel Sharon, and his sons received from a South African Jewish businessman, Sharon's advisors launched a fierce attack on "the media," which, they claimed, were trying to undermine the administration. In 2006, Netanyahu attacked the media once again, accusing them of "targeting" him for attack in order to harm him and his party. Similar arguments regarding the left-wing political orientation of the media are consistently made by Republican Party candidates in the U.S., accusing the American media of favoring the Democratic Party. Both Israeli and American politicians justify their claims by pointing to the lack of impartiality embodied in the liberal-left worldview of most journalists (Niven, 2001). In other words, the purported political identity of journalists is used by politicians on the right to account for their impression that they are not given fair media coverage. The underlying assumption here is that journalists' political views find expression in their work and the manner in which they cover an election campaign. As to the political identity of journalists, the accusations made by politicians on the right would seem to be justified, at least as far as the U.S. is concerned. Surveys and studies have consistently demonstrated that the vast majority of U.S. journalists hold left-wing-liberal views, and vote for the Democratic Party and its candidates (Lichter, Rothman, and Lichter, 1986; Patterson, 1993; D'Alessio and Allen, 2000; Niven, 2001).

No study has been undertaken in Israel to examine the distribution of political attitudes among journalists. It is generally assumed that most journalists support the left (Wolfsfeld, 1997), with public opinion supporting this assumption, but such assumptions do not constitute proof that the work of journalists is indeed biased. In a 2003 survey of a representative sample of Israeli journalists, 84 percent of respondents rejected the claim that the media constitute a "left-wing mafia" (Tsfati and Livio, 2003). Journalists reject the accusation that the media are left-wing, claiming that their approach is professional and objective, leading to balanced coverage of political events. In Israel, as well as in other democracies, politicians on the right focus on the political identity of journalists, claiming that the "media are left-wing," while journalists stress that their approach to reviewing the political contenders is professional and even-handed.

The Extent of the Public's Trust in the Media Coverage

To fulfill their function in the democratic process, the media must operate in an atmosphere in which they enjoy public trust. Lack of this trust may cause the public to feel alienated from the political process and subsequently reduce its political involvement. According to the findings of the Israel Democratic Index in 2003 (Arian et al., 1999), only 49 percent of the public trusts the news media, compared with 83 percent who trust the IDF, 70 percent who trust the Supreme Court, 68 percent who trust the president, 66 percent who trust the police, 58 percent who trust the attorney general, 55 percent who trust the government, 53 percent who trust the prime minister, 52 percent who trust the General Federation of Labor (Histadrut), and 51 percent who trust the Knesset. Only the Rabbinate (43 percent) and the political parties (32 percent) are trusted less than the news media. When the public's trust in the various institutions were ranked, media fell 4 or 5 ranks from their position in 2002, a steeper drop than even that of the attorney general, who had been severely criticized during the previous year. Since 2003 the Chaim Herzog Institute of Communications has prepared an index of the Israeli public's media trust. This series of studies demonstrates a fairly consistent low level of trust, generally hovering between 2.9 and 3 on a scale of 1 to 5 (Tsfati and Tukachinsky, 2005).

The quality and impartiality of election coverage in Israel can be assessed from a series of studies that examined the coverage and content of the election campaigns in 1996, 1999, 2001, and also recently in 2003 (Arian, Weimann and Wolfsfeld, 1999; Wolfsfeld and Weimann, 1999, 2001; Weimann and Wolfsfeld, 2002; Weimann and Sheafer, 2004; Sheafer and Weimann, 2005). These studies were based on systematic examinations of the content of television news broadcasts as well as television election coverage in the period just prior to the election campaigns. However, an important dimension—the public itself, its expectations, needs, and attitudes—is missing from these studies. By focusing on specific issues and areas, coverage may respond to the public's needs and expectations. The above criticism derives primarily from two sources: academic research and politics. The news media generally defend themselves by claiming that they are attempting to give the public what it wants and that they are trying to interest an audience in the content they are providing by meeting its needs. What, then, does the public need and expect from media during elections and to what extent are these needs actually met?

The Audience Survey: Expectations, Needs, Disappointments

The first stage of our research examined the public's attitudes toward, and expectations of, the news media. Five hundred and nine respondents were surveyed by phone, 437 of them Jews (including immigrants from the former USSR) and 72 of them Israeli Arabs. A bit more than half of those surveyed, 50.3 percent, were men, and their average age was 43.88 (SD = 17.05), with an average of 13.55 years of schooling (SD = 5.7). Their satisfaction with media coverage was examined relative to two aspects: the content of broadcasts and the intensity of the coverage. Respondents were asked to rank the extent of their satisfaction with the general media coverage of the elections on a 4-point scale (1, not at all; 4, to a great extent).

An analysis of the results demonstrated that the public was dissatisfied with the coverage: 61.9 percent of those interviewed noted that they were not at all, or not very satisfied, and only 38.1 percent said they were satisfied. A comparison between the research findings for the 2006 and 2003 elections demonstrated

Figure 1
Extent of Satisfaction with Media Coverage of 2006 Elections

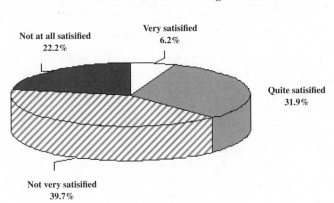

Not at all satisified
22.2%

Very satisified
6.2%

Quite satisified
31.9%

Not very satisified
39.7%

little change in the level of satisfaction among the general public (2.22 in 2006 compared with 2.24 in 2003, on a scale of 1–4), and in 2003, 60 percent of the public was dissatisfied with media coverage of the elections.

About one third of the population feels that media coverage does not contribute to its political knowledge. This finding does not significantly differ from research regarding the 2003 elections. In addition to measuring general satisfaction with the media coverage, satisfaction with the coverage of specific content was also examined (on a scale of 1–4). Topics included in this category related to the coverage of the personal characteristics and biographies of the principal candidates; the programs and platforms of the various parties; the leadership and administrative qualities of the principal candidates; the attitudes and voting intentions of athletes, writers, and actors; facts associated with Israel's security situation; and facts connected with Israel's economic and social situation (see figure 2, below).

A low level of public satisfaction with the coverage is evident in most areas. The media receive fairly mediocre grades in all topics (an average of 2.2 to 2.4) and slightly higher grades relative to the coverage of Israel's security situation.

The public's needs were also examined to the extent that these needs were met by the media. Each respondent was asked to choose the type of news content that he or she felt was important for the media to cover and then to assess what the media actually focused on. As figure 3 below shows, there is a considerable disparity between the news that the public would like to see in media and the news that it feels is given prominence in their coverage.

The largest group (31.7 percent) of respondents is interested in obtaining information about the attitudes and programs of the candidates and the parties,

Figure 2
Satisfaction with Media Coverage of 2006 Election Campaign, by Subject

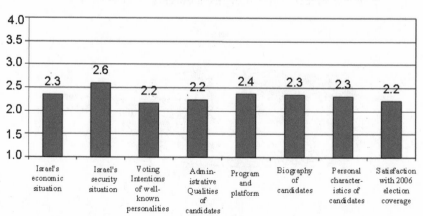

Figure 3
Desired vs. Actual: What the Public Thinks It Wants and What Media Provide

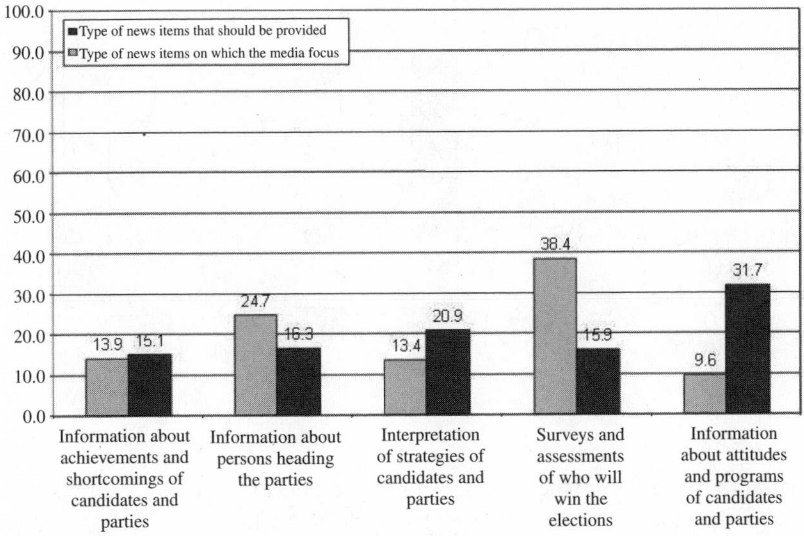

but only 9.6 percent believe that the news media focus on these topics. However, almost 40 percent of the public believes that the media are concerned primarily with reviewing and assessing the results of the elections, more than twice as many as those who defined these items as being the most important. In effect, a comparison of the topics listed as being preferred, with those defined as actually being presented, demonstrates that the vast majority of the public (80 percent) does not find that media coverage meets their needs on the subjects they feel are important, and only 20 percent of respondents feel that the media deal with topics that are important to them.

Thus far we have discussed the public's needs and expectations relative to the content of coverage. There is, however, another aspect that should be discussed, namely the balance or bias of coverage, as assessed by the public. Respondents were asked to describe their views regarding media coverage of the three major parties (Likud, Labor, and Kadima) and Shas (ultra-orthodox) party. As can be seen from figure 4 below, most of the public believes that media coverage is biased in one way or another. Shas, closely followed by Likud, are both perceived as parties to which the media are particularly hostile (52.6 percent feel that the media are hostile to Shas, and 48 percent that they are hostile to Likud). On the other hand, 56.5 percent of the public believes that the news media strongly favor Kadima.

A link was found between a respondent's political position and his or her view of media bias: the more right-wing a respondent's definition of him or herself, the more the news media were perceived to be hostile toward Shas. The

Figure 4
To What Extent, in Your Opinion, Are the Israeli Media Hostile or Favorable Towards Each of the Following Parties?

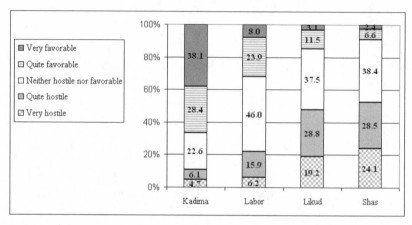

contrary also held true: the more left-wing a respondent's definition of him or herself, the more he or she perceived the media as hostile toward Labor. Many respondents also felt that the media were hostile toward the party for which they intended to vote: 66.7 percent of those who supported Shas, 45 percent of those who supported Likud, 26 percent of those who supported Labor, and 12.7 percent of those who supported Kadima believed that the media were hostile to their party. Respondents who defined themselves as supporters of Likud, Kadima, or Shas felt that the media were more hostile toward their party than did supporters of other parties. This finding is consistent with research regarding the "hostile media phenomenon," which indicates that people tend to perceive the media as biased against their political view (Vollone, Ross, and Lepper, 1985). The criticism of media coverage with regard to its quality, response to needs, and balance is also associated with the third aspect—trust in media coverage.

The entire population expressed a rather low level of trust in the work of the news media: the general index of trust stood at 2.3, only slightly above the mid-point, while large groups of the population expressed an even lower level of trust. The greater the sense of social alienation, the lower the level of trust in media coverage of the elections. Consequently, groups that are characterized by a sense of social alienation tend to have a very low level of trust in the media. For example, the level of media trust of Haredi (ultra-orthodox) and orthodox Jews (1.9 and 1.7 respectively) is less than that displayed by traditional and secular Jews (2.2 and 2.3 respectively), while respondents who place themselves at the right-hand extreme of the political spectrum tend to have the lowest level of trust in the media (2.0) compared with respondents who define themselves as being in the middle (2.3) or on the left (2.5).

Analysis of Media Coverage

Public criticism of media coverage focuses on three aspects: quality, impartiality, and credibility. A systematic examination of the actual coverage can test the accuracy of these criticisms. We therefore undertook a content analysis of media coverage (as was done in the four preceding election campaigns) of the three main national television networks (Channels 1, 2, and 10). All the newscasts and election campaign specials broadcast on these channels during the month leading up to the election were recorded and analyzed. The analysis was performed by skilled coders who were equipped with precise coding instructions and had been trained in content analysis. During the training period the encoders were tested for reliability. We compared the results of the various encoders and solved any resultant problems with inconsistencies. Most of the variables yielded high interpersonal reliability coefficients (0.9 or more). The lowest reliability was found for the variables whose purpose was to assess the level of criticism of candidates in media texts (coefficient of 0.76).

In the month prior to the 2006 elections, all three television channels broadcast 438 news items dealing with the upcoming elections. Relative to the last few election campaigns, this constituted widespread coverage. The extent of coverage given to the 2003 elections was not impressive; in the month before the election the two channels (only Channels 1 and 2 were examined then) broadcast 286 items dealing with the elections. In the 2001 elections (in which only the prime minister was elected) approximately 570 items were broadcast in the two months prior to the election, i.e., about 285 items per month. Both the 2001 and the 2003 election campaigns received slightly less coverage than the 2006 election campaign. Even taking into account the fact that there was another channel (Channel 10), each channel broadcast many more items in the 2006 elections. It is important to note that the Intifada and its terror attacks constituted the backdrop to the 2001 and 2003 election campaigns. It appears that public apathy and the low voter turnout in the 2006 election were not the result of low-level media coverage, or any lack of media interest. On the contrary, there was extensive and very visible coverage, but it did not arouse the public's interest or participation. It is necessary, therefore, to focus on the content, quality, and impartiality of the coverage.

The Coverage: What the Public Wants and What It Gets

As noted, the public displays low levels of satisfaction with election coverage, claiming that the coverage does not meet its needs with regard to content. Our examination of the coverage also addressed various aspects relative to quality, such as fairness, impartiality, and the focus of the reporting. A distinction should be made between "substantive" subjects, namely, those that are on the agenda of Israeli society, including its problems and challenges, on the one hand, and "campaign subjects," such as references to election slogans, polls, and political party broadcasts on the other. This distinction derives from the findings of studies of elections conducted in the U.S., which differentiate between two types of framing in news coverage: strategic framing and issue framing (Patterson, 1993; Capella and Jamieson, 1997). By definition, framing deals with "how," namely, the way things are said (not what is said). Strategic framing focuses less on content and stresses aspects such as election strategy, the election campaign, and the nature of the speakers' external appearance instead. Issue framing, however, focuses on the essence or substance of what is said. Public opinion polls tell us that the news media deal primarily with those aspects of the election campaign that interest them. To examine this criticism, we studied the issues covered, the focus of the coverage, and the distinction made between substantive topics and campaign issues in the election coverage of all three channels.

Only 18.7 percent of the 438 news items devoted to the election focused largely on content, while 74.7 percent focused on campaign issues, and 6.6 percent related equally to both. Obviously, most of the coverage was devoted to campaign issues and less to matters of substance. What were the content issues covered? Television coverage in 2006 included 344 items relating to public issues. Their distribution is presented in the last column of table 1 below, where their coverage is compared with that of previous election campaigns. It is important to note that the classification of subjects was determined in accordance with the analysis of previous election campaigns, so that in the category of "other," the subject of "Iran and the nuclear bomb" assumed prominence in the 2006 campaign, accounting for 7.8 percent of the items, but figured little in previous campaigns.

Most of the coverage of substantive issues in the 2006 elections focused on internal topics, such as welfare, social equality, crime, corruption, and their investigation. Together these areas accounted for 40.2 percent of the issues covered. This emphasis demonstrates the success of Amir Peretz in amending the public agenda. When he was elected head of the Labor Party, he declared that the party would concentrate on internal matters, particularly social justice, the war on poverty, and a new welfare policy, thereby forcing both his rivals and the news media to focus on those issues. The coverage of the 2006 elections therefore, focused less on crime, corruption, and violence than did that of the 2003 election campaign (19.1 percent in 2006 compared with 33.2 percent in 2003), while the frequency with which such subjects as education, health, welfare, and social justice were mentioned rose steeply in 2006, reaching a peak level over the previous five election campaigns examined. On the other hand, security and political subjects, such as terror, the security fence, the Palestinians, the removal of the settlements, and negotiations with the Palestinians, were given less prominence in the 2006 election campaign. This is extremely interesting in view of the fact that the disengagement had occurred not long before the elections, while the subjects of terror and the division of Jerusalem were frequently raised by Binyamin Netanyahu in his election campaign and public appearances.

Table 1
Distribution of Substantive Subjects in Election Coverage, 1996-2006

Subject	1996 elections	1999 elections	2001 elections	2003 elections	2006 elections
Terror, attacks, Intifada, security	11.5	9.6	6.2	3.9	15.3
Palestinians, negotiations with Palestinians	13.0	7.2	30.3	11.4	22.4
Jerusalem, dividing Jerusalem	1.2	0.8	8.6	8.3	5.3
Golan Heights and Syria	0	0	1.5	5.7	8.7
Settlers, settlements	5.8	0.2	2.7	2.5	19.7
Economics, finance	3.5	4.9	1.1	5.9	11.2
Religion and state	10.5	5.5	8.4	5.5	4.1
Education, health, welfare, social justice	20.3	5.8	1.6	0.7	2.3
Israeli Arabs	3.8	4.9	8.6	4.2	7.4
Crime, corruption, and their investigation	19.1	33.2	4.3	25.1	0
Immigration, immigrants	0	0	1.1	5.5	2.3
Other	11.3	27.9	25.6	25.5	1.3
Total	100%	100%	100%	100%	100%

Note: The categories occurring most frequently in each campaign are emphasized.

What is problematic about the quality of media coverage is the focus on issues that are not substantive in the strategic coverage. The media prefer to deal with relatively unimportant issues that can be incorporated under the rubric of "campaign subjects," e.g., polls, forecasts, speculation about who will be appointed to which position, "deals" between parties, internal quarrels, and actual campaign propaganda. In our analysis of the election campaign, we found 646 references to campaign issues, almost twice as many as to substantive issues (344). Media coverage of the last five election campaigns focused more on campaign issues than on substantive ones, the latter being included in only a few news items. Campaign issues were included in all the items, however, and a single news item would often include more than one kind of campaign issue. Moreover, a comparison of the election campaigns demonstrates a clear increase in the coverage devoted to campaign issues, which peaked in 2006. Table 2 below compares the distribution of campaign issues in the coverage of the various election campaigns.

Table 2
Distribution of Campaign Issues in Media Coverage of Election Campaigns, 1996-2006

Subject	1996 elections	1999 elections	2001 elections	2003 elections	2006 elections
Publicity strategy, propaganda, image, marketing	63.4	44.4	67.6	52.1	55.8
Polls, surveys, sample polls	28.8	26.8	26.7	6.5	8.1
Internal quarrels and disagreements	8.2	18.5	6.9	9.8	6.8
Possible coalitions, "deals," appointments	13.2	25.2	32.4	12.5	16.1
Mutual attacks and accusations by candidates	27.6	18.5	15.8	13.5	13.2

Note: The numbers sometimes add up to more than 100 percent because items may sometimes fit more than one category, e.g., a candidate is accused of publishing fraudulent poll results.

According to the data in table 2, when dealing with campaign subjects there is a preference on the part of news broadcasts to concentrate on election propaganda, public relations strategy, and allied subjects. This is always the most frequent category in election coverage and occurs more often than any other substantive topic broadcast in any of the five election campaigns. Election journalists and newscast editors devote, on average, about half their news coverage to election broadcasts—criticizing them, their content, objectives, and messages. This trend reached new heights in the 2001 and 2006 election campaigns, when two-thirds of the strategic coverage items focused on this issue. The second most frequent topic in election coverage was opinion polls (see below). News coverage of the attacks, accusations, and vilifications launched by one side against rival parties or candidates were in third place in the 2006 election campaign. This trend, which also increased prior to the last election campaign, peaked in 2006 when one-quarter of the news items included this type of negative reference.

It is interesting to compare these findings with the public's understanding of the issues that it felt ought to be covered and those that actually were. Figure 3 above shows that almost 40 percent of the public felt that the media dealt primarily with opinion polls and assessments of the election results—more than twice as many as the proportion of respondents who regarded these subjects as most important. About 20.9 percent claimed that the media focused on election campaigning and strategy, while only 13.4 percent viewed this as an important topic. The largest group of respondents (31.7 percent) wanted information on substantive issues, such as the attitudes and programs of the candidates and the parties. However, only 9.6 percent found that the media focused on these issues. Of course, it can be claimed that the public gives the most "appropriate" replies about the content it desires, in accordance with "socially desirable" patterns, while the media identify the public's real desire for more "entertaining" coverage. Nonetheless, the data verify the public's disappointment with the multitude of items that tend to deal with strategy, namely, focusing on campaign items and especially on analyzing election broadcasts, opinion polls, and accusations.

Fairness of Coverage: Balance in the Amount of Coverage

The question of "who gets the most coverage" represents another aspect of the fairness of coverage, the dimension that deals with the frequency with which an issue appears in the news media, i.e., the number of times it is mentioned. Another aspect discussed further on is whether a candidate or party is presented in a positive or negative light. As previously mentioned, most of the public believes that media coverage is biased, and that the media favor Kadima, with a more balanced treatment of the Labor party, and more hostility toward the Likud and Shas parties (see Figure 4 above). Our study of news coverage of previous election campaigns provided clear evidence that a balance was maintained relative to the accessibility of media coverage: in 1996 the Labor party received exposure in 198 news items and Likud in 190; in 1999 Likud received exposure in 426 items and One Israel in 423; in 2001 One Israel received exposure in 351 items and Likud in 340; in 2003 Likud received exposure in 173 items and Labor in 148 (Weimann and Sheafer, 2004). The data show that there was an almost perfect balance in the coverage accorded to the two major parties, with the ruling party always holding a slight advantage over its opposition rival. There is relatively less balance in the coverage accorded to candidates. In 1996 Shimon Peres received exposure in 341 news items while Binyamin Netanyahu received exposure in only 183; in 1999 Netanyahu received exposure in 514 items and Ehud Barak in 412; in 2001 Barak received exposure in 405 items and Ariel Sharon in 375; in 2003 Sharon received exposure in 147 items and Amram Mitzna in 111. These findings indicate that in every election campaign the candidate who was the incumbent prime minister had greater access to the news media (Peres in 1996, Netanyahu in 1999, Barak in 2001, and Sharon in 2003). While this finding attests to a systematic bias in accessibility, the reason for this bias stems from the fact that candidates' newsworthiness is a result of their political position, not their political affiliation.

The situation was different in the 2006 elections, if only because there were three major parties participating—Likud, Labor, and Kadima. Furthermore, while Likud was the ruling party after the 2003 elections, Kadima was established shortly before the 2006 elections and had an incumbent prime minister (Sharon). Sharon's illness led to his replacement by his successor (Ehud Olmert), and the defection of several ministers to the newly formed party. Table 3 below presents the rate at which the major parties and their prime ministerial candidates were featured in news items.

We find a slight preference for Kadima relative to the number of appearances in the coverage of the major parties over the other parties in 2006, as well as for Olmert over Peretz and Netanyahu, but the disparity is not large. Here, too, the explanation can for the most part be attributed to the fact that Kadima was the ruling party in the period prior to the elections, and Olmert was acting prime minister after Sharon fell ill. The almost perfect balance found between the coverage accorded to Labor and Likud is consistent with the almost perfect balance between the coverage accorded to Peretz and Netanyahu. The amount of coverage is only one measure of balance, however, with another measure being the nature of the coverage—who is admired or criticized?

Fairness of Coverage: Balanced Criticism

Methodologically speaking, it is difficult to make a valid and reliable assessment of the positive content "inherent" in a news item. As noted earlier, lower intercoder reliability coefficients were found for these variables. Consequently, in our research, as with the entire series of election studies, we have examined the extent to which an item contains criticism of a candidate or party. A news item is characterized as critical if it includes a negative reference (by the writer or a featured spokesperson) to the candidate, his or her honesty or past failures, as well as references to a party or a critical reference to its list of candidates, the integrity of its internal election process, or problems with its financial management. Most of the news items included a negative reference to a candidate or party, and sometimes to more than one candidate or party. In effect, 228 out of 438 news items contained negative comments about one of the three major parties (Likud, Labor, Kadima). This finding continues the increasing trend in the rate of critical remarks made on television about candidates and parties. In the 1996 election campaign, only five percent of news items that dealt with

Table 3
Balance in Appearance of Parties and Candidates in Election Coverage, 2006

Party	No. of items in which featured	% of items	Candidate	No. of items in which featured	% of items
Kadima	247	56.4	Ehud Olmert	155	35.4
Labor	192	43.8	Amir Peretz	129	29.5
Likud	203	46.3	Binyamin Netanyanhu	139	31.7

Note: The numbers may add up to more than 100 percent of all items in which more than one party appeared.

parties or candidates included criticism or attacks. The rate of criticism rose slightly in the 1999 elections and exceeded 20 percent in the 2001 elections. There was a marked increase in the 2003 election, with almost 60 percent of news items concerning the two major parties and their candidates containing attacks and criticisms. A large proportion of negative remarks were also found in the 2006 election (52 percent of all coverage included criticism).

The findings indicate that over time media coverage of Israel's elections campaign has become increasingly negative and critical. The odds that television viewers will be exposed to information presenting the parties and their candidates in a negative light is greater than their odds of being exposed to information presenting the parties and their candidates in a positive light. The media play an important role in exposing the faults, mistakes, and failures of candidates and parties. However, by stressing the negative aspects of the campaign, the media may contribute to a spiral of cynicism followed by the alienation of the public from politicians and the political process, thereby seriously damaging the functioning of the democratic regime.

Is the negative coverage of all the parties and candidates even-handed? Table 4 below compares the frequency of criticism in news items.

Table 4 presents the increased frequency of critical comments in the coverage, but the negative coverage is not balanced among the major parties and their candidates: there were more critical items about Kadima (52.6 percent of all news items contained a negative reference to the party) and its candidate for prime minister, Ehud Olmert (64.5 percent of all items included criticism), compared to criticisms of Likud (43.8 percent) and its candidate, Binyamin Netanyahu (51.8 percent), with a relatively small proportion of negative comments about the Labor party (28.6 percent) and its candidate, Amir Peretz (37.9 percent). The media coverage was most critical of Kadima and its leader, critical to a moderate extent of Likud and its leader, and moderately critical of the Labor party and its leader.

The public's perception of media bias therefore is not fully accurate. Although the public's assessment is correct in that coverage is more critical of

Table 4
Balance in Criticism of Parties and Candidates in the 2006 Election Coverage

Party	No. of items with criticism	% of items of the party	Candidate	No. of items with criticism	% of items of the candidate
Kadima	130	52.6	Ehud Olmert	100	64.5
Labor	55	28.6	Amir Peretz	49	37.9
Likud	89	43.8	Binyamin Netanyanhu	72	51.8

Likud than of Labor, the amount of criticism leveled against Kadima and its candidate does not mesh with the public's perception that the media tend to support Kadima. Kadima may have received an inordinate amount of criticism because the other two major parties, Likud and Labor, attacked it during the election campaign, and those attacks were reflected in media coverage. Another possible reason could be the events that took place during the election campaign: the exposure of scandals connected to Kadima's leading candidates (Ehud Olmert's real-estate transactions, Tzachi Hanegbi's political appointments); disappointment that Ariel Sharon, Kadima's founder, was still in a coma, and Olmert's announcement that he would continue the process of disengagement from the Palestinians.

We also examined the content of the critical statements made about prime ministerial candidates. As in our past studies, we focused on the nature of media attacks on the leaders of the major parties. We examined the critical comments made regarding the issues they dealt with. Were these criticisms concerned primarily with the ideological-political sphere or with the leaders' personalities, their lack of experience, or negative incidents from their past? Table 5 below compares the extent of criticism leveled against each candidate, both as a group and separately.

The data in the left-hand column in table 5 indicate that media criticism in general was divided almost equally between the personal dimensions (inexperience, unsuitability, past failures—25.3 percent of all items about the candidates), ideology and political attitudes (27.1 percent), and communicative behavior (23.5 percent—gimmicks, maneuvering, spins, communicative dishonesty). However, when the candidates are compared on the extent of coverage, real differences emerge. The criticism of Olmert focused on the ideological-political sphere (41 percent: zigzagging, incoherent attitudes, ideological vagueness,

Table 5
Extent of Criticism in Coverage of Prime Ministerial Candidates in 2006 Elections

Extent of criticism	% of items of Olmert	% of items of Peretz	% of items of Netanyahu	% of items of all candidates
In experience, personal unsuitability, past failures	25.3	33.3	36.7	14.0
Ideology, political attitudes	27.1	18.0	12.2	41.0
Gimmicks, maneuvering, spins, communicative dishonesty	23.5	25.0	24.4	22.0
Other	24.0	23.6	26.5	23.0

Note: The numbers in bold type indicate the most frequent category of criticism of each candidate.

switching from right to left, etc.), while the criticism of Peretz focused on his lack of experience and negative incidents from his past (36.7 percent: inexperience in senior positions, failures as a labor leader). Netanyahu, on the other hand, was attacked in two areas. The first was incidents from his past (33.3 percent), primarily his abandonment of the Likud party when he was defeated by Barak in 1999, and his actions as minister of finance, which allegedly harmed the weaker sections of society. The other dimension—his media manipulation (25 percent)—included criticism of the negative aspects of his campaign and his repetition of messages from past campaigns (terror, dividing Jerusalem).

Quality of Coverage: From a Horse Race to Marketability

The most frequent criticism about election coverage, both in Israel and abroad, concerns the trivialization and contempt displayed toward the political process, which is portrayed as an entertaining horse race with opinion polls functioning as a stopwatch employed to assess the relative positions of the candidates at any given moment. This is the claim put forward by Broh (1980: 515): "For journalists, the horse race metaphor provides a framework for analysis. A horse is judged not by its absolute speed or skill but in comparison to the speed of other horses and especially by its wins and losses. Similarly, candidates are pushed to discuss other candidates; events are understood in the context of competition..., the race—not the winner—is the story." The tendency to report on the campaign in terms of a horse race is expressed by the frequency of sporting images found in these reports as well as in the number of expressions taken from the world of competitive sports, such as neck and neck, a close-run race, impressive start, gathering speed, crossing the finishing line, exchange of blows, and gaining or losing points (Cantril, 1976, 1991). The disquieting outcome of this style of reporting is the trivialization of the political process, with the struggle between principles, ideologies, worldviews, and values portrayed as a sporting event, a personal competition, or a clash between personal ambitions.

We examined the use of metaphors taken from other semantic fields, such as war, sports, and commercial marketing. A little under half—195 items (44.5 percent of all election coverage items)—included references borrowed from these fields. The most frequently borrowed were war expressions (23.7 percent), among them: battle, weapon, election bombshell, battling, and cannons. The second most frequently employed were sporting expressions (11.9 percent), among them: the game has begun, batting, race, finish line, gathering speed, and slow start. Marketing and sales terms, used less frequently (8.9 percent), included terms such as package, sale, and progress. A comparison of these three areas demonstrated a large and significant difference between them relative to their frequency of use and, contrary to expectations, the public channel (Channel 1) did not differ from the commercial ones (Channels 2 and 10) in this regard.

As stated, framing an election campaign in terms of a horse race is achieved through the use of public opinion polls, which serve as a stopwatch, providing continuous data on the status of the competitors. Election polls have become ubiquitous in the news media, taking center stage in news broadcasts and election specials. A comparison of the data of the last five election campaigns (see table 2 above) indicates a rising trend in references to, and presentation of, election polls. Aptly described as an "obsessive concern with polls," this focus reached new heights in Israel's last election campaign, in 2006. A series of studies on election polls in the Israeli media documented the growing preoccupation with these polls, with almost every news broadcast referring to them during the election campaign (Weimann, 1990, 1994, 1998, 2003). In the 1996 elections, 8.1 percent of election news items included references to election polls, in the 2001 and 2003 elections their frequency was greater, 26 percent, and they reached new heights in the 2006 elections (28.8 percent, with almost one third of all election items including a reference to polls, as did all the news broadcasts). The growing popularity of polls in media reports might be viewed as entertaining were it not for the damaging effects they have on the political process and the quality of political discourse.

Political Party Election Broadcasts

There are those who feel that election propaganda wastes public money and corrupts the political discourse, enabling politicians to cynically exploit the resource of media time and space at their disposal. This allegation is countered by those who maintain that election propaganda is necessary because it familiarizes the public with the candidates, the parties, the platforms, and the differences between competitors. This contention was reinforced to some extent during the many years when media coverage of competitors was forbidden in the month prior to the election. In the absence of coverage of this kind it was difficult for the candidates to establish contact with the public. It was believed that election propaganda could compensate for this inequity by providing an alternative podium enabling the candidates to present their attitudes and vision. The removal of this prohibition eliminated the need for expensive political party election broadcasts, but they enabled political issues to be discussed and placed on the public agenda, and also functioned as a popular method of "civic education." They also helped familiarize the public with the candidates and examine their claims and vision. Moreover, political party election broadcasts often serve to increase the public's involvement in the election process, raising public interest and placing issues on the agenda of public debate.

Public criticism, both active and passive, has been leveled against the political election broadcasts. Active criticism was expressed in a debate that claimed that the broadcasts were unnecessary, wasteful, and shallow. Passive criticism found expression in low exposure figures, which plummeted to the lowest level of any Israeli election campaign in 2006. The combined average rating for all the days of propaganda broadcast on all three channels was 14.6 percent (7.8 percent on Channel 2, 3.6 percent on Channel 10, and 3.2 percent on Channel

1). In effect, in each evening of election broadcasts, including the opening night of the TV campaign, the viewing figures were lower than in any previous election campaign. There were no ratings in the 1970s and 1980s. However, there was only one channel at that time, and it may therefore be assumed that anyone watching television viewed the political party election broadcasts, so that exposure to them has been assessed at 60 percent to 70 percent. Ratings were first measured when Channel 2 began broadcasting. In 1996 the average rating in one evening was 30 percent, declining consistently in subsequent elections and reaching the lowest point in 2006. Figures for the first evening, when viewing rates peaked, also indicated a decline: in 1999 the first evening attained an average rating of 38.8 percent, in 2001 it was 25 percent, in 2003 it was 21 percent, and in 2006 it was only 19 percent.

We examined the content of all the political party election broadcasts aired prior to the 2006 election. In the last three weeks before the election, 434 such broadcasts were aired, and each party was allocated time in accordance with its size in the last Knesset (on the basis of a key of ten minutes per party and another three minutes for each of its incumbent Knesset members). As a result, most of the election broadcasts were for the major parties (42 for Labor, 39 for Likud, 29 for Kadima, and 26 for Shas). Systematic content analysis was used to examine the issues the broadcasts dealt with and the distribution of these issues, along with an examination of the distribution of the issues in media coverage. The results are presented in table 6 below, which also indicates the importance assigned to the subjects by the public before the election campaign. (In a survey conducted between February 12 and 16, 2006, 509 respondents were asked to rank subjects by their importance for Israeli society today. (The replies to the open-ended question were placed in categories by the researchers in accordance with the categories used in the content analysis.)

News media coverage of the election campaign focused primarily on social issues (the leading topic), as did the party broadcasts—almost half of them (47.9 percent) related to social issues (welfare, poverty, social equality, benefits for pensioners). The correlation between the rank order of frequency of the subjects covered and the rank order of importance of the propaganda subjects was high (0.63), but the question remains as to which agenda was leading the other—do the parties guide the public's agenda or vice versa? In the 1996 elections, Weimann and Wolfsfeld found evidence of Netanyahu's success in influencing the public and media agenda, noting that subjects raised by Netanyahu in his TV broadcasts (dividing Jerusalem, terror attacks) gradually entered into the public media discourse (Weimann and Wolfsfeld, 2002). In 2006, however, we found no evidence of this. When the election campaign was examined by various time periods (weekly periods), and the correlation between the propaganda agenda and the media agenda was calculated, we found that the correlation between them was maintained. One is therefore correlated with the other without one preceding the other. However, as indicated by the left-hand columns of Table

Table 6
Distribution of Subjects in Party-Political Election Broadcasts, in Media Coverage, and in Public Opinion, 2006

Subject	% in party broadcast	Rank order in propaganda	% in media coverage	Order of importance in coverage	% in public opinion before election*	Rank order in public opinion
Terror, attacks, Intifada, security	3	16.9	4	11.5	2	15.9
Palestinians, negotiations with Palestinians	5	7.7	3	13.0	6	11.5
Jerusalem, dividing Jerusalem	9	0	9	1.2	9	0.7
Settlers, settlements	8	0.3	6	·5.8	3	14.3
Economics, finance	2	18.5	8	3.5	8	7.6
Religion and state	6	1.8	5	10.5	4	14.0
Social issues, poverty, education, health, welfare, social justice	1	36.7	1	20.3	1	47.9
Israeli Arabs	7	1.1	7	3.8	5	13.8
Crime, corruption, and their investigation	4	10.4	2	19.1	7	8.9

*In a poll conducted between February 12–16, 2006, about one month before the election.

6 above, the public—even before the election campaign began—ascribed the greatest importance to social issues. The election of Amir Peretz as the Labor party's prime ministerial candidate (in the primaries in which he defeated Shimon Peres) in effect determined the social agenda. The media discourse, and its attendant commentary, focused on social issues, enabling prominent journalist Shelly Yechimovich to be included in the Labor party list. Opinion polls conducted during the election campaign (see Dialogue polls under the supervision of Professor Camille Fox)[1] demonstrated the stability of the rank order of importance of the issues by the public throughout the campaign. The election campaign did not greatly alter, and essentially tried to adapt to, the mood of the public. The high correlation between the public agenda and the propaganda agenda (0.77) derives from the adaptation of the latter in the last month to the social agenda (which preceded it), rather than from its success in determining the public agenda.

A further criticism that may be leveled against the election propaganda, especially the propaganda which focused on negative aspects, is that it appealed to emotions rather than to intellect, accentuating fears and threats in place of vision and hope, and using cheap, manipulative appeals (Marmor-Lavie and Weimann, 2006). The 2006 political party broadcasts did not mold or influence the news media and public discourse, nor did they manage to hold the public's attention. They merely dragged the parties into extremely wasteful campaign productions. Moreover, they appeared to reflect most of the criticisms leveled against them: they were influenced by the attacks (if the broadcast contained an attack—criticism, accusation, disparagement, presentation of errors—on another party or one of its leaders): 39.4 percent of the broadcasts contained attacks, directed mainly against Kadima or Olmert (19.1 percent of broadcasts), while others were directed against Likud or Netanyahu (6.7 percent), and against Labor or Peretz (2.1 percent). The attacks were largely of a personal nature. About 64.7 percent of the broadcasts contained criticism of or attacks on the leader of a party, with only 31.5 percent criticizing a party, its platform, or its principles. This pattern is also evident relative to the dimension of time: most of the political party broadcasts (52.5 percent) dealt with the past, and only a minority of them (32.7 percent) addressed the future, or dealt equally with both the past and the future (14.7 percent).

The election broadcasts were replete with appeals to emotions, especially to fear: 23.5 percent of the broadcasts included words that connote fear (fear, destruction, killing, disaster, slaughter, danger, devastation, death, etc.); 12.2 percent of broadcasts contained fear-inducing audio elements (ambulance sirens, explosions, gunshots, distorted human voices); 17.7 percent of the broadcasts used expressions associated with terror (terrorists, suicide bombs, victims of terrorism, etc.); 23.7 percent of the broadcasts used expressions associated with strength (a strong people, a strong leader, a strong army, etc.); 27 percent of the broadcasts included military elements (soldiers, military ranks, uniforms, the IDF, and the candidates' military record); and about 50 percent of the broadcasts featured children and teenagers.

Conclusion

Media coverage of the political process assumes increasing importance in an election campaign. At other times the media are important in mediating between the public and its representatives, monitoring the way politicians function as public appointees, and transferring large quantities of political information to the public (Barber, 1980; Patterson, 1993; Mancini and Swanson, 1996; Galnor, 1998; Blumler and Kavanagh, 1999; Mazzoleni and Schulz, 1999). During an election campaign, however, the media's roles of mediating, monitoring, updating, and criticizing are even more important. In this study we examined the attitudes of the Israeli public towards media coverage as well as the realization of its expectations and needs in media coverage, and the accuracy of these public criticisms. A systematic analysis was conducted to determine the quality, fairness, and bias of the coverage.

A comparison of the public's criticism of the quality and fairness of the coverage with the findings of the content analysis demonstrates that most of the criticisms—though not all of them—are justified. The public's criticism regarding the quality of coverage was found to be valid: media coverage focuses inordinately on subjects that are not substantive, such as campaign strategies. The news media prefer to deal with relatively unimportant issues—campaign issues—including polls, forecasts, speculation about appointments, deals between parties, internal quarrels, and the election propaganda itself. This pattern constitutes a disturbing verification of the claim made by most of the public (61.9 percent), namely, that the coverage does not provide essential information; it also bears out the public's criticism of media coverage for focusing on entertainment and personal issues. We found a significant discrepancy between the information the public would like to obtain from media coverage during an election campaign and the issues that receive most of the media coverage. It can, of course, be claimed that this constitutes "social desirability," and that respondents prefer to give replies that present them in a positive light, as people who are interested in serious information. However, the public does not only express its criticism of the election coverage in its attitudes: reduced exposure to coverage, less interest in the election campaign, a low rate of viewing campaign broadcasts, and a lower voter turnout rate than ever before in the actual election attest to the fact that the public's criticism is not merely for purposes of show.

The public also frequently levels criticism against the fairness of media coverage: is it objective and impartial, or is it biased toward one party or another? Despite the tendency of large sections of the public to accuse the media of being politically biased, the findings from our analysis of the coverage do not support this accusation. As to the quantity of appearances during the coverage of the major parties in 2006, there is a slight preference for Kadima over the other parties, as well as for Olmert over Peretz and Netanyahu, but the differences are not that great. As stated, Kadima became the ruling party in the period prior to the election, and Olmert became acting prime minister after Sharon was hospitalized. As to the favorable and unfavorable comments, our findings demonstrate that the public's criticisms are not justified: Kadima as a party, and Olmert as a prime ministerial candidate, actually were on the receiving end of more critical coverage, with more frequent negative expressions and remarks. On the other hand, the coverage was more critical of Likud than it was of Labor, in line with the public's assessment that Likud was a more frequent target of media criticism.

We found a tendency in the previous elections toward a greater balance in coverage of the two major parties and their candidates (see Weimann and Sheafer, 2004). In the 1996, 1999, 2001, and 2003 elections a similar proportion of items contained criticisms of both Labor and Likud. Only in 2006 was there more criticism of Olmert and Kadima, whereas the public's perception was that the media favored them. How can these discrepancies regarding Kadima be explained? It is important to note first that the public was asked about the bias of the news media as a whole, while our study focused solely on television coverage. In addition, Kadima was a new party, so while the public's assessment of media bias in its favor was speculative, the coverage of Labor and Likud (as well as other parties) could be assessed on the basis of past experience. A third explanation is connected to the "precious object" syndrome displayed by the media and the public.[2] Kadima, and especially its founder Sharon, benefited from the media's positive attitude because of their support for the disengagement process. This was the contention put forward by journalist and commentator Amnon Abramowitz. According to Abramowitz, the media were prepared to ignore unsavory revelations about the Sharon family's business transactions because of their support for disengagement. This perception of the "precious object" was expressed many times by journalists and may have permeated public awareness. The findings, however, indicate the opposite effect, with more media criticism leveled against Kadima and Olmert. In this instance it is also important to understand that the research period was subsequent to Sharon's hospitalization. The campaign was in effect led by Olmert, and the "precious object" effect that had surrounded Sharon dissipated. The findings of the content analysis regarding the critical tone directed towards Kadima may also stem from the fact that Kadima was attacked by politicians from many parties, on both the right and the left, and the findings reflect these attacks, rather than any oppositional journalistic bias.

Considerable public criticism was leveled against the political party broadcasts on the grounds that they were unnecessary, wasteful, and shallow. Passive criticism was expressed in extremely low viewing figures, which fell to their lowest level ever in Israel in the 2006 elections. Our research findings also endorse this criticism. Our systematic content analysis of the political party broadcasts demonstrated that they affected neither the media nor the public agenda. The propaganda campaign adapted to general public opinion and neither molded nor changed it. This pattern contrasted with several previous election campaigns, especially that of Netanyahu in 1996, which succeeded in directing the media and public discourse to such issues as the division of Jerusalem and terrorist attacks. The tendency of the broadcasts to focus on emotions, negativity, and personal issues, as indicated by the content analysis, bears out the public's criticism and explains why people avoided watching them.

These findings are not unique to the Israeli media. Other democratic societies have displayed similar tendencies. Several U.S. studies found that media coverage of election campaigns is characterized by an escalation in negative coverage of parties and candidates—media coverage that included attacks, accusations, and negative information (Robinson, 1976; Patterson, 1993; Cappella and Jamieson, 1997). Patterson (1993) identified the beginning of the gradual increase in negative coverage of parties and candidates in the U.S. in the early

1960s. Media research has shown that the rise in negative coverage at that time was connected to the seminal role played by television in covering the political campaign and to the replacement of political party communications by independent media (Blumler and Kavanagh, 1999).

The damage inflicted by negative coverage has been well documented: discrediting the public's image of the political process, reducing the desire to participate in the political process, and undermining trust in both politics and the media are all closely associated with the imperfect functioning of the news media as an intermediary. Cappella and Jamieson (1997) found that political coverage in U.S. media was mainly strategic. Our findings regarding television coverage in Israel are similar. The focus on campaign items and the preference for them over substantive issues, the inordinate concern of the Israeli media with election polls, propaganda, and the personal aspects of the contest all characterize pronounced strategic framing. This type of framing has important consequences. Cappella and Jamieson titled their study "Spiral of Cynicism," because in their view strategic framing precedes a cynical, alienated attitude to politics on the part of the public. This cynical approach is characterized by a perception of politics as a corrupt, devious, manipulative, exploitative, and unfair process. Politicians are regarded as individuals with narrow or personal interests, motivated by the desire to win rather than the aspiration to achieve true leadership status or implement any far-reaching vision. Strategic coverage constitutes framing, which then causes the general public to view politics as a system based on personal interests, as a manipulative process whose objective is the politician's well-being rather than that of the general public.

The public's lack of faith in media and its criticism of the quality of media coverage in Israel, as indicated by the findings presented at the beginning of this article, give rise to grave apprehensions regarding the media's role as an intermediary between voters and their representatives. When a large section of the public feels that the media are unreliable, unfair, and unable to provide essential information, especially in the context of crucial elections, there is a real and present danger that this attitude will impact not only on the legitimacy of the media and the information they provide, but also on the legitimacy of Israeli democracy.

Notes

1. Polls conducted for *Haaretz* newspaper during the election campaign and published daily.
2. A term ("sacred ethrog" in Hebrew) coined by Amnon Abramowitz and taken up by many other journalists.

References

Ansolabehere, Stephen, and Iyengar Shanto. 1995. *Going Negative: How Political Advertisements Shrink and Polarize the Electorate*, New York: The Free Press.

Arian, Asher, Gabriel Weimann, and Gadi Wolfsfeld. 1999. "Balance in Election Coverage," In: Asher Arian and Michal Shamir, eds. *The Israeli Elections 1996*, New York: SUNY Press, 295–312.

------, David Nahmias, Doron Navot, and Daniel Shani. 2003. *An Index of Israeli Democracy, 2003*, Jerusalem, The Israel Democracy Institute [Hebrew].

Barber, James David. 1980. *The Pulse of Politics: Electing Presidents in the Media Age*, New York: W.W. Norton and Co.

Blumler, Jay G. and Dennis Kavanagh. 1999. "The Third Age of Political Communication: Influences and Features," *Political Communication* 16(3): 209–230.

Broh, Anthony C. 1980. "Horse-Race Journalism: Reporting the Polls in the 1916 Elections," *Public Opinion Quarterly* 44: 514 –529.

Cantril, Albert H. 1976. "The Press and the Pollster," *Annals of the American Academy of Political and Social Sciences* 427: 52–54.

------. 1991. *The Opinion Connection: Polling, Politics, and the Press*, New York: CQ Press.

Cappella, Joseph N. and Kathleen H. Jamieson. 1997. *Spiral of Cynicism*, New York: Oxford University Press.

D'Alessio, Dave and Mike Allen. 2000. "Media Bias in Presidential Elections: A Meta-Analysis," *Journal of Communication* 50(4): 133–156.

Galnur, Yitzhak. 1998. "Parties, Communications, and Israeli Democracy," in Danny Koren, ed. *The End of Parties: Israeli Democracy in Distress*, Tel Aviv, Kibbutz Hameuhad, Red Line, 195-214 [Hebrew].

Joslyn, Richard A. 1990. "Election Campaigns as Occasions for Civic Education," in David L. Swanson, and Dan Nimmo, eds. *New Directions in Political Communication*, Newbury Park, CA: Sage, 86-119.

Just, Marion A., Ann N. Crigler, Dean E. Alger, Timothy E. Cook, Montague Kern, and Darrell M. West. 1996. *Crosstalk: Citizens, Candidates, and the Media in Presidential Election*, Chicago: University of Chicago Press.

Kaid, Lynda Lee and Christina Holtz-Bacha, eds. 1995. *Political Advertising in Western Democracies: Parties and Candidates on Television*, Thousand Oaks, CA.: Sage.

Lewis, Justin and Karin Wahl-Jorgensen. 2003. *Does TV Turn People off Politics?* Report Prepared for the Economic and Social Research Council, United Kingdom.

Lichter, S. Robert, Stanley Rothman, and Linda S. Lichter. 1986. *The Media Elite*, Bethesda, MD: Adler and Adler.

Mancini, Paolo and David L. Swanson. 1996. "Politics, Media and Modern Democracy: Introduction," in David L. Swanson, and Paolo Mancini, eds. *Politics, Media and Modern Democracy*, Westport, CT: Praeger, 1–26.

Marmor-Lavie, Galit and Gabriel Weimann. 2006. "Measuring Emotional Appeals in Israeli Election Campaigns," *International Journal of Public Opinion Research* 18(3): 1–26.

Mazzoleni, Gianpietro and Winfried Schulz. 1999. "'Mediatization' of Politics: A Challenge for Democracy?" *Political Communication* 16(3): 62–247.

Niven, David. 2001. "Bias in the News: Partisanship and Negativity in Media Coverage of Presidents George Bush and Bill Clinton," *Harvard International Journal of Press/Politics* 6(3): 31–46.

Norris, Pipa. 1998. "Introduction: The Rise of Postmodern Political Communications?" In idem, ed. *Politics and the Press: The News Media and Their Influences* , Boulder, CO: Lynne Reinner Publishers, 1–26.

Patterson, Thomas E. 1993. *Out of Order*, New York: Vintage Books.

Perry, Yoram, Yariv Tsfati, and Rivka Tukachinsky. 2005. *News Consumption on Internet Sites: An Index of the Public's Faith in the Media,'* Report no.4, Tel Aviv; Chaim Herzog Institute of Communications, Tel Aviv University [Hebrew].

Robinson, Michael J. 1976. "Public Affairs Television and the Growth of Political Malaise: The Case of 'The Selling of the President,'" *American Political Science Review* 70(3): 32–409.

Sheafer, Tamir, and Gabriel Weimann. 2005. "Agenda-Building, Agenda-Setting, Priming, Individual Voting Intentions and the Aggregate Results: An Analysis of Four Israeli Elections," *Journal of Communication* 55: 347–365.

Tsfati, Yariv, and Oren Livio. 2003. "A Study of the Image of the Israeli Journalist," *The Seventh Eye*, 43, 4-9 [Hebrew].

Vollone, Robert P., Lee Ross, and Mark L. Lepper. 1985. "The Hostile Media Phenomenon: Biased Perception and Perception of Bias in Coverage of the Beirut Massacre," *Journal of Personality and Social Psychology* 49: 577–585.

Weimann, Gabriel. 1990. "The Obsession to Forecast: Pre-Election Polls in the Israeli Press," *Public Opinion Quarterly* 54: 396–408.

------. 1994. "Caveat Populi Quaestor: The 1992 Pre-Election Polls in the Israeli Press," in Asher Arian and Michal Shamir, eds. *The Elections in Israel 1992*, New York: State University of New York Press, 255–271.

------. 1998. "Beware of Polls? The Coverage of Election Polls in the Israeli Media," in Camille Fuchs and Saul Bar-Lev, eds. *Truth and Polls*, Tel-Aviv, Kibbutz Hameuhad Publishers, Red Line, 123-146 [Hebrew].

------. 2002. "The 2001 Elections: Propaganda that Changed Nothing," in Asher Arian and Michal Shamir, eds. *The Elections in Israel 2001*. Jerusalem:The Israel Democracy Institute, 101-126 [Hebrew].

------. 2003. "Beauty is in the Eye of the Beholder," *The Seventh Eye* 42, 18-19 [Hebrew].

------, and Tamir Sheafer. 2004. *The Media Coverage of Elections in Israel: Soul-Searching Regarding Studies of Four Campaigns*, Tel Aviv, Chaim Herzog Institute of Communications, Society, and Politics, Tel Aviv University [Hebrew].

------, and Gadi Wolfsfeld. 2002. "Struggles over the Electoral Agenda," in Asher Arian and Michal Shamir, eds. *The Elections in Israel 1999*, New York: State University of New York Press, 269–288.

Wolfsfeld, Gadi. 1995. "Voters as Consumers: Audience Perspectives on the Election Broadcasts," in Asher Arian and Michal Shamir, eds. *The Elections in Israel 1992*, New York: State University of New York Press, 234–235.

------. 1997. *Media and Political Conflict: News from the Middle East*, Cambridge: Cambridge University Press.

------. 2001. "The Struggle for the Agenda in the 1996 and 1999 Election Campaigns," in Asher Arian and Michal Shamir, eds. *The Elections in Israel, 1999,* Jerusalem: The Israel Democracy Institute, 383-410 [Hebrew].

------, and Gabriel Weimann. 1999. "The Struggle for the Agenda in the 1996 Election Campaign," *Politics* 4, 9-26 [Hebrew].

The Internet Race: Parties and the Online Campaign in the 2006 Elections[1]

Nir Atmor

Introduction

In his opening address to the winter session of the Sixteenth Knesset on October 30, 2005, Prime Minister Ariel Sharon announced: "We are embarking on an election year, and it is natural for both interparty disputes and personal disagreements to increase. I call on everyone here to act responsibly and remember that life also goes on after elections."[2] That same day an interesting item appeared in the daily newspaper *Haaretz*. It was titled, "New on the Internet: Funeral Arrangements Can be Made Gratis, and Without Leaving Home." The article informed readers of a new website, *Kadisha-Net*, which provided all-encompassing advice and information about the burial process.[3] There was, in the end, a strong link between the two articles; the one detailing the coming elections and the intrusive nature of the Internet, accompanying us even unto death.

Very few subjects relative to Israeli politics have not been closely studied. The Internet, however, is one of them, especially its use by political parties during an election campaign. The 2006 general election was the first in which most parties set up websites to convey their political messages. The messages themselves, and their presentation on the websites, served as a channel of communication between campaign leadership, on the one hand, and supporters and Internet surfers, on the other. In some cases the sites were somewhat interactive. Web users could submit requests to party leaders. The parties were attempting to simulate the appearance of a lively political exchange even if this was not necessarily the case. Interparty political competition on the Internet, however, became an integral part of the election campaign, and was noted for the first time as being a significant venue which could impact on the success of an election campaign.

It is possible to analyze the use of the Internet in the election campaign from two standpoints. First, from that of the voters surfing the web looking for

295

information on the candidates and their parties. Research of this kind should focus on the behavior of the voters, the interaction between them at the time of the elections, and their involvement in the election campaign (i.e., the focus is on the demand aspect). This type of study was undertaken in Israel and examined the 2003 elections, focusing on the talkback in several discussion forums (Lehman-Wilzig, 2004). The second approach would be to examine Internet use during the election from the standpoint of the party institutions and their use of the Internet during the campaign. Here the focus should be on the "supply" provided by the various parties, namely, the Internet channels used in the course of the election campaign to reach the largest number of supporters in the voting population.

This section analyzes the content of the parties' websites in the 2006 election campaign. The theoretical aspect of this study consists of a comparative analysis of party websites (Gibson and Ward, 2000), taking into account the following four aspects:

- **Information provision**, seeking to ascertain whether party websites in Israel provide their voters with ample information about the party
- **Resource generation and recruitment**, examining whether party websites succeed in recruiting new voters, activists, and even financial contributions
- **Promoting participation**, investigating whether parties attempt to use the Internet to increase public involvement in the campaign
- **Networking and party organization**, examining whether parties attempt to strengthen both internal and external party ties

The primary assertion of this analysis is that planning a political campaign on the Internet has become an important element in determining election success or failure but is not yet deemed crucial. On the one hand, there are substantial differences between the parties in Israel insofar as ideology and voter-base. On the other, during the 2006 election campaign the parties demonstrated considerable similarities in their Internet use and their attempts to set up interactive websites. Did the parties follow a similar pattern? What did party websites offer Internet users during the election campaign? Does an election campaign conducted on the Internet possess identifiable characteristics? Using a content analysis of the parties' websites, we attempt to identify the principal characteristics of the 2006 election campaign. Concurrent with the analysis is a discussion of the significance of Internet use within the broader context of the institutional and social changes affecting the political system in recent years, and how they impact on the parties.

Parties and Election Campaigns on the Internet

The past few decades have witnessed the growing importance of the mass media and the increasingly prominent role they play in Israeli politics. This has, to some extent, sidelined the political party, traditionally the intermediary between society and state institutions. The political environment has changed. The political arena is highly competitive, the trust placed in political parties by modern society is declining, and widespread public support—actively courted during an election campaign – is not easily obtained (Arian, Atmor, and Hadar, 2006). The parties invest tremendous effort in gaining exposure to the general public at election time. An increasing use of television and radio broadcasts by party functionaries, extensive advertising campaigns in the daily papers, and a massive use of marketing strategy which entails using advisers and opinion polls, are all geared to strengthening the parties and assisting them in the competition for power in the political arena. The Internet, part of the ICT technologies,[4] is viewed as neutral, as it permits various kinds of information to flow unencumbered and freely. Within this context the Internet provides a new political arena, as activated primarily prior to an election.

Three main periods can be delineated in the history of political campaigns, each offering its own type of campaign: traditional, modern, and post-modern (Norris, 2000).

The traditional campaign was prevalent in the U.S. and advanced democracies until the late 1950s. The methods used by parties promoted their door-to-door campaigns, disseminating their election message at the local level and motivating supporters to attend election meetings and rallies. The party leaders achieved prominence by addressing party meetings and public rallies attended by thousands of volunteers, activists, and supporters. These methods characterized traditional campaigns and were prevalent until the late 1950s.

The modern campaign, which emerged in the 1960s and endured until the 1990s, was highlighted by the professionalization of politics. It utilized outside political advisors as well as professional teams and advertising agencies from the world of marketing, business, and communications as well as public opinion polls. Television shifted the focus to "air time." The parties needed to invest considerable resources, time, and money in demanding election campaigns (Farrell and Webb, 2000). These processes, known as the "Americanization of politics," took place in Western democracies (Dalton, 2002) and in Israel (Aronoff, 2000; Rahat and Sheafer, 2005). The growth in the importance of Internet sites since the 1990s should be viewed within the wider context of these processes.

The post-modern campaign symbolized the transition to the Internet age. Party websites, talkback, and e-mail characterize this important stage. The use of interactive media is still in its infancy, but these channels are assuming greater prominence in many countries (Norris, 2000: 313).

Various studies have examined how parties and candidates make use of the Internet as it becomes more widespread. Research initially focused on U.S. elections (D'Alessio, 1997; Davis, 1999), analyzing candidates' sites for the congressional election (Margolis et al., 1997) and U.S. presidential candidates' sites (Margolis and Resnick, 2000). Studies soon followed in other countries, e.g., Australia (Gibson and Ward, 2002; Ward and Gibson, 2002), Germany (Schweitzer, 2005), Italy (Newell, 2001), Japan (Tkach-Kawasaki, 2003), and the U.K. (Coleman, 2001; Coleman and Ward, 2005; Gibson, Lusoli, and Ward, 2005). There were also studies conducted comparing this subject on an international level (Margolis et al., 1999; Gibson et al., 2003; Norris, 2003).

The question as to how the various political players use the Internet can be answered as follows: most parties do not have clear guidelines regarding Internet campaign activity beyond the need to create an image of professionalism and present themselves as technologically up-to-date (Gibson and Ward, 2000: 302). In addressing these questions, some studies developed methodological tools, primarily theoretical ones (Margolis et al., 1997). Others presented more sophisticated, quantitative methods to analyze parties' websites, focus on their design, the information they present, and their interactive possibilities (Gibson and Ward, 2000; Gibson and Ward, 2002; Norris, 2003). Whether they concentrated on analyzing an individual country (Gibson and Ward, 2002; Gibson et al., 2005) or focused on inter-country comparisons (Norris, 2003), these studies made it possible to undertake a systematic analysis of online election campaigns.

The Analytical Framework

Research literature indicates that parties use Internet sites throughout their election campaigns, with varying levels of success, for both official and functional purposes; on the official level parties can disseminate their ideas by means of the websites, listing their platform or their candidates, while on the functional level parties may use their sites to further their election campaign, attempting to recruit new members, and develop various organizational ties (Schweitzer, 2005).

The present study expands the discussion of these uses and examines whether the parties in Israel succeeded in establishing a significant Internet presence during the 2006 election campaign. A broader examination makes it possible to map the parties' websites with the aid of the aforementioned four main dimensions:

1. Information provision: Do the parties use their websites to present and disseminate information which Internet surfers need? Several studies have criticized the parties' websites, claiming that most of them tend to be slow and conservative in their approach, without adapting to the needs of Internet users, and not all that creative relative to form and style (Stone, 1996). This is in contrast to the websites of Internet groups which were characterized as leaders in the field (Margolis and Resnick, 2000; Davis, Elin, and Reeher, 2002). However, all the researchers felt that the parties' websites should provide a wealth of data, focus on intelligent information, and furnish surfers with the necessary tools, from official documents to announcements and updates about the party. The prevalent view is that political parties worldwide employ their websites more for purposes of publicity and spreading information than to promote their identity and policies (Gibson and Ward, 2000).

The present study attempts to examine to what extent the information presented by the parties in Israel's general election of 2006 was essential. We therefore analyzed the content of ten party websites, following a list of twenty criteria linked to the provision of information, the presentation of the party's platform and policy, links to the party's history, the biography of the party's chairman and other candidates, and any information about election campaign data on the party's branches, press releases, speeches, results of opinion polls, which might aid a party in spreading its message to the broader public and attract more supporters *(ibid.)*. This dimension was coded in accordance with the implementation (√) or non-implementation (-) of each criterion, thereby reaching a general conclusion about the parties' websites relative to the information provision dimension.

2. Resource generation and recruitment: Are party websites a means of recruiting new supporters and attracting Internet surfers? The recruitment and mobilization of supporters are challenging in light of the general shift away from politics (Dalton and Wattenberg, 2000). The skeptical approach views parties' websites as a means of reinforcing existing ties between involved and updated activists on the one hand, and the party on the other. The mobilization of voters is perceived by those who adhere to this opinion as "preaching to the converted," and they do not view the Internet as a viable means of attracting potential voters (Norris, 2003).

Another approach focuses on the advantages inherent in the Internet, with parties attempting to adapt to the political, communication, and social changes of the last decade. These attempts are overshadowed by marked differences between the parties relative to Internet use in the period just prior to the election. There were those who felt that the Internet era has made it possible to identify another stage in the development of parties, with a new prototype known as a cyber party. The outstanding feature of a cyber party is its strong link to its voters, achieved by means of Internet technology, with little regard for the traditional ways of recruiting supporters (Margets, 2006: 531). The Internet in general, and party websites in particular, help to reach the population of young voters (known as the e-generation), who have grown up with Internet technology but tend to be less politically involved. Discourse on the Internet aids in strengthening a relatively unknown party, providing it with exposure.

When criticism as to how parties conduct campaigns is positioned at the center of public discourse and scrutiny, it is difficult to obtain resources and contributions (Hofnung, 2006). But the Internet is a new venue, with independent candidates and parties aspiring to recruit fresh supporters and activists, as well as the money to fund their election campaigns. This was particularly apparent in the campaign conducted in the U.S. by Howard Dean in the primaries held for the U.S. presidency in 2004. He managed to raise a total of $50 million, obtaining approximately half this amount via the Internet by requesting contributions of less than $100 each (Hindman, 2005).[5] This new dimension represents some of the methods available for recruiting voters and for the resources used by parties in the 2006 election campaign.

3. Promoting participation: Do parties operate via the Internet to increase civic participation? Do their sites offer interactivity and engender dialogue, providing access and enabling grassroots participation?

A research trend which gained prominence in the mid-1990s stressed the advantages implicit in the Internet, expressing admiration for its success in augmenting the interaction between people and enabling them to express their views in public as well as to elicit responses (Norris, 2003: 23). This research trend indicated that the Internet succeeded in contributing to the public debate and created a new arena for public discussion on political topics of general interest. As noted by Selnow (1998), before the Internet era an individual's only option for a response was by turning off the television or throwing the daily paper into the trash. The Internet offered the individual additional modes of response, whether in sending an e-mail or participating in a talkback, thereby effectively expressing his or her concerns.

Other researchers, prominent primarily in the late 1990s, were more skeptical about Internet use during an election campaign. They felt that while the Internet has the potential to bring about change in electoral politics, it was still premature (Margolis and Resnick, 2000; Norris, 2003). Those researchers felt that most party websites were notable for their extensive use of multimedia and one-way messages, and therefore were no different than publicity campaigns which utilized billboards or newspaper advertisements. In their opinion, few websites truly facilitated public debate (Margolis and Resnick, 2000). There has been considerable debate about access to the Internet. It has been stated that it is not as global and all-encompassing as it purports to be (Davis, 1999; Norris, 2001), and some researchers offer an even more pessimistic view of what is known as the "virtual community" (Sunstein, 2001).

One of the most accepted assumptions is that during an election campaign parties operate primarily in an attempt to augment civic involvement (Farrell and Webb, 2000; Coleman, 2001). The dimension of promoting participation focuses on the Internet's interactive facility, enabling a dialogue to be conducted not only between members of a party but also between them and the party leadership as well as political forces managing the election campaign (Gibson and Ward, 2000: 306). Sending electronic messages, conducting chats, and using blogs are just some of the functions parties employ to gauge the mood of the public and public opinion on controversial subjects (the party's platform and policy) as well as responses to the election campaign at the grassroots level (Cornfield, 2004). Parties' websites were also examined for this dimension relative to the implementation or non-implementation of ten criteria, among them voluntary activities proposed by the parties, the possibilities of being placed on a mailing list, discussion groups, and other involvement possibilities.

4. Networking and party organization: Do parties operate to strengthen their internal connections (between regional organizations and the local activists, on the one hand, and the party leadership, on the other), and reinforce their external ties (between parties and organizations, such as interest groups)?

The costs of running a website are lower than those of a billboard advertising campaign, and the Internet can help parties to organize their election campaign, primarily in decentralizing organizational authority. Party websites make it possible to reduce the work of many functionaries and focus on expert teams equipped with technological devices, all this in an attempt to reach as many people as possible. The costs are the same, in terms of time and money, to send e-mails to a thousand or one hundred thousand people by technological means, without requiring the involvement of large numbers of devoted party activists *(ibid.)*. Within the framework of the discussion of this aspect, we present several examples of parties that utilized networking and party organization in the course of the 2006 elections.

Party websites were analyzed from a comparative perspective, focusing on parties which succeeded in getting representatives elected in the 2006 elections. For four months—from the day the prime minister announced that the Sixteenth Knesset was being disbanded (November 21, 2005) to election day (March 28, 2006)—the official sites (org.il) of ten parties were examined at specific points in time.[6] Each party website was examined relative to the four aspects mentioned above: information provision, resource generation and recruitment, promoting participation, and networking and party organization.

The Internet Election Campaign: The Information Provision Dimension

The analysis of interparty competition on the Internet relative to the information provision dimension compares methods of marketing the identity and policies which each party seeks to promote. What content is transmitted to the public via the parties' websites, and to what extent are parties successful in reaching their target audience? How do the parties adapt to this new environment? In this section we describe the parties' efforts to display an Internet presence, and we attempt to identify the principal patterns they employed during the election campaign. We begin with providing a general picture of the ten major parties, and then focus on Labor and Likud, comparing them with the rest of the parties.

It is important to note, within the context of the analysis of the situation in Israel, that the information highway is anarchic. In contrast to the control and monitoring evident in the traditional communications media, the Election (Methods of Publicity) Law does not regulate the Internet. The initial precedent was set by the Central Election Committee in 2001, when the Shas party faction appealed to the chairman of the Election Committee, Justice Mishael Cheshin, against Knesset Member Ofir Paz-Pines of the Labor party faction. The appellants asked Justice Cheshin to prevent MK Paz-Pines from appearing on a video chat on the *Maariv* newspaper's website. On January 30, Justice Cheshin ruled that "what is not explicitly forbidden by law is permitted; therefore publicity via the Internet is permitted as there is no law forbidding it."[7] This decision effectively determined that in the absence of an explicit law regulating Internet use, there could be no restrictions on its use even for election purposes.

In the 2006 election campaign the Meretz and Hetz party factions asked the chairman of the Central Election Committee, Justice Dorit Beinish, to issue a restraining order preventing the Shas party faction from distributing books of Psalms to new members registering via the party's website.[8] They claimed that this constituted election bribery via the Internet, since "it is forbidden by law to distribute gifts, including sacred objects, to voters, and this would appear to amount to election bribery."[9] Shas thus creatively sought to recruit adherents via the Internet. Ten days after the appeal, Justice Beinish permitted Shas to distribute Psalm books, noting: "I do not think that the distribution of a book can be regarded as bestowing a forbidden gift or offering a bribe, and the presentation of the book does not constitute an attempt to exert illicit influence on voters' considerations."[10] She did, however, determine that the book should not be given together with a blessing from Rabbi Ovadia Yosef. These two events highlight the lack of regulation and the parties' freedom to campaign on the Internet, even during an election campaign.

Table 1 below presents the analysis of the sites of ten parties relative to the twenty criteria pertaining to the aspect of information provision. Eight of the ten parties examined scored more than half the points in this category. The websites of three parties—Labor, Meretz, and Israel Beiteinu—scored the highest points (17), followed by Kadima, Shas, and National Front (16). Likud scored 13, followed by Hadash, Yahadut Hatorah, and Gil, with only 10, 5, and 3 respectively. The average score of the ten party websites was 13 (Standard Deviation 5.2), and indicates that most of the parties did in fact present surfers with varied information. Most of the party websites contained historical and general information about the elections, including important events in their past as well as significant incidents in the life of the party. At different points in time the parties posted their manifestos on their sites, offering a general outline of their policies and views on the following subjects: security, economic policy, and social issues. All the parties presented their list of candidates for election to the Knesset, seven provided biographical details on the chairman of the party, and only five incorporated information about the other candidates. Six parties presented speeches made by their members on various occasions, six offered information on the party's institutions, and five provided information about their branches. Seven parties posted sites in more than one language, and six described their ties to other social organizations and provided links to other sites; the Hadash site, for example, gave links to the sites of Maki (Israel Communist

Party), Banki (Communist Youth in Israel), "the Left Bank," and the Hadash site in Arabic. The Shas website gave links to the sites of Rabbi Ovadia Yosef's sermons and Uri Zohar. Three parties (Kadima, Shas, and Israel Beiteinu) gave data on opinion polls presented in the media or conducted by the parties. Three parties (Israel Beiteinu, Meretz, and Kadima) gave information on their websites about donations they had received from citizens, even though according to the State Comptroller "in an election year every party should publish any donation larger than NIS 1,000 on an ongoing basis on its website."[11]

Only three of the ten parties (Labor, Shas, and Likud) invested in a photo archive, but all of them used publicity broadcasts. It is important to note that one of the most outstanding features of the 2006 election campaign was the prevalence of publicity video clips on the Internet. By law, television and radio political party broadcasts begin twenty-one days before the elections. The parties displayed video clips on their websites in February 2006. In effect, these were the political party broadcasts that had been prepared for television. Some of these, which were broadcast on television only on March 9, were shown on the Internet more than a month beforehand, as if on a trial basis. The parties examined the response to the films on the Internet before emerging with a new campaign. Displaying the clips on the Internet was not merely a question of audacity. It enabled the parties to display fearlessness (e.g., Meretz's "Seedlings" clip), and even insensitivity (Shinui's publicity clip, which was banned),[12] without apprehension over an extreme reaction of any kind. With no regulation of election publicity on the Internet, or any monitoring which could prevent this publicity, the parties were free to act without restraint.[13]

Some video clips were especially notable during the campaign: the Likud's first clip, *Fatal Finances*, was posted on its website on February 8, even though the party's site was still in the process of being built. "The film gives visual expression to the opposition to transferring money to Hamas, since it is clear that it will be used for the purposes of terrorism and incitement against the state of Israel,"[14] claimed the chairman of Likud's publicity campaign headquarters, MK Gideon Sa'ar. Shas went even further when it presented an hour-long clip entitled *Burning Heart*,[15] portraying scenes of abysmal poverty and urging viewers to vote for the party which promised to reduce the social gap. Likud's election clip, which was first aired on February 20, was unusual in its sharp criticism of Russian President Vladimir Putin for inviting Hamas representatives to Russia. Various Internet sites and Likud's official website offered a clip in which Putin's face was replaced by that of Ehud Olmert. The clip was quickly removed from Likud's official site, after the Russian ambassador to Israel protested to Likud party chairman, Binyamin Netanyahu, about the use of Putin's image in the party's campaign.[16]

One of the most prevalent and established methods of Internet use is e-mail, enabling any user to send data (primarily verbal) to any other user with an Internet connection, providing they have a known address. Only four of the

Table 1
The Parties and Information Provision*

Information	Labor	Israel Beiteinu	Meretz	Kadima	Shas	National Front-Mafdal	Likud	Hadash	Gil	Yahadut Hatorah
Historical information about the party	✓	✓	✓	✓	✓	✓	✓	✓	-	✓
General information about elections	✓	✓	✓	✓	✓	✓	✓	✓	✓	-
List of Knesset candidates	✓	✓	✓	✓	✓	✓	✓	✓	✓	✓
Party manifesto	✓	✓	✓	✓	✓	✓	✓	✓	✓	-
Publicity broadcasts	✓	✓	✓	✓	✓	✓	✓	✓	✓	✓
Articles and official documents	✓	✓	✓	✓	✓	✓	✓	✓	-	-
Calendar and events in election campaign	✓	✓	✓	✓	✓	✓	-	✓	✓	-
Biography of party chairman	✓	✓	✓	✓	✓	✓	✓	-	-	-
Information about organization's institutions	✓	✓	✓	-	✓	✓	✓	-	-	-
Biographies of party candidates	-	✓	✓	✓	✓	✓	-	-	-	-
Archive of press releases	✓	✓	✓	✓	-	✓	-	✓	-	-
Speeches	✓	✓	✓	✓	✓	✓	-	-	-	-
Downloading possibilities	✓	✓	✓	✓	✓	✓	✓	-	-	-
Other languages	✓	✓	✓	✓	-	✓	✓	✓	-	-
Photo archive	✓	-	-	-	✓	-	✓	-	-	-
Information about party branches	✓	✓	✓	-	-	✓	✓	-	-	-
Information about donations and economic data	-	✓	✓	✓	-	-	-	-	-	-
Results of public opinion polls	-	✓	-	✓	✓	-	-	-	-	-
Sending e-mails to mailing list	✓	-	✓	✓	-	✓	-	-	-	-
Links to social organizations and additional sites	✓	-	✓	-	✓	✓	✓	✓	-	-
Score per party (out of 20)	17	17	17	16	16	16	13	10	5	3

*The data are based on the number of entries into the party websites between November 22, 2005, and March 28, 2006, election day.

ten parties used this service in the 2006 elections. Every four days Labor sent out various e-mails; National Front sent out an updated list of managers of the branches nearest to recipients' homes, together with a calendar of upcoming party events; Meretz kept its approximately 11,000 subscribers up-to-date with a weekly notification of information on the party's election campaign activities, its principal messages, comparisons between its platform and those of the other parties, and links to its election video clips as well as personal letters. Two months before the elections Kadima began a similar campaign of sending out e-mails and a weekly newsletter. The first of these stated "We in Kadima attach tremendous importance to the relationship with our supporters, members, and admirers."[17] The party sent out a newsletter (for a total of nine weekly updates). The other parties did not send out e-mails, and their websites focused on disseminating information by the traditional methods.

It is also possible to learn about the differences in investment in party websites and in implementing sites by comparing the two oldest parties, Labor and Likud, during the election in choosing their list of candidates for election to the Knesset.

During the election campaign Labor ran three websites: the first operated along the lines of the old one [the website from the 2003 election] and included photos of Amir Peretz's victory in the primaries for the party leadership. This site was mainly informative and included only limited links. The second site was launched on December 30, 2005, about two weeks before the Labor party election, and was used in an interesting fashion: when the vote counting began, the site presented the results in real time. Every few minutes the vote count was updated, and surfers could view the current results for the top spots on both the national and regional levels (number of votes and support rates) on the main page. When the counting process was over, the headline on the main page of the site read: "63,888 Voters Voted for Labor's Social Agenda. Only 2,760 Voted in the Likud Election. And in Kadima Only One Person Counts."[18] In the 2006 elections Labor was indeed the only party that enabled all its members to participate in choosing its Knesset candidates, and the fact that the site was frequently updated indicates an educated use of the Internet.

The Likud website was not prominent in the election campaign.[19] Prior to Ariel Sharon's resignation from Likud, the site operated along the same lines as in the 2003 election. Even after Likud's Knesset Members removed Sharon's picture from the Knesset faction's room, his portrait continued to remain at the center of the party's website for several days. Three weeks after Sharon was hospitalized, Likud erased all trace of his existence from its website. Under the heading "Milestones," there was no mention of Sharon heading the party, and the review culminated in 1998, when Binyamin Netanyahu took office. The Likud spokesman, Ronen Moshe, told journalists: "These are ridiculous and unfounded accusations. The Likud website has been upgraded in the last three days, and the process of upgrading and renewal has not yet been concluded. In the next few days all the missing content will be completed."[20] However, in the primaries for Likud party chairman (December 19, 2005) the website was not changed, save for the addition of a posting of "An amendment to Likud's list of Knesset candidates," and the addresses of voting stations. On election day not a single item of information appeared on the website about the results of the internal elections nor was any current data provided on the vote count. In effect, the Likud website was not active during the election for the party's list of candidates for the Seventeenth Knesset.

The Labor party's new (third) website was launched on January 31, 2006, fifty-six days before the Knesset elections. The site contained stylized links, a wealth of information about the party's candidates, and considerable humor, all intended to present the shift that had taken place in the Labor party and to primarily attract young Internet surfers. The message the party sought to convey was that "it's time for a turnaround," in the words of the party's first campaign slogan. The website contained a great deal of general information, such as the address given by the party chairman, Amir Peretz,[21] as well as the main points of the party's platform, headed "The Moral Road Map." The main points stressed features on equality and social welfare, including the fair wage and package of services that the state should guarantee, although this was not yet part of its systematic manifesto. At the bottom of the page there was a link for joining, for finding the nearest polling station, and for sending the data to a friend. No additional information, e.g., candidates, calendar, future plans, articles, press releases, etc., appeared on the party website at this stage. The new Likud site was launched on February 14, 2006, forty-two days before election day, and included many video clips, but the possibilities it offered were extremely limited.

Like the disparities between the three major parties regarding Internet use, there were also differences in this respect between the medium-sized and small parties. Some of them (Israel Beiteinu, Meretz, and National Front) maintained up-to-date websites, while the rest invested less effort in this feature. Not all the parties invested the necessary resources for setting up varied and lively websites. The prevalent feeling throughout the election campaign was that the results were a foregone conclusion, due mainly to public opinion polls preceding the election campaign. This led some of the parties to conclude that it was futile to direct money and resources to funding an extensive Internet network. Parties close to the electoral cut-off threshold (2 percent) felt the investment was not worthwhile. The Gil party, which, until just before the elections, had not been predicted by any opinion poll to pass the threshold, maintained a party website that offered only a few possibilities. And finally, many parties did not consider the Internet to be of particular importance, and therefore did not invest efforts in setting up websites. This was also linked to their voter base, which tended not to use the Internet.

The most extreme example of a party whose voters did not use the Internet was Yahadut Hatorah, whose site was launched on March 22, less than a week before the election, and it was the last of the party websites to be inaugurated.[22] Yahadut Hatorah had not used the Internet until then, fearing that this would be interpreted as support for the web. The inauguration of the website represented a significant shift for the ultra-orthodox population, which—at least officially—avoids using this medium.

It would appear, therefore, that the decision to not dedicate time and money to a party website stemmed in some cases from cost-benefit considerations. There is evidence that small parties are better able to reach an audience in the online arena than in the traditional ones—e.g., via television broadcasts, newspaper advertisements, or billboards (Norris, 2001)—nevertheless not all the small parties in Israel utilized the advantages offered by the Internet.

To what extent did the parties in Israel make use of the Internet to provide information? In light of these findings a mixed picture emerges, with competition between the two major parties, Kadima and Labor, clearly demonstrating that considerable time, money, and thought was invested in providing Internet surfers with a variety of data and information. The Likud party, however, tended to use the party websites to a lesser degree, although it invested in propaganda films. The competition between the medium-sized parties was evident in Israel Beiteinu, Meretz, Shas, and National Front-Mafdal, and they gained high marks in the information provision dimension. Hadash, Gil, and Yahadut Hatorah resorted less to the party websites, with the latter hardly using theirs at all since their target audience does not surf the net.

A New Source for Recruiting Supporters and Generating Resources?

The second dimension deals with the parties' efforts to recruit new members and gain the financial support required to conduct an election campaign. The Internet's characteristics, immediacy, and interactivity, as well as its global dispersion, enable it to effectively recruit members and raise funds (Gibson and Ward, 2000: 305). The following examples highlight just how the Internet may be used to generate resources and augment membership.

Two main periods characterized Kadima's election campaign: the first was the period of Ariel Sharon, beginning with his announcement of the establishment of the party on November 21, 2005, and ending on the night of January 4, 2006, when the prime minister was rushed to the hospital. The second period began with the prime minister's hospitalization and ended with the general election on March 28, 2006. During those four months Kadima ran two Internet sites, a temporary one launched one week after the party was registered with the Registrar of Parties, and a permanent one launched at the end of December 2005. The temporary site was extremely limited and featured a picture of Ariel Sharon with the slogan, "A strong leader for peace." The site welcomed visitors and offered only two links: one to the speech announcing the establishment of the party, and one to a membership form. Visitors who entered the party's website and became members received a letter of thanks, which read as follows:

"At this time we are establishing a network of members. In the framework of our efforts to increase our numbers and recruit new members we are glad to welcome you into our ranks and salute your participation in this important process."[23] That marked the beginning of the first stage of the campaign. The focus was then on recruiting members and attempting to attract visitors to the website to build a large base of supporters and activists. At that time the public opinion polls showed Kadima gaining support, but information about the party was available to interested Internet surfers only through newspaper articles or political websites. The temporary website did not contain updates from the field, information that was relevant to members, or any other current data. Kadima's initial efforts focused solely on augmenting its mailing list and recruiting as many members as possible.

In the four months between the end of November 2005 and March 28, 2006, the parties endeavored to recruit supporters. The most prevalent method for doing this via the Internet was by building a database of people who had signed up by compiling a long list of I.D. numbers. Kadima's campaign managers were astonished to find that 12,000 people had joined within three weeks (Arden, 2006: 23). When Kadima's permanent website was launched the registration process continued, and the number of new recruits reached 40,000.

The decline in support reflected in opinion polls generated a new kind of recruitment campaign about two weeks before the election. An e-mail entitled "Get a friend to join" was sent to the members with the following request: "Anyone who talks, explains, influences, and causes a friend to emerge from his state of apathy and vote for Kadima will win some amazing prizes: permanent borders, a Jewish majority, and stability in government, the economy, and society…. So get up from that chair, call a friend, and go out to convince, influence, and vote!"[24] The Labor party went even further, sending an e-mail to members in February entitled "Contact someone. Convince them. We'll win!" It contained the following passage:

> You don't have to leave home, hang around busy intersections, or devote whole days or even hours to political activity…. Many people want to be involved in Israel's political life, to take part in the 2006 turnaround, but feel that they simply don't have the time. What with earning a living, and dealing with the burdens of everyday life, it's very difficult to find the time to lend a hand. "Contact someone. Convince them. We'll win!" answers that need.[25]

What we have here, therefore, is an initiative intended to recruit supporters for a party via the Internet. Anyone who was interested in helping the election campaign could join and receive a list of twenty phone numbers of people in their neighborhood, whom they were then asked to call and try and convince them to vote for the party in the elections to be held on March 28. The party announcement also stated: "You can act at the time and place that suits you, and give as much time as you can spare. Labor's new system enables you to play an important role in the campaign, and instead of just talking about how much the country needs change, you can do something about bringing about change yourself." According to party data, 4,000 individuals registered in the first week alone.[26]

Meretz also initiated a similar campaign twenty days before election day: "We are all mobilizing in order to make a joint effort: campaign for the last ten days before the election: call the floating voters, and paint the country in Meretz's colors."[27] The e-mail stated that the party had located several thousand floating voters, and anyone who wanted to help convince and recruit people could receive a list of twenty individuals to "call and convince." Individuals who were registered on the National Front website received a list of regional campaign administrators, and anyone who was willing to contribute was asked to contact his or her local administrator.

However, despite the attractive use of the Internet, and regardless of the attempts to convince others directed towards web surfers, it is difficult to point to a general influx of supporters to the parties' websites in the 2006 election campaign. No party included on its website a counter indicating the number of entries. In the course of the election campaign, the parties took care to maintain a certain degree of secrecy in publishing up-to-date figures about the number of registered members and visitors to their websites. The only exception was Meretz, which published part of the figures for entries to its website during February. The number of entries to the Meretz website (see figure 1 below) presents a general picture of interest in the parties' websites in general, and in that of Meretz in particular: in December 2005 there were about 4,000 entries to the party website in one week: in January 2006 the number of entries rose to 8,000, and during February, when the new website was launched, the number of entries to the party's site remained low—averaging between 1,000 and 2,000 a day, approximately 8,000 a week. On February 12, Meretz posted its party manifesto on the site, and on that day there were 4,820 entries; on Sunday, February 19, at the event marking the launch of Meretz's 2006 election campaign, the party revealed its election jingle and presented its billboard campaign and video clips—all in an election atmosphere. On that day there were 1,640 visitors to the party site; the day before the election the party headquarters sent out an e-mail to "the apathetic left-winger,"[28] in which it appealed to the many floating voters to go to the polling booth on election day. An opinion poll taken by the Netvision Institute in March 2006 of a representative sample of the population, found that in the month before the elections, between 5 percent and 6 percent of the adult population in Israel visited party websites.[29]

Obtaining donations to fund an election campaign via parties' websites is vital in the U.S. and to some extent also in the U.K., but in most European countries the amount of money raised via the Internet is negligible (Gibson et al., 2003). In this respect Israel's parties behave much as their European counterparts do, because their campaigns are based almost solely on public funding,

Figure 1
Entries to the Meretz Party Website in February 2006

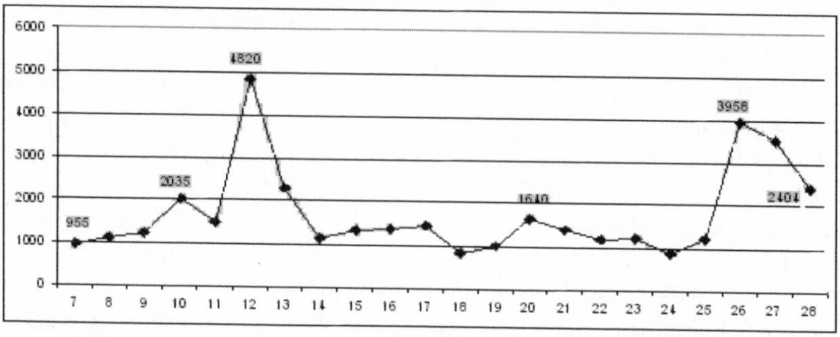

SOURCE: Reports of entries to the Meretz party website during February 2006.

with private donations accounting for only between 1 percent and 2 percent of parties' expenditure in an election campaign (Hofnung, 2004). The parties hardly engage in any fundraising, and this is also reflected by their websites in the 2006 elections. Meretz and Labor were the only two parties which included (protected) links for donating money via the Internet. Meretz reported only one donation (of NIS 1,950) via the Internet in the course of the three months of the campaign. The low number of donations reported may attest to the fact that in this election campaign many parties failed to attract large donors. This could be a result of the public's preference to contribute to individuals vying for spots at the head of their parties or for Knesset seats, rather than to parties themselves. Furthermore, the parties may prefer to release the names of donors only after the election. In any event, the websites did not constitute a fundraising source during the 2006 election campaign.

The Election Campaign on the Internet:
The Dimension of Promoting Participation

The Internet's most outstanding feature is its interactivity. Constituting a two-way channel of communication between voters and their representatives, it facilitates grassroots participation and enables demands and wishes to be expressed. In the traditional communications media the connection between voter and representative is primarily one-way, namely, the public reads reports of what its representatives have said, watches them at work, and passively listens to them, without being able to respond immediately by means of this very same media. The information which flows "from above" is directed by a limited group of politicians and journalists, and they are the ones who determine the agenda. But the rapid evolution of high-tech media in the past decade has led to the emergence of a new kind of politics (Coleman and Gotze, 2001).

The Internet enables voters to obtain information and respond to it on demand, enabling voters to communicate directly with candidates who are seeking their support. It is now possible to participate in an election campaign and direct criticism at party leadership. This opens up an entirely new public domain in which activists and supporters can voice their concerns to the candidates. The parties, for their part, can listen, learn, and respond to grassroots requests or, alternatively, simply ignore them.

There was little interactivity between the parties and web surfers in the 2006 election campaign. Knesset members and other candidates appeared daily to

Table 2
Possibilities of Participation*

Participatory possibilities	Labor	Meretz	Kadima	Israel Beiteinu	National Front-Mafdal	Hadash	Shas	Likud	Yahadut Hatorah	Gil
Sending mail to the system	✓	✓	✓	✓	✓	✓	✓	✓	✓	✓
Joining the mailing list	✓	✓	✓	✓	✓	✓	✓	-	-	-
Volunteering via the Internet	✓	✓	✓	-	✓	✓	✓	-	-	-
Party youth	✓	✓	✓	✓	✓	✓	-	✓	-	-
Games and various publicity gimmicks	✓	✓	✓	✓	✓	-	-	✓	-	-
Other possibilities	✓	✓	✓	-	-	-	-	-	-	-
Blogs	✓	-	-	-	-	✓	-	-	-	-
Participation in party opinion polls	-	-	-	✓	-	-	✓	-	-	-
Donating money via the website	✓	✓	-	-	-	-	-	-	-	-
Discussion groups (forums) on the party website	-	-	-	✓	-	-	-	-	-	-
Grade per party (out of 10)	**8**	**7**	**6**	**6**	**5**	**5**	**4**	**3**	**1**	**1**

*The data are based on entries to party websites between November 22, 2005, and March 28, 2006, election day.

answer questions on the most-visited Internet sites—Walla, Nana, msn, ynet and nrg—but the party websites were for the most part lacking in interactivity possibilities or any genuine dialogue between candidates and surfers.

Table 2 above presents the participatory possibilities offered by ten parties on their websites. Only four of them scored more than half the points awarded in terms of participatory possibilities, and the average grade of all ten was 4.6 (Standard Deviation 2.4). All the parties enabled requests to be sent to them via e-mail (although not all of them responded); seven made it possible to join their mailing list (although only four of them sent out e-mails), and six included the possibility of volunteering on their behalf in their website. With the exception of Israel Beiteinu, no party set up a permanent forum on the party website, but instead they directed visitors to the discussion groups of the Tapuz website;[30] only two parties (Labor and Meretz) included a (protected) link enabling money to be donated to the party. Two parties (Labor and Hadash) included links to members' blogs on their sites, while the other participatory possibilities (sometimes defined as gimmicks) were not particularly inviting.

Underlying the table of participatory possibilities is a variety of methods to encourage involvement and participation via the Internet. A tried and tested procedure is to respond in writing to information put out by the party (talkback), appearing primarily in online journals and newspapers and enabling readers to link their reaction to a specific article. This was one of the most important arenas in the 2006 election campaign. Anyone who closely analyzed the responses could see that most of them had been "planted" by dedicated professional surfers who may even have been hired by the various parties to "strike a blow" at their rivals. While none of the parties admitted to using agents of this kind,[31] the parties are convinced that talkbacks do influence public opinion, especially floating voters. Another example was the campaign presented by Kadima on its website, one day after Ariel Sharon's condition worsened. The campaign slogan was changed to "Continuing to go Forward" (*kadima* in Hebrew), replacing the previous slogan "Forward (kadima) Sharon." Within the framework of the campaign, Kadima endeavored to enable the thousands of citizens who were concerned about Sharon's health to send the prime minister their wishes for his speedy recovery. In the space of a few hours hundreds of citizens posted wishes for the prime minister's return to good health. In the first 20 hours over 7,000 get well wishes poured in from citizens seeking to share their feelings and pain with other surfers (Arden, 2006, 48).

Another possibility was to use online forums or communities. These are basically websites enabling surfers to air their views and beliefs on a given topic. The site does not rely on content posted in real time. Participants enter the site, express their opinions on a certain topic, and reply in their own time to comments that appear on the site. The replies appear as a chain, each response being linked to the statement to which it pertains. The lifetime of any such opinion is but a few days, but sometimes older posted statements may be found.

Participants in Internet talkbacks conduct discussions among themselves and do not always agree with one another about the topic under review. An additional possibility is provided by chat rooms, where surfers meet on a website to which they are all simultaneously connected, writing their opinions and responding to the views of others.

With the exception of Israel Beiteinu, the websites of the parties in the 2006 elections did not provide access to discussion forums or chat rooms, but referred surfers to the "Tapuz Communities" site. They therefore effectively prevented surfers from expressing their views and participating in a public debate to which both surfers and politicians could contribute. The Labor party facilitated interactivity that was closest to a forum or chat room via its "Tribal Campfire" link. Surfers could upload a photo or clip onto the site that they had photographed during the election campaign, and post it under such categories as "Funny," "Annoying," or "Inspiring." Other surfers could grade the photos and video clips, with the most popular ones posted on the party website.

The 2006 election campaign witnessed the tentative beginnings of the use of a new interactive tool which is rapidly becoming more widespread—the web log, or *blog*. These personal diaries enable an individual to express his or her views in a dynamic and current fashion (i.e., on a daily basis). In contrast to the party websites, which were largely static, the advantage of a blog is that its author, in this case Knesset members, can express his or her opinions, experiences, and personal thoughts about the election campaign quite freely. The traditional communications media restrict the space or time allotted to politicians, requiring them to respond to an interviewer's questions, whereas blogs place no limits on their authors. Informal writing, as well as the ability to communicate directly with Internet surfers and share experiences that have not been given exposure in the mass media, can help generate support for a candidate. While a blog is far from being a guaranteed route to success, it helps politicians disseminate their ideas and receive a response (which may be negative). This constitutes an interactive dialogue between the candidate and the web community.

The use of blogs expanded in the U.S. in 2002, when the war in Iraq was the focus of attention. Soon afterwards blogs also found expression in the election campaign.[32] In Israel the Isra-Blog website was established in August 2001 and has gained immense popularity as the place where blogs are concentrated (it was bought by the Nana site in June 2004). Since its establishment it has provided a platform for over 55,000 blogs, 5,000 of which are updated at least once a month. The first Israeli Knesset Member to use a blog was Likud's Ehud Yatom, who launched his in 2004 but closed it shortly after that, when surfers reproved him for his involvement in the Bus 300 incident.[33]

In the 2006 election campaign most of the parties' websites did not incorporate links to their members' blogs, except for the Labor and Hadash sites. The Labor party website had links to two blogs, those of Shelly Yechimovich and Ami Ayalon. Hadash included a link to Dov Hanin's blog. Only an additional three Knesset Members kept blogs: Arieh Eldad, Roman Bronfman, and Shaul Yahalom. The latter has had a blog since 2005, and wrote in it: "I invite you to visit my website and keep track of my parliamentary activity in order to make your comments and suggestions. Everything will be welcomed and given attention."[34] Nevertheless, few politicians or Knesset candidates had personal sites and blogs, and only a fraction of them updated them frequently.[35] A gap also emerged between the blogs of candidates and longer-standing ones, with most candidates not enabling surfers to respond to what they had written. In the end, the average Israeli web surfer was able to contact candidates via the Internet and could expect to receive a personal response even if it was the candidate's advisors who replied. However, blogs were not at the center of the 2006 election campaign, and only a few candidates used them.

Alongside the accepted ways of attracting voters, mention should also be made of several new ideas. Kadima, for example, implemented a project known as "Legal Issues," aimed at involving the public in the legislative process. The site portrayed the youth candidate Yoel Hasson saying to surfers: "For the first time in history a party is going to ask you what laws will be promulgated in the next Knesset. Enter the Legal Issues website today, propose laws or parliamentary questions.... We will rank them.... and bring the laws you propose before the next Knesset."[36] Kadima's youth site thus invited the surfing community to submit proposals for laws and rank the proposals of others. Even as a populist project, its originality prompted 1,300 proposals for laws to appear on the site prior to the elections. The question remains whether anything actually was done with these proposals. Another idea put forward by Kadima was a virtual demonstration, with a map of Israel portraying tiny figures of demonstrators. Surfers could select a figure and decide its features: gender, hairstyle, clothing, age, and area of activity, design a support placard, and place it on the map at a spot of their choosing. The National Front party presented "One Million Orange Spots," in which it asked surfers to light "another warm spot for a strong National Front party in the Knesset."[37] At that time the Labor party website called upon visitors to "Join the Tribal Campfire!... If you're out in the field helping in the election campaign and you see something funny or inspiring, photograph it and send it to the Tribal Campfire, your photograph section on the Labor party's website."[38]

Our inspection of the parties' sites during the 2006 election campaign demonstrates a lack of innovation relative to interactivity. Most party websites were not innovative in general, and the ones that tried to promote participation used different sifting methods to avoid real bottom-up communication. For example, if the site invited surfers to discuss topics on the general agenda and respond to published material, the party site webmasters reviewed the material that came from the public, and the screening process focused on content as well as on style.

In conclusion, the Internet, like any technology, cannot fulfill the individual's desire to be politically active. While the parties attempted to encourage participation via the Internet, the possibilities were limited. Most of the party websites in the 2006 election campaign did not display advanced interactivity, and functioned solely as publicity sites (giving information from the top down).

The Online Organization of the Election Campaign

In recent decades the organization of an election campaign has been based on two main features: a planning team and an implementation team.

The planning team: In the past parties were supported by a campaign organization consisting mainly of non-professional party members. In the past few years, however, there has been a growing tendency to rely on a team of skilled professionals. The team often includes communications advisors, public relations and marketing experts, and public opinion pollsters, all of whom help to organize, formulate, and design the election campaign, and control events on the ground.

The implementation team: This consists of volunteers and paid employees working on behalf of the party and putting the decisions of the planning team into action in an efficient and economic way (Farrell and Webb, 2000). The Internet can serve as an important tool in connecting the two teams, providing a bridge between party members and activists, on the one hand, and the activists in the field, on the other.

The advantages of organizing an election campaign via a party's websites have been noted above: the Internet helps to keep members and supporters up-to-date about events (e.g., meetings) initiated by the party. Information sent via the Internet is quick and cost-effective. In the past campaigns concentrated on sending out the party's mail and newsletters and getting as many activists as possible to go from door to door, while the Internet has reduced the need for these activities. It would appear that the Internet is meant to utilize the potential embodied in technology to reduce costs and limit the need for human involvement, thereby providing a convenient infrastructure for the organization of a campaign.

In the 2006 election campaign most of the parties presented a wealth of material about their activities—meetings, rallies, petitions, and demonstrations—on their websites. All these were merely part of the organization of an election campaign, and information about them appeared on the parties' websites in the framework of news or a calendar of events and updates, or were sent as e-mails to the mailing list (see table 1 above).

An interesting example in the 2006 election campaign was provided by Kadima, a new party whose members and ministers had defected from Likud and Labor and had to become quickly accustomed to working in the field in the election campaign, even before the party had managed to establish branches. Three weeks after the party was founded, the "Malam Group" finished computerizing the party website and preparing its networks to absorb members and supporters. Instead of the traditional system of branches, Kadima established an advanced computerized network, based on four portals supported by manned telephone stations ready to register new members. The system, which cost about $0.5 million, was designed to track the various regional registration centers and the payment of membership dues. In addition, a system for sending e-mails and SMS messages[39] was set up, alongside a general administration system for registering volunteers, accepting donations, managing the campaign budget, and making payments via the Internet and advanced phone messaging systems. On December 25, Malam began operating a website for Kadima which was to be the focal point for managing the party's online campaign and to help keep computerized track of all the aspects of the election campaign. The infrastructure thus incorporated a dedicated system for running the party's website. All these facilitated in organizing the election campaign efficiently.[40]

The Labor party gained prominence when the women's headquarters in the party, headed by Shelly Yechimovich, organized the "Baby Buggy March" for women's rights on March 3, 2006. The march was announced in an e-mail sent by Yechimovich to the Labor party's mailing list ten days prior to the event. The slogan of the march was "We'll run for you, even in high heels."[41] The content of the letter stated that babies in buggies should be brought to the march, and that it was to begin at 1 p.m. at the junction of Rothschild and Balfour Boulevards in Tel Aviv. In addition, by means of the party website, the women's headquarters had visitors sign a "Women's Manifesto," which in effect constituted the party's commitment to work for equality between the sexes.[42]

Anyone interested in volunteering to help Meretz was invited to send their particulars to the party's website and state in which sphere they wanted to work: organizing protests, distributing informational material, conducting student activities in universities, providing administrative assistance, etc. Through its website Meretz also recruited volunteers who were prepared to be present at polling centers on election day.[43] The website also noted planned events, such as demonstrations to express support for Arab inhabitants of Jaffa, or participation in Amnesty International's demonstration against white slavery, want ads, organizing meetings in private homes, and even publishing meeting points for the Women in Black protest movement. But with the exception of the websites of Kadima, Labor, and Meretz, the organization of the 2006 election campaign on parties' websites was limited.

Conclusion

A democracy is characterized by the existence of two basic conditions: a high level of competition and widespread participation (Schumpeter, 1944: 269-283). Competition exists between parties and politicians who vie for government positions, but this is not enough. Extensive civic participation, especially on election day, is integral to competition. The modernization process and technological progress of the past few decades have brought about a greater transparency as well as increased political awareness. The result is the entry of new players concurrent with a wide circle of interests. The Internet, like the press, is another player in the political arena, and also assumes a more prominent place in elections. Contrary to a commonly held view, the Internet embodies many more possibilities than simply the dispatch of e-mails. Its global distribution, the information passing through it, its availability, speed, and low cost all make it into an asset for anyone able to utilize it.

In the four months prior to the elections to the Seventeenth Knesset we monitored the websites of ten parties to obtain an overall idea as to how they were utilized. This field is still in its beginning stages relative to the study of politics in Israel. The analysis of the content of the websites focused on four aspects: information provision; resource generation and recruitment; promoting participation; and networking and party organization. These aspects enabled party websites to be compared with one another. The research findings indicate that party websites presented surfers with a wide range of attractive possibilities—from obtaining information about the campaign to providing opportunities to become actively involved. Not all the parties utilized their websites in similar ways, however.

Several conclusions can be drawn from these results. All the party websites in the 2006 elections possessed a common denominator, focusing to a greater or lesser extent on the information provision dimension, stressing the party, its candidates, and its principles. The websites resembled the traditional media in this aspect, presenting election propaganda via television, newspaper advertisements, and billboards. The resemblance between the party websites was particularly obvious in the extensive use of multimedia and publicity video clips, with the websites serving as a trial run before the television broadcast. The websites provided surfers with a wealth of information, but appear to have focused on preaching to the converted, thereby reinforcing the connection between the party and activists, who wanted to be involved. Limited space was allotted on the websites to any genuinely interactive, two-way debate, enabling a lively discussion to be held by supporters and critics, and by candidates and net surfers, but some parties did attempt to stimulate discussions of this kind on their websites. As to the participation and recruitment of members and resources, it appears that for the most part the party websites did not serve to augment citizens' motivation to be politically involved and contribute their time and money.

There were, however, broad differences between party websites. Not all the parties succeeded in using the advantages offered by the Internet: some provided user-friendly sites, employing talented and able teams of professionals, while others did not attach much importance to the new medium. This is highlighted by the fact that some websites were rebuilt over a considerable amount of time, while some were only launched in the last few weeks before the elections. Another difference relates to cultural and group factors, which play a pivotal role in Israeli society. The attractive websites of the Kadima, Labor, and Meretz parties served to attract the population of young Internet surfers. Shas set up a site which included a link to "Anniversaries of the deaths of sages" to attract the audience of orthodox Jewish surfers. The election broadcasts of Israel Beiteinu, also offered on its website (Niet-Niet-Da), were directed primarily at new immigrants from the former USSR, whereas Yahadut Hatorah hardly used the party's website, as few of its supporters used the Internet.

Was there a difference between the large parties and the small and medium-sized ones relative to Internet use and the investment of resources in websites? Israel's reality teaches us that the answer to this question is unclear. Only a few of the smaller parties invested considerable resources in building sophisticated websites. Even the websites of the large parties varied, reinforcing the conclusion that the Internet does not appeal to everyone. It is even more difficult to assess the extent to which the Internet can attract new supporters, and how it can lead to significant achievements in the election results. The success of the pensioners' party (Gil) in the 2006 elections proves that success can be achieved without a website.

The relations between voters and parties in Israel, as in most Western democracies, are growing weaker (Dalton, 2002). The marked decline in party membership and the low voter turnout in the 2006 elections emphasize this point. In the absence of a stable electoral base, parties must seek new methods of reinforcing their position. Does building an interactive website attest to a new, post-modern period in election campaigns, in which clever, sophisticated, and brief segments extracted from recorded interviews dominate the public debate? The experience of the 2006 elections in Israel demonstrates that this medium operated primarily as a one-way channel of transferring information from the leadership to the grassroots level, namely, from the top down to those surfing the web.

Although the Internet offers many possibilities of sustaining participatory democracy, it has not yet succeeded in bringing about a change in the behavioral patterns of the parties and the voting public. Many questions remain unanswered: Is the Internet useful? Is it perceived by those involved in politics as a phenomenon which is genuine or ephemeral? Further study is required to evaluate the significance of the link between the political system and the general public. It would appear, however, that the transition to the information era signals that parties that do not learn how to use the Internet in the future will be left behind.

Notes

1. I would like to thank Asher Arian, Michal Shamir, Gidi Rahat and several anonymous readers for their useful and encouraging comments.
2. Gideon Allon and *Haaretz* service, "Sharon: Government Will Strive to Implement Road Map and Continue to Hit Terrorists," *Haaretz*, November 1, 2005.
3. Yuval Azulai, "New on the Internet: Funeral Arrangements Can be Made Gratis, and Without Leaving Home," *Haaretz*, November 1, 2005.
4. ICT (Information and Communication Technologies) is a general term for the field of technological communications and services, including transmitting information, start-ups, and certain communications services.

5. Dean's success in obtaining funds is known as the "$100 revolution." In contrast to Bush, who announced that his target was $200 million in large contributions from wealthy individuals in the U.S., the objective of Dean's $100 revolution was to get two million contributors, each of whom would donate $100. With many small contributions of $50 and $100 Dean believed it would be possible to defeat Bush in the presidential race. This was proved to be unfounded, but at the end of February 2004, Dean was at the top of the list of fundraisers and had garnered an unprecedented $50 million.

6. Within the framework of this study the focus was on the following party websites: Kadima (www.kadimasharon.org.il), Labor (www.avoda2006.org.il), Shas (www.shasnet.org.il), Israel Beiteinu (www.beiteinu.org.il), Likud (www.likud.org.il), National Front-Mafdal (www.leumi.org.il), Gil (www.gil.org.il), Yahadut Hatorah (www.gimel2006.com), Meretz (www.myparrty.org.il), Hadash (www.hadash.org.il). The websites of Balad and Ra'am-Ta'al were in Arabic only, and because of language constraints were not included in this study. The other parties, e.g., Shinui, Hetz, Tafnit, The Green Party, Green Leaf, etc. had active websites but were not included in the research.

7. For further information, see the decision of the chairman of the Central Election Committee, Mishael Cheshin, "Election Publicity Via the Internet," January 30, 2001, http://www.knesset.gov.il/spokesman/heb/election01.asp

8. "MK Abraham Poraz and the Hetz party list submitted a request to the chairman of the Central Election Committee to issue a restraining order against the Shas party faction for distributing books of psalms to the public in the framework of its campaign for election to the Seventeenth Knesset," *Press Release of the Central Election Committee*, February 21, 2006. http://www.knesset.gov.il/elections17/heb/CecNotice.asp?Notice1d=22.

9. Roi Nahmias and Ilan Marciano, "Meretz vs. Shas: Distribution of Psalm Books, Election Bribery," *ynet*, February 20, 2006. http://www.ynet.co.il/articles/0.7340.1.-3218845.00.html.

10. Gideon Allon, "Shas to Remove Rabbi Kadouri's Blessing from the Psalm Books it Distributes," *Haaretz*, March 3, 2006.

11. Anyone with the right to vote may donate money to the parties. The amount that could be donated in 2005 was not to exceed NIS 900 (per person and his/her dependents), and in 2006—the year of the elections—the amount was NIS 1,900. To increase transparency the State Comptroller determined that the parties would publish the names of their donors on their websites. See, "Party Funding Law and the role of the State Comptroller," *website of the State Comptroller*. http://www.mevaker.gov.il/serve/site/elections17-mimun.asp.

12. The chairman of the Election Committee, Justice Dorit Beinish, rejected Shinui's broadcast which portrayed ultra-orthodox men clinging to the ankles of a secular person like "leeches." The Supreme Court upheld the decision, and Chief Justice Aharon Barak wrote: "The images portrayed in the film clip are horrifyingly akin to anti-Semitic propaganda, turning orthodox Jews into faceless creatures" (Abraham Zeno, "Supreme Court on Shinui's Election Broadcast: Like Anti-Semitic Propaganda," *ynet*, June 28, 2006).

13. Mazal Muallam, "The New Public Square: Election Broadcasts on the Internet," *Haaretz*, February 14, 2006.

14. Ilan Marciano, "The Likud Presents *Fatal Finances*, Starring Olmert," *ynet*, February 8, 2006. http://www.ynet.co.il/articles/0.7340.L-3206017.00.html.

15. Link from Shas site to *Burning Heart* site: http://www.levboher.com.

16. Lily Galili, "Likud Clip Attacking Putin Removed," *Haaretz*, February 20, 2006.

17. "Kadima's First Internet Newsletter Launched," *Kadima party website* (see note 5 above), January 23, 2006.
18. *Labor party website* (see note 5 above).
19. *Likud party website* (see note 5 above).
20. Allon Marciano, "Likud Removes Ariel Sharon from its Website," *ynet*, January 25, 2006. http://www.ynet.co.il/articles/1.7340.L-3206017.00.html.
21. "It's time for a turnaround! A turnaround in government, a turnaround in policy, a turnaround in priorities, a turnaround in reducing gaps, a turnaround in health, a turnaround in education, a turnaround in welfare, a turnaround in employment... a turnaround for the good. Labor led by Amir Peretz will put the individual first in national priorities! Economics will serve the individual, the individual will work for peace, and peace will help the economy. The time has come to look after our future. Let's make history together in the 2006 turnaround!" *Labor party website* (see note 5 above).
22. Gilead Shinhav, "Now on the Internet too: Last Night Yahadut Hatorah Launched a Special Election Website,'" *nrg*, March 22, 2006, http://www.nrg.co.il/online/11/ART1/063/742.html.
23. E-mail from Zvika Dagan, head of the membership drive, February 21, 2006.
24. E-mail from the Kadima party headquarters, "Get a friend to join," March 23, 2006.
25. E-mail from Labor party headquarters, "Contact someone. Convince them. We'll win!" February 20, 2006.
26. Lilach Weisman, "The Labor Party Gives Out Personal Information Freely," *Haaretz*, February 27, 2006.
27. E-mail from Meiron Shor, Meretz campaign manager, "Who's going to be sent out? Campaign for the last ten days before the election," March 19, 2006.
28. E-mail from Meretz campaign headquarters, "Letter to the apathetic left-winger," March 27, 2006.
29. The opinion poll taken by the Netvision Institute in March 2006 polled 1,024 individuals, constituting a representative sample of the adult population in Israel (aged 18 or more), the sample error was 4.5 percent, see http://www.niis.tau.ac.il.
30. The *Tapuz* communities website (http://www.tapuz.co.il/forums) serves as a meeting place enabling web surfers to exchange information, opinions, and ideas on a variety of topics. Among the many forums under the "On the Agenda" link, was one which directed surfers to discussion forums on Israel's political parties.
31. Dudi Goldman, "Talkback for Sale," *Yediot Ahronoth, Weekend Supplement*, December 23, 2005.
32. In 2003 the candidate Howard Dean was notable for being the first to use a blog in his election campaign. His popularity increased to a level unrivalled by any other candidate (Cornfield, 2004).
33. Ehud Keinan, "Blogs: Kadima's Politicians Fall Behind," *ynet*, 21 March 2006.
34. Shaul Yahalom's blog: http://www.shaulyahalom.co.il/yahalom.
35. Many of those with blogs were new candidates, e.g., Labor party candidate Einat Wilf, who was not successful in her bid to gain a realistic spot in the party's internal election. http://www.wilf.prg/blog.html.
36. *Kadima party website*, "Legal Issues," http://www.kadimasharon.co.il/law/gal.asp?page=129.
37. *Website of the National Front party* (see note 5 above).
38. *Website of the Labor party* (see note 5 above).
39. Mazal Muallam, "A Computerized System Instead of Branches," *Haaretz*, December 25, 2005.

40. Hezi Sternlicht, "Malam Goes Forward with Sharon: Computerizes the Party HQ," *Bizportal*, December 25, 2005. http://www.bizportal.co.il/shukhahon/biznews02. shtml?mid=109772.
41. E-mail from Shelly Yechimovich, *Labor party website*, February 23, 2006, http://www.avoda2006.org.il/Amana.asp?cc=0126.
42. Women's Manifesto, *Labor party website*, http://www.avoda2006.org.il/Amana. asp?cc=0126.
43. "Sitting in the Polling Center," *Meretz party website*, http://www.myparty6.org. il/elections/s_volunteers.php?id=8.

References

Arian, Asher, Nir Atmor, and Yael Hadar. 2006. *The 2006 Israeli Democracy Index— Changes in Israel's Political Party System: Dealignment or Realignment?* Jerusalem: Israel Democracy Institute.

Arden, Eran. 2006. Kadima Click: Winning the Battle on new Consumer's mind. Tel-Aviv: Yediot Aharonot, Chemed Books [Hebrew].

Aronoff, J. Myron. 2000. "The 'Americanization' of the Israeli Politics: Political and Cultural Change." *Israel Studies* 5(1): 92–127.

Coleman, Stephen. 2001. "Online Campaigning." *Parliamentary Affairs* 54(4): 679–688.

Coleman, Stephen and John Gotze. 2001. *Bowling Together: Online Public Engagement in Policy Deliberation*. London: Hansard Society.

Coleman, Stephen, and Stephen Ward, eds. 2005. *Spinning the Web: Online Campaigning in the 2005 General Election*, London: Hansard Society.

Cornfield, Michael. 2004. *Politics Moves Online*, New York: The Century Foundation Press.

D'Alessio, Dave. 1997. "Use of the World Wide Web in the 1996 US Election." *Electoral Studies* 16(4): 489–500.

Dalton, Russell. 2002. *Citizen Politics: Public Opinion and Political Parties in Advanced Western Democracies*, New York: Chatham House Pub (3rd edition).

------, and Martin Wattenberg. 2000. "Partisan Change and the Democratic Process." In Russell Dalton and Martin Wattenberg, eds. *Parties Without Partisans*, Oxford: Oxford University Press, 261–285.

Davis, Richard. 1999. *The Web Politics: The Internet's Impact on the American Politics*, Oxford: Oxford University Press.

Davis, Steve, Lary Elin, and Grant Reeher. 2002. *Click on Democracy: The Internet's Power to Change Political Apathy into Civic Action*, Boulder: Westview.

Farrell, David and Paul Webb. 2000. "Political Parties as Campaign Organizations." In Russell Dalton and Martin Wattenberg, eds. *Parties Without Partisans*. Oxford: Oxford University Press, 102–128.

Gibson, Rachel. 2002. "Virtual Campaigning: Australian Parties and the Impact of the Internet." *Australian Journal of Political Science* 37(1): 99–129.

------, Wainer Lusoli, and Stephen Ward. 2005. "Online Participation in the UK: Testing a 'Contextualized' Model of Internet Effects." *British Journal of Politics and International Relations* 7(4): 561–583.

------, Michael Margolis, David Resnick, and Stephen Ward. 2003. "Election Campaigning on the WWW in the USA and UK: A Comparative Analysis." *Party Politics* 9(1): 47–75.

------, and Stephen Ward. 2000. "A Proposed Methodology for Measuring the Function and Effectiveness of Political Web-Sites." *Social Science Computer Review* 18(3): 301–319.

Hindman, Matthew. 2005. "The Real Lessons of Howard Dean: Reflections on the First Digital Campaign." *Perspectives on Politics* 3(1): 121-128.

Hofnung, Menachem. 2004. "Fat Parties—Lean Candidates: Funding Israeli Internal Party Contests." In Asher Arian and Michal Shamir, eds. *The Elections in Israel—2003*. Jerusalem: Israel Democracy Institute, 63-84.

------. 2006. "The Cream and the Cat, Monitoring and Motoring: Funding and Monitoring Internal Party Elections Using the Relative Method." In Gideon Rahat, ed. *Choosing Candidates in Israel: Actual and Factual*. Tel Aviv: Institute for Economic and Social Studies, 106-123 [Hebrew].

Lehman-Wilzig, Sam. 2004. "Worth an Agora? The 2003 E-lections Party Sites and Public Discourse." *Israel Affairs* 10(4): 242–262.

Margets, Helen. 2006. "Cyber Parties." In Richard Katz and William Crotty, eds. *Handbook of Party Politics*. London: Sage Publication, 528–535.

Margolis, Michael, and David Resnick. 2000. *Politics as Usual: The Cyberspace Revolution*, Thousand Oaks: Sage Publications.

------, David Resnick, and Ching-chang, Tu. 1997. "Campaigning on the Internet: Parties and Candidates on the World Wide Web in the 1996 Primary Season." *Harvard International Journal of Press/Politics* 2(1): 59–78.

------, David Resnick, and Joel De Wolfe. 1999. "Party Competition on the Internet: Minor versus Major Parties in the UK and USA." *Harvard International Journal of Press/Politics* 4(4): 24–47.

Newell, James. 2001. "Italian Political Parties on the Web." *Harvard International Journal of Press/Politics* 6(4): 60–87.

Norris, Pippa. 2000. *A Virtuous Circle*. Cambridge: Cambridge University Press.

------. 2001. *The Digital Divide: Civic Engagement, Information Poverty and the Internet in Democratic Societies*. Cambridge: Cambridge University Press.

------. 2003. "Preaching to the Converted? Pluralism, Participation and Party Websites." *Party Politics* 9(1): 21–45.

Rahat, Gideon, and Tamir Sheafer. (2007). "The Personalization(s) of Politics: Israel, 1949–2003." *Political Communication* 24(1): 65:80.

Schumpeter, Joseph. 1944. *Capitalism, Socialism and Democracy*. London: Allen and Unwin.

Selnow, Garry. 1998. *Electronic Whistle-Stops: The Impact of the Internet on American Politics*. Westport, CT: Praeger.

Schweitzer, J. Eva. 2005. "Election Campaigning Online: German Party Websites in the 2002 National Elections." *European Journal of Communication* 20(3): 327–351.

Stone, Brad. 1996. "Politics 96." *Internet World* 7(Nov.): 44–50.

Sunstein, Cass. 2001. *Republic.com*. Princeton, NJ: Princeton University Press.

Tkach-Kawasaki, M. Leslie. 2003. "Politics@Japan: Party Competition on the Internet in Japan." *Party Politics* 9(1): 105–123.

Ward, Stephen, and Rachel Gibson. 2002. "Virtual Campaigning: Australian Parties and the Impact of the Internet." *Australian Journal of Political Science* 37(1): 99–129.

List of Contributors—
The Elections in Israel 2006

Institutional affiliations are generally with departments of political science unless noted differently.

Paul R. Abramson, Professor, Michigan State University; abramson@msu.edu

John H. Aldrich, Pfizer-Pratt University Professor, Duke University; aldrich@duke.edu

Asher Arian, Israel Democracy Institute and distinguished professor, the City University of New York; arian@idi.org.il

Nir Atmor, the Hebrew University of Jerusalem and the Israel Democracy Institute; nir_atmor@idi.org.il

Roni Baum, Ph.D. in Jewish history, Tel-Aviv University; ronibaum@netvision.net.il

André Blais, Canada Research Chair in Electoral Studies, Université de Montréal; andre.blais@UMontreal.CA

Orit Kedar, Assistant Professor, Massachusetts Institute of Technology; okedar@mit.edu

Viacheslav Konstantinov, Ph.D., Hebrew University of Jerusalem; viachesl.konstantino@mail.huji.ac.il or vk58@netvision.net.il

Daniel Lee, Duke University; djl10@duke.edu

Renan Levine, Assistant Professor, University of Toronto; renan.levine@utoronto.ca

Jonathan Mendilow, Professor, Rider University; jmendilow@rider.edu

Doron Navot, the Hebrew University of Jerusalem; doronn@netvision.net.il

Michael Philippov, the University of Haifa, and the Israel Democracy Institute; mphilippov@idi.org.il

Gideon Rahat, Lecturer, The Hebrew University of Jerusalem; msgrah@mscc.huji.ac.il

Elie Rekhess, Senior Research Fellow, The Dayan Center, Tel Aviv University; relie@post.tau.ac.il

Michal Shamir, Alvin Z. Rubinstein professor, Tel Aviv University; m3600@post.tau.ac.il

Tamir Sheafer, Lecturer, Departments of Communication and Political Science, the Hebrew University of Jerusalem; msstamir@mscc.huji.ac.il

Sultan Tepe, Assistant Professor, University of Illinois at Chicago; sultant@uic.edu

Yariv Tsfati, Senior Lecturer, Department of Communication, the University of Haifa; ytsfati@com.haifa.ac.il

Raphael Ventura, PhD, Tel Aviv University. The Guttman Center at the Israel Democracy Institute; rafi@idi.org.il

Gabriel Weimann, Professor, Department of Communication, the University of Haifa; weimann@com.haifa.ac.il

Index